# The Archaeology of the West Midlands

## A framework for research

Edited by

## Sarah Watt

UNIVERSITY OF
BIRMINGHAM

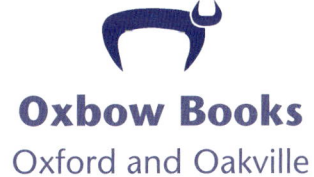

**Oxbow Books**

Oxford and Oakville

Published by Oxbow Books
on behalf of the University of Birmingham

ISBN 978-1-84217-427-2


A CIP record for this book is available from The British Library


*This book is available direct from*

Oxbow Books, Oxford, UK
(Phone: 01865-241249 Fax: 01865-794449)

*and*

The David Brown Book Company
PO Box 511, Oakville, CT 06779, USA
(Phone: 860-945-9329 Fax: 860-945-9468)

*or from our website*

www.oxbowbooks.co.uk


Printed in Great Britain by
Cambrian Printers, Aberystwyth
Wales

# Contents

# Figures

# Abbreviations

| | |
|---|---|
| Agric Hist Rev | Agricultural History Review |
| Anglo-Saxon Studies in Archaeol & Hist | Anglo-Saxon Studies in Archaeology and History |
| Antiq J | The Antiquaries Journal |
| Archaeol News Letter | The Archaeological News Letter |
| Archaeol J | Archaeological Journal |
| Avon-Severn Valley Res Proj Rep | Avon-Severn Valley Research Project Report |
| Brit Mus Occ Paper | British Museum Occasional Paper |
| Bull Board Celtic Stud | Bulletin of the Board of Celtic Studies |
| CBA Res Rep | Council for British Archaeology Research Report |
| Centre for Archaeol rep | Centre for Archaeology Report |
| Comm for Archaeol in Gloucestershire and CBA | Committee for Archaeology in Gloucestershire and Council for British Archaeology |
| Derbyshire Archaeol J | Derbyshire Archaeological Journal |
| East Anglian Archaeol Rep | East Anglian Archaeology Report |
| English Heritage Arch Rep | English Heritage Archaeological Report |
| English Heritage Centre Archaeol Rep | English Heritage Centre for Archaeology Report |
| Essex Archaeol and Hist | Essex Archaeology and History |
| European J Archaeol | European Journal of Archaeology |
| Geol Soc London Spec Rep | Geological Society London, Special Report |
| Herefordshire Stud Archaeol | Herefordshire Studies in Archaeology |
| J Anthrop Archaeol | Journal of Anthropological Archaeology |
| J Engl Place-Name Soc | Journal of the English Place-Name Society |
| J Quaternary Science | Journal of Quaternary Science |
| J Social Archaeology | Journal of Social Archaeology |
| J South-West Shropshire Hist Archaeol Soc | Journal of the South-West Shropshire Historical & Archaeological Society |
| Leicester Archaeol Monogr | Leicester Archaeology Monograph |
| Lithic Studies Soc Occ Papers | Lithic Studies Society Occasional Papers |
| McDonald Institute Monogr | McDonald Institute Monograph |
| Neolithic Stud Grp Sem Papers 4 | Neolithic Studies Group Seminar Papers |
| North Staffordshire J Field Stud | North Staffordshire Journal of Field Studies |
| Nottingham Studies in Archaeol | Nottingham Studies in Archaeology |
| Oxbow Monogr | Oxbow Monograph |
| Oxford Univ Comm Archaeol Monogr | Oxford University Committee forArchaeology Monographs |
| Oxford-Wessex Archaeol Rep | Oxford-Wessex Archaeology Report |
| Proc Brit Acad | Proceedings of the British Academy |
| Proc Prehist Soc | Proceedings of the Prehistoric Society |
| Sottish Archaeol Rev | Scottish Archaeological Review |
| Scot Trust Archaeol Res Monogr | Scottish Trust for Archaeological Research Monograph |
| Sheffield Archaeol Monogr | Sheffield Archaeological Monograph |
| Soc Antiq Scotland | Society of Antiquaries of Scotland |

| | |
|---|---|
| Thames Valley Landscapes Monogr | Thames Valley Landscapes Monograph |
| Trans Birmingham Warwickshire Archaeol Soc | Transactions of Birmingham and Warwickshire Archaeological Society |
| Trans Bristol Glouc Archaeol Soc | Transactions of the Bristol & Gloucestershire Archaeological Society |
| Trans Shropshire Archaeol Hist Soc | Transactions of the Shropshire Archaeological and Historical Society |
| Trans South Staffordshire Archaeol Hist Soc | Transactions of the South Staffordshire Archaeological and Historical Society |
| Trans Staffordshire Archaeol Hist Soc | Transactions of the Staffordshire Archaeological and Historical Society |
| Trans Woolhope Natur Field Club | Transactions of the Woolhope Naturalists' Field Club |
| Trans Worcestershire Archaeol Soc | Transactions of the Worcestershire Archaeological Society |
| Univ Birmingham Dep Geogr Occ Pap | University of Birmingham Department of Geography Occasional Papers |
| Univ Birmingham Hist J | University of Birmingham Historical Journal |
| Univ Bournemouth School Conserv Sci Res Rep | University of Bournemouth School of Conservation Sciences Research Report |
| Univ Leicester Depart Engl Local Hist Occas Pap | University of Leicester Department of English Local History Occasional Papers |
| Wessex Archaeol Rep | Wessex Archaeology Report |
| West Midlands Archaeol | West Midlands Archaeology |
| Worcestershire Archaeol Soc | Worcestershire Archaeological Society |
| World Archaeol | World Archaeology |

# Foreword

The publication of this volume marks the culmination of several years of coordinated research, seminar presentations and the personal contribution of many individuals; it also represents a major step forward in the future management of our archaeological heritage in the west midlands. This was a project started in 2001 with a series of open meetings in the region, drawing together archaeologists from local societies, universities, local authorities and field units as well as interested individuals both professional and amateur. The initiative and the funding belonged to English Heritage and the purpose was to provide a research framework for the region in order to ensure that future archaeological work, the majority of which was developer-led, might be better aligned to research purpose and to the resolution of academic goals.

The committee that evolved from these open meetings took upon itself to identify appropriate chronological periods for study and gathered information from local museums and collections, sites and monuments records/historic environment records, excavation reports published and unpublished, artefact specialists and experts in a host of subject areas ranging from geology to place-names. This data was then drawn together and presented in a series of period seminars, discussed, synthesised, and finally published in this volume. Although ostensibly a simple process, it involved many individuals working in their own time, fitting in the research around other commitments, and collaborating with individuals with other areas of interest. It was a process that additionally served to bring together the various components of a sometimes fragmented archaeological community. It is a great credit to the enthusiasm and energies of the coordinator Sarah Watt, and to the patience of the English Heritage representative Ian George, that the work has been completed so superbly.

The results of this work have provided us with an audit: it has defined our strengths and weaknesses, in some cases quite frighteningly; it has shown where the gaps in our knowledge lie both geographically and chronologically, and it has demonstrated where we may need to exert greater research effort. This is a volume which we hope will find many homes throughout the region and will be used to underpin the research designs and commercial specifications of archaeology throughout the next decade and beyond. The editor, the contributors and the many individuals whose efforts underpinned the papers here are to be congratulated on setting the archaeology of the west midlands on a new footing.

John Hunter
Professor of Ancient History and Archaeology
University of Birmingham

# Acknowledgements

The organisation and production of the Research Framework has relied on the support and hard work of a wide range of individuals and organisations. As well as the authors of the chapters in this volume, who have done a superb job of assimilating an enormous amount of data and supplementing it with their own research and knowledge, I would like to thank all those who participated in the process, especially the authors of the county resource assessment papers and themed regional papers presented at the series of Resource Assessment seminars held in 2002-2003. These included local authority and university archaeologists as well as independent archaeological practitioners, who took on the task of auditing the region's archaeology:

Andy Boucher of Archaeological Investigations Ltd.; Mike Hodder of Birmingham City Council; Paul Garwood, John Halsted, Della Hooke, Alex Jones, Roger White and Ann Woodward of the University of Birmingham, and Simon Buteux, Sally Crawford, Jane Evans, Iain Ferris, James Greig, Annette Hancocks, John Hunt and Alex Lang formerly of the University of Birmingham; Peter Guest of Cardiff University; Iain Soden formerly of Coventry City Council; Nathan Pittam of Coventry University; Andy Myers of Derbyshire County Council; Pete Boland and John Hemingway of Dudley Metropolitan Borough Council; Martyn Barber, Mark Bowden, Paul Stamper and Chris Welch of English Heritage; Julian Cotton, Tim Hoverd and Keith Ray of Herefordshire County Council, and Paul White and Rebecca Roseff formerly of Herefordshire County Council; Paul Belford of Nexus Heritage; Richard MacPhail of University College London; Jeremy Milln of the National Trust; Gavin Kinsley of Nottingham University; Paul Booth of Oxford Archaeology; Mike Watson and Andy Wigley of Shropshire County Council; Chris Wardle and Bill Klemperer formerly of Staffordshire County Council; David Barker formerly of Stoke-on-Trent City Council; David Jordan of Terra Nova Ltd.; Nicholas Palmer, Stuart Palmer and Jonathan Parkhouse of Warwickshire County Council; Stephen Hill formerly of Warwick University; Angie Bolton of the West Midlands Portable Antiquities Scheme; Mike Shaw of Wolverhampton City Council; James Dinn of Worcester City Council; Malcolm Atkin, Victoria Bryant, Hal Dalwood, Derek Hurst, Robin Jackson and Liz Pearson of Worcestershire County Council, and Neil Lockett formerly of Worcestershire County Council; Nigel Baker; Hilary Cool; Bob Meeson; Stephanie Rátkai; Barrie Trinder; Alan Vince; John van Laun. Lawrence Barfield of the University of Birmingham, who sadly died in July 2009, also made a significant contribution.

Thanks also to all the delegates who attended the seminars and contributed to the discussions, particularly the invited chairs and discussants (all included above) and those invited to fulfil the daunting task of summarising each seminar, setting the west midlands in its wider national context: John Hines and Niall Sharples of Cardiff University, Glyn Coppack of English Heritage, Jeremy Taylor and Marilyn Palmer of the University of Leicester, and Richard Bradley of the University of Reading.

The seminar papers cam be found at http://www.iaa.bham.ac.uk/research/projects/wmrrfa/index.shtml

English Heritage has generously funded the project and special thanks go to their representative Ian George for his help and support throughout. Thanks also to John Hunter for his overall management of the project and to Caroline Sturdy for her support in the final stages of coordination for publication and for collating the illustrations. Henry Buglass of the Institute of Archaeology and Antiquity, University of Birmingham, produced the original distribution map template used throughout this volume and all the distribution map figures, and prepared the illustrations for publication. The distribution maps are based on data collated from all the region's Sites and Monuments Records at the beginning of the project; thanks to all the SMR and HER officers who supplied this information and to all the local authority archaeologists who took the time to meet me and talk about the archaeology of their respective areas.

Thanks are also due to the members of the project's Management Committee for their invaluable support and assistance (and good ideas). The committee consisted of: Andy Boucher, Victoria Bryant, Vince Gaffney, Ian George, Mike Hodder, Della Hooke, John Hunt, John Hunter, Lisa Moffett, Cathy Patrick, Stephanie Rátkai, Mike Shaw and Mike Stokes. Mike Stokes, who died in February 2005, is sadly missed.

Sarah Watt

# Introduction

This volume represents the result of several years of work to produce an Archaeological Research Assessment and Research Agenda for the west midlands region, which embraces the counties of Herefordshire, Staffordshire, Shropshire, Warwickshire, Worcestershire and the former West Midlands County. This large region covers a disparate landscape from the southern edge of the Peak District in the north, to the Welsh border region to the west, and a major industrial conurbation in the centre, surrounded by a rich archaeological and historical agricultural landscape.

Despite this disparate landscape the region has a strong tradition of informal liaison within its diverse archaeological 'community'. This includes County Archaeologists and other Local Authority Archaeological Officers, Sites and Monuments Record (and Historic Environment Record) Officers, cathedral and diocese archaeologists, academics, contracting units and consultants, independent archaeologists, professionals and non-professionals, all of whom make an active contribution to the archaeology of the region. There is also a number of representative groupings, including the West Midlands Regional Group of the Council for British Archaeology (CBA WM), the West Midlands Group of the Institute for Archaeologists (IfA WM), the West Midlands regional office of English Heritage, the West Midlands Archaeological Collections Research Units (WEMACRU), and the Association of Local Government Archaeologists (ALGAO).

It was these existing links and lines of communication that were critical in the success of the research framework process, ensuring a high attendance and level of engagement at the Research Assessment seminars and a diverse wealth of knowledge and experience to draw upon in the preparation of this volume.

The overall aim of the Research Framework process was to produce an archaeological research framework for the region (including the proper integration of artefactual and ecofactual interests) that will provide a viable, realistic and effective academic basis for undertaking archaeological intervention, either as the result of development-related operations or to underpin future research designs. The outcome will enable curators to integrate appropriate research strategies within their specifications, and ensure that contractors tender and operate in full awareness of local designs. Equally, it will inform museum curators, education officers and university staff and students with regard to the research parameters of the region.

The starting point was the Department of the Environment's *Planning Policy Guidance No 16* (DoE 1990), dealing with archaeology and planning, which emphasised the need for proper research frameworks within which archaeological work might be located, and raised issues that were explored further in the English Heritage survey *Frameworks For Our Past* (Olivier 1996). Here, it was further argued that the public perception of archaeology and the need for acceptable public accountability 'make it essential that the discipline acquires a proper means of selecting and targeting local and regional priorities in order to justify curatorial policies and decisions' (*ibid*, 2). The context for dealing with planning issues should be clearly and explicitly informed by the needs of archaeological research.

In the west midlands, subsequent English Heritage guidance, through two public meetings (in June and September 2000), underlined the necessity of producing a regional research framework not only as a 'flexible research tool', but also one which would serve to maintain a necessary academic basis to developer-related archaeology.

A working party (or steering group) was selected and confirmed through the two public meetings and through consultation within the interested parties represented.

This group (which became the project's Management Committee) reflected the wider forum of archaeological interest and expertise within the region, and drew its membership from English Heritage, the SMRs, ALGAO, contracting units and consultants, Higher Education, CBA WM, the IfA WM, museums, archaeological sciences, artefactual specialists and independent archaeologists. The group was tasked with producing an outline framework, and with providing an information cascade mechanism. Its proposals were reported and validated in a further public meeting (in March 2001) representing the diverse archaeological interests within the region.

The need to develop a research framework has long been acknowledged within the region. Local authority archaeological services have been actively engaged in producing their own strategic plans, and representative groups such as WEMACRU, ALGAO and the IfA have also engaged with the process. Even before *PPG 16* and *Frameworks For Our Past* highlighted these issues, specialist groups were attempting to address the need for coherent research approaches. The CBA WM has also produced a research plan, with its own membership in mind (1999, 2-10).

At the time the process was initiated in the west midlands, research frameworks had already been produced (or were in production) for the East Midlands, the Eastern Counties, and the Greater Thames Estuary among others. West midlands archaeologists have therefore enjoyed the considerable benefit of having been able to review the approaches to this process adopted in other regions and, thus informed, to consider the particular needs and characteristics of their own region.

The Research Agenda for the west midlands is the result of a two-stage process:

1. a *Resource Audit,* which identified the nature and extent of the known database

2. a *Research Assessment,* which interrogated and interpreted this resource in order to evaluate strengths, weaknesses and biases in the record.

## Resource Audit

Although not originally anticipated to form part of the work undertaken for the Resource Audit, the major part of this stage of the project involved the collation and amalgamation of data from all of the County and City Sites and Monuments Records (now for the most part Historic Environment Records) across the region (11 separate databases in all) in order to produce period-based distribution maps of recorded sites and findspots for the entire region using GIS software, something which had not been attempted previously. These maps form the basis for the distribution maps contained throughout this volume. The production of the maps was supported by other information, including the compilation of bibliographies (including grey literature), and a summary audit of museum collections.

There were various problems of incompatibility between the different SMR databases (for instance, the names of site and find types differed between databases, as did the level of subdivision within periods, many databases also using the 'catch-all' period 'prehistoric', and there was inconsistent recording of artefacts, something which will be addressed in the future (see Chapter 9)). It was thus a labour-intensive and time-consuming piece of work but it was considered that the end justified the means and that the results of this exercise were worthwhile, particularly for the pre-medieval periods.

Despite the various biases and other problems, the HERs represent the most important source of archaeological data for the region, and the distribution maps also served the purpose of identifying where problems were in terms of compatibility across the region. The datasets that were used to prepare the maps were current in early 2001 (with the caveat that there were data-entry backlogs across the region ranging from a few weeks to an estimated four years) but have been updated when appropriate for the production of the maps in this volume.

## Research Assessment

The Research Assessment stage of the project comprised seven period-based seminars (with the period divisions drawn as per the separate chapters of this volume) held between June 2002 and June 2003. Over 25% of the seminar papers were written and delivered by ALGAO/SMR Officers. Another 25% were undertaken by Contracting Units or Consultancies. The rest were undertaken by academics, independent parties and English Heritage officers. It was intended to make the scope of the seminars broad in order to include as many participants as possible and, in order to facilitate constructive comparison across the region, each paper was prepared to a brief, which included the following elements:

- Assessment of present knowledge and gaps in knowledge
- Sources
- Key excavations and surveys
- Methodologies and techniques
- Economy
- Landscapes
- Social frameworks
- Continuity and transition
- Specific regional issues
- Potential cross-period themes

The seminars were held at different venues across the region and saw an average attendance of c 65 people (with the largest number of people, 81, attending the Roman period seminar). Between 13 and 16 papers were presented at each day-long seminar: the first half of each seminar consisted primarily of county-based papers, with the afternoon generally consisting of thematic papers followed in most cases by a national overview given by an invited speaker from outside the region. Time for discussion was programmed in throughout and at the end of the day.

The papers presented at each seminar were then posted in draft on the project's website: (http://www.iaa.bham.ac.uk/research/projects/wmrrfa/index.shtml),where they remain. This was in order to invite comments from all interested parties, which could then be incorporated into the papers where appropriate. The revised papers were then collated and circulated to the authors of the chapters in this volume as an essential basis for the production of the period-based chapters.

## Research Agenda

A subsequent series of seven smaller period-based discussion groups were held between July 2003 and June 2004, focusing on the Research Assessment papers. These were held at the University of Birmingham and were chaired by the respective future authors of the chapters of this volume. The object of these meetings was to focus the contributions from the general meeting, define a draft list of research topics, and generate cross-period themes. The chapter authors then embarked upon writing the Research Assessment/ Research Agenda chapters, for which they drew on the papers presented at the Research Assessment and the discussions (which were recorded) at the Research Agenda meetings. Chapters 8, 9 and 10 of this volume were originally circulated by e-mail to those on the project's extensive mailing lists for comment.

## Other Outcomes

It was of course recognised that the county-based and thematic papers presented at the Research Assessment seminars formed a useful resource in their own right and, as well as publishing the draft versions of these on the web, another early outcome of the research framework was the idea for a new series of volumes entitled *The Making of the West Midland*s, the first volume of which, on the early prehistory of the region, has now been published (Garwood 2007); the series is to comprise the full papers presented at each research framework seminar in a series of period-based volumes.

This separate series of volumes is an added bonus to come out of the framework process, will 'plug' a large gap in the current availability of texts on the archaeology of all periods in the west midlands, and will represent a landmark series in the drawing together and publication of the archaeological evidence for this region.

From discussions held at the Research Agenda meetings, it became clear that there was a desire to maintain the informal networks of people who had been brought together by the research framework process. For example, it was suggested for some periods that interested parties continue to meet at organised seminars held at regular intervals in order to maintain the momentum that the research framework process has started. A related material outcome of this, for instance, was the establishment of the West Midlands Palaeolithic Network (or Shotton project).

The maintenance of such networks would be a very positive outcome for the region which has been born out of the Research Framework process.

## Addendum

The unintended delay between the initial preparation of the chapters forming this volume and their publication means that, despite some revisions in the interim, the contents of the published volume make no reference to recent significant events, two of which in particular should be mentioned here.

First is the much-publicised discovery of the 'Staffordshire Hoard' in a field near Lichfield in July 2009, an Anglo-Saxon hoard comprising more thatn 1500 (mostly military-related) items of gold and silver. The implications for the west midlands region of this nationally significant find will be addressed in the Early Medieval volume of the *The Making of the West Midlands* series referred to above (edited by Della Hooke).

Second, the replacement of planning Policy Guidance notes 15 and 16 with the new Planning Policy Statement 5 (PPS5) in March 2010, and the implications this has for the management of the historic environment within the region, should also be noted.

Sarah Watt

## Bibliography

CBA West Midlands, 1999 Frameworks For Our Past: A Regional Strategy for the West Midlands, in *West Midlands Archaeology Vol 42*, 2-10

Department of the Environment, 1990 *Planning Policy Guidance 16: Archaeology and Planning* HMSO

Garwood, P (ed), 2007 *The Undiscovered Country: The Earlier Prehistory of the West Midlands,* Oxford: Oxbow

Olivier, A, 1996 *Frameworks For Our Past. A review of research frameworks, strategies and perceptions.* London: English Heritage

# 1. Geology of the west midlands: a summary

## Dr Jonathan D. Radley

jonradley@warwickshire.gov.uk

The west midlands is taken to cover the West Midlands metropolitan area and the counties of Herefordshire, Shropshire, Staffordshire, Warwickshire and Worcestershire. Covering a large part of central England and the Welsh Borderlands, this area incorporates a variety of 'solid' geological formations that range in age from late Precambrian to Jurassic (British Geological Survey, 2001; Fig 1.1).

These provide evidence for approximately 400 million years of Earth history and a continental drift from about 40-50 degrees south of the equator, to southern Britain's present position within the northern, temperate climatic belt. Accordingly the geology of the west midlands provides evidence for large-scale climatic change through time (Anderton et al 1979; Duff and Smith 1992; Ellis et al 1996; Woodcock and Strachan 2000). Quaternary deposits, ranging from glacial clays, sands and gravels to river terrace deposits, solifluction deposits and modern river alluvium, locally mantle these rocks (Wills 1948; Hains and Horton 1969; Earp and Hains 1971; Ragg et al 1984; Keen 1989; Fig 1.2).

Sedimentary rocks dominate the west midlands. Igneous and metamorphic rocks occur locally, as within the Precambrian terrains of the Malvern Hills and the Church Stretton area (Fig 1.3). In essence, the west midlands area divides the substantially post-Carboniferous, weakly deformed geological terrain of the east midlands from the highly-folded and faulted Lower Palaeozoic terrain of mid Wales (British Geological Survey 2001).

Precambrian terrains have locally undergone considerable geological deformation. For instance, the late Precambrian Malvernian rocks of the Malvern Hills and the Rushton schists of the Church Stretton area, have suffered varying degrees of metamorphism, locally resulting in high-grade schistose and gneissic metamorphic rock types, while the late Precambrian Longmyndian rocks of the Longmynd, Shropshire, for example, are less deformed and include sandstones, mudstones and volcanic ashes.

The well-preserved Lower Palaeozoic marine successions of the region are dominated by sandstone, shale and limestone, deposited on the stable basement of the Midland Platform and in adjacent parts of the Welsh Basin. These are developed for example in the Welsh Borderland, Black Country inliers (eg Wren's Nest, Dudley) and the Nuneaton Inlier of northern Warwickshire. These strata have yielded many invertebrate fossils, indicating marine environments ranging from shallow-water reef settings to deep-sea basins, between around 540 and 415 million years before present.

The west midlands were only mildly deformed by a major episode of Earth movement and deformation in mid Silurian-early Devonian times – the so-called 'Caledonian Orogeny'. This remarkable event resulted from the closure of the Iapetus Ocean, causing

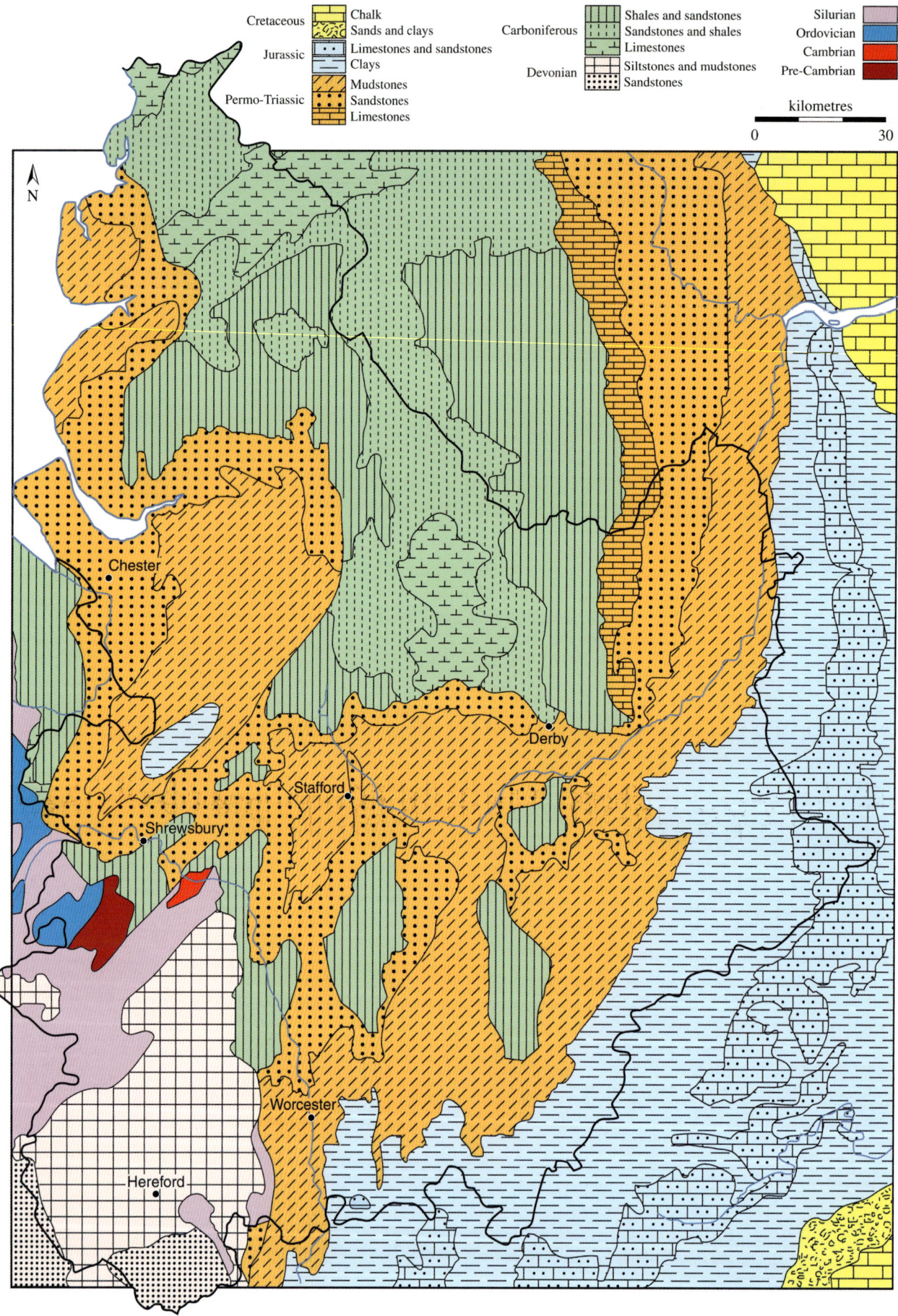

**Fig 1.1** Outline 'solid' geology of the west midlands area

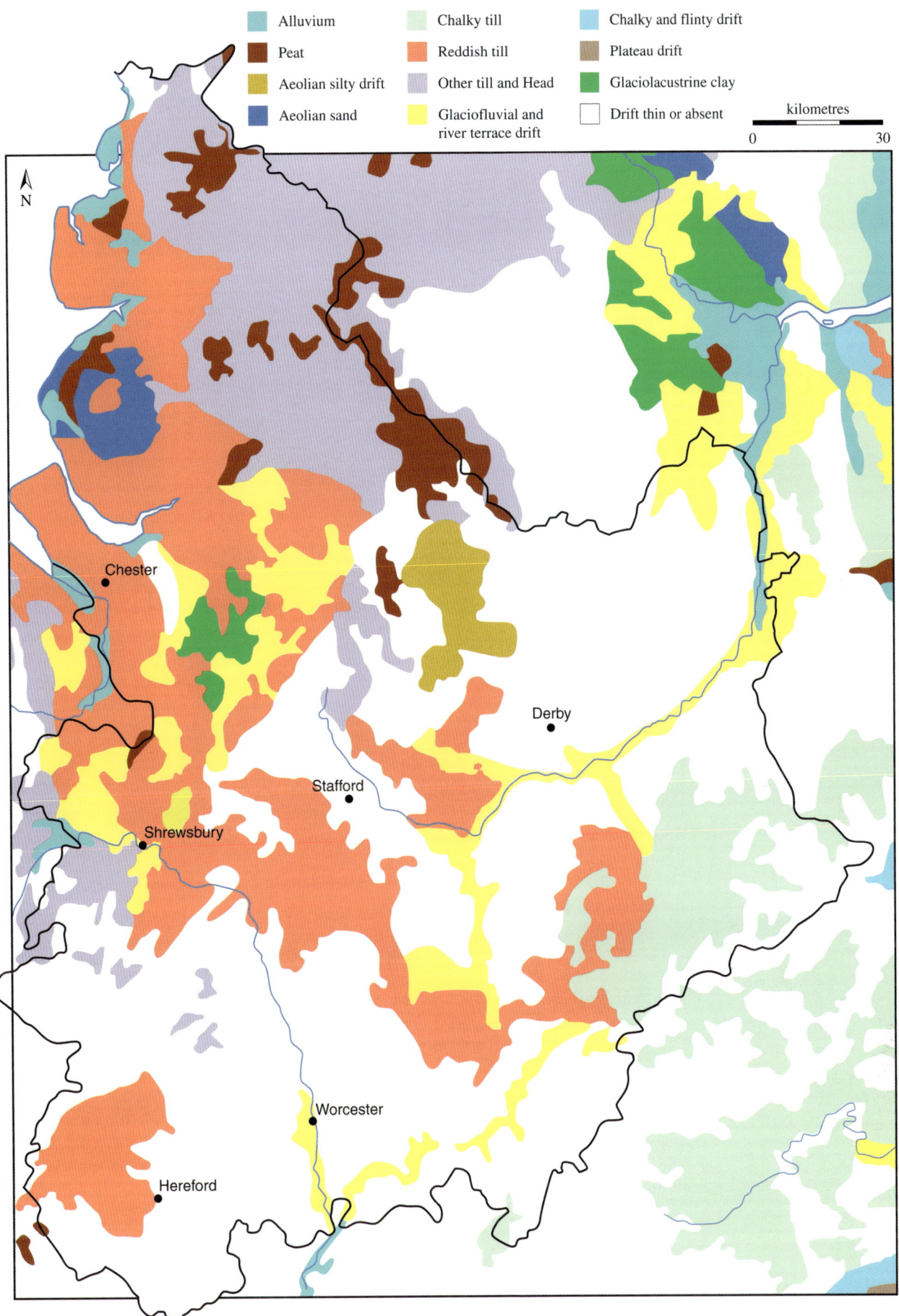

**Legend:**

- Alluvium
- Peat
- Aeolian silty drift
- Aeolian sand
- Chalky till
- Reddish till
- Other till and Head
- Glaciofluvial and river terrace drift
- Chalky and flinty drift
- Plateau drift
- Glaciolacustrine clay
- Drift thin or absent

kilometres

0    30

N

Chester

Derby

Stafford

Shrewsbury

Worcester

Hereford

**Fig 1.2** Outline Quaternary geology of the west midlands area

**Fig 1.3** The Church Stretton valley looking north-east from the flanks of the Long Mynd. The hills on the east side of the Valley (The Lawley, Caer Caradoc, Helmeth, Hazler and Ragleth) are of Precambrian (Uriconian) volcanic rock, approximately 650 million years old. They are the eroded remnants of up-faulted blocks within the Church Stretton fault complex. The main line of the Church Stretton Fault – at its most conspicuous through the valley from which it takes its name – is marked on Caer Caradoc at the boundary between the cultivated land and open hillside. Photo courtesy of Andrew Jenkinson (copyright Scenesetters – countryside interpreters and publishers)

the collision of 'Scotland' and 'England' and the Caledonian mountain-building episode. Following this, the Devonian Old Red Sandstone of the Welsh Borderland comprises a thick pile of predominantly red sandstones and mudstones, deposited largely on arid river floodplains to the south of the eroding Caledonian foothills, at about 15-20°S latitude. The Old Red Sandstone contains abundant evidence of early non-marine life, notably the remains of primitive freshwater fish.

Limestones of Lower Carboniferous age are well developed in parts of Staffordshire and the Welsh Borderland. They originated as lime-rich muds and sands, shell and coral banks in a clear, tropical sea that flooded the area north of the Midland Platform during an early Carboniferous sea-level rise. Overlying the Carboniferous Limestone, the Millstone Grit is especially well developed in North Staffordshire as coarse-grained sandstones interbedded with shales. These were deposited as part of a complex of deltas that invaded the Carboniferous sea. The Upper Carboniferous Coal Measures Group is known from the Wyre Forest, Coalbrookdale, Shrewsbury, North Staffordshire, South Staffordshire and Warwickshire Coalfields. These economically important strata originated as mud, sand and peat, deposited in and around hot, humid equatorial swamps, lakes and river floodplains roughly 300 million years ago. They are overlain by the so-called 'Barren Measures' of late Carboniferous age – poorly fossiliferous, predominantly red-coloured mudstones, sandstones and conglomerates that are mainly of semi-arid alluvial origin.

The west midlands area underwent gentle folding and faulting during the Variscan mountain-building episode, which peaked during the Upper Carboniferous and into the early Permian. This resulted from the continent of Gondwana moving northwards against Laurussia, to form the 'supercontinent' of Pangaea. The west midlands area was

**Fig 1.4** Permian Bridgnorth Sandstone in which the old cave houses were excavated at Holy Austin Rock, high on Kinver Edge, Staffordshire. The sandstone represents part of a desert dune field, approximately 250 million years old. The cave houses were occupied from the 16th century until the 1960s. Photograph courtesy of Tony Waltham (copyright Tony Waltham Geophotos)

additionally affected by extensive faulting during the early part of the Permian Period, attributable to regional stretching of the continental crust in response to early opening of the Atlantic Ocean. Much of the Permian and Triassic succession of the west midlands accumulated among the resultant terrain of hills and rift valleys. Permian strata are well developed in Warwickshire and the Bridgnorth area of Shropshire, comprising reddish mudstones, sandstones and conglomerates, laid down in hot, arid conditions, at approximately 10-20°N latitude. Amongst these, the thick Bridgnorth Sandstone (Fig 1.4) includes the remains of large-scale aeolian (wind-blown) sand dunes.

Triassic strata are more extensively developed in the region. A lower, sandy and pebbly succession (Sherwood Sandstone Group) is widespread, and includes the well-known Bunter Pebble Beds that are seen, for example, on Cannock Chase, Staffordshire. The so-called 'Bunter' quartzite pebbles are widespread in the west midlands, either derived directly from Triassic pebble beds or recycled via Quaternary deposits. They are thought to have been derived ultimately from the ancient Armorican massif of Brittany-Cornwall. The Sherwood Sandstone Group is overlain by the Mercia Mudstone Group – rather featureless, unfossiliferous red mudstones (formerly known as 'Keuper Marl') enclosing thin sandstones such as the Arden Sandstone of Worcestershire and Warwickshire. The Permian and Triassic rocks were deposited partly in semi-arid environments, ranging from alluvial fans to wind swept salt flats. The very youngest Triassic rocks (Penarth Group) include black shales (Westbury Formation) and thin limestones (Langport Member) of marine origin.

Overlying the Triassic, Jurassic rocks are well developed in Worcestershire and Warwickshire but are also known from the Prees outlier of Shropshire. The Lower Jurassic is dominated by the mudstone-dominated successions of the Lias Group, interspersed with sandstones and ironstones. Middle Jurassic 'Cotswold' limestones of the Inferior Oolite and Great Oolite groups represent the youngest 'solid' geology of the west midlands area. The Jurassic strata are almost wholly of marine origin, deposited in a shallow epicontinental sea of subtropical aspect that covered much or all of the west midlands, at latitudes of between 30° and 40°N.

During the Quaternary Period a range of unconsolidated clays, sands and gravels was deposited. During glacial phases, ice invaded the west midlands from the Welsh Mountains, Irish Sea, southern Scotland, Pennines and Vale of York, introducing varied suites of erratic pebbles amongst the boulder clays and fluvio-glacial sands and gravels. Post-glacial river terrace deposits, consisting mainly of sand and gravel, are widespread in the modern river valleys. Amongst the most recent geological deposits, alluvium forms modern river floodplains. Peat deposits locally occur, both in lowland and upland settings. The mosses and meres of North Shropshire and Staffordshire are a series of water or peat-filled hollows. They originated as 'kettle holes' – flooded topographic depressions representing the sites of melted ice blocks. Shropshire's northern plain is additionally characterised by ranges of glacial morainic hills and smaller drumlins. Variation throughout the region in underlying geology, landscape, climate and vegetation has given rise to a wide variety of soil types.

The west midlands region is topographically varied, though predominantly a lowland area below 250m above sea level. The harder, commonly older rock formations, give rise to upland areas such as the Malvern Hills and the Shelve district and Longmynd of Shropshire. The Black Mountain escarpment, Herefordshire, is composed of a thick Devonian Old Red Sandstone succession and rises to more than 600m above sea level. Upper Carboniferous (Coal Measures) rocks produce varied topography, including the subdued, rolling topography of the Warwickshire Coalfield, the dolerite-capped upland of the Clee Hills, Shropshire, and the higher ground of the western Peak District. The extensive outcrops of Triassic Mercia Mudstone form low-lying country, as in North Shropshire. Sandstone outcrops that locally give rise to landscapes of low hills and incised valleys vary the Mercia Mudstone lowlands. The Lower Jurassic Lias Group clays and thin limestones form low-lying agricultural vales, fringed by escarpments, plateaux and outlying hills formed by the sandstones and ironstones of the Dyrham Formation and Marlstone Rock Formation, and the Middle Jurassic Cotswold limestones of the Inferior Oolite and Great Oolite groups. Such outcrops characterise Warwickshire and Worcestershire's Cotswold fringe. Post-glacial and Recent deposits, including terrace gravels and alluvium, are widespread features of modern river valleys.

Historically, the area has been central to the early development of geological science. The historic and scientific importance of geological sites in the west midlands is underpinned by the Sites of Special Scientific Interest (SSSI) network, protected and administered by Natural England. Pioneers such as Robert Plot (1640-1696), John Farey (1766-1826) and William Smith (1769-1839) are all associated with the region. Sir Roderick Murchison, a former Director of the Geological Survey of Great Britain, provided a detailed account of the geology of Staffordshire, Worcestershire and Shropshire in 'The Silurian System', published in 1839. Eminent 19th-century palaeontologists such as Richard Owen founded studies on locally collected fossils. The Geological Survey initiated systematic geological mapping in the 19th century. 'Old Series' one inch maps have been superseded by the 'New Series', currently published at 1:50,000 scale. The maps have been accompanied by a series of sheet memoirs, providing comprehensive detail of surface and subsurface geology. Other eminent field geologists who have worked in the region include Charles Lapworth (1842-1920), Leonard Wills (1884-1979), and Fred Shotton (1906-1990).

Rock, fossil and mineral specimens from the west midlands have been dispersed into recognised collections throughout Britain and beyond. Notable amongst these are the Silurian invertebrate faunas of the Welsh Borderlands and the Black Country, Coal Measures plants, and Triassic-Jurassic vertebrates. Local collections, including important holdings of west midlands specimens, are listed in Appendix 1.1. The rocks of the west midlands contain strata of considerable economic importance, notably coal, limestone, ironstone, building stone, brick clay, cement materials, gypsum, salt, sand and gravel. Intensely industrialised areas have consequently developed, notably the Black Country and The Potteries. Ironbridge Gorge, the birthplace of the Industrial Revolution, owes its significance to locally available deposits of coal, clay, limestone and iron ore.

## Acknowledgements

Paul Smith (School of Geography, Earth and Environmental Sciences, University of Birmingham) and Don Steward (The Potteries Museum and Art Gallery) commented on an early version of the text.

## Bibliography

Anderton, R, Bridges, P H, Leeder, M R, and Sellwood, B W, 1979  *A dynamic stratigraphy of the British Isles,* London

British Geological Survey 2001  *1:625,000 Scale Solid Geology Map, UK South Sheet (South of National Grid Line 500 km N), 4th Edn*

Duff, P, McL, D, and Smith, A J, 1992  *Geology of England and Wales,* London

Earp, J R, and Hains, B A, 1971  *British Regional Geology: The Welsh Borderland,* London

Ellis, N V (ed), Bowen, D Q, Campbell, S, Knill, J L, McKirdy, A P, Prosser, C D, Vincent, M A, and Wilson, R C L, 1996  *An Introduction to the Geological Conservation Review. GCR Series No 1,* Peterborough

Hains, B A, and Horton, A, 1969  *British Regional Geology: Central England,* London

Keen, D H, 1989  *West Midlands Field Guide.* Quaternary Research Association, Cambridge

Ragg, J M, Beard, G R, George, H, Heavan, F W, Hollis, J M, Jones, R J A, Palmer, R C, Reeve, M J, Robson, J D, and Whitfield, W A D, 1984  *Soils and their use in Midland and Western England. Soil Survey of England and Wales, Bulletin 12,* Harpenden

Wills, L J, 1948  *The Palaeogeography of the Midlands,* Liverpool

Woodcock, N, and Strachan, R (eds) 2000  *Geological History of Britain and Ireland,* Oxford

## Appendix 1.1: Local geological collections

The West Midlands Natural Science Collections Group provides information and advice on geological collections within the region. Further details are available on their website at: www.naturalsciencewm.org.uk

The following collections are especially rich in local material:

*Birmingham Museum and Art Gallery, Chamberlain Square, Birmingham B3 3DH, tel. 0121 303 2834, www.bmag.org.uk*

Major strengths of the collection include Palaeozoic and Mesozoic rock and fossil specimens from the west midlands.

*Dudley Museum and Art Gallery, St James's Road, Dudley DY1 1HU, tel. 01384 815575, www.dudley.gov.uk*

Includes a comprehensive collection of Wenlock and Ludlow (Silurian) fossils from the Dudley and Walsall areas. There are also representative specimens from the local Coal Measures, including fossil plants and remains of terrestrial animals.

*The Lapworth Museum of Geology: University of Birmingham, Edgbaston B15 2TT, tel. 0121 414 7924/4173, www.lapworth.bham.ac.uk*

The collections include fossils, rocks and minerals from the midlands region, including the archive collection of Charles Lapworth.

*Ludlow Library and Museum Resource Centre, Parkway, Ludlow SY8 2PG, tel. 01584 813666, www.shropshireonline.gov.uk/llmrc.nsf*

Includes a comprehensive collection of fossil and rocks from the Palaeozoic rocks of south Shropshire and the Welsh Borders, and Shropshire mammoths.

*Stoke-on-Trent: Potteries Museum and Art Gallery, Bethesda Street, Hanley, Stoke-on-Trent ST1 3DE, tel. 01782 232323, www.stoke.gov.uk/museums*

The collection is notably rich in locally collected Carboniferous and Triassic rocks and fossils. Highlights include Coal Measures fish and local minerals.

*Warwickshire Museum, Market Place, Warwick CV34 4SA, tel. 01926 412500, www.warwickshire.gov.uk/museum*

Strengths include locally collected Triassic and Jurassic fossils.

# 2. The earlier prehistory of the west midlands

## Paul Garwood

p.j.garwood@bham.ac.uk

## 2.1. Introduction

The earlier prehistory of the west midlands was once seen as an unrewarding subject for serious archaeological research. This region was usually represented on distribution maps of earlier prehistoric sites and finds as an almost blank area; a vast tract of the British landscape virtually devoid of 'significant' material remains. The region was characterised archaeologically as a 'barren waste' (C W Phillips, cited by Seaby 1949, 85), and for much of prehistory was thought to have been 'culturally backward' (ibid, 87). Despite his earnest efforts to put 'the Birmingham plateau and its margins' back on the archaeological map, Seaby had to admit that between the Rollright Stones and the Wrekin 'there was scarcely a prehistoric monument that even the most ardent antiquarian would turn aside to inspect' (ibid, 85).

The first attempts to rewrite the earlier prehistory of the region were closely linked to major discoveries and investigations of crop mark sites in the Avon and Severn valleys (Webster and Hobley 1964; Hunt 1982), and more extensive regional surveys that tried to integrate the results of 'rescue archaeology' work in the mid 1960s to mid 1980s with contemporary overviews and interpretative studies (eg Stanford 1980, Hunt 1982, Vine 1982, Gibson 1989, Loveday 1989). Most county-scale summaries of the evidence, however, were written before 1970 (eg Gunstone 1964, 1965; Smith 1957) and were already out of date by the time that larger-scale studies were undertaken. The notable exceptions are Richard Hingley's review of prehistoric Warwickshire (1996) and Mike Hodder's study of the archaeology of Birmingham (2004). Recent large-scale landscape studies in the west midlands have been restricted to the north-western part of the region (eg Leah et al 1998, Mullin 2003), while thematic studies of specific categories of evidence have barely impinged on the region, the most valuable being Barnatt and Collis' survey of Peak District barrows (1996). There have been a few more recent attempts to redefine and resituate the prehistoric archaeology of the west midlands in relation to broad research themes and new appraisals of the *nature* of earlier prehistoric evidence. The most important of these have focussed on the Neolithic and Bronze Age of Shropshire (Carver 1991, Watson 1991; Buteux and Hughes 1995), and on the Lower and Middle Palaeolithic of the region as a whole (Lang and Keen 2005).

A remarkable feature of much of this literature is the overt way in which archaeologists attempted to challenge what they regarded as prejudiced and misleading characterisations of west midlands earlier prehistory as somehow unimportant, materially invisible or culturally impoverished. Just as Hunt once dismissed the notion that the region was an 'archaeological wasteland' (1982, 1), Buteux and Hughes have more recently rejected the view that lowland Shropshire was a 'wilderness' (1995, 159). Similarly, Hodder has suggested that rather than being a 'barren waste' the Birmingham area has produced evidence for significant earlier prehistoric activity (2004). At the same time, concerted attempts have been made to account for the absence or scarcity of prehistoric evidence. These typically draw attention to geological and environmental constraints on the identification and investigation of prehistoric sites (eg soils and land use regimes that are not conducive to air photographic survey; or alluvial processes that have concealed ancient land surfaces), destruction of prehistoric sites by urban development and agricultural and industrial activities (especially ploughing and gravel extraction), and a lack of archaeological fieldwork and research (Carver 1991, 1; Hunt 1982; cf assessments in Barber 2007, Myers 2007, Ray 2007). It has also been suggested that earlier prehistoric social organisations and cultural practices within the region were distinctive, with extensive kinds of economic activity, a high degree of residential mobility, limited investment in durable architecture' and forms of cultural expression that involved little in the way of formal material deposition (eg Buteux and Hughes 1995; cf Ray 2007).

The need to revisit these themes again and again over the last 30 years seems at first sight to provide a measure of the *persistence* with which west midlands prehistory is still materially and interpretatively 'marginalised', despite the ardent endeavours of those who have tried to redress the situation. It is now time, however, to re-evaluate this appraisal, especially in the light of the period assessments discussed in the following sections. These show that some of the most striking features of the earlier prehistoric archaeology of the region *are* the relative scarcity of evidence, the rarity of prominent monuments, the small-scale nature of many artefact assemblages, thin and uneven distributions of sites and finds, and areas which appear consistently to be devoid of earlier prehistoric evidence of any period. It is especially notable how often recent large-scale excavation projects have produced almost no earlier prehistoric remains or only the occasional isolated pit group, including the Wroxeter Hinterland Project (V Gaffney, pers comm), the Mid-Shropshire Wetland Survey (Leah et al 1998), the Birmingham Northern Relief Road (Denison 2002; Powell et al 2008), and the Arrow Valley project in Warwickshire (Palmer 1999).

In this context, it is becoming increasingly difficult to account for the scarcity of earlier prehistoric evidence in the terms outlined above, or simply to claim that 'absence of evidence is not evidence for absence'. The west midlands has been subject to hundreds of archaeological investigations since the 1960s, at a greatly accelerated pace since the advent of PPG16, with few areas untouched by fieldwork of some kind (eg see Darvill and Russell 2002, 28-9), yet the overall pattern of earlier prehistoric finds distributions and site identifications has for the most part changed only in detail.

This does not, however, mean that the region is unimportant in research terms. In fact, there are good reasons to argue that the opposite is the case. Despite the *overall* scarcity of earlier prehistoric evidence, there are parts of the west midlands with significant concentrations of sites of one or several periods (eg the Staffordshire Peak District, the middle Trent valley, the Avon valley in Warwickshire, the upper Severn valley and parts of upland Herefordshire and Shropshire close to the Welsh border). These are comparable with similar site concentrations in other regions such as Wessex, south-east England and the east midlands. In addition, while some 'classic' site types (of various periods) are rare or absent, it is apparent that monument groups in the region (eg Neolithic ceremonial complexes and Early Bronze Age dispersed round barrow groups) and specific site categories (eg cave sites, occupation sites, enclosures, cursus monuments and round barrows) have clear research significance in national terms. In some cases, individual sites easily bear comparison in terms of surviving material evidence and research potential with similar sites elsewhere. Most notably, recent reassessments of the Lower and Middle Palaeolithic of the west midlands highlight the research potential of the evidence in international as well as national terms (Lang and Keen 2005; Lang and Buteux 2007).

The uneven distributions of earlier prehistoric evidence within the region, especially between central areas (with low densities of surface finds and known sites), and outer parts of the region (with often dense monument and/or artefact distributions), also have considerable potential for investigating intra- and inter-regional variation in the nature and intensity of social and economic activity. Indeed, it can be argued that while the region lacks a coherent geographical identity and is an arbitrary unit of study in cultural terms, it is especially well situated for comparative study of prehistoric societies, cultural repertoires and the activities of many different social groups. This is not only because of the great diversity of cultural forms, practices and sequences of change evident in each period, particularly around the periphery and in different river systems, but also because of the geographical position of the region. It is centrally located in southern Britain between the Welsh mountains and east midlands plains, between the south-west peninsular and the Yorkshire Wolds and Moors, and between the chalk and limestone hills and river valleys of southern England and the Pennine and Cumbrian uplands. Cultural exchanges between these varied regions in prehistory must have involved forms of social action and movement that traversed the west midlands.

In this light, the desire to 'champion the cause' of west midlands earlier prehistory by simply seeking more sites and finds to fill distributional gaps, and thus redress the biases of previous fieldwork and geo-environmental conditions, now appears to be misguided. A particular problem with this approach is the tendency for fieldworkers to operate at local or county rather than regional (let alone national) scales of enquiry and to devote insufficient attention to comparative analyses or research themes that transcend local concerns. In this way it is easy to miss what is *really* distinctive about the evidence and to lose sight of what is – and is not – important in wider research terms.

The enormous value of the West Midlands Regional Research Framework earlier prehistory seminar, and the significant research outcomes that have followed from it (see the wide range of papers in Garwood (ed) 2007d), has been to look at the full geographical extent of the region and to produce synthetic, critical evaluations of specific periods and categories of evidence across the entire region with reference to current national research agenda. For the first time it is possible to obtain a reliable and balanced assessment of the nature, scale, types, qualities and distributions of the material evidence for each earlier prehistoric period, and an evaluation of current interpretative frameworks and the research potential of earlier prehistoric sites and material culture in the region.

This work has revealed what appears to be real variation in earlier prehistoric activity and strongly suggests very sparse occupation in some areas, but this can only contribute to a mature understanding of the nature of prehistoric social and cultural life in the west midlands. At the same time, as the following period-based reviews will demonstrate, the evidence is extraordinarily diverse, often of extremely high quality in terms of site preservation, surviving monuments, dating evidence and artefact assemblages, and that there are widespread opportunities for detailed studies of prehistoric landscapes of all periods. There is no question that earlier prehistoric studies in the west midlands, effectively guided by clear research agenda, will contribute to current and future research at a national scale of enquiry, and that there is great potential for dedicated research programmes, research-led initiatives in curatorial archaeology and research-guided developer-funded archaeological fieldwork in the region.

## 2.2. Lower and Middle Palaeolithic

### 2.2.1. Introduction

*The Lower and Middle Palaeolithic in the west midlands: previous research*
In comparison with the south and east of England there are relatively few Lower and Middle Palaeolithic finds recorded in the west midlands. Before the 1960s, amateur collectors, archaeologists and geologists (with the notable exception of Professor F.W. Shotton; Lang and Keen 2005, 66-7) showed little interest in the Palaeolithic archaeology of the region. More recently, although some significant field collection has been carried out, especially around the Severn/Avon confluence in Worcestershire by P. Whitehead, and at Wolvey in north Warwickshire by R. Waite, considerably increasing the number of known finds (Lang and Keen 2005; Lang and Buteux 2007, 13), there have been no systematic research-led programmes of artefact recovery. The most significant site discovery, made by quarry workers at Waverley Wood near Warwick in the 1980s (handaxes in a pre-Anglian palaeochannel deposit), was reported by Shotton (Shotton and Wymer 1989, Shotton et al 1993) and has been studied in more detail recently (Lang and Keen 2005).

In wider terms, the recent survey of the Palaeolithic archaeology of English river valleys deals with the west midlands in a relatively cursory manner (Wessex Archaeology 1996; Wymer 1999, 114-21, 176-78), although it does provide a helpful correlation of the Severn and Avon river terrace deposits, together with summaries of the archaeological evidence from the Avon Valley, Waverley Wood, and the Wolvey area (the only part of the region that warrants a finds distribution map; Wymer 1999, 178, map 54). The Lower and Middle Palaeolithic archaeology of the west midlands was assessed by Simon Buteux in 2001 for the Regional Research Framework earlier prehistory seminar. This led to a one year research programme (The Shotton Project) commissioned by English Heritage (funded by the Aggregates Levy Sustainability Fund) to evaluate the nature and research potential of Palaeolithic evidence in the west midlands. Our understanding of the Lower and Middle Palaeolithic of the region, and its research potential, has been significantly enhanced by this work, published in papers by Lang and Keen (2005) and Lang and Buteux (2007). The present discussion of the evidence is based mainly on these papers, and on the data presented previously by Wymer (1999).

*Current research agenda in Lower and Middle Palaeolithic archaeology*
Lower and Middle Palaeolithic archaeology in Britain has risen in prominence in recent years in both academic circles and popular perception. The discoveries at Boxgrove, in particular, have captured the public imagination and emphasised the international research significance of the British evidence (Roberts and Parfitt 1999). It is important to recognise that research aims and methods in Palaeolithic archaeology are in many respects different to those prevailing in studies of later periods. Above all, Palaeolithic archaeology cannot be separated from Quaternary climatology, geology and human evolutionary studies (Lang and Buteux 2007, 8-10). The chronological framework for the period, for example, is based on the Marine Oxygen Isotope Stage (MIS) sequence derived from Pleistocene climatological and geological studies, in relation to which biostratigraphical and archaeological sequences and specific assemblages are ordered (Barton 2005, 16-29; Wymer 1999, 2-4, 29-31). The archaeological evidence for the period is also distinctive in that it consists almost entirely of lithic artefacts (see Barton 2005, 6-14, for a basic introduction), produced by pre-modern humans whose cognitive capabilities and social practices may have been profoundly different to those of modern humans (ibid; cf Gamble 1996; Mithen 1996).

Current research themes in British Lower and Middle Palaeolithic archaeology are set out in a Prehistoric Society research document (1999), and key issues and debates have been reviewed in several recent books and articles (eg Gamble and Lawson 1996; English Heritage 1998; Gamble 1999; Wymer 1999; Ashton et al 2002; Barton 2005; McNabb 2006). There are also major national research programmes currently in progress concerned with Palaeolithic archaeology (notably the *Ancient Human Occupation of Britain* project funded by the Leverhulme Trust). These identify a number of general research themes, all to a greater or lesser extent relevant to the west midlands:

1.  The date and character of the earliest human occupation of Britain: this has for some time focused on the short versus long chronology debate (see Gamble 1999, 115-23); recent discoveries now clearly favour a long chronology (Wymer 2001; Parfitt, et al 2005).

2.  The geographical distribution and adaptations of human populations, including the impact of climate change, colonisation processes and population replacements (Prehistoric Society 1999, 4; cf Ashton and Lewis 2002; Barton 2005; Stringer and Gamble 1993).

3.  Technical and cognitive capabilities of early human populations in Britain (Prehistoric Society 1999, 4-5; cf Gamble 1996, 1999; Barton 2005, 57-73).

4.  The social organisation and behaviour of early human populations, including patterns in the scale, spatial organisation, density and landscape contexts of inhabited locales and particular practices (Prehistoric Society 1999, 4-5; Gamble 1996, 1999).

### Period subdivision

Although there is broad agreement about British Pleistocene chronology and the course of environmental change based on the MIS geo-climatological sequence, and about the relationship of many regional chrono-stratigraphies to the MIS framework (eg Bridgland 2000), there is no consensus in Lower and Middle Palaeolithic archaeology with regard to the most appropriate periodisation of evidence for human activity. There is, in particular, a basic contrast between MIS-based frameworks that give primacy to *environmental* sequences, and material culture-determined *archaeological* chronologies which assume that assemblage types relate to distinctive kinds of human behaviour, resource exploitation and cognition. The recent review of the west midlands evidence by Lang and Keen (2005), for example, organises the evidence in relation to MIS stages. In contrast, Wymer (1999, 4) subdivides the British Lower and Middle Palaeolithic into three archaeological periods. This approach was adopted and modified by McNabb for his four-period division of the Lower and Middle Palaeolithic of the east midlands (2006, 13-16: Wymer's 'Period 3' being subdivided for archaeological and geo-climatological reasons into Periods 3 and 4). McNabb's framework is summarised below (with reference to British Middle and Late Pleistocene eras and the MIS sequence), and is used in the discussion that follows to describe the west midlands evidence. Dates are given in years Ka (thousand years ago).

*Period 1*: Cromerian and Anglian (MIS 19-12), *c* 800–423 Ka. The earliest human occupation (*H. heidelburgensis*) associated with early Lower Palaeolithic artefacts (Acheulian handaxe and flake tool industries). Humans were probably absent during most but not necessarily all of the Anglian glaciation (*c* 478-423 Ka).

*Period 2*: Hoxnian to middle Wolstonian (MIS 11-8), *c* 423-245 Ka. Occupation by humans from MIS 11 to 8 (*H. heidelburgensis* to early *H. neanderthalensis*; Barton 2005, 74-5); most of the Lower Palaeolithic finds in Britain date to this period (Acheulian handaxe and Clactonian flake tool industries), found primarily in river terrace deposits.

*Period 3*: Middle Wolstonian to Early Devensian (MIS 7-4); *c* 245-60 Ka. Limited early Middle Palaeolithic human presence during MIS 7, followed by the apparent absence of human populations from MIS 6 to late MIS 4.

*Period 4*: Early to Middle Devensian (first half of MIS 3); *c* 60-40 Ka. Reoccupation of Britain by *H. neanderthalensis* from the end of MIS 4 to mid-MIS 3, associated with late Middle Palaeolithic (Mousterian) industries.

## 2.2.2. Research assessment: current knowledge and understanding of the evidence

### Geological and palaeontological evidence

An important development in recent Lower and Middle Palaeolithic studies in the west midlands is the identification of major pre-Anglian river systems (Period 1; before 480 Ka). The largest of these, the Bytham, traversed the region from south-west to north-east: from south Worcestershire, crossing Warwickshire, and then continuing across the east midlands and East Anglia to reach the North Sea basin near Lowestoft in Suffolk (Lang and Keen 2005, 64, fig 1; Lang and Buteux 2007, 20; cf Rose 1989, 1994). A second ancient river, the Mathon, represented by deposits in eastern Herefordshire and part of Shropshire, was either a tributary of the Bytham or flowed into an as yet unidentified pre-Severn river (Lang and Buteux 2007, 15-16; cf Maddy 1999).

Identification of these rivers is important for several reasons. In particular, mapping of the river systems is essential for understanding the geography of the early human occupation of Britain (during MIS 13-12). As Lang and Buteux (2007, 15-16) observe, human populations would have relied on constant access to the water and food sources that river valleys provided and are likely to have followed river valleys in moving through the landscape. They suggest that there were two major entry routes into central Britain prior to the Anglian: from the east along the Bytham and the pre-Anglian Thames (cf Wymer 1999, 130-31), and from the south along the coast (eg at Boxgrove) and into the ancient Solent and its tributary river valleys (although Wymer notes that there is little evidence for pre-Anglian activity in the Hampshire Basin; ibid, 109). The pre-Anglian finds in the west midlands, including the Waverley Wood material, can in this context be seen as part of a more extensive distribution of pre-Anglian material along the Bytham, including the important site at High Lodge (Lang and Keen 2005, 73; Ashton et al 1992). The research potential of these deposits is extremely high, with major implications for Lower and Middle Palaeolithic studies in Britain.

Recent discoveries of artefacts in the Cromer Forest-bed Formation deposits at Pakefield (Suffolk) and Happisburgh (Norfolk) (Parfitt et al 2005) appear to pre-date the Bytham river in this area and may provide evidence for an even earlier human presence in Britain at various times during MIS 19-14, with major implications for our understanding of the earliest human colonisation of northern Europe. It is important to note that if precursors to the Bytham flowed in roughly the same direction during MIS 19-14, and humans moved along the river as they appear to have done later on, it is possible that similar early material may occur in central Britain.

The Anglian glaciation, which commenced around 480 Ka (MIS 12), obliterated the pre-Anglian river systems and destroyed most of the deposits associated with them (Lang and Keen 2005, 75). The major rivers of the west midlands that exist today - the Trent, Severn and the Avon in Warwickshire and Worcestershire - have all developed since the end of the Anglian glaciation (Lang and Buteux 2007, 15). The terrace sequences of the Avon and the Severn, which contain evidence for human activity during Periods 2 and 3, can now be provisionally dated and related to the MIS sequence on the basis of palaeontological and archaeological evidence (ibid; for a detailed summary see Wymer 1999, 117-19, tbl 11, fig 45). These terrace deposits have in some places provided important information for reconstructing local environments and climatic conditions (eg at Cropthorne, Eckington and Strensham along the lower Avon; Lang and Buteux 2007, 16). It is important to note, however, that the Middle and Late Pleistocene geological sequence in the west midlands, and the structure of regional drainage patterns, are still little understood. The possible occurrence of a major glaciation during the Wolstonian (MIS 10-6), for example, which would have destroyed Anglian (MIS 12) and post-Anglian (Hoxnian; MIS 11) river systems, has not yet been resolved and the implications of such processes for understanding human occupation in the region remain unexplored (Wymer 1999, 115-19).

### Lower and Middle Palaeolithic sites and lithic artefacts

Several hundred Lower and Middle Palaeolithic artefacts have been found in the west midlands, mostly from the terrace deposits of the River Avon in Warwickshire and Worcestershire, and from the terraces of the Severn (Lang and Buteux 2007, fig 2.1, tbl 2.2). There are, however,

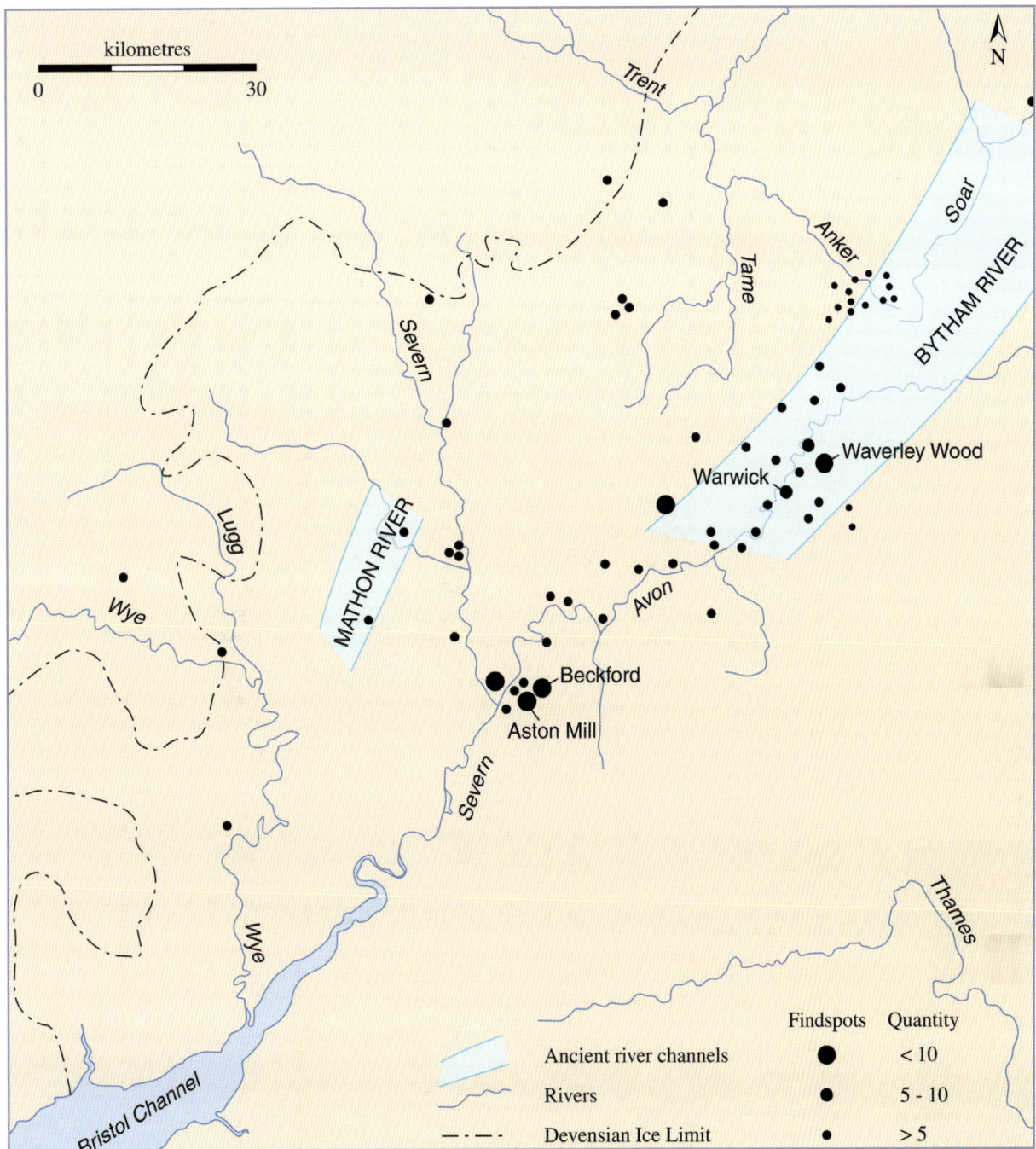

**Fig 2.1** The distribution of Lower and Middle Palaeolithic artefacts and finds concentrations in the West Midlands (after Lang and Buteux 2007, fig 1)

no known sites in the region with *in situ* archaeological deposits such as knapping debris (Lang and Keen 2005, 71). Notable concentrations of lithic artefacts have been found close to the Avon/Severn confluence at Beckford and Kemerton, around Warwick in the Avon valley and at Wolvey in north Warwickshire (Fig 2.1). In contrast, few artefacts have been found in the Severn valley above Worcester or in central, western and northern parts of the region. As Lang and Buteux (2007, 13) demonstrate, such distribution patterns are largely a product of uneven fieldwork: the groups of finds known from the Avon/Severn confluence and the Wolvey area, for example, were mostly collected by individual fieldworkers. The current distribution map of Lower and Middle Palaeolithic artefacts is clearly not, therefore, a reliable guide to early human activity in the region as a whole.

The raw materials used for lithic tool manufacture in the west midlands are distinctive. There are no outcrops containing flint in the region and most stone tools were made of poor quality 'drift' flint and local materials, especially quartzite from the Kidderminster Conglomerate found to the north and west of Birmingham (Lang and Keen 2005, 70-1; cf Hardaker and MacRae 2000 on the use of quartzite along the Bytham river). The other most common material used was andesitic tuff, derived from glacial erratics or transported into the region from outcrops in the Lake District (Wymer 1999, 115; Lang and Keen 2005, 70-1). This diversity of raw materials is unusual at a regional scale in the British Palaeolithic (Lang and Buteux 2007, 14).

The Lower and Middle Palaeolithic finds recorded in the west midlands are summarised below following the Period division outlined above (cf McNabb 2006).

*Period 1 (Pre-Anglian and Anglian; MIS 19-12; c 800-423 Ka)*
There is a cluster of extremely important pre-Anglian finds in north-east Warwickshire which date to MIS 13 or before. The most significant site in the region is Waverley Wood, to the north of Warwick, where an assemblage of five handaxes in fresh condition (four made of andesite), several quartzite tools and the remains of straight-tusked elephant (*Palaeoloxodon antiquus*), have been found in organic palaeochannel deposits sealed beneath Baginton Sand and Gravels (Thrussington Till) of Anglian date (Shotton and Wymer 1989; Wymer 1999, 115, 118, 178; Lang and Buteux 2007, 13). The palaeochannel is believed to be associated with the River Bytham and date to MIS 13 (c 500 Ka; Lang and Keen 2005, 73), roughly contemporary with the key site of High Lodge further along the Bytham to the east. It is possible that several finds from Baginton in the Avon valley, not far from Waverley Wood, may also belong to the pre-Anglian period (Lang and Buteux 2007, 13). The fresh condition of the Waverley Wood artefacts and their association with animal remains suggest that this site, and perhaps others in the vicinity, has considerable research potential for investigating the chronology and character of very early human activity, both regionally and nationally.

The artefacts recovered from surface deposits in the Wolvey area in Warwickshire (by R. Waite; Saville 1988) are more difficult to evaluate. They derive from the Oadby Till laid down during the Anglian glaciation and from the overlying Wigston (Dunsmore) Gravel, which is regarded as an outwash deposit from the Oadby Till (Wymer 1999, 178). These artefacts may be pre-Anglian, broadly contemporary with activity at Waverley Wood but redeposited in the course of the Anglian glaciation, or they may relate to activity during an unknown warmer interstadial that occurred during the Anglian period (ibid).

*Period 2 (Hoxnian to middle Wolstonian; MIS 11-8; c 423-245 Ka)*
In contrast to the large number of sites in southern and eastern England dating to the Hoxnian interglacial (MIS 11) and the sequence of cold – warm – cold stages of the first half of the Wolstonian period (MIS 10-8), there are virtually no well-dated artefacts of these periods in the west midlands (Lang and Keen 2005, 75). at present, only the very small number of handaxes from Avon terrace 5 and Severn terrace 5 (three in total; ibid, tbl 2), which are correlated with MIS 9 (Wymer 1999, 114-21, tbl 11, fig 45), suggests there was human activity in the west midlands in Period 2.

*Period 3 (Middle Wolstonian to Early Devensian; MIS 7-4; c 245-60 Ka)*
Evidence for Middle Palaeolithic activity in Britain is extremely limited. There appears to have been sparse inhabitation by humans during MIS 7 (a warm stage), c 245-186 Ka, and humans were totally absent in the period c 186-60 Ka during MIS 6 (a cold stage at the end of the Wolstonian), MIS 5e (the Ipswichian warm stage) and MIS 5a-d (the cold and temperate stages of the early Devensian). Only at the end of MIS 4 did humans, presumably Neanderthals, re-colonise Britain. In the west midlands, the handaxes found in Avon terrace 4 and Severn terrace 4 (23 in total; Lang and Keen 2005, 76-7, tbl.2), belong to MIS 7 (though the lower terrace 4 deposits may correlate with MIS 8: Wymer 1999, 114-21, tbl 11, fig 45). The large handaxe assemblage from Avon terrace 4 at Twyning pit, located just outside the region, is probably the same age as the west midlands material (Lang and Keen 2005, 77; Wymer 1999, 117-18, tbl 11).

*Period 4 (Early to Middle Devensian; first half of MIS 3; c 60-40 Ka)*
The reoccupation of Britain, and the presence of later Neanderthal populations from c 60 Ka, is evident in the west midlands only in the lower Avon valley, where handaxes

and other lithic artefacts such as prepared cores have been recovered from Avon terrace 2, especially from Beckford and Kemerton (Aston Mill Pit) (a total of 52 bifaces; Lang and Keen 2005, tbl 2; Wymer 1999, 117-18, tbl 11). These include a number of late Middle Palaeolithic small flat-based flint handaxes and Levallois-type cores (Lang and Keen 2005, 77-8). Most of these artefacts were found in re-worked late MIS 3 or MIS 2 terrace gravels (dating to *c* 30 Ka) derived from deposits laid down at the beginning of MIS 3, *c* 60-50 Ka (ibid).

### 2.2.3. Research agenda and specific research questions

As work at Boxgrove has demonstrated, the discovery of just one well–preserved Lower or Middle Palaeolithic site with *in situ* remains has the potential to transform our understanding of these periods nationally and to contribute to research at an international scale. There is no reason to regard the west midlands river terrace deposits, where these survive, as having any less potential than similar deposits elsewhere in southern Britain.

The research aims for Lower and Middle Palaeolithic archaeology in the west midlands identified by Lang and Buteux (2007, 18-20) form the basis for the research agenda presented here. They observe that the presence of human populations in the west midlands was discontinuous in time and space and that a key general aim must therefore be to determine the chronology, geographical extent and relative intensity of human activity, and to identify possible colonisation routes. This may further help to define the preferred environmental zones inhabited or traversed by early human populations. As both routes and favoured habitats were probably mostly riverine, it is clearly of primary research importance to identify, map and investigate the pre-Anglian river systems of the Bytham, the Mathon and the 'pre-Severn' (as well as possible precursors), and the post-Anglian riverscapes of the Severn, Avon, Lugg, Tame and Trent valleys. Investigation of *in situ* lithic assemblages, and recovery of high quality palaeo-environmental evidence from river terraces and other deposits (even in the absence of archaeological remains), should be research priorities wherever such evidence is encountered.

Specific research aims and questions that should take priority in Lower and Middle Palaeolithic studies in the region are discussed below under period headings.

### *Period 1*

The presence of pre-Anglian (MIS 18-13; *c* 800-480 Ka) material in the west midlands has considerable importance in research terms. The Waverley Wood finds (*c* 500 Ka), in particular, are significant in relation to national and international research questions concerning the chronology and extent of the earliest human occupation of northern Europe. Further work on this site, and identification and investigation of contemporary sites in the region, is clearly a research priority. The suggestion of human migration along the Bytham river system from the North Sea basin, and the apparent contemporaneity of the Bytham and Mathon rivers, point to the possibility that similar evidence will exist in pre-Anglian river terrace and palaeochannel deposits right across the region (cf McNabb 2006, 18-20, 41). The recent discovery of earlier human activity on the North Sea coast in Suffolk and Norfolk (*c* 800-500 Ka) 'close to the Bytham channel deposits' may also have implications for the Lower Palaeolithic of the west midlands, especially if an early course of the Bytham or other pre-Bytham rivers were used as migration routes by early humans. Identification and investigation of deposits in the region datable to MIS 18-13 may prove to be especially significant for future research.

The concentration of pre-Anglian or Anglian material around Wolvey in Warwickshire also deserves serious investigation to establish the date and character of the artefacts, their geological and environmental contexts and the research potential of the area. The presence of this material outside the main river systems raises the possibility that Lower Palaeolithic material may be present far more widely in the region than hitherto supposed. The recovery of Palaeolithic artefacts in areas that are promising in geological terms should be an explicit aim of all surface collection programmes.

### Period 2

#### (i). Hoxnian Interglacial (MIS 11), 423-362 Ka

The absence of Hoxnian sites in the west midlands, in contrast to the very rich evidence from deposits of this period elsewhere in southern and eastern England, is surprising and demands particular investigation. It is possible that the Wolstonian glaciation event posited by Shotton (at some point during MIS 10-6; Wymer 1999, 115-19) may have destroyed Hoxnian deposits, but there is presently no evidence to support this. These issues should be priorities for both archaeological and geological research in the region.

#### (ii). Early Wolstonian occupation (MIS 10-8), 362-245 Ka

It is uncertain whether the few artefacts datable to MIS 10 to 8, recovered from the river terraces of the Avon and Severn, reflect small-scale and episodic occupation or limited field investigation. The significance of this material, its precise dating, processes of terrace formation and reconstruction of the changing environment, all require integrated archaeological and geological study (ibid).

### Period 3

The early Middle Palaeolithic handaxes found in Avon terrace 4 and Severn terrace 4 suggest human activity in the west midlands during the early part of MIS 7 (Lang and Keen 2005, 79), but the rarity of artefacts with evidence for Levallois technology, the earliest occurrence of which is broadly associated with the Lower-Middle Palaeolithic transition (Barton 2005, 81), raises questions about the chronology extent and nature of occupation. The apparent abandonment of Britain by human populations during MIS 6-5 and most if not all of MIS 4 remains little understood: there is considerable potential for geological and bio-stratigraphic evidence from the west midlands, especially from river terrace contexts, to shed light on environmental conditions in this period (Lang and Buteux 2007, 19).

### Period 4

The extent to which the west midlands region was occupied by Neanderthals at the end of the Middle Palaeolithic, after the re-colonisation of Britain at the end of MIS 4 (from *c* 70 Ka at the earliest) and the early part of MIS 3 (*c* 59-40 Ka), is unknown. The only major group of finds of this period in the region was found by just one fieldworker in south Worcestershire and it is unlikely that this is representative of the wider picture. The rich palaeo-environmental evidence from sites of this period, especially along the Avon valley river terraces, certainly point to the potential for discovering contemporary archaeological sites in similar contexts throughout the west midlands (Lang and Keen 2005, 79).

### 2.2.4. Research aims and methods

The research agenda and key research questions outlined above have major implications for methods of resource assessment, curatorial practices, fieldwork methods and networks of communication and data gathering in the region.

- There is a need for more detailed evaluation of the research potential of the Palaeolithic archaeology and Pleistocene palaeo-environments of the region, especially in river gravel contexts (cf English Heritage 1998). This should certainly be undertaken at local and county levels, although larger regional and inter-regional scales of analysis are especially appropriate for investigating major river systems.

- Continuing assessment of quarry sites and further evaluation of museum and private collections are also essential for defining in more detail the nature, scale and research potential of the archaeological resource in the region.

- It is evident that Palaeolithic archaeology should be brought more effectively into the domain of developer-funded archaeology and the planning process guided by PPG16. In particular, finds of non-archaeological fossils and deposits do not fall within the current remit of curatorial archaeology, yet these are central to Quaternary studies and the investigation and interpretation of Palaeolithic remains (Lang and Buteux 2007, 19). In this context, perhaps the most important issue for curatorial archaeologists relates to how archaeological and palaeo-environmental data of this period can be effectively incorporated into the region's Historic Environment Records (HERs).

- An important methodological development that can be facilitated by HER databases is 'predictive modelling' of sites and finds (cf English Heritage 1998; Wymer 1999). This should be combined with systematic and regular monitoring of sand and gravel workings for Palaeolithic finds and Pleistocene deposits, combined with a programme of site prospection. Contacts among fieldworkers, quarry companies and workers, and professional archaeologists, geologists and other specialists should be an essential feature of such work.

- Lang and Buteux (2007, 6) observe that most field and curatorial archaeologists in the region, as elsewhere in England, are unfamiliar with Lower and Middle Palaeolithic archaeology and that there is a need to establish protocols for dealing with this evidence and to provide training in appropriate sampling and analytical techniques. Recommended prospection, investigation and evaluation procedures in Palaeolithic archaeology outlined recently by Collcut (in McNabb 2006; app 2) provide some important guidelines in this area.

### 2.2.5. Conclusion

The Lower and Middle Palaeolithic periods in the west midlands are perhaps especially important in regional and wider terms. The geographical position of the region at the furthest northern limits of Lower Palaeolithic settlement, at a global scale, is clearly important for exploring early human adaptations in what must often have been an extreme environment for human occupation. Indeed, evidence for activity dating to these periods immediately has potential *international* research significance: the discovery of a single well-preserved *in situ* deposit of pre-Anglian date, for example, is relevant to far reaching research questions concerning early human migration, social behaviour and cognition. There is scope within the region to address basic questions concerning the chronology, spatial distribution and ecological and landscape settings of early activity, and how these relate to Quaternary climate change, river terrace formation and bio-stratigraphic sequences. There is potential here for significant new discoveries that could radically transform our wider understanding of the Lower and Middle Palaeolithic in Britain. The recent publications by Lang and Keen (2005), and Lang and Buteux (2007), plainly set out the research opportunities and challenges ahead.

It is also important to note that there are two major national projects that will contribute significantly to all aspects of Lower and Middle Palaeolithic archaeology in the west midlands in the next decade. The National Ice Age Network, which aims to foster contacts and collaborative research in Pleistocene studies, especially in relation to sand and gravel extraction sites, operates from several centres including the University of Birmingham and has a strong presence in the region. This is funded by the Aggregates Levy Sustainability Fund and administered jointly by English Heritage and English Nature. The Leverhulme Trust funded Ancient Human Occupation of Britain project, concerned specifically with key research questions in British Palaeolithic archaeology, will also clearly contribute in a fundamental way to the development of future national and regional research agenda.

## 2.3. Upper Palaeolithic

### 2.3.1. Introduction

*The Upper Palaeolithic in the West midlands: previous research and research agenda*
There has been very little research concerned with the Upper Palaeolithic of the west midlands, and the most recent national review (Campbell 1977) provided only summary descriptions of the west midlands evidence. In this context, the assessment of the Upper Palaeolithic for the West Midlands Regional Research Framework earlier prehistory seminar is an important contribution to our understanding of this period in the region (Myers 2007). The present discussion of the evidence is based largely on that paper, together with additional assessment of the data presented by Campbell (1977) and recent work on the British Upper Palaeolithic (eg see Barton 1999, 2005).

The time span of the Upper Palaeolithic encompasses profound cultural changes: from the appearance of anatomically modern humans with wide range of new materials, practical and symbolic (*c* 40 Ka), to the development of early Holocene hunter-gatherer societies (by *c* 10 Ka). It is also important to recognise that Upper Palaeolithic societies in Britain cannot be understood separately from the wider northern European context of population movement, social and economic systems, and complex climatic and environmental changes.

Current research themes in British Upper Palaeolithic archaeology are set out in a Prehistoric Society research document (1999) and key issues and debates have been reviewed in several recent books and articles (eg Barton et al 1991; Smith 1992; Housley et al 1997; Gamble 1999; Barton 1991, 1999, 2005). These identify a number of general research themes that are relevant to the west midlands:

1.  The chronology of the first colonisation of Britain by anatomically modern humans, and the chronology and duration of later re-colonisation episodes during the Last Glacial (Prehistoric Society 1999, 4; cf Barton 2005, 115-38).

2.  The geographical distribution and adaptations of modern human populations in relation to climate change and particular environmental zones and conditions (Prehistoric Society 1999, 4; cf Barton 2005, 115-38; Gamble 1999, 268-302; Smith 1992, 159-80).

3.  The spatial organisation of settlement, subsistence and other practices, and patterns of everyday life (Prehistoric Society 1999, 4-5; cf Barton 2005, 115-38; Gamble 1999, chs 3, 6-7; Smith 1992, 10-39, 159-80).

4.  Large-scale organisation of Upper Palaeolithic societies: territories, migration ranges and regional cultural groups (Prehistoric Society 1999, 5; cf Gamble 1999, 351-87; Smith 1992, 159-80).

*Period subdivision*
Barton's chronological outline of the Upper Palaeolithic occupation of Britain and representative lithic types (2005) is a convenient way of organising the west midlands evidence. This framework is summarised below (cf Gamble 1999, tbl 6.5, 6.9). Dates are given in years Ka (thousand years ago).

*Early Upper Palaeolithic*

39-36 Ka: Leaf point industries; Jerzmanovican points.

*36-32 Ka: Cold phase: no human presence.*

32-28 Ka: Aurignacian II; nosed (shouldered) scrapers.

28-25 Ka: Gravettian; *Font Robert* points.

*25-13 Ka: Full Glacial conditions (MIS 2): no human presence (Last Glacial Maximum (LGM), c 18 Ka).*

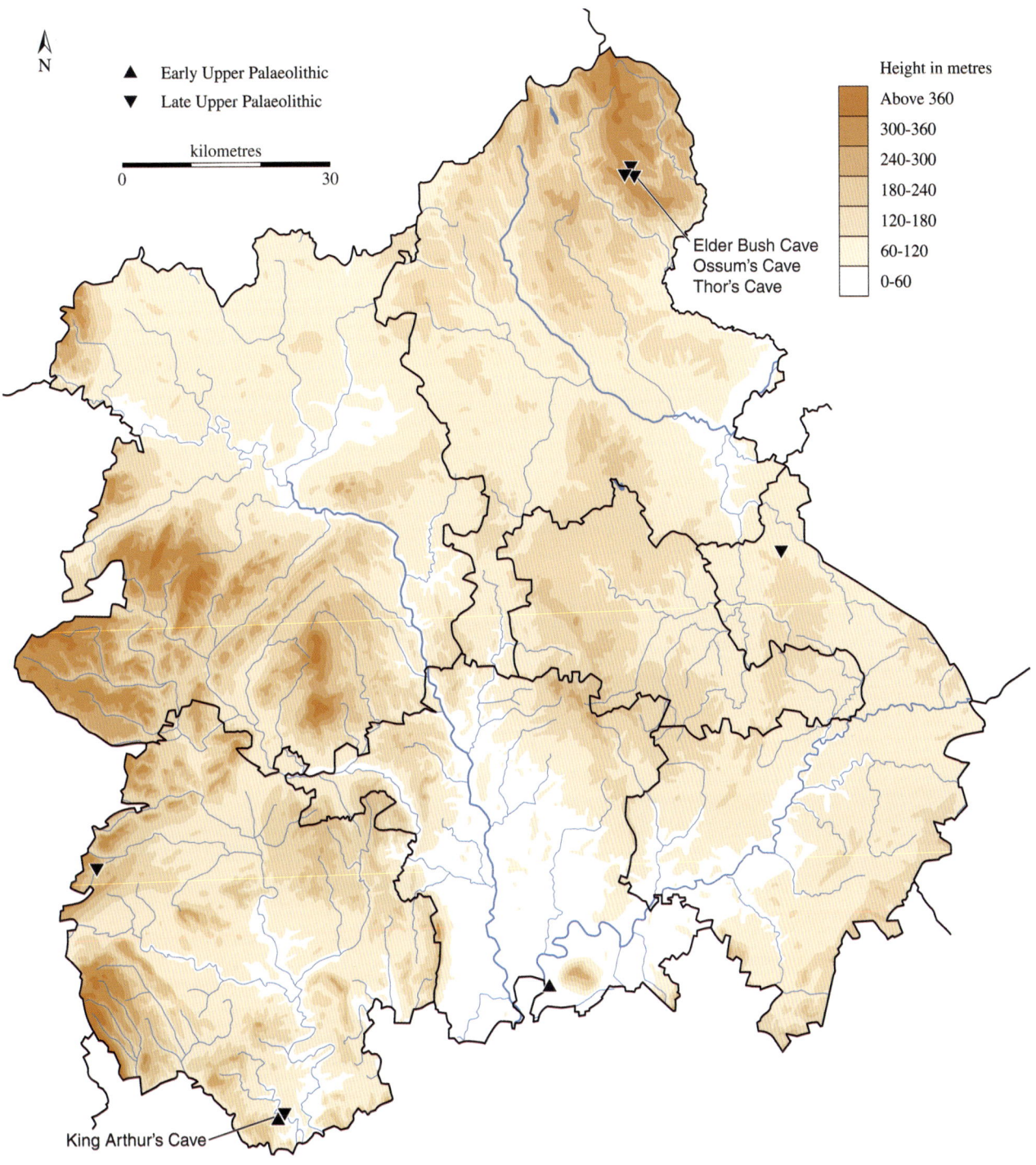

**Fig 2.2** Upper Palaeolithic sites and artefacts (after Myers 2007, fig 1)

*Late and Final Upper Palaeolithic*

    13-12 Ka: Creswellian (late Magdalenian); straight-backed blades, Cheddar points.

    12-11 Ka: Final Upper Palaeolithic; curve-backed blades and points, and penknife points.

    *11-10 Ka: Loch Lomond interstadial: extreme cold conditions; no human presence.*

    10.3-10 Ka: Final Upper Palaeolithic; long-blade industry.

    After *c* 10 Ka (*c* 8000 BC): Mesolithic industries.

### 2.3.2. Research assessment: current knowledge and understanding of the evidence

*Early Upper Palaeolithic sites and artefacts*

There are very few Early Upper Palaeolithic (EUP) finds from the west midlands (Fig 2.2) and only one site with known stratified deposits: King Arthur's Cave, Herefordshire (Campbell 1977, 41-3). This site produced a small lithic assemblage that included a Jerzmanovice leaf blade-point (Barton 2005, 115-16). Another possible leaf-shaped point has been identified from Tiddington, Warwickshire. It is uncertain whether these items, which date to the period 39–36 Ka, relate to late Neanderthal activity or mark the earliest presence of anatomically modern humans in Britain (ibid, 114). Two probable Aurignacian scrapers (*c* 32-28 Ka), found at Aston Mill Quarry in the Carrant valley, Worcestershire, can be associated more confidently with modern human settlement. No Gravettian artefacts have been recorded in the region (Myers 2007, 25).

*Late and Final Upper Palaeolithic sites and artefacts*

The earliest reoccupation of Britain following the LGM is associated with Creswellian artefacts, dating to *c*13-12 Ka. The only sites with definite Late Upper Palaeolithic (LUP) finds in the west midlands are King Arthur's Cave (Myers 2007, 25; cf Campbell 1977, 41-3) and Arrow Court, Kington, Herefordshire (two backed tools: Campbell 1977, 167-8) (Fig 2.2). There are also several sites in the region with final Upper Palaeolithic material such as penknife points: King Arthur's Cave, Herefordshire (Barton 2005, fig 127); Ossum's Cave, Elder Bush Cave and Thor's Cave in the Staffordshire Peak District (Campbell 1977; Myers 2007, 25); and Purley Park, Warwickshire (ibid, 26). No long-blade assemblages associated with the Final Upper Palaeolithic re-colonisation of Britain (from *c* 10.3 Ka), at the end of the cold Loch Lomond interstadial, have been found in the west midlands (ibid).

*Spatial patterns and regionality*

Regional contrasts are not discernible in the distribution of the few EUP artefacts in Britain, but the larger numbers of LUP finds reveal a distinctive spatial pattern. Campbell (1977, 158-60, map 46) suggested that they fall into two major groups: in northern/eastern England and southern/western England, divided by an extensive area across the midlands and central Wales that is largely devoid of LUP artefacts. This 'empty' area is interpreted as either a 'socio-ecological buffer zone' between distinct communities, or as an area traversed by a single population during a seasonal round (ie between winter encampments to south and west, and summer hunting stations to north and east; ibid, 159). Similar observations have been made by Smith (1992, 165-7), who interpreted the occupied zones as areas of settlement by groups migrating from different parts of Europe, and the intervening midlands area as a birch and willow scrub landscape with 'less to offer' in economic terms (ibid, 166). Although recent finds in areas such as Leicestershire (see below) may modify this picture to some extent, distribution maps continue to reproduce the general spatial pattern (eg Barton 2005, figs 127-26). From this perspective, the sites in the south-west of the west midlands (including King Arthur's Cave), and those in the north of the region in the Peak District, may have belonged to separate cultural regions in the LUP, or were occupation sites that related to very different economic practices at different times of the year.

### 2.3.3. Research agenda and specific research questions

The west midlands has the potential to contribute in several ways to national research agendas in Upper Palaeolithic archaeology. The geographical situation of the region at the margins of known distributions of EUP material culture, and between what appear to have been distinct LUP regions (cultural and/or economic), provides opportunities for investigating the chronology, scale, extent and spatial pattern of Upper Palaeolithic occupation in Britain, including phases of re-colonisation and abandonment in response to climatic and environmental changes. The Upper Palaeolithic communities that occupied this region, at the northernmost fringes of human population distributions, would have been especially sensitive to changes of this kind. Moreover, the wide range of topographic zones in the region, with adjacent areas of upland and lowland terrain, provides opportunities for investigating relationships between upland and lowland occupation and economic activity, and between cave and open-air sites.

Specific regional research aims and questions that should take priority are discussed below under period headings.

### Early Upper Palaeolithic

Reinvestigation of King Arthur's Cave, Herefordshire, and a search for EUP sites of similar date in the same area, are clear priorities for investigating the earliest presence of anatomically modern humans in the west midlands and their relationship with late Neanderthal communities. Assessment and prospection work to identify EUP occupation in the limestone caves of Staffordshire may also be rewarding. In wider terms, the thin distribution of artefacts currently known in lowland areas need not reflect either the research potential of EUP sites in the region nor the extent and intensity of occupation. The hunting station site recently excavated at Glaston, Rutland (Barton 2005, 116; Myers 2006; 2007, 25), demonstrates the existence of EUP remains in open-air locations, with important implications for the possibility of future discoveries of this kind elsewhere in the English midlands (Myers 2007, 27).

### Late and Final Upper Palaeolithic

The presence of Creswellian material at King Arthur's Cave, and the concentrations of sites just outside the west midlands, to the south-west in the Cheddar area and to the north-east in the Creswell area, suggests that work on LUP sites in the region may contribute significantly to studies of the rate and extent of re-colonisation of Britain after the LGM. A clear research priority in regional terms should be to determine the spatial pattern of LUP activity, especially in relation to the interpretative frameworks proposed by Campbell (1977) and Smith (1992). Identification of open-air sites in the west midlands would raise questions about the validity of existing spatial models, besides offering opportunities to explore the social organisation and resource procurement and consumption practices of LUP communities. The important open-air sites investigated recently at Bradgate Park (Creswellian assemblage) and Launde (long-blade assemblage) in Leicestershire, point to the potential presence of LUP material in open-air locations in the west midlands (Myers 2007, 26). The long-blade assemblage at Launde also raises questions about the extent to which central Britain was occupied during the first phase of re-colonisation after the Loch Lomond interstadial (ibid; Cooper 2006, 86-90).

### 2.3.4. Research aims and methods

The research agenda and questions for Upper Palaeolithic archaeology in the west midlands discussed in the previous section point to some important methodological and practical issues in current and future archaeological work in the region.

- Myers (2007) notes that most field and curatorial archaeologists are unfamiliar with Upper Palaeolithic archaeology and Late Glacial environmental studies. Guidance for field and curatorial archaeologists in dealing with Upper Palaeolithic sites is called for (cf Myers 2007, 27), especially in terms of the potential of lithic studies and site recognition/data recovery methods (eg Collcut, in McNabb 2006, App.2; English Heritage 2000; Lithic Studies Society 2004; Pollard 1998).

- Existing lithic artefact collections in museums should be re-evaluated as Upper Palaeolithic artefacts may have gone unrecognised (Myers 2007, 26).

- As much of what is known about the Upper Palaeolithic in Britain derives from cave deposits, a programme of cave prospection offers considerable potential for the identification of new sites. Discoveries of human remains and/or dating evidence in association with stratified artefact assemblages and palaeo-environmental evidence would be of exceptional importance (ibid). It is also important to note that the recent recognition of late glacial parietal art at Creswell, Nottinghamshire (Ripoll et al 2004), invites detailed survey of cave interiors in the west midlands.

- Recent discoveries in the east midlands have shown the existence of important Upper Palaeolithic open-air sites, with major implications for Upper Palaeolithic archaeology in the west midlands. Curatorial and field archaeologists should be aware of this potential, and take active measures through appropriate site evaluation strategies to locate Upper Palaeolithic sites (Myers 2007, 27). This should include an awareness of potential deposits in what are now urban areas (ibid). The intensity of surface collection and other sampling strategies is especially significant for effective identification of Upper Palaeolithic sites in open-air settings (cf Hey and Lacey 2001).

### 2.3.5. Conclusion

The Upper Palaeolithic period in the west midlands is clearly of great potential importance to future research at regional, national and international scales. The discovery of well-preserved *in situ* deposits would be especially relevant to research questions concerning the migration and social behaviour of anatomically modern humans in relation to the extreme environmental changes that took place in Europe during MIS 3 and 2. The geographical position of the region at the furthest northern limits of Upper Palaeolithic settlement in Europe is clearly important as a context for investigating modern human adaptations and social and cultural life in extreme environmental conditions.

Particular priorities, in this context, are to define more clearly the earliest presence of modern humans in the west midlands during the EUP and their relationship with late Neanderthal communities, and to identify LUP sites in the region that may contribute to an understanding of the re-colonisation of Britain after the Late Glacial Maximum. The importance of cave sites in the region should not be forgotten and more of these deserve serious investigation using modern techniques, but perhaps especially important for future developer-funded field archaeology is the potential for discoveries of Upper Palaeolithic open-air sites throughout the west midlands. Like the Lower and Middle Palaeolithic periods, the Upper Palaeolithic has been neglected in regional research terms and there is potential for major new discoveries that could change wider perceptions of modern human communities in Britain during the last Ice Age. It is again important to note that the National Ice Age Network, and the Ancient Human Occupation of Britain project will contribute significantly to the development of Upper Palaeolithic studies in the region.

## 2.4. Mesolithic

### 2.4.1. Introduction

#### The Mesolithic in the West midlands: previous research

The Mesolithic has been little studied in the west midlands and in some respects has been neglected at a national scale. The most recent gazetteer of known finds, for example, was published nearly 30 years ago (Wymer 1977) and is now out of date. The only regional-scale studies are Saville's (1981) analysis of the Mesolithic tool industries of central England and Bevan's (1995) doctoral thesis on aspects of later Mesolithic settlement. Although there have been several excavations of Mesolithic sites and widespread surface collection of artefacts since 1980, there has been no attempt to collate or evaluate this evidence until very recently. It is notable that local and regional accounts of the Mesolithic in the west midlands are almost completely absent from recent interpretative studies and period reviews (eg see Young 2000).

In this context, Myers' (2007) review of the Mesolithic for the Regional Research Framework earlier prehistory seminar is an important contribution to our understanding of this period in the region. The present discussion of the evidence is based on that paper, Greig's (2007) discussion of Holocene environmental evidence and references to the midlands evidence in a range of other interpretative studies.

#### Current research agenda in Mesolithic archaeology

The Mesolithic was a period of profound social and cultural changes, from the development of early Holocene hunter-gatherer societies to the adoption of farming, and it important to emphasise that the societies represented cannot be understood separately from their environments and the processess of rapid climatic warming, sea level rises and afforestation that took place in the period *c* 8000-4000 BC. The material record consists almost entirely of lithic assemblages, although there is also some evidence for built structures and other remains (see Mithen 1999 for an introduction to the nature of the evidence).

Current research themes in British Mesolithic archaeology are set out in a Prehistoric Society research document (1999), and key issues and debates are reviewed in several recent books and articles (eg Bevan and Moore 2003; Conneller and Warren 2006; Larsen et al 2003; Mithen 1999; Panter-Brick et al 2001; Smith 1992; Young 2000). These identify a number of general research themes that are relevant to the west midlands:

1.  Environmental change and settlement at the Pleistocene/Holocene (Late Upper Palaeolithic/Mesolithic) boundary, *c* 9000-7000 BC (Prehistoric Society 1999, 4; Mithen 1999, 35-43; Smith 1992; Tolan-Smith 2003a).

2.  The geographical distribution and local adaptations of Mesolithic populations in relation to changing environmental conditions, resource availability and diet during the early Holocene (Prehistoric Society 1999, 4-5; cf Mithen 1999; Smith 1992).

3.  Large-scale organisation of Mesolithic societies: territories, migration ranges, and regional cultural or ethnic groups (Prehistoric Society 1999, 5; cf Bergsvik 2003; Jacobi 1976; Reynier 1998; Saville 2003; Smith 1992).

4.  Settlement, subsistence and other practices, including the nature of occupation sites, residential mobility and perceptions of landscape (Prehistoric Society 1999, 4-5; cf Grøn 2001; McFadyen 2006; Milner 2006; Mithen 1999, 49-55; Moore 2003; Whitelaw 1994; Zvelebil 2003).

5.  Lithic technologies, tool function and behaviour (Prehistoric Society 1999, 5; cf Lithic Studies Society 2004; Mithen 1999, 49-52; Warren 2006).

#### Period subdivision

The Mesolithic can be divided broadly into early and late phases on the basis of both artefactual and environmental evidence (Mithen 1999, 43):

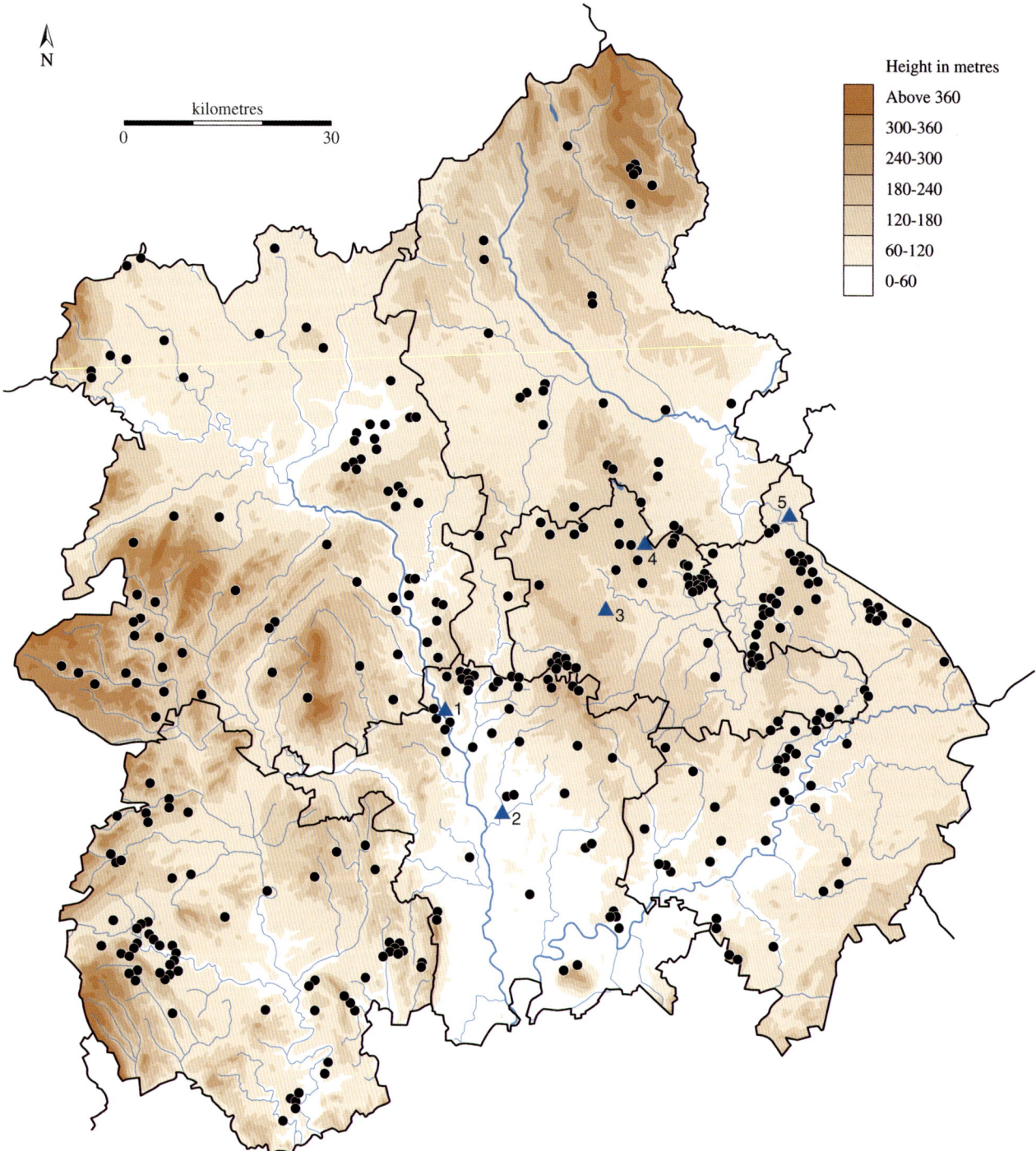

**Fig 2.3** Distribution of Mesolithic finds in the west midlands (after Myers 2007, fig 2). Sites in the region with occupation features are numbered: 1. Lightmarsh Farm, Trimpley; 2. Dodderhill; 3. Sandwell Priory, West Bromwich; 4. Bourne Pool, Aldridge; 5. Kisses Barn Farm, Polesworth

*Early Mesolithic, c* 8000-6500 BC: typified by 'broad blade assemblages' with large microliths such as obliquely blunted points. Subsistence practices appear to have been dominated by terrestrial large game hunting. Climatic warming resulted in sea-level rises, which led to the separation of Britain from the continent (*c* 6500 BC), and an afforestation process that transformed open landscapes into mixed broadleaved woodland.

*Late Mesolithic, c* 6500-4000 BC: typified by 'narrow blade assemblages' with small microliths to make tools suitable for a diverse range of hunting and processing tasks. Broad-spectrum subsistence practices included the hunting of woodland game such as red and roe deer and wild pig, and intensive exploitation of both woodland plant resources and marine resources.

## 2.4.2. Research assessment: current knowledge and understanding of the evidence

The distribution of Mesolithic finds in the west midlands is shown in Fig 2.3 (from Myers 2007). Finds densities in the region (especially of Early Mesolithic material) are relatively low in comparison with other parts of Britain (see Smith and Openshaw 1990). Most Mesolithic artefacts have been found in surface contexts, but systematic collection has rarely been undertaken and finds locations are usually imprecise. Surface finds are also very uneven in spatial terms, with significantly more recorded in Warwickshire and Worcestershire than other counties in the region. A major problem identified by Myers (2007) is the questionable value of HER databases for studying the distribution of Mesolithic artefacts, which are all too often listed simply as 'prehistoric', and there have been few attempts to study museum or private collections to identify Mesolithic artefacts among larger lithic assemblages. Excavations of Mesolithic sites are also exceptionally rare, although a few have produced evidence for features and possible structures.

### Environmental data

Three well-dated palaeo-environmental sequences from sites at Crose Mere, Shropshire (Beales 1980), The King's Pool, Stafford (Bartley and Morgan 1990), and Wilden Marsh, Worcestershire (Brown 1988), provide the main sources of information for climate change and environmental conditions during the early Holocene in the west midlands (Greig 2007, 42-3). Although there is variation from one site to another, the west midlands evidence conforms to the generally recognised sequence of woodland colonisation in Britain after the last glaciation: marked by the spread, successively, of birch, hazel, pine, elm and oak, and finally lime and alder. This culminated in mixed broadleaved woodland known as the 'wildwood', consisting primarily of oak, alder, hazel and elm (ibid; cf Rackham 1980). In chronological terms, this process in the west midlands spanned the period c 9500/8500 BC to c 7200/7000 BC, by which time mixed broadleaved woodland was fully developed at all three sites (Greig 2007, 42). It is important to emphasise, however, that there was considerable local variation in the extent of clearings, the density and appearance of woodland cover and the types of woodland present (eg carr woods dominated by oak, alder and willow in valley bottoms; while woodlands on drier land were possibly dominated by lime; ibid).

Faunal evidence of Mesolithic date is very sparse, with only one site in the region producing a significant assemblage of large ungulate remains (King Arthur's Cave, Herefordshire: aurochs, elk, red deer, roe deer, wild pig and horse). Examples of wolf and beaver, and small mammals, have been found at other sites (ibid). There is also very little evidence for the impact of human populations on the environment, although woodland burning is suggested at King's Pool, Stafford, and Impney Farm, Droitwich (ibid).

### Mesolithic sites and lithic artefacts

Most of the Mesolithic finds recorded in the west midlands are the result of unsystematic surface collection, although a few areas have attracted more systematic programmes of fieldwork, often carried out by amateurs (Myers 2007, 31), including the Clun and Kinver areas in Shropshire, the Weaver Hills, Staffordshire, Halesowen and Sutton Coldfield, Birmingham, and the New Red Sandstone Hills and Wolvey area in Warwickshire. It is notable, in contrast, that the extensive North-West Wetlands survey in north Shropshire produced very few Mesolithic artefacts (Leah et al 1998). In general terms, the distribution of Mesolithic artefacts from surface contexts suggests a preference for well-drained elevated terrain close to water sources (Myers 2007, 31), This pattern may, however, be a product of uneven fieldwork (which has concentrated on ploughed fields in areas with free-draining soils) and post-depositional processes, especially in river valleys where erosion and alluviation may have led to widespread destruction or concealment of Mesolithic sites. The presence of Mesolithic artefacts in areas with clay soils (ibid) suggests that Mesolithic activity may have been more widespread and in more diverse topographical and geological locales than generally assumed.

Excavations that have deliberately targeted known Mesolithic sites are very rare in the west midlands, although there are some examples of excavations of later sites that have produced significant Mesolithic evidence. The excavation of a multi-period lithic scatter at Bourne Pool, near Aldridge, West Bromwich, produced over 2000 artefacts including basally-retouched points that suggest an Early Mesolithic phase of activity in the mid to late 7th millennium BC (Saville 1972-3; Myers 2007, 32). Significant artefact assemblages, mostly Late Mesolithic, have also been recorded in excavations at Sandwell Priory in West Bromwich (Hodder 1991), Lightmarsh Farm Camp, Worcestershire (over 1400 artefacts; Jackson et al 1996), Dodderhill, Worcestershire, and at Kisses' Barn Farm, Corley Camp and Rollright in Warwickshire. Smaller assemblages have been found beneath round barrows in the Staffordshire Peak District, the Roman road at Chaddesley, Worcestershire, and medieval deposits at the Durrance moat site in Worcestershire (including an Early Mesolithic tranchet axe) (Myers 2007, 29-30, 32). Features such as stakeholes, gullies and hollows associated with Mesolithic artefacts have been recorded at several sites in the region, including Lightmarsh Farm and Dodderhill, Worcestershire; Sandwell Priory; Bourne Pool, Aldridge; and Kisses' Barn Farm, Warwickshire (see Fig 2.3 for site locations). Although these are mostly poorly preserved, they suggest the presence of settlement structures and activity areas, which are rare at a national scale.

Excavations of caves and rock shelter sites in Staffordshire have also produced small quantities of lithic material (Myers 2007, 29), including Early Mesolithic artefacts from Wetton Mill Rockshelter in the Manifold valley, and Late Mesolithic artefacts from a small rockshelter site at Rugeley.

### Spatial patterns and regionality

It has been suggested that a distinctive regional pattern of settlement can be recognised in the British Mesolithic, with relatively intense occupation of both northern/eastern England and southern/western England, separated by an extensive area across the midlands and central Wales in which Mesolithic artefacts are sparse (Tolan-Smith 2003b, 116; cf Smith and Openshaw 1990). This in some respects reproduces the model proposed for the Later Upper Palaeolithic by Campbell (1977, 158-60, map 46) and Smith (1992, 165-7), although Tolan-Smith (2003b, 116-17) suggests that the midlands was not simply a 'buffer zone' or 'resource reservoir' between distinct populations, but may have been a dangerous area of conflict and competition that was rarely traversed even by hunting parties. Myers (2007) strongly rejects this view, arguing that the character and scale of Mesolithic activity in the midlands remains under-investigated, and that low finds densities may in any case relate to distinctive regional patterns of resource procurement and settlement mobility. The distribution map of Mesolithic find spots derived from HER data (Fig 2.3) certainly shows no increases in densities towards the north/east and south/west peripheries, which might be expected given that the region more than spans the 'unoccupied' zone defined by Tolan-Smith (extending 100 km north-south; 2003b, 116). Instead, the distribution map shows a relative concentration of Mesolithic activity in the central uplands and eastern part of the region.

### Processes of long term change in the Mesolithic of the west midlands

At present, very little is known about social and economic changes in the west midlands during the Final Upper Palaeolithic/Mesolithic transition, Early to Late Mesolithic phases, or the Mesolithic/Neolithic transition (discussed in detail in the next section). The rarity of Early Mesolithic material, in particular, prevents comparisons with Final Upper Palaeolithic and Late Mesolithic evidence, and the general absence of well-stratified archaeological sequences and absolute dating evidence for any part of the period *c* 9000-4000 BC (Myers 2007) undermines detailed study of long-term change in settlement patterns, economic practices and social organisation.

### 2.4.3. Research agenda and specific research questions

### Social and economic change

Research priorities in Mesolithic studies in the west midlands include investigation of the Upper Palaeolithic to Early Mesolithic transition, the nature of social, economic and cultural changes during the Mesolithic, and the transition from hunting and gathering to farming during the Late Mesolithic. Colonisation processes (see Tolan-Smith 2003a) and changing modes of occupation demand particular attention, especially the change suggested from Early Mesolithic seasonal residence systems that were part of long distance migratory cycles in open grassland landscapes, to Late Mesolithic 'tethered mobility' settlement patterns within relatively fixed local territories in woodland landscapes. These have very different implications for the scale and spatial organisation of social groups and community dispersal and aggregation (Smith 1992, Spikens 2000). This will require a good deal more detailed investigation of occupation sites (especially of Early Mesolithic and Late Mesolithic/Early Neolithic date) and the recovery of detailed evidence for changes in environmental conditions, resource availability and diet (Myers 2007, 28, 34; cf Prehistoric Society 1999, 4-5).

### Settlement, economy and community

There is considerable potential in the west midlands for investigating local adaptations by Mesolithic communities to particular environmental conditions and landscape settings. Key research aims must be to identify and investigate occupation sites, to characterise different kinds of settlements and activities, and relate these to wider residence patterns, social groups and systems of resource exploitation. This will require landscape studies organised at an appropriate analytical scale (see Darvill 2003) to integrate the evidence for social practices from well-preserved occupation sites with the evidence from surface lithic scatters (Myers 2007, 32-5). The presence of possible structures and activity areas at Mesolithic sites in the region suggests that there is considerable research potential for analyses of social practices within occupation areas and perhaps settlement organisation (cf Grøn 2001; Smith 1992, 29-34; Whitelaw 1994). Other important research themes in this context include the perception and meaning of landscape (see: Moore 2003; Zvelebil 2003), environmental manipulation by Mesolithic communities (eg deliberate burning to facilitate hunting in open clearings; Moore 2003), and diet and population mobility (eg based on stable isotope studies of human skeletal material; Richards and Schulting 2003).

### Lithic artefacts

A fundamental aspect of Mesolithic research in the west midlands should be systematic study of the principal archaeological resource, lithic artefacts, especially in relation to technologies, tool function and behaviour. Analysis of existing lithic artefact collections in museums and full publication of excavated site data would considerably enhance the research potential of this material (Myers 2007, 35). A number of key research aims in lithic studies in the region can be identified (ibid; cf Lithic Studies Society 2004):

1.  Refinement of lithic artefact chronologies, especially in relation to Early Mesolithic variants, possible intermediate industries containing basally-trimmed microliths and early to mid 4th millennium BC types.

2.  Chronological evaluation of technological and typological changes in comparison to changes in the locations and sizes of sites (which elsewhere in Britain appears to be closely related; Myers 2007, 34).

3.  Identification of 'assemblage-types' (and thus consistent technical and behavioural categories in site use) in Early and Late Mesolithic assemblages through quantitative and comparative analysis of artefact assemblages.

4.  Definition of raw material types and artefact reduction sequences to study stone tool manufacturing technologies, and investigation of intra-site discard patterns and tool use (cf Lithic Studies Society 2004, 4-5).

### Spatial patterns and regionality

A clear research priority in regional terms should be to determine the overall spatial pattern of Mesolithic activity in the west midlands, especially in relation to the interpretative framework proposed by Tolan-Smith (2003b) and recent discussions of territoriality, regionality and the possible presence of distinct ethnic or cultural groups in the European Mesolithic (cf Bergsvik 2003; Jacobi 1976; Reynier 1998; Saville 2003; Smith 1992). Central research aims, in this context, should be to determine whether the midlands was a sparsely inhabited region during the whole or part of the Mesolithic (Tolan-Smith 2003b), and to identify typologically distinctive assemblages and artefact types in the region (such as 'midlands basally-trimmed microliths') that may represent distinct cultural identities, social groups or demographic relationships (Myers 2007, 32, 34). A major methodological issue in this context is the reliability of existing HER databases for constructing distribution maps of Mesolithic find spots, and how these may (or may not) reflect the original density and intensity of occupation at different times during this period (ibid; cf Lithic Studies Society 2004, 3; Smith 1992, 27-43).

### 2.4.4. Research aims and methods

The research agenda and key research questions outlined above have major implications for methods of resource assessment, curatorial practices, fieldwork methods, and networks of communication and data gathering in Mesolithic archaeology in the west midlands.

- Myers (2007) observes that many field and curatorial archaeologists are unfamiliar with current themes in Mesolithic archaeology and Early Holocene environmental studies, and may need specific guidance for dealing with Mesolithic sites, especially with regard to the potential of lithic artefact analysis and site recognition and data recovery methods (eg English Heritage 2000, Lithic Studies Society 2004, Pollard 1998).

- A fundamental requirement for future research on the Mesolithic of the west midlands is improvement of local authority HER databases so that they include all known finds and sites (Myers 2007, 34-5). These provide the primary sources of archaeological data used in the development control process yet in some cases appear not to have taken account of available gazetteers of known evidence (ibid). It would assist research if these databases categorised artefactual material in more detail, at the very least in broad chronological terms.

- The preparation of *precise* specifications for projects that are likely to encounter Mesolithic sites or artefacts is essential, especially with regard to appropriate surface collection and excavation methods for recovering Mesolithic evidence (ibid).

- It is important that strategies are put in place for recognising and/or prospecting for Mesolithic material during excavations of later sites, including urban locations (high quality evidence, for example, has been recovered from urban sites in London; ibid).

- Systematic surface collection of Mesolithic artefact assemblages is needed throughout the west midlands, especially in areas which have attracted little previous work and/or where little is known about Mesolithic activity (eg river valleys). Surveys of different soil-types and topographic locations to identify preferred occupation or activity sites would be of considerable value, especially for predictive modelling of site locations.

- There is considerable potential for more widespread and intensive use of systematic test-pitting methods as a means of prospecting for and evaluating Mesolithic sites. However, a critical requirement of such surveys is the need to use narrow intervals between both surface collection and test-pitting transects in order to locate small lithic artefact concentrations of 10m diameter or less (Myers 2007, 33-4; see Hey and Lacey 2001, for a discussion of sampling procedures on prehistoric sites).

- Scatters of Mesolithic artefacts defined by surface collection and test pitting should be excavated as a standard procedure to recover artefacts in the topsoil and to explore possible features beneath (which may be relatively insubstantial and thus easily destroyed by machining) (English Heritage 2000).

- Careful and detailed recording of the character, content and spatial distribution of lithic assemblages is essential. The development of excavation methods appropriate for investigating and analysing artefact-prolific scatters produced by numerous repeat visits to the same location, would be especially valuable (Myers 2007, 34-5).

- Well-preserved Mesolithic sites with stratified artefact assemblages, structural remains and/or high quality environmental and dating evidence are of primary research importance in regional, national and international terms.

- Systematic evaluation of cave sites in the region to identify stratified Mesolithic deposits, recover artefact assemblages and human remains, and collect radiocarbon dating samples, may be particularly rewarding (ibid).

- The recovery of human remains would be exceptionally important for dating purposes, dietary and demographic studies, and for investigating mortuary and ritual practices (cf Conneller 2006).

### 2.4.5. Conclusion

The Mesolithic period is perhaps the least understood of the earlier prehistoric periods in the west midlands, and has certainly suffered from a lack of concerted research at anything other than local scales. The region has relatively low densities of recorded Mesolithic finds in comparison with other parts of Britain, but Myers (2007, 28-9) argues strongly that this does not necessarily mean that occupation was sparse or that the region comprised a 'buffer zone' or 'resource reservoir' (cf Tolan-Smith 2003b, 116-17). Instead, he observes that current HERs have been especially ineffective in recording Mesolithic material, and that the character and scale of Mesolithic activity in the west midlands remains under-investigated in all aspects (Myers 2007, 28-9, 31, 34-5).

In this context, there are clear priorities and areas of research potential for Mesolithic studies in the region. A key avenue of research at a large spatial scale is to determine whether the west midlands was sparsely inhabited during all or part of the Mesolithic. Particular attention needs to be paid to colonisation processes and local adaptations to particular environmental conditions and landscape settings by Mesolithic communities (especially through landscape studies of lithic artefact scatters and excavation of occupation sites). There is also potential for investigating changes in the large-scale spatial organisation of residential, migrational and territorial patterns, and for studying social behaviour within occupation areas. Curatorial and field archaeologists in the west midlands will have an extremely important part to play in redressing the history of under-investigation of this period in the region, especially by being aware of current research agenda, the need to recover Mesolithic artefacts in all depositional contexts, and the need to identify and excavate occupation sites.

## 2.5. Early Neolithic

### 2.5.1. Introduction

*The Early Neolithic in the west midlands: previous research*
The Early Neolithic (*c* 4000-3400 BC) is defined by the first appearance in Britain of domesticated animal and plant species and associated agricultural technologies, a range of substantial and/or durable material culture categories, including monumental architecture and ceramics, and a diverse range of new social practices including complex mortuary ritual leading to formal burial deposition. These changes are usually thought to mark far-reaching social and economic changes, although the nature and chronology of these are much disputed (discussed below).

There has been very little previous research work specifically devoted to the Early Neolithic in the west midlands. Regional and county-based syntheses of the evidence are limited in scope, there have been few systematic artefact collection surveys and material culture studies relating to the west midlands are rare. Vine's (1982) survey of the Neolithic of the Middle and Upper Trent Basin, for example, is now rather dated and restricted to Staffordshire, north Warwickshire and the old West Midlands county, while Hingley's (1996) short, incisive review of the Warwickshire evidence inevitably lacks detail and does not take account of significant recent publications and new discoveries. Neolithic ceramics in the region have been summarised briefly by Ann Woodward (in Hughes and Woodward 1995, 15-18) but no detailed synthesis of the material exists. Surveys of prehistoric evidence at a smaller 'landscape' scale are almost non-existent: the only significant example being an assessment of the prehistory of lowland Shropshire (Buteux and Hughes 1995). Large-scale fieldwork projects have been undertaken in several parts of the region, but with the notable exception of the Avon valley in Warwickshire these have not produced major groups of Early Neolithic sites (see below).

In this context, the wide range of papers entirely or partly concerned with the Early Neolithic that were prepared for the Regional Research Framework earlier prehistory seminar (Garwood 2007d), provides an important new basis for investigating this period in the region. These include general descriptive and interpretative syntheses (Ray 2007, Greig 2007), thematic studies (Barfield 2007, Woodward 2007), data-set assessments (Barber 2007) and site-specific studies (Jackson 2007, Palmer 2007). The present discussion of the evidence is based on these papers, and on current interpretative frameworks and debates in wider discussions of the British Early Neolithic.

*Current research agenda in Early Neolithic archaeology*
Apart from the broad themes defined by Kinnes (1994) over a decade ago, there has been no recent attempt to identify research agenda in Early Neolithic archaeology at a national scale. Prehistoric Society research documents (1984, 1988) focus mainly on fieldwork and conservation priorities. Key research themes are highlighted, however, in several recent books (eg Bradley 1998, 2007; Thomas 1991, 1999; Whittle 1996), and there is an exceptionally large and growing research literature concerned with Early Neolithic topics. Especially important research themes in current Early Neolithic archaeology include:

1. *The nature of the 'Neolithic' and the Mesolithic-Neolithic transition.*
   Prevailing interpretative frameworks reject the traditional 'Neolithic package' model and instead represent the Neolithic primarily as a cultural rather than an economic phenomenon (eg Thomas 1993, 1999, 2003; Whittle 1996; Bradley 2004). The recognition of regional diversity, uncertainty about the economic importance of farming, lack of consensus about the temporalities of cultural and economic changes and suggestions of continuity in hunter-gatherer practices, have raised fundamental questions about the nature of Early Neolithic society (eg see: Thomas 1999, 7-33; King 2003; Pollard 2004). In this context, the emergence of an increasingly precise, fine-grained absolute chronology for the early Neolithic has far-reaching implications for social and cultural

interpretation (and already suggests a series of sub-phases marked by rapid cultural changes) (see Whittle 2007).

2. *The significance of agriculture.* The relative importance of farming to subsistence and social organisation remains a key research issue (Bradley 1984a; Kinnes 1988, 1994; Thomas 1999). There is, at present, strong disagreement between those who argue that farming was of central economic importance (eg Entwistle and Grant 1989, Richards and Hedges 1999, Rowley-Conwy 2003, Schulting 2000), and those who argue that farming was just one part, often of limited importance in subsistence terms, of a more variegated economy (eg Bradley 2004; Fairbairn 2000, Jones 2000; Moffett et al 1989; Robinson 2000; Thomas 1993, 1999, 2003; Whittle 2000).

3. *Environmental change.* The impact of Early Neolithic communities on the environment is widely debated, with increasing evidence for only limited woodland clearance (eg see Allen et al 2004, Austin 2000, Brown 2000, Pollard 2004).

4. *Monuments.* Tombs, barrows and enclosures and the practices associated with them have always been central to interpretations of Early Neolithic society in Britain (eg Piggott 1954; Renfrew 1973; Bradley 1984a, 1998; Barrett 1988; Kinnes 1994; Thomas 1999). There are recent surveys of earthen long barrows (Kinnes 1992, Field 2006), chambered tombs (Darvill 2004) and causewayed enclosures (Oswald et al 2001). Recent research has focused on the role of monuments and mortuary practices in the construction of social and cultural identities, the reification of classificatory and cosmological schemes, and phenomenological studies of monuments in the landscape (eg Bradley 1998, 2004; Cummings and Whittle 2003a, 2003b; Darvill 1997b; Oswald et al 2001, 107-32; Thomas 1999, 34-61, 126-51; Tilley 1994, 1998; Whittle and Pollard 1999).

5. *Settlement.* There are some strongly opposed views of Early Neolithic settlement. The limited evidence for houses in England, and rejection of the farming/sedentism model (eg Thomas 1993, 1996) have led to a new emphasis on residential mobility (eg Whittle 1997a; Evans et al 1999, Grogan 2002, Pollard 1999, 2000, 2004; cf Scarre 2001, for a north-west European perspective). This is contested by those who still favour a significant sedentary element in Neolithic settlement patterns, pointing to the evidence for substantial houses in Ireland while drawing attention to wider problems of site preservation and visibility (eg Cooney 2000a, Darvill 1996, Gibson 2003, Rowley-Conwy 2003).

6. *Material culture and depositional practices.* Recent discussions of artefact categories such as lithics (Lithic Studies Society 2004; cf Edmonds 1995, Pitts 1996), and ceramics (Cleal 1992, Hamilton 2002, Woodward 2002b), emphasise the distinctive characteristics of Early Neolithic extractive and production technologies, and exchange and consumption practices (eg Bradley and Edmonds 1993; Barber et al 1999). Perhaps the most significant area of interpretative debate, however, concerns depositional practices and their meaning, especially in relation to the deliberate placement of artefacts in ditches, pits and middens (Thomas 1999, 62-125; cf Evans et al 1999, Pollard 2002, Woodward 2002c).

7. *Regionality and cultural diversity.* There is growing research interest in cultural identity and diversity (eg 'ethnicity') and in the large-scale spatial structuring of social action, especially in terms of territoriality and regionality (eg Bradley 1984b; Harding 1995; Thomas 1998; Barclay 2000; Cooney 2000b; Armit et al 2003). Widespread recognition of significant regional diversity in the Early Neolithic has major implications for investigating the origins and development of farming communities and interactions within and between prehistoric cultural and economic regions (eg in relation to the long-distance exchange of flint and stone axes).

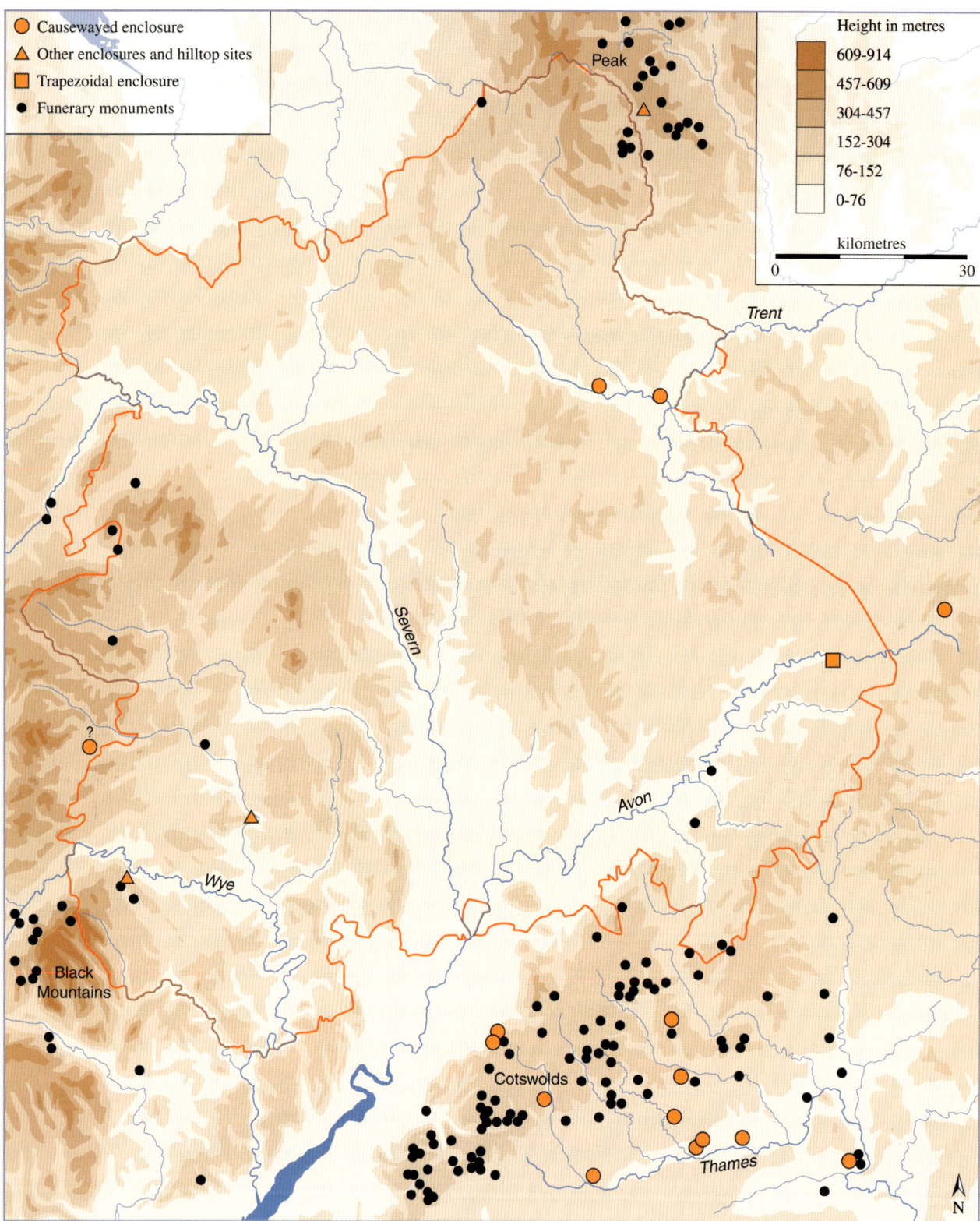

**Fig 2.4** Early Neolithic monuments in the west midlands (after Garwood 2007c, fig. 1)

## 2.5.2. Research assessment: current knowledge and understanding of the evidence

Early Neolithic sites and finds in the west midlands are unevenly distributed, mostly concentrated around the margins of the region, and sites and finds densities are low in comparison with distributions in neighbouring areas (Ray 2007, 57-60; Barfield 2007, 103-4). Although there have been large-scale fieldwork projects in parts of the region, Early Neolithic evidence is encountered only rarely. The most intensively studied area is the Avon valley in Warwickshire, where widespread rescue work took place under

the auspices of the Avon-Severn Valleys Research Committee from 1963 to 1973 (Hunt 1982), including important excavations of Early Neolithic monuments at Barford (Oswald 1969, Loveday 1989; cf Woodward 2007, 188-9) and Charlecote (Ford 2003). More recent excavations have taken place at Wasperton (Hughes and Crawford 1995), and Church Lawford (Palmer 1999; 2007, 126-9). Elsewhere in the region, Early Neolithic features have sometimes been investigated in the course of multi-period excavation projects: for example, at Sharpstones Hill, Shropshire (Barker et al 1991), and Wellington, Herefordshire (Jackson 2007). It is important to note, however, that other large-scale fieldwork projects in the region have produced very little or no Early Neolithic evidence. These include the North Shropshire wetlands survey (Leah et al 1998), the Wroxeter Hinterland project in west Shropshire (Lawrence Barfield, pers comm; project archive), the M6 Toll route in west Warwickshire and south Staffordshire (Denison 2002, Powell et al 2008), and the Arrow valley project in south-west Warwickshire (Palmer 1999).

**Fig 2.5** Arthur's Stone chambered tomb, Herefordshire (copyright Paul Garwood)

### Environment, landscape change and subsistence economy

Evidence for environmental conditions in the west midlands during the 5th and 4th millennia BC is patchy geographically and temporally imprecise (Greig 2007, 42-3). It is also striking that there is very little evidence from any site in the region for Early Neolithic agriculture, either in terms of its impact on the wider environment or in the form of direct evidence for domesticates or agricultural practices (ibid). Detailed pollen diagrams are available from several sites, including Wellington Quarry, Herefordshire (Jackson 2007, 112; Dinn and Roseff 1992), Crose Mere, Shropshire (Beales 1980), sites in the Shropshire wetlands (Leah et al 1998), the King's Pool, Stafford (Bartley and Morgan 1990), and Hartlebury Common, Wilden Marsh and Cookley in Worcestershire (Greig 2007, 43-5). Only Warwickshire lacks significant pollen evidence of Neolithic date (ibid).

The Wellington and Cookley sequences, in particular, provide a broad picture of environmental change during the Early Neolithic: both sites show evidence for woodland disturbance and increased presence of weeds in the early 4th millennium BC, with cereal

**Fig 2.6** Early Neolithic enclosures in the Trent valley at Alrewas and Mavesyn Ridware, Staffordshire (after Oswald et al 2001, figs 4.9, 4.18, app 76, 77)

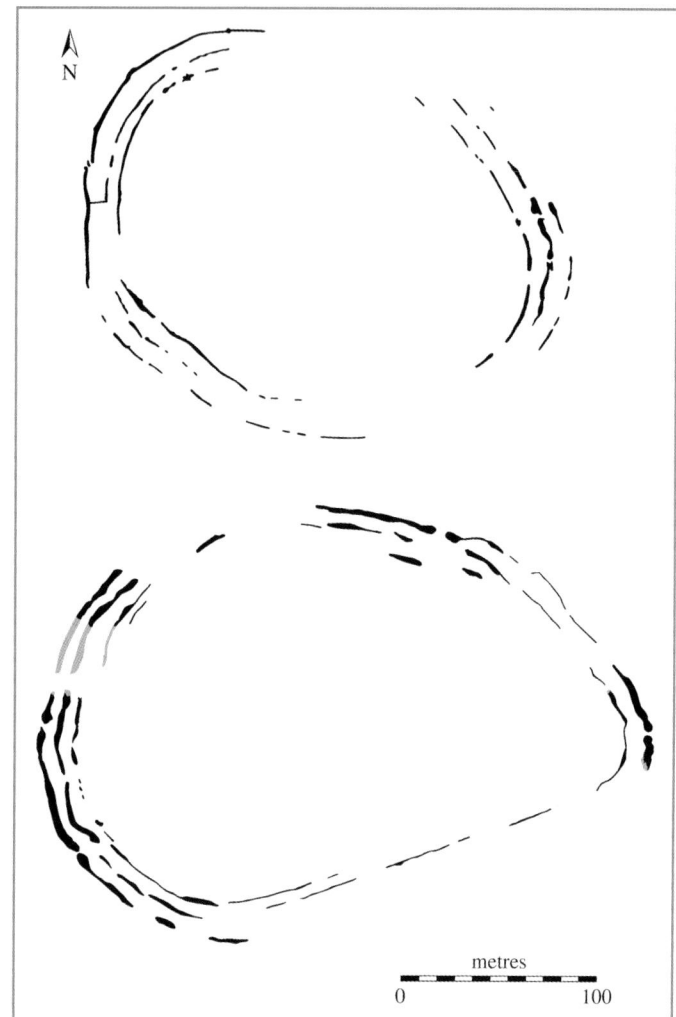

pollen at Cookley from *c* 3500 BC and at Wellington from *c* 3000 BC (Greig 2007, 45). There is no indication of large-scale woodland clearance at either site, however, until the 3rd millennium BC, which is consistent with the evidence from sites elsewhere in the west midlands and from other major river valleys in southern Britain (discussed in more detail below in relation to Middle and Late Neolithic landscapes). The argument that hunting and gathering may still have been important to the subsistence economy is reinforced by plant assemblages from Wellington, Herefordshire, Broom, Warwickshire and Kemerton, Worcestershire, which are dominated by wild plants such as hazelnuts, with little evidence for cultivated species such as wheat, barley and flax (Moffett 1999).

### *Monuments*

Early Neolithic monument types are very rare in the west midlands (Fig 2.4). There are no definite earthen long barrows in the region, although there are probable examples at Cross Lodge, Herefordshire, and Long Hill, Alderminster, Warwickshire (Ray 2007, 63), and another possible site at Hampton-in-Arden, also in Warwickshire. There are also several 'long' or 'mortuary' enclosures that are probably Early or Middle Neolithic in date (see discussion in Barber 2007, 85, 89-90), including examples at Mavesyn Ridware, Staffordshire (Loveday 2003, fig A1), Barford (Loveday 1989; Barber 2007, 89-90), Charlecote (Ford 2003), Wasperton Field 3 (Ray 2007, 63) and Church Lawford, Warwickshire (Palmer 2007, 126-9), and Norton, Worcestershire (Loveday and Petchey 1982). Of these, only the small rectilinear enclosure at Charlecote has significant dating evidence, indicating construction 'toward the close of the Earlier Neolithic' (Loveday 2003, 37). The Charlecote evidence also suggests that a low mound originally existed within the enclosure, which raises the possibility that at least some of the other rectilinear enclosures in the region were originally long mound sites (ibid).

Two definite chambered tombs are known in the west midlands: Arthur's Stone, Herefordshire (Fig 2.5), a north-eastern outlier of the Black Mountains group in Breconshire (Ray 2007, 63; cf Cummings and Whittle 2003a, 198), and the Bridestones site on the Staffordshire-Cheshire border (Ray 2007, 63). There are two more possible examples on the Warwickshire-Oxfordshire border at Chastleton (Hingley 1996, 7) and Rollright Stones Site 2 (Hingley 1996, 7; cf Lambrick 1988, 68-70), and another in the Lugg valley at The Tarrs, Kingsland, Herefordshire (Ray 2007, 63, fig 5.8). There may also be a number of partly stone-built Early Neolithic funerary monuments in the Staffordshire Peak District, including Long Low, Wetton and Grub Low, Waterhouses (ibid). Identifications of other possible funerary monuments at the northern end of the Golden Valley in Herefordshire, and at Hales on the Shropshire-Staffordshire border, are now thought to be dubious or are demonstrably erroneous (ibid).

Early Neolithic enclosure sites are also exceptionally rare in the west midlands. There are two probable causewayed enclosures recorded on air photographs in the Trent valley at Alrewas and Mavesyn Ridware, Staffordshire (Oswald et al 2001, figs 4.9, 4.18, app 76, 77), both of which consist of ovate triple ditch circuits with multiple causeway breaks (Fig 2.6). The presence of enclosures has also been suggested at Woolston, Shropshire (Oswald et al 2001, app 73; Ray 2007, 58; Barber 2007, 88) and at the Early Neolithic site on Dorstone Hill, Herefordshire (although published details are sketchy: Oswald et al 2001, 48, app 42; Ray 2007, 58; Barber 2007, 88-9). The likelihood that many more enclosure sites will come to light is strengthened by the recent discovery (in 2006) of an Early Neolithic single-circuit hill-top enclosure with a single entrance at Hill Croft Field, Bodenham, Herefordshire: excavation of the western ditch terminal revealed plain bowl ceramics, flintwork and animal and human remains (Ray 2007, 60). The other definite Neolithic circular enclosure in the region, at Wasperton, Warwickshire (Hughes and Crawford 1995), although causewayed, is probably Middle Neolithic in date (Oswald et al 2001, 133-34; discussed in more detail below in the Middle and Late Neolithic section).

It is possible that some other hilltop enclosures in the region are Neolithic or have Neolithic phases (on the basis of occasional artefact finds, constructional features and/or location), but most recorded examples have not been investigated or have produced evidence only for Iron Age occupation (Ray 2007, 59-60; cf Ray 2001, 62). The Early Neolithic trapezoidal enclosure excavated recently in the Avon valley at Church Lawford, Warwickshire (Palmer 2007, 126-9), similar in some respects to the enclosure at Godmanchester, Cambridgeshire, which dates to c 4000-3500 BC (McAvoy 2000), also emphasises the likely presence of non-circular Neolithic enclosure forms. This point is reinforced by the recent excavation of a small rectilinear enclosure of Neolithic date at Lower Luggy, just outside the region in the Severn valley near Welshpool (Gibson 2006). Similar enclosures known from aerial photography in the west midlands, including several in Herefordshire, may well prove to be Neolithic (Ray 2007, 58-60).

There are no obvious large groups of Early Neolithic funerary monuments and enclosures in the west midlands similar to those found in other regions, such as Wessex and Sussex (Renfrew 1973; Drewett et al 1988, 34-44; Oswald et al 2001, 108-18). This picture will probably change, at least in some parts of the region, as air photographic data is assessed in more detail and new sites evaluated (Barber 2007, 94). The distribution of Early Neolithic monuments is discussed further below.

### Settlement and occupation sites

The evidence for Early Neolithic settlement in the west midlands is both extremely limited and ambiguous. There are no definite examples of house structures anywhere in the region (Ray 2007, 68), and apart from lithic artefact distributions (see below) and occasional finds in cave and rock shelter sites (ibid), the only direct evidence for Early Neolithic activity comes from pit contexts and from finds within colluvial and alluvial deposits. Pits containing significant assemblages of Early Neolithic lithic artefacts and plain bowl pottery have been found in several parts of the region, notably at Causeway Farm, Hereford, and Wellington, Herefordshire (Jackson 2007, 112-14; Ray 2007, 70);

Bromfield (Stanford 1982, Hughes et al 1995) and Sharpstones Hill, Shropshire (Barker et al 1991), and Baginton (Hobley 1971) and Barford, Warwickshire (Oswald 1969). Assemblages with both plain bowl and early, decorated pottery have also been found in Warwickshire at Church Lawford and King's Newnham (Palmer 2007), and Brook Street, Warwick (Cracknell and Bishop 1992).

The pit group at Wellington is especially important because of the size of the artefact assemblages (both ceramic and lithic), the presence of radiocarbon sample materials, and the well-preserved nature of the site, which was sealed beneath river alluvium in the 1st millennium BC (Jackson 2007, 112-14). The nature of the activities associated with pit digging and deposition at this and other sites is open to debate: it indicates short-duration 'occupation' of particular locales, but the deliberate deposition of selected materials, sometimes in considerable quantities, suggests that these were not routine practices (Ray 2007, 71-2; cf Thomas 1999, 62-80).

A notable feature of the distributions of most Early Neolithic flint and stone artefacts in the west midlands is their concentration in particular areas (see below). Although flint scatters of broadly Neolithic date are found in surface contexts across the region, suggesting an extensive pattern of occupation, relatively few areas have high densities of finds that might indicate long-term settlement or repeated occupation events (Barfield 2007). The most significant exception to this is the Clun area, close to the Welsh border in south-west Shropshire, where there is a high density of Neolithic flint finds (the flint probably derived from distant sources to the south) (ibid, 101-2; Barfield 2003, 18-19; cf Chitty 1963). It is interesting that stone axe studies in the region also show that these originated mainly outside the region, predominantly from Welsh and Cumbrian sources (Shotton 1988; cf Wise 1990; Ray 2007, 57). Axe distributions in general are far more dispersed than other artefact types, which may reflect distinct extensive patterns of use and associated social activities.

### Regionality and cultural diversity in the Early Neolithic of the west midlands

A striking feature of regional distribution maps is the virtual absence of Early Neolithic sites and finds from large areas of the west midlands and the low overall density of artefact finds in comparison with surrounding regions (Barfield 2007, 103-4; Garwood 2007c; Ray 2007, 52-3). In particular, known funerary monuments, enclosures and concentrations of lithic artefacts are all found around the fringes of the west midlands, in areas such as south-west Herefordshire (the Golden valley), south Warwickshire (the Avon valley and the Cotswold ridge), and north Staffordshire (the Peak District and middle Trent valley). In contrast, there are no known monuments and no significant groups of Early Neolithic artefacts anywhere in the central part of the region, including the middle Severn valley, the upland area between the Severn and Avon, the Birmingham plateau, north and east Shropshire, and south and west Staffordshire.

It is possible that environmental processes (eg alluviation of ancient land surfaces in river valleys) and the limited nature of previous fieldwork in these areas may have led to the under representation of Early Neolithic sites, and/or that cultural activities in the region more generally were marked by relatively rare use of durable material culture types and by practices that did not demand monument construction. It has also been noted that soils in some parts of the west midlands are not conducive to air photographic survey (Barber 2007, 81-3), which may help to explain the apparent lack of monuments in these areas. Even so, the continuing absence or low incidence of Early Neolithic sites and finds in recent widely distributed research projects and developer-funded evaluations and excavations (eg the Wroxeter Hinterland Project, the Mid-Shropshire Wetland Survey, and the M6 Toll route), suggests that the overall spatial pattern is genuine and that it does reflect relatively sparse and/or low-intensity occupation of the central west midlands in this period (Barfield 2007, 103-4; Garwood 2007c).

Where monuments and artefact concentrations do exist, around the fringes of the region, it is evident that these represent peripheral parts of wider distributions of sites and finds that lie mainly outside the west midlands (eg in the Black Mountains to the south-west;

the Cotswolds and upper Thames valley to the south; the Welland, Nene and Ouse valleys to the east; and the Peak District and middle Trent valley to the north). From this perspective, not only does the modern west midlands region embrace parts of several adjacent areas that were quite different from each other in the Early Neolithic (both in geographical and material culture terms), but it also appears to have no distinctive cultural 'character' of its own unless this is described in terms of the absence of 'classic' Early Neolithic site categories and related practices (Ray 2007, 72-3).

### 2.5.3. Research agenda and specific research questions

*Social and economic change*

There is considerable research potential in the west midlands for investigating the Mesolithic to Neolithic transition, especially with regard to the chronology and character of agriculturalisation, the construction of durable funerary and ceremonial architecture, the adoption of and use of ceramics, and changes in social practices and organisations. (cf Bradley 2007, 27-87, Whittle 2007). Although monuments and pit deposits are very rare, the extensive distribution of Early Neolithic ceramics and lithic artefacts (such as leaf-shaped arrowheads and polished stone axes) does suggest that material culture categories usually associated with farming lifestyles were widely adopted across the region. At the same time, the rarity of sites and most artefact types in the central part of the west midlands, if not a product of biases in the recovery and/or accessibility of Early Neolithic evidence, may point to sparse and/or low intensity occupation by farming communities, or perhaps the continuity of Mesolithic lifestyles and thus late or low-level adoption of new cultural practices.

*Monuments and landscape*

The small number of Early Neolithic monuments identified in the west midlands should be reappraised with reference to recent reviews of monument types and artefact categories. Above all, new dating, artefactual and environmental evidence is needed to situate monuments and other sites within their broader palaeo-environmental and cultural landscape settings (Ray 2007, 73-4). This should be undertaken, where possible, as part of extensive landscape projects involving air photographic survey, remote sensing and surface collection work, and targeted excavation of key sites. There are three areas with known concentrations or groups of Neolithic monuments that are obvious candidates for intensive landscape-scale and site-based studies of this kind.

First, the upper and middle Trent valley between Stone and Burton-on-Trent, and especially the area around the two probable causewayed enclosures at Alrewas and Mavesyn Ridware, would clearly benefit from intensive survey work to establish the landscape contexts of these sites and to identify contemporary monuments and settlement evidence. Studies of enclosure groups in other parts of England have shown that these were usually part of relatively densely occupied landscapes with concentrations of settlement activity and associated groups of funerary and other monuments (Oswald et al 2001, 108-18). Investigation of the enclosures to confirm an Early Neolithic date, to recover high quality artefactual and palaeo-environmental data, and to establish sequences of construction and use, is a clear research priority.

Second, the Avon valley catchment area in Warwickshire and Worcestershire deserves further large-scale survey and trial excavation of possible sites (cf Hunt 1982, 11). The apparent rarity of Early Neolithic monuments in this area is surprising given the presence of settlement evidence and several Middle Neolithic monuments. In this context, the recent discovery and investigation of the trapezoidal enclosure at Church Lawford, Warwickshire (Palmer 2007) not only has major implications for our understanding of the Early Neolithic landscape of the upper Avon but also suggests that more sites of this period await discovery at other places along the valley.

Third, Arthur's Stone chambered tomb in Herefordshire remains little understood in terms of its cultural context and landscape setting. A research priority must be to reassess the tomb site itself and possible contemporary monuments nearby (cf Cummings and Whittle 2003a, Nash 2002; Ray 2007, 63), and to investigate the wider context of Early Neolithic occupation along the Wye valley and on the eastern margins of the Black Mountains, including the settlement and possible enclosure at Dorstone Hill.

It is likely that Early Neolithic mortuary sites and enclosures of various kinds will be identified in the future using air photography (Barber 2007; Ray 2007, 63). Ray (ibid, 60) has also drawn attention to the need to evaluate hilltop enclosure sites in the western part of the region, some of which may be Neolithic in date and perhaps similar in purpose to 'tor enclosures' in south-west Britain and upland enclosure sites in areas such as Cumbria and Derbyshire (cf Oswald et al 2001, 85-9). The potential significance of such work is highlighted by the recent discovery of a new Early Neolithic enclosure site at Hill Croft Field, Bodenham, Herefordshire (Ray 2007, 60). In more general terms, it is of course essential that every effort is made to evaluate possible Early Neolithic monuments wherever these are encountered in the region, especially in areas where monuments of this period appear to be absent altogether, most notably in the Severn valley and the Birmingham area. Discovery of new sites in these areas would have major implications for characterising and interpreting the Early Neolithic period in the region as a whole.

### Settlement and landscape

The nature of settlement is central to current debates in Early Neolithic studies, especially with regard to residential mobility, the relative permanence and scale of occupation sites, sedentism and farming practices, relationships between monuments and settlements, and social organisation and change in the early to mid 4th millennium BC. There is scope in the west midlands for investigating the character of settlement in areas with known monuments, but also to compare these with areas in which durable and/or prominent architectural structures are absent. The main question is whether these areas differed in terms of the adoption of farming and other 'Neolithic' technologies, resource exploitation strategies, demographic patterns, social ranking and/or contrasting cultural identities.

The nature of occupation sites deserves particular attention, especially with regard to the interpretation of 'pit clusters' of the kind excavated at Wellington. Despite being the most common, and in most parts of the English midlands the most artefact-rich of Early Neolithic site categories, it is uncertain whether these represent everyday residential sites, specialised activity areas concerned with resource procurement and processing, or 'special' locales for more formal social practices involving the exchange, consumption and deliberate disposal of objects and materials. The high quality of the evidence from Wellington and other sites demonstrates the considerable research potential of this aspect of Early Neolithic occupation in the region. However, pit groups are unlikely to be wholly representative of settlement and occupation practices. The growing number of Early Neolithic buildings known in southern Britain (Darvill 1996), especially the substantial timber 'longhouses' or 'halls' at sites such as Lismore Fields, Derbyshire, Yarnton, Oxfordshire, and White Horse Stone, Kent, suggests the presence of foci for settlement and other kinds of social activity (whether they were actually houses or not) that were more durable than the occupation events represented by pit groups (Thomas 1996; cf Cooney 2000a, 52-7). Discovery and investigation of buildings of all kinds in the west midlands should clearly be a research priority, with special attention given to floor layers, hearths, and internal and external activity areas (about which very little is known).

Fieldwork projects in areas being destroyed by mineral extraction have provided important information about Early Neolithic sites in the region (eg at Wellington), but these sites are usually isolated from their wider landscape contexts and it is unclear how representative they are in relation to wider patterns of activity, both locally and regionally. Landscape projects and comparative studies of contrasting landscape areas are needed to address these issues. The outstanding research potential of well-preserved occupation sites in sub-alluvial or sub-colluvial contexts has been amply demonstrated at Wellington (Jackson 2007), and there are likely to be many more sites with significant deposits of organic materials and artefacts awaiting discovery. In this light, reconstruction of the sedimentation histories of river valleys and the identification of sub-alluvial ancient land surfaces and organic remains should be a priority.

There is clearly a need, in this context, for comparative studies of Early Neolithic settlement sites and evaluation of the character of settlement and landscape organisation in different geo-environmental and topographic zones (cf Knight and Howard 2004, Allen et al 2004). This should aim to establish the presence/absence of Early Neolithic activity in specific landscape settings and to investigate diverse settlement and economic systems in different parts of the region (Ray 2007, 73-4). One of the site types that requires particular attention in this context is the 'hilltop settlement': at present, only Dorstone Hill in Herefordshire has been identified as a site of this kind, although Ray (ibid, 58-60) has suggested that others probably exist in the western parts of the region, if not more widely.

The exceptionally large concentrations of lithic finds in parts of the region also deserve special attention (Barfield 2007, 99-103). A key research issue is whether these represent large settlement complexes or places where communities repeatedly gathered in the course of annual residential mobility cycles over long periods of time. If the latter, it is especially important to investigate the particular significance of these locales in socio-political and/or cultural terms. It is notable that these 'prolific' sites appear to contain unusually high proportions of finished and finely made artefacts (ibid, 99).

### Material culture

Early Neolithic material culture in the region deserves more synthetic and detailed analysis (Ray 2007, 74; Barfield 2007, 106-7). Above all, there is a need to define ceramic and lithic chronologies more precisely, produce more detailed distribution maps, investigate artefact functions and 'biographies', and to study sourcing, production, exchange and depositional aspects of a range of material categories (eg stone axes) (ibid; cf Lithic Studies Society 2004). Studies of this kind are relevant to a wide range of research questions concerning the nature of social identities and relations embodied in production practices, material exchanges and depositional events. For example, the social organisations and relationships concerned with the procurement of essential lithic raw materials or artefacts remain uncertain (Ray 2007, 57, 74). This is especially interesting in the west midlands given the large-scale use of flint despite the lack of good quality primary flint sources (most strikingly in the Clun area: Barfield 2003; 2007).

The appearance and widespread use of ceramics in the Early Neolithic is perhaps especially interesting in terms of the radical nature of the technological innovations involved and the changes in social agency that are implicated in the transference of technological skills, the social organisation of production practices (Hamilton 2002; Woodward 2002b) and consumption practices using ceramic vessels (Pollard 2002). The presence of significant pottery assemblages at Wellington, Herefordshire, and several sites in the Avon valley in Warwickshire, suggests that the technological transfers and new social practices associated with ceramic manufacture and use occurred as early in the west midlands as other parts of Britain. Detailed analysis of pottery assemblages of this period in the region should clearly be a research priority.

### Spatial patterns and regionality

The main research issue at a regional scale is the apparent absence of Early Neolithic monuments from many parts of the region, and the rarity of well-defined monument groups that are a familiar feature of Neolithic landscapes elsewhere in Britain. In particular, there is a need to assess the extent to which the known distribution of monuments is a 'real' reflection of Early Neolithic occupation and monument building, or a consequence of previous research limitations (Barber 2007, 80-3, 94; Ray 2007, 71-3). If monuments really were as rare in the west midlands as the present evidence suggests, then this raises fundamental research questions about why settlement patterns and social organisations in the region were so different from those in neighbouring areas where Early Neolithic monuments and other sites were more densely clustered (ibid; Garwood 2007c).

### 2.5.4. Research aims and methods

The research agenda and questions for Early Neolithic archaeology in the west midlands discussed in the previous section point to some important methodological and practical issues in current and future archaeological work in the region.

- A major problem identified by contributors to the Regional Research Framework earlier prehistory seminar is the limited value of HER databases. Most of the local authority HERs provide very incomplete records of known finds, rarely define them consistently in formal or chronological terms and many records do not include quantification of finds, preventing effective study of finds distributions and artefact concentrations (e.g. Barfield 2007, 97-9). The HER resources in the west midlands require significant enhancement.

- There is an urgent need to review the available air photographic record and for further air photographic survey, especially in areas that have received little attention in the past and/or where crop marks are rarely seen (Barber 2007, 94).

- Sample excavations of crop mark sites in all parts of the region should be a high priority in future fieldwork, including those sites that do not conform easily with accepted categories in morphological terms (ibid). This work should aim to determine the dating, design and purpose of enclosures and other sites, and compare these with other examples known from air photographs (ibid; Ray 2007, 74).

- The development of fieldwork strategies to investigate Early Neolithic sites in all kinds of landscape contexts is a high priority (Ray 2007, 73-4). In particular, the significance of lithic scatters should be recognised and far more care taken over their identification and study (English Heritage 2000).

- Recent assessments of sampling strategies have demonstrated that surface collection and plough zone test pit surveys should use narrow sample intervals to identify earlier prehistoric artefact concentrations (ibid), and that evaluation methods for earlier prehistoric sites (eg by trenching) require a minimum 6-10% sampling level (eg Hey and Lacey 2001).

- The development of predictive modelling and new site prospection and excavation methods is also clearly essential for investigating Early Neolithic sites that are buried in sub-alluvial or sub-colluvial contexts (Challis and Howard 2003; Hey 1998; Jackson 2007, 120-1). The work at Wellington shows what can be achieved when appropriate methods are devised for investigating sites of this kind (ibid).

- Methods for recognising and recording Early Neolithic material should be included in specifications for excavations of sites of *later* periods, including those in urban locations.

- Fieldwork designs should take account of the significant spatial structuring of Early Neolithic social practices (eg in terms of adjacency and proximity, alignments, orientations and oppositions: Darvill 1997b; Pollard 2002; Woodward 2007, 189-92).

- Extensive open-area excavation is essential for understanding the spatial contexts of social practices. The 'strip, map and sample' process (Hey and Lacey 2001, 55-7) appears to be the most effective method for defining the scale of fieldwork tasks and for planning and implementing appropriate excavation strategies.

- Where well-defined Early Neolithic sites such as monuments and pit groups are identified, it is exceptionally important that they are *totally* excavated, at least within the areas to be affected by development. This is the only way to understand overall architectural designs or layouts, constructional features and the spatial structuring of depositional practices, artefacts and materials. Special attention needs to be paid to the recovery of dating evidence of all kinds, especially radiocarbon sample materials.

- Excavation methods used on sites with Early Neolithic evidence should take full account of the structured and often purposeful deposition of artefacts and other kinds of materials (Hill 1995; Pollard 2000, 2002; Richards and Thomas 1984; Thomas 1999, 62-88). All too often it is apparent that pit deposits, for example, are treated as if they represent 'rubbish' disposal rather than meaningful deposits of spatially organised cultural materials. Early Neolithic features of all kinds require context sensitive three-dimensional recording methods. Practices such as half sectioning of pits and other features, and anything less than 100% recovery of artefacts and other materials from specific depositional contexts (ie representing specific depositional 'events'), fail to address the nature and significance of the evidence at a fundamental level.

- Early Neolithic material culture studies are in need of considerable attention in the west midlands if the research agenda discussed above are to be addressed. The construction of reliable chronologies is a priority, requiring comprehensive programmes of radiocarbon dating and fine-grained typo-chronological study. Depending on the preservation and contextual quality of the artefactual evidence, residue and microwear analyses may also be possible.

- Further work on the sourcing and spatial distribution of stone axes would enhance our understanding of dispersal and exchange patterns, and depositional practices (Barfield 2007, 106; Ray 2007, 74; cf Lithic Studies Society 2004). It may also be possible to investigate the sources, technological and functional characteristics, and distribution of objects made of distinctive types of flint and chert, and to compare these with artefacts derived from local raw materials (Barfield 2007, 106).

- Analysis of museum and private collections of Early Neolithic stone, flint and ceramic artefacts is essential, with the results incorporated in local authority HERs.

- As Ray (2007) argues very strongly, recognition of the significance and potential of Early Neolithic sites depends on the familiarity of both curatorial and field archaeologists with the nature of the material evidence and current research priorities. The development of expertise in these areas amongst the archaeologists working in the region should be a priority, especially those who are in a position to *specify* strategies and methods appropriate to current research agenda in fieldwork designs, briefs and planning applications.

### 2.5.5. Conclusion

The Early Neolithic period in the west midlands has been relatively neglected in comparison with the Middle and Late Neolithic, despite the presence of some early ceramic assemblages, extensive lithic artefact distributions and several major monuments. It is surprising that there has been no recent attempt to investigate known or suspected Early Neolithic monuments and their wider landscape settings in lowland parts of the region, especially the causewayed enclosures in the Trent valley. This is probably a reflection of the lack of research interest shown in the west midlands by period specialists.

As Ray (2007) points out, there is also considerable potential in the west midlands for future discoveries of monuments of all kinds, especially enclosure sites and hilltop settlements. Even so, it is apparent that classic Early Neolithic monument types are sparsely distributed across the region and that this pattern is unlikely to change radically. In this context, perhaps the typical, and in many respects most important, Early Neolithic site category to be investigated in the region is the 'pit group' (ibid).

There is no question that the west midlands does have a significant contribution to make to Early Neolithic research at a national scale. In particular, the rarity of monuments and the relatively sparse distribution of artefacts raise important questions about the continuity of Mesolithic lifestyles and adoption of new farming practices and material culture in the region. This has particular relevance to national and Europe-wide debates concerning the Mesolithic-Neolithic transition, and regional and local variation in the creation of agricultural communities, sedentism and the adoption or invention of formal ceremonial practices and monumental architecture.

In addition, there are many opportunities in the region for investigating Early Neolithic landscapes, both in areas with known monuments and significant evidence for occupation and material deposition (notably in the Avon valley in Warwickshire, the middle Trent valley, the Dorstone area and Wellington and the Lugg valley in Herefordshire), and in areas that have attracted little previous fieldwork. The Early Neolithic landscapes of the west midlands are especially interesting because of the ways in which they seem to differ from the 'classic' Early Neolithic landscapes of the southern English downlands. The striking diversity and uneven spatial distribution of Early Neolithic sites and cultural practices within the region, around its periphery, and in comparison with adjacent regions, also suggests that the west midlands will have a prominent part to play in future research concerning cultural diversity, identities and interactions at both regional and national scales of enquiry.

## 2.6. Middle and Late Neolithic

### 2.6.1. Introduction

*The Middle and Late Neolithic in the west midlands: previous research*

The Middle Neolithic (*c* 3400-2800 BC) and Late Neolithic (*c* 2900-2100 BC) are distinguished from the Early Neolithic primarily by new artefact categories, the appearance of new monument forms (some built on a massive scale) and the development of large ceremonial centres and 'sacred landscapes'. The Middle Neolithic is associated, in particular, with cursus monuments, oval barrows and Peterborough Ware ceramics, and the Late Neolithic with henge monuments, stone circles and avenues, timber circles, palisade enclosures and Grooved Ware ceramics. The latter half of the Late Neolithic is also marked by the appearance of single grave funerary traditions associated with Beaker pottery and the earliest copper and bronze metalwork.

Research work devoted specifically to the Middle and Late Neolithic periods in the west midlands has been limited, although recent large-scale fieldwork projects have made a significant contribution to the study of monument complexes and depositional practices in several parts of the region (especially the Avon valley in Warwickshire and the Middle Trent valley in Staffordshire: Ray 2007, 54-6; Woodward 2007, 187-92). Existing regional and county-based syntheses of the evidence (the same as those listed for the Early Neolithic) are limited in scope and mostly out of date, and there have been very few landscape surveys. In this context, the wide range of papers entirely or partly concerned with the Middle and Late Neolithic prepared for the Regional Research Framework seminar (Garwood (ed) 2007d) provide an important new basis for investigating these periods in the region. These reveal the distinctive character of the west midlands evidence and provide important insights into the nature of regionality and long-term change in the British Neolithic (Ray 2007, Barfield 2007, Garwood 2007c). The present discussion of the evidence is based partly on these papers, additional research relating to the spatial organisation and character of monument groups and occupation sites, and a wider review of current interpretative frameworks and debates in British Middle and Late Neolithic archaeology.

*Current research agenda in Middle and Late Neolithic archaeology*

There has been no recent attempt to establish a comprehensive research framework for British Neolithic archaeology at a national scale (already discussed in relation to Early Neolithic studies) and there is a lack of consensus regarding temporal boundaries and the extent to which these mark cultural, social and economic changes. Even the basic descriptive terminologies that are used to characterise material culture assemblages and monument types have undergone significant revisions and chronological shifts in the last 30 years. The idea of a British Middle Neolithic, for example, has become fashionable again only recently, now that more precise dating of long barrows, causewayed enclosures, cursus monuments and ceramic types has clarified the material and cultural contrasts between the earlier and later parts of the 4th millennium BC. Even so, it is still apparent that long mound/long enclosure structures and late activity at causewayed enclosures span the Early/Middle Neolithic boundary (usually set at *c* 3500/3400 BC), whilst pit circles, the earliest 'henge' sites and the use of Peterborough Ware span the Middle/Late Neolithic boundary (usually set at *c* 2900/2800 BC).

There are also problems with defining and dating the diverse monument types, artefact categories and social practices of the 3rd millennium BC. The period 2500-2000 BC, in particular, has been prone to terminological confusion, being variously described as 'Late Neolithic', 'Final Neolithic', 'Early Bronze Age' and combinations of these, such as 'Late Neolithic/Early Bronze Age'. One of the reasons for this is the appearance from *c* 2500 BC of Beaker burials and increasing numbers of round barrows that are often assumed to be emblematic of the 'Bronze Age'. The presence of metal artefacts from *c* 2500 BC has also sometimes been seen as a way of defining the beginning of the 'Early Bronze Age' (eg Parker Pearson 1999), even though this would place henges and most stone and timber circles, traditionally regarded as the archetypal monuments of the Late Neolithic, within a hugely extended Early Bronze Age spanning a period of a thousand years or more. Given the rapid changes in monument building and ceremonial practices that took place during the 3rd millennium BC there is clearly a need for more detailed and more precise chronological schemes, although attempts to construct these (eg Burgess 1980, Needham 1996) have not met with general agreement. In this context it is important that archaeologists working on material belonging to the late 4th and 3rd millennia BC discriminate carefully between alternative chronological and interpretative frameworks, and define as precisely as possible the temporal range of the evidence under discussion, preferably with reference to absolute age ranges based on calibrated radiocarbon dates.

In the west midlands, the boundary between Early and Middle Neolithic is marked by the widespread occurrence of large-scale monument construction (especially cursuses) for the first time and by the development of ceremonial centres. The end of the 'Neolithic', in contrast, is less clearly marked (eg the cessation of henge construction is not a helpful threshold because these monuments are largely absent from the region), but even so a major change is evident from *c* 2100 BC when round barrow construction increased very rapidly, especially in areas around the margins of the region (Garwood 2007b, 154; cf Garwood 2007a, 37-46). This is associated with the appearance of new material culture types and may be associated with wider evidence for woodland clearance and agriculture.

Although there is presently no agreed national framework or consensus with regard to research priorities in Middle and Late Neolithic archaeology, some key research questions and themes relevant to the west midlands have been highlighted in several recent books (eg Bradley 1998, 2000, 2002, 2007; Thomas 1991, 1999; Whittle 1996, 1997b) and a wide range of interpretative studies:

1. *Social and cultural change.* Evolutionary models, which describe a transition from minimally ranked societies in the Early Neolithic, to increasingly hierarchical chiefdoms (Renfrew 1973) or 'prestige goods' societies (eg Braithwaite 1984) in the Late Neolithic, have been questioned from a variety of perspectives (eg Shennan 1982, Barrett 1994). Alternative explanatory frameworks have not, however, been forthcoming and descriptions of increasingly complex social organisations and political institutions appear still to have value (eg Whittle 1997b, 139-70). The interpretation of change over time in the structures and spatial scales of different kinds of social agency, and of group identities and relationships (cf Richards 1998, Fleming 2004) remain key research themes.

2. *Agriculture and economy.* The current debate concerning the relative importance of farming in the Early Neolithic (discussed above) is also relevant to Middle and Late Neolithic studies, with the same kinds of opposed views (eg contrast Richards and Hedges 1999 and Rowley-Conwy 2003, with Jones 2000, Robinson 2000 and Thomas 1993). There are, however, additional research questions concerning the scale of agrarian production and cereal consumption, practical and organisational changes relating to the adoption of plough and traction technologies, and the economic and cultural significance of pastoralism (Sherratt 1981, Entwistle and Grant 1989, Legge 1989).

3. *Environmental change.* The impact of Middle and Late Neolithic communities on the environment, although less widely debated than in Early Neolithic studies, is an important research issue given the evidence for increasingly widespread and sustained woodland clearance, extensive grasslands and cereal cultivation (eg Allen et al 2004; Entwistle and Grant 1989; Legge 1989; Smith 1984; cf Knight and Howard 2004, 51-3, 70).

4. *Monuments and burials.* Monuments and the practices associated with them still tend to dominate interpretations of Middle and Late Neolithic

society. There have been excellent recent surveys of several major classes of monuments, notably cursuses (Barclay and Harding 1999, Loveday 2006), henges and timber circles (Gibson 1998, Harding 2003) and palisade enclosures (Whittle 1997b, Gibson 2002b). Less well understood are Middle Neolithic oval barrows and 'long enclosures' (Loveday 2003), Middle/Late Neolithic pit circles and round barrows (Kinnes 1979) and Beaker funerary monuments (Garwood 1999a, 288-89). Research has focused mainly on the following themes: (i) chronology; (ii) monument scale and construction methods, (iii) architectural designs, especially in relation to the symbolic ordering of space, cosmography and ceremonial practices (eg Richards and Thomas 1984; Barrett 1994, 9-69; Richards 1996; Bradley 1998); (iv) the significance of 'structured' deposition (eg Richards and Thomas 1984; Pollard 1995; Bradley 1998, 2000; Thomas 1999, 34-88); and (v) the significance of conceptions of time and history in the design, alteration and use of monuments (Bradley 2002). There have also been contrasting approaches to the funerary evidence: in particular, while studies of Middle Neolithic and non-Beaker Late Neolithic mortuary practices are rare (see Kinnes 1979 for a review of the evidence; cf Thomas 1999, 151-56), early Beaker graves have attracted a great deal of attention (eg Thomas 1991; Mizoguchi 1993; Barrett 1994, 86-108; Garwood 1999a, 281-84; Thomas 1999, 151-62), with particular emphasis on the symbolic significance of burial deposits and artefact assemblages.

5. *Ceremonial centres/landscapes.* The development, spatial organisation and social significance of monument concentrations, usually characterised as 'ceremonial centres' or 'sacred landscapes', are key research themes in Middle and Late Neolithic studies, attracting a diverse range of interpretative approaches (especially well represented in studies of the Stonehenge landscape: eg Cleal et al 1995; Allen 1997; Darvill 1997a; Parker Pearson and Ramilisonina 1998; Bradley 1998, 116-31; Thomas 1999, 163-83; Exon et al 2000). Recent research has focused, in particular, on cosmographic schemes (eg Darvill 1997b; Field 2004), the phenomenology of architectural forms and landscapes (eg Tilley 1994), and relationships between monument groups and settlement organisation (eg Barnatt 1998, 2000). Less prominent in recent studies are interpretations of change within such landscapes; for example, in relation to the appearance of Beaker funerary monuments within established Late Neolithic ceremonial landscapes (cf Thorpe and Richards 1984; Thomas 1984; Parker Pearson and Ramilisonina 1998).

6. *Settlement.* The opposed views that characterise Early Neolithic settlement studies also pervade discussions of the Middle and Late Neolithic evidence. Interpretations that emphasise short-lived occupation episodes, residential mobility and the rarity of durable houses (eg Thomas 1996; Whittle 1997a; Pollard 1999, 2000), can be contrasted with those that focus on a few well-preserved buildings and problems of site preservation and visibility (eg Darvill 1996, Gibson 2003). It is important, however, not to assume 'continuity' of settlement forms and functions throughout the Neolithic simply because of similar contrasts between durable/visible monuments and insubstantial/invisible settlements. The very different forms, scales and spatial arrangements of monuments at different times during the Neolithic, and evidence for economic and environmental changes, suggest that settlements in the Middle and Late Neolithic existed in very different social, economic and cultural landscapes to those of the Early Neolithic. Key research themes, in this context, include the relationship between settlements and monuments, especially within and around monument concentrations, and the changing nature of settlement (see Barnatt 1996, 2000; Allen 1997, Smith 1984; Pollard 2000).

7.  *Material culture and depositional practices.* Research issues in Middle and Late Neolithic artefact studies are similar to those defined for the Early Neolithic (eg Bradley and Edmonds 1993, Edmonds 1995, Lithic Studies Society 2004; Hamilton 2002, Woodward 2002b). Perhaps the most significant area of debate concerns the nature of depositional practices: especially in relation to pits and middens (Thomas 1999, 62-125; cf Pollard 2002, Woodward 2002c) and 'structured deposition' at henges and timber circles (Richards and Thomas 1984, Pollard 1995). The three principal Middle and Late Neolithic ceramic types have attracted varying attention: there has been little general analysis of Peterborough Ware except for a reassessment of chronology (Gibson and Kinnes 1997); while Grooved Ware and Beakers, in contrast, have been subject to a good deal of recent study (see especially: Cleal and MacSween 1999; Kinnes et al 1991; Case 1993, 1995, 2001; Boast 1998; Needham 2005).

8.  *Regionality and cultural diversity.* There is growing research interest in the large-scale spatial structuring of Neolithic cultural practices and the creation of distinctive regional identities (eg Harding 1995; Barclay 2000; Armit et al 2003). Widespread recognition of significant regional diversity in the Middle and Late Neolithic has major implications for investigating the development of ceremonial centres and interactions within and between prehistoric cultural and economic regions (eg in relation to long distance exchange).

### 2.6.2. Research assessment: current knowledge and understanding of the evidence

Middle and Late Neolithic sites in the west midlands, like those of the Early Neolithic, are mostly concentrated around the margins of the region and finds densities are again generally low in comparison with distributions in neighbouring areas (Ray 2007, 52-3). It is possible, however, to recognise some intensification and expansion of settlement during this period. The most intensively studied area is the Avon valley in Warwickshire, where several important excavations of monuments and other sites have taken place, notably at Barford (Oswald 1969; Loveday 1989; Woodward 2007, 188-9), Charlecote (Ford 2003), Wasperton (Hughes and Crawford 1995), King's Newnham and Church Lawford (Palmer 1999; Palmer 2007). Elsewhere in the region, significant Middle and Late Neolithic sites have been excavated at Catholme and Whitemoor Haye, Staffordshire (Bain et al 2005; Coates 2002; Woodward 2007, 189-91; Buteux and Chapman forthcoming), Kemerton, Worcestershire (Dinn and Evans 1990), Wellington, Herefordshire (Jackson 2007, 114-16), and Meole Brace, Shropshire (Hughes and Woodward 1995). It is important to note, however, that other large-scale fieldwork projects in the region have produced very little Middle or Late Neolithic evidence (eg the M6 Toll route: Powell et al 2008).

#### *Environment, landscape change and subsistence economy*
Knowledge of environmental conditions in the west midlands during the late 4th and 3rd millennia BC is very limited. The pollen sequences from Wellington, Herefordshire and Cookley, Worcestershire, indicate woodland clearance, grassland and farming in the late 4th millennium BC, although extensive clearance is not evident at either site until the 3rd millennium BC or later (Greig 2007, 45). More widely in the Severn valley, lowland Shropshire and Worcestershire, and the upper Trent valley and its tributaries, there is little evidence for large-scale clearance until at least the mid 2nd millennium BC (Barber and Twigger 1987, Bartley and Morgan 1990, Brown 1982, Buteux and Hughes 1995, Shotton 1978). It is notable that significant alluviation in the larger river valleys, probably related to the effects of clearance and farming on drainage patterns, also appears to date to the Late Neolithic or Bronze Age (eg at Beckford, Worcestershire; Greig 2007, 44). Overall, a gradual increase in open grassland areas during the 3rd millennium BC is suggested, perhaps indicative of a pastoral emphasis in the subsistence economy, and there is evidence for limited arable farming and some continuing reliance on hunting and gathering (Grieg 2007; cf Moffett 1999, 211). This is very similar to the pattern evident

in the Thames valley (Allen et al 2004; Barclay and Hey 1999, 70-1), and other major river valleys in southern Britain such as the Trent (Knight and Howard 2004).

*Monuments*

Middle and Late Neolithic monuments are rare in most parts of the west midlands; only in the Avon valley and around the Trent-Tame confluence are there significant concentrations of sites of this period (Fig 2.7). Although over 20 *possible* cursuses have been identified in the region, these are mostly unexcavated and several are doubtful (Barber 2007, 84, 89). The most convincing examples (see Fig 2.8 for comparative site plans) are those at Catholme, Staffordshire (Woodward 2007, 189-91; Buteux and Chapman forthcoming); Fladbury in the lower Avon, Worcestershire (Ray 2007, 61-2, fig 5.6); Barford (Loveday 1989), Sherbourne and Charlecote (Ford 2003, fig 1) in the middle Avon valley, Warwickshire; and the Walton cursus, Powys, the east end of which is in Herefordshire (Ray 2007, 61-2; Gibson 1999). These sites generally have rectangular termini, are often oriented south-southwest/north-northeast, and are all at the smaller end of the size range for cursus sites (less than 400m in length). Monuments of this kind have been characterised by Loveday (1999, 55) as 'local centres'. These are contrasted with larger 'regional centres' organised around monuments such as the Aston cursus, Leicestershire (shown in Fig 2.8), and 'cult centres' focused on exceptionally large monuments such as the Dorchester-on-Thames cursus (ibid; cf Harding 1995, 124-27). There are also several much smaller rectilinear or oblong enclosures in the region ('long' or 'mortuary enclosures', in some cases probably eroded mound sites) that may be Middle Neolithic in date (Loveday 2003; Barber 2007, 85). Only the small rectilinear enclosure at Charlecote (site A; see Fig 2.8) has significant dating evidence, indicating construction in the late 4th millennium BC (Loveday 2003, 37).

The enclosure at Wasperton, Warwickshire (Hughes and Crawford 1995), which has a single circular ditch circuit *c* 150m in diameter, with few causeways, is similar to the slightly smaller enclosures at Flagstones, Dorset (Healy 1997), and Stonehenge 1, Wiltshire (Cleal et al 1995), and like them is probably Middle Neolithic in date (Oswald et al 2001, 133-34). Surprisingly, given the wider range of Middle and Late Neolithic evidence and the large number of recorded ring ditches in the region, there is only one definite pit circle, Barford Site A, Phase 1, Warwickshire (Oswald 1969). This complex multi-phase site consists of a sequence of ring ditch and pit ring structures, very similar in several respects to some of the Middle/Late Neolithic multi-phase ring ditch and pit circle sites at Dorchester-on-Thames (especially Site XI; Whittle et al 1992) and at Etton in the lower Welland valley, Cambridgeshire (Etton Landscape Site 2; French and Pryor 2005). A similar site is known from air photographs at the National Memorial Arboretum, Staffordshire (Coates 2002). Smaller pit circles that may be Middle or Late Neolithic have been excavated at Wasperton, Warwickshire, and at Winforton and Wellington Quarry, Herefordshire, but in each case they lack precise dating evidence (Ray 2007, 66-7).

Of the classic Late Neolithic monument 'types' of southern Britain, henges and stone and timber circles are almost completely absent from the west midlands (Fig 2.7). Although several possible henge monuments have been identified from air photographs, few have been investigated and many are doubtful on typological grounds (Barber 2007, 85-6, 90-2; Ray 2007, 64-5). There are only two sites that may be henges on the basis of their distinctive surviving earthworks: at Eardisley in the Wye valley, Herefordshire and at Piles Coppice, Binley, Warwickshire (ibid; Planas and Wilson 2006). There are also a number of ring ditches with single, opposed or multiple entrances, or beaded ditch circuits, that may belong to the diverse range of Late Neolithic enclosures sometimes characterised vaguely as 'hengiform' monuments. A flat-based penannular ring ditch with a probable external bank at Stapleton in the Lugg valley, Herefordshire, is probably a site of this kind although definite dating evidence is presently lacking (Ray 2007, 65, fig 5.10). The ring ditches excavated recently at Bredon's Norton, Worcestershire (ibid, 56, 65), and Catholme, Staffordshire (Area A, F127; Area B, F100: M Hewson, pers comm), and in the early 1980s at Fatholme, Staffordshire (apparently associated with Grooved Ware deposits: unpublished; see Losco-Bradley 1984; Ray 2007, 68), may also be Late Neolithic

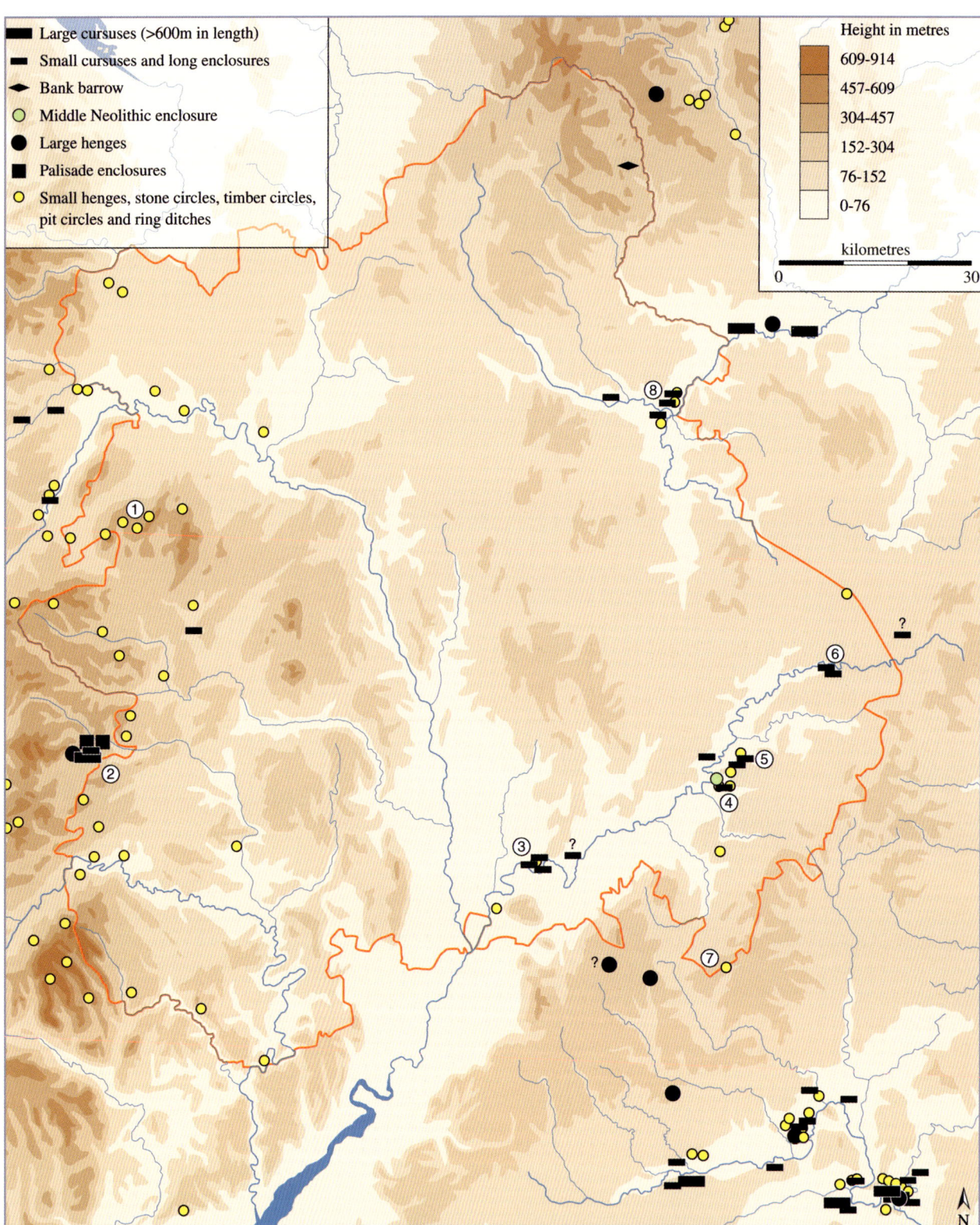

**Fig 2.7** Middle and Late Neolithic monuments and ceremonial landscapes in the west midlands (after Garwood 2007c, figs 2, 3). Ceremonial landscapes numbered: 1. Stapeley Hill; 2. Walton/Hindwell; 3. Fladbury; 4. Wasperton/Charlecote; 5. Barford; 6. King's Newnham/Church Lawford; 7.Rollright Stones; 8. Catholme and Whitemoor Haye

although both dating and structural evidence is imprecise or ambiguous. The range of architectural forms and material deposits, and in some cases the complex multi-phase histories represented, suggests great diversity in the purpose, practical use and cultural significance of these enclosures, both from one site to another and over time.

Timber circles and related structures, which are often assumed to be closely associated with henges (ie as structures built within henges, or as separate 'open' ceremonial arenas) and which mostly date to the Late Neolithic (Gibson 1998), are also virtually non-existent in the region, with the notable exception of the multiple post circle and the 'sunburst' pit

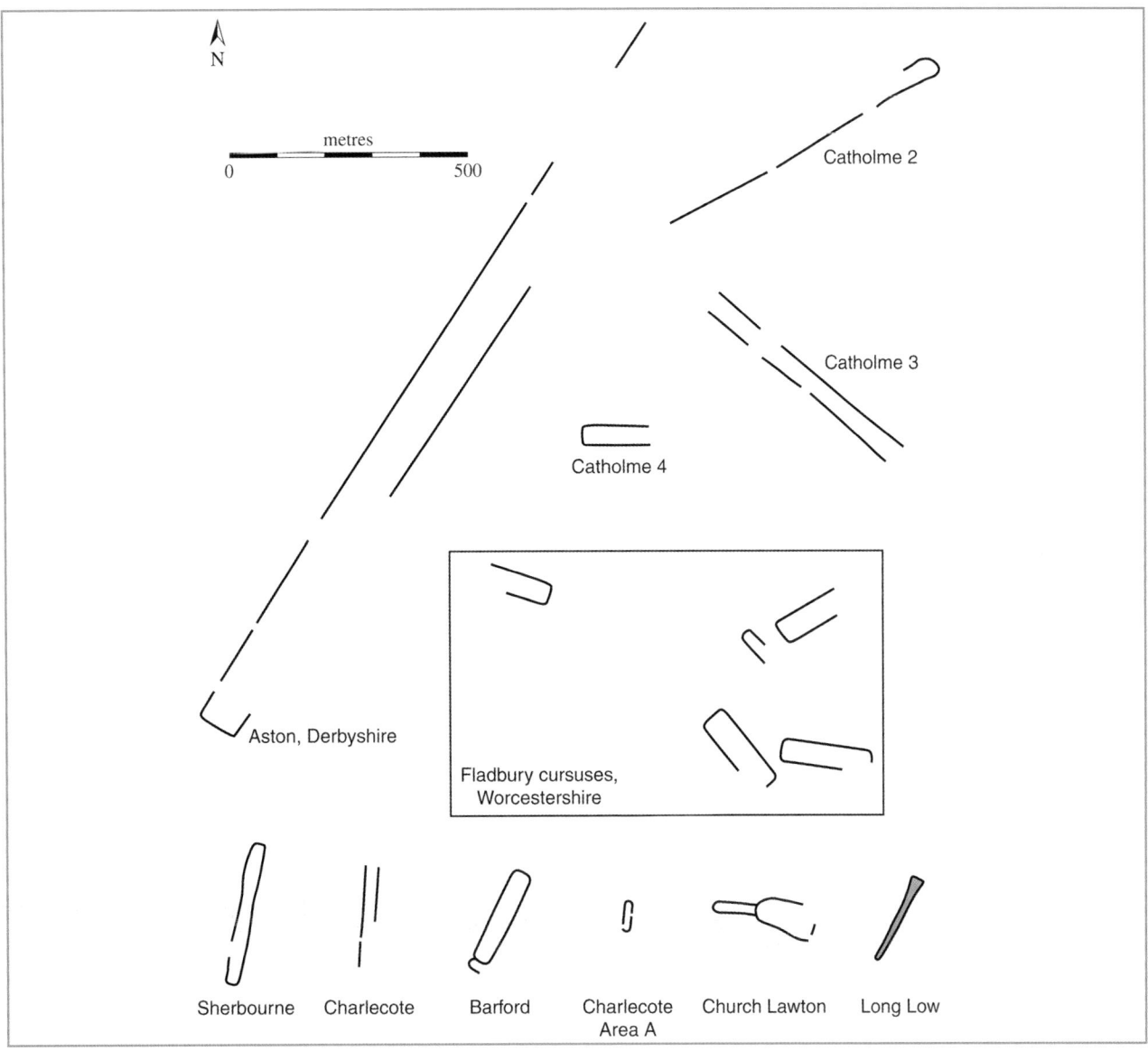

**Fig 2.8** Cursus monuments in the west midlands: site plans. The very large cursus at Aston, Derbyshire, is included for comparison

arrangement investigated recently at Catholme in the Trent valley, Staffordshire (Bain et al 2005; Woodward 2007, 189; Buteux and Chapman forthcoming). There are, however, several standing stones and stone circles (which may be the stone-built counterparts of timber structures) recorded in the upland areas around the western and southern fringes of the region. These include a group of sites at Stapeley Hill on the Shropshire-Montgomeryshire border (Fig 2.9), including Mitchell's Fold stone circle (Fig 2.10), the Carreg-y-Big monolith near Selattyn, Shropshire (Ray 2007, 69), the Queen's Stone monolith at Symond's Yat in the Wye valley, Herefordshire (ibid, 69-70) and the Rollright Stones, straddling the Warwickshire-Oxfordshire border (Lambrick 1988).

At present, Late Neolithic wooden-walled enclosures are absent from the west midlands, although the exceptionally large Hindwell 2 palisade enclosure and the Walton post-pit enclosure are located just outside the region in the Lugg Valley, Radnorshire (Gibson 1999; Gibson et al 2001). The crop mark site at Staunton-on-Arrow, Herefordshire, once thought to be a palisade enclosure, has now been shown to be ditched rather than palisaded and is probably Iron Age in date (White 2003, 25-8). Another site tentatively identified from air photographs as a possible palisade enclosure, near Milton Cross, also in the Arrow valley, Herefordshire, has not yet been investigated (Ray 2007, 65-6).

There is very little evidence for Middle and Late Neolithic funerary monuments in the west midlands. It is possible that some of the Peak District monuments in Staffordshire (Barnatt and Collis 1996) and one or more of the mounds and ring ditches at King's

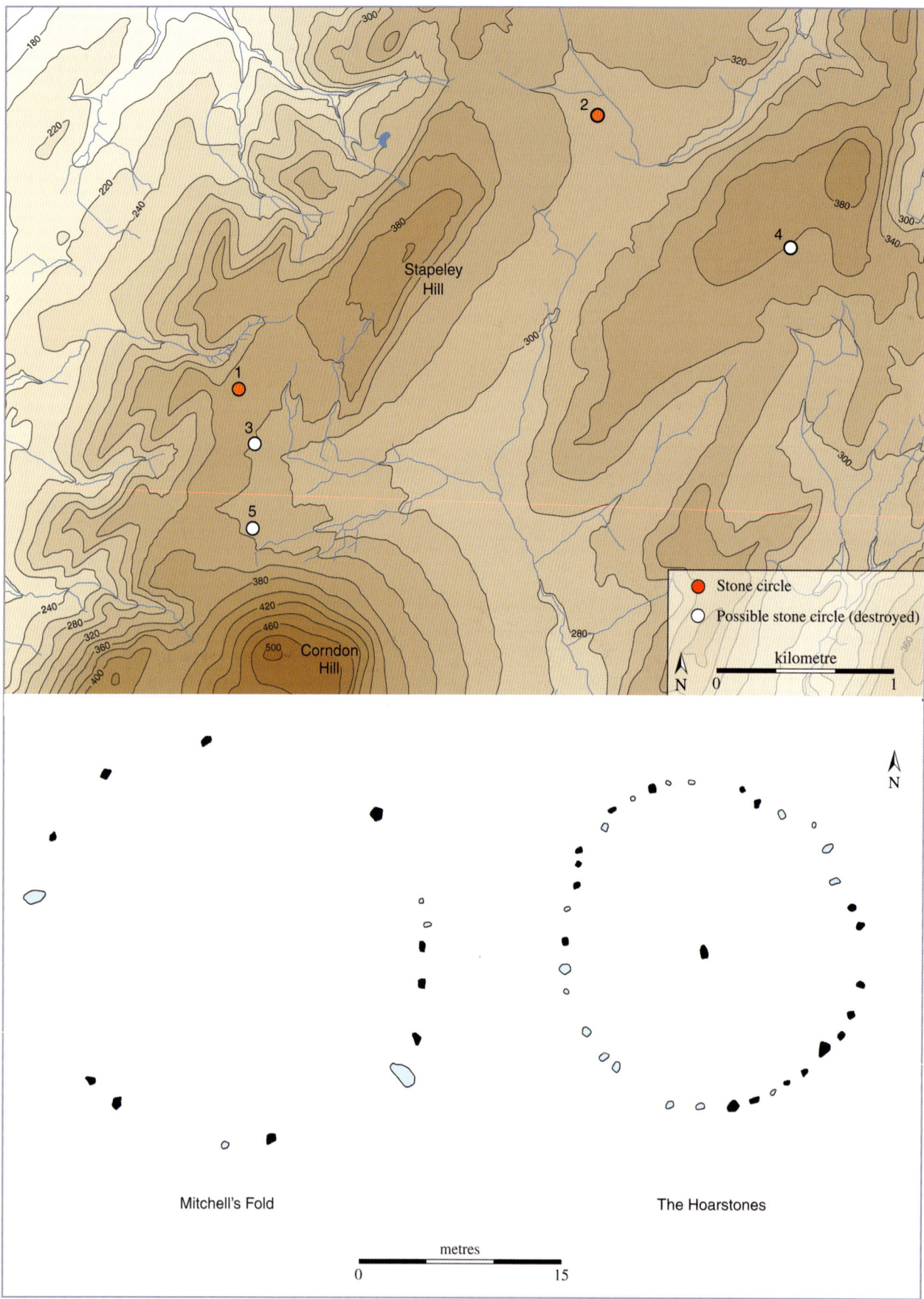

**Fig 2.9** Top: The Stapeley Hill monument group, Shropshire/Montgomeryshire. Sites numbered: 1. Mitchell's Fold; 2. Hoarstones; 3. Druid's Castle; 4. Shelve; 5. Whestsones. Bottom: plans of Mitchell's Fold and Hoarstones stone circles (after plans from Burl 1976, fig 45).

Newnham, Warwickshire (Palmer 2007, 123-6), belong to this period, but the dating evidence is far from certain. Early Beaker funerary monuments and burials are also very rare and restricted spatially to the south-western part of the region. An important early burial, possibly a 'flat grave', has been excavated recently at Wellington Quarry, Herefordshire (Harrison et al 1999). This was probably an adult male, with a funerary assemblage consisting of a European Bell Beaker, tanged copper dagger, stone wristguard fragment and 16 flint objects, including four barbed-and-tanged arrowheads (Fig 2.11). There are other early Beaker burials in the Olchon valley, Herefordshire (Marshall 1932), and at Bredon Hill, Worcestershire (Thomas 1965). The finds contexts of early Beakers found at Normacott, Staffordshire, and Meriden, Warwickshire, are uncertain and they may not have been associated with burials (Clarke 1970, cat. 832, 1014).

**Fig 2.10** Mitchell's Fold stone circle, Shropshire. View south towards Corndon Hill (copyright Paul Garwood)

### Ceremonial landscapes

Despite the overall rarity of Middle and Late Neolithic monuments in the west midlands, it is possible to recognise the development of several distinctive 'ceremonial landscapes' in the region during this period (Ray 2007, 54-6; Woodward 2007). These consist of relatively large clusters of monuments and pit groups, sometimes with evidence for complex spatial organisation and the deliberate deposition of artefacts and other materials (eg at Wasperton and Barford; Woodward 2007, 187-9). The most convincing examples (Fig 2.7) can be summarised by county as follows:

#### Shropshire

Stapeley Hill: located on the Shropshire-Montgomeryshire border. This group of megalithic monuments consists of two surviving stone circles, at least one more destroyed circle just across the Welsh border, possibly two more destroyed circles or monoliths and several round cairns (see Figs 2.7 (1), 2.9, and 2.10; cf Burl 1976, 264-66; Ray 2007, 69).

#### Herefordshire/Radnorshire

Walton/Hindwell: located in the Lugg valley, mostly on the Radnorshire side of the border but just extending into Herefordshire. The main sites include the largest known palisade

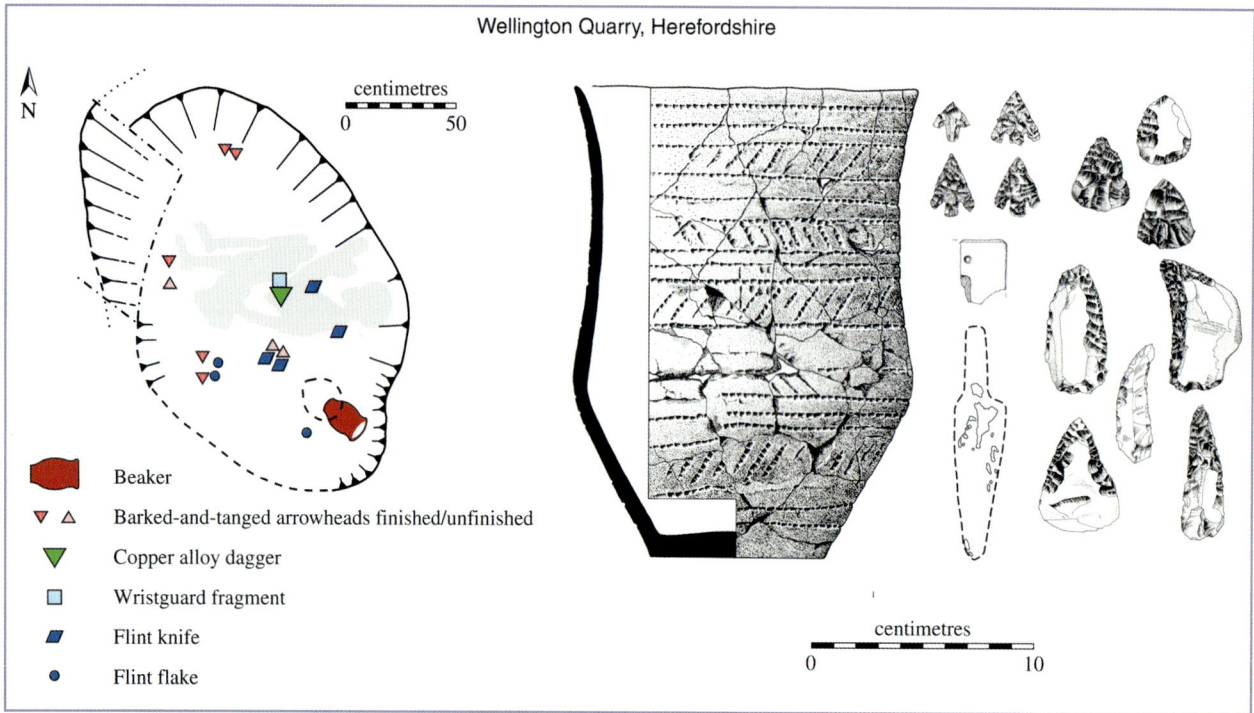

Wellington Quarry, Herefordshire

centimetres
0          50

**Beaker**

▽ △ Barked-and-tanged arrowheads finished/unfinished

▽ Copper alloy dagger

☐ Wristguard fragment

◢ Flint knife

● Flint flake

centimetres
0          10

**Fig 2.11** The early Beaker burial at Wellington Quarry, Herefordshire (after Garwood 2007b, fig.3; Harrison et al 1999, fig 11; other artefact illustrations supplied by Robin Jackson)

enclosure in Britain (Hindwell 2), the Walton post-pit enclosure, two cursuses, a probable henge and several ring ditches (Fig 2.7 (2); Gibson 1999; Gibson et al 2001).

### Worcestershire

Fladbury: at least four small cursuses or rectilinear enclosures and a possible 'hengiform' enclosure and other crop mark sites on the other side of the rover to the east (see Figs 2.7 (3), 2.8; cf Ray 2007, 61-2).

### Warwickshire

1. Wasperton/Charlecote: located on the east side of the Avon about 3.5km south of Barford, consisting of a circular enclosure, pit circle, long enclosure, ring ditches, pits and other features (Fig 2.7 (4); Hughes and Crawford 1995, Ford 2003, Loveday 2003, Woodward 2007, 187-8).

2. Barford: located on the east side of the Avon south of Warwick, with a cursus, possible 'long enclosure', multi-phase ring ditch/pit circle site, pit groups and ring ditches (Fig 2.7 (5); Oswald 1969; Loveday 1989; Woodward 2007, 188-9). The cursus nearby at Sherbourne on the west side of the Avon (Ford 2003, fig 1) may form part of the same monument complex, similar to the spatial arrangement of monuments at King's Newnham/Church Lawford.

3. King's Newnham/Church Lawford: located on either side of the upper Avon just to the west of Rugby, consisting of enclosures, pit groups and possible Middle Neolithic mounds (Fig 2.7 (6); cf Palmer 2007).

4. The Rollright Stones: located on the Warwickshire-Oxfordshire border, with a stone circle, monolith, round cairns and round barrows (Fig 2.7 (7); Lambrick 1988).

### Staffordshire

Catholme/Whitemoor Haye: located at the confluence of the Trent and Tame, with at least three cursus monuments, a multiple timber circle, 'sunburst' pit arrangement and numerous ring ditches (Fig 2.7 (8); Woodward 2007, 189-92; cf Bain et al 2005, Coates 2002; Buteux and Chapman forthcoming).

### Settlement and occupation sites

Direct evidence for Middle and Late Neolithic occupation in the form of settlement sites and houses is very rare throughout southern Britain, and the west midlands is no exception. It is possible that some of the features recorded at Barford in Warwickshire may have been buildings: a sub-rectangular enclosure and posthole group, associated with a Peterborough Ware bowl, has been interpreted as a Middle Neolithic 'house' (Site C, Enclosure 4; Oswald 1969, 19-27), while several less well dated groups of stakeholes, postholes and pits have been interpreted as Neolithic huts, the most convincing of which is an oval stakehole structure (Site B, Hut 13; ibid, 16-19, fig 8). A possible Middle Neolithic 'post and wall-slot' building has also been excavated at Stretton-on-Fosse, Warwickshire (Site 5: Darvill 1996, 106; Gardiner et al 1980, 9-13). Evidence for Late Neolithic buildings is even more scarce, although recent excavations on the line of the Rotherwas Access Road near Dinedor Camp, Hereford, have produced evidence for at least one four-post structure associated with sherds of Beaker pottery, in an area with apparent settlement traces including pits and further postholes associated with Peterborough Ware and Grooved Ware pottery (Ray 2007, 68).

Generally, however, occupation sites of this period appear to be represented mostly by pits, other non-structural features such as gullies' and surface scatters of lithic artefacts. The purpose of Middle and Late Neolithic pits and pit deposits is uncertain, although in many cases the deliberately placed nature of the deposits suggests practices that were 'special' rather than a matter of everyday routine (Thomas 1999, 64-74). Sites in the region with Peterborough Ware pit deposits include King's Newnham, Warwickshire (Palmer 2007), Wellington, Herefordshire (Jackson 2007, 114-5), and Meole Brace (Hughes and Woodward 1995) and Brompton, Shropshire (Woodward 2007, tbl 12.1). A large assemblage of Peterborough Ware was also found in a gully at Whitemoor Haye, Staffordshire (ibid; Coates 2002). Middle and Late Neolithic sites with both Peterborough Ware and Grooved Ware pit deposits include Church Lawford (Palmer 2007) and Wasperton, Warwickshire (Hughes and Crawford 1995). Late Neolithic sites with only Grooved Ware pit deposits include Barford Site B (Oswald 1969; Woodward 2007, 188) and Broom Area E in Warwickshire (Palmer 1999, 22-37), and Aston Mill Farm, Kemerton, Worcestershire (Dinn and Evans 1990). The recent discovery of several Grooved Ware pit deposits at Severn Stoke, just south of Worcester, including one consisting of a large pottery assemblage and several stone axes (Ray 2007, 68), is especially important as this is the first well-dated Late Neolithic site to be found in the lower Severn valley.

Some of the Beaker pit deposits in the region may date to the later 3rd millennium BC (eg at Longmore Hill Farm, Astley, Worcestershire; Dinn and Hemingway 1992, 111-17) but without radiocarbon dates it is difficult to be certain. Early Beaker pottery is sometimes found in pits that also contain late Beaker material (eg Whitemoor Haye Area P, Pit F122; Ann Woodward pers comm). There are also occasional finds of early Beaker ceramics redeposited in later features (eg in probable Iron Age pits at Bromfield, Shropshire; Stanford 1982, 287-89). This material was probably derived from surface spreads of occupation debris or middens that have since been destroyed by ploughing.

There are occasional finds of Middle and Late Neolithic material in other contexts. For example, Peterborough Ware has been found at several round barrow sites (eg at Burton Hastings 1, Warwickshire; Garwood in prep) and in ring ditch fills (eg Wasperton, southern ring ditch; Hughes and Crawford 1995). Although it is possible that some of these are Middle Neolithic sites, in most cases it is likely that this material was redeposited, either accidentally in the course of mound construction or deliberately in order to incorporate ancient cultural materials within new monuments. It is also important to note the presence of Middle and Late Neolithic sites found beneath alluvial and colluvial deposits, notably at Wellington, Herefordshire (Jackson 2007; Dinn and Roseff 1992). This raises the possibility that settlements in valley locations may be far more numerous than currently recognised (ibid; Knight and Howard 2004). The recent discovery in Herefordshire of two late Beaker middens close to streams (Ray 2007, 68) also suggests that midden sites of Neolithic date may exist more widely in the region, as in other parts of southern Britain (cf Allen et al 2004).

In addition to the Middle and Late Neolithic lithic scatters found throughout the west midlands, which indicate widespread if generally low intensity occupation, some localities around the fringes of the region have produced exceptionally large finds assemblages, notably the Clun district in Shropshire (Barfield 2003; Chitty 1963), the Golden Valley in Herefordshire, the Staffordshire Peak District and Wolvey in Warwickshire (Barfield 2007, 99-103). The distributions of flint axe heads, barbed-and-tanged arrowheads (ibid) and stone axe heads (Woodward 2007, 184-7) follow this general pattern, although the latter has a more even distribution that includes finds in the central part of the region and along the Avon valley. Stone axe heads in the west midlands derive primarily from Welsh sources (Groups VII, VIII and XXI; especially in Worcestershire, Herefordshire and Shropshire), a Cumbrian source (Group VI; especially in Staffordshire, Warwickshire and Shropshire) and a Cornish source (Group I; especially in Warwickshire). In contrast, shaft-hole implements such as battle-axes and axe-hammers, which are Late Neolithic or Early Bronze Age in date (ibid), are mostly derived from more local sources in North Warwickshire (Group XIV) and the Shropshire-Montgomeryshire border (Group XII), or from a south Cumbrian source (Group XV) (see Fig 2.15).

### Regionality and cultural diversity

There are clear contrasts between the central and outer parts of the west midlands in the distribution of Middle and Late Neolithic sites and finds (Barfield 2007, 103-4; Garwood 2007c, 200-1; Ray 2007, 52-3). All of the definite cursuses, enclosures, funerary monuments and major lithic artefact concentrations are found around the fringes of the west midlands, in areas such as the Peak District and middle Trent valley in north Staffordshire, the Wolvey district, the Avon valley and the Cotswold ridge in Warwickshire, the Golden valley in south-west Herefordshire, and the Clun area and other places along the Shropshire-Wales border. In contrast, there are no monuments and very few significant artefacts groups in the central part of the region, including east Shropshire, the Birmingham area, south and west Staffordshire, the lower Severn valley and the area between the Severn and Avon. The rarity of Middle and Late Neolithic finds in large-scale research and developer-funded projects in these areas suggests that the overall spatial pattern does reflect relatively sparse and/or low intensity occupation of the central west midlands (Barfield 2007, 103-4; Garwood 2007c, 201, 202).

This seems to sustain the overall pattern of occupation and finds densities evident in the Early Neolithic. It is also possible, however, to recognise some expansion in the distribution of both monuments and pit deposits (eg in the Severn valley), as well as greater clustering of monuments and pit groups in some areas. This suggests that certain kinds of social practice and organisation, represented by more intensive occupation and ceremonial activity, not only became geographically more widespread but gave rise to the development of ceremonial centres in especially significant and favoured locales (Garwood 2007c, 202-4).

It is also evident that Middle and Late Neolithic monuments and artefact concentrations located around the periphery of the region, like those of the Early Neolithic, were parts of wider distributions that lie mainly *outside* the west midlands (Garwood 2007c, 200-1). The forms and spatial distributions of cursus monuments in the Avon valley, for example, are paralleled most closely in the upper Thames valley to the south (Barclay and Hey 1999, Loveday 1999) and the Ouse valley to the east (eg see Malim 2000). It is also notable that monument concentrations in central Britain that include exceptionally large and/or elaborate monuments are all located outside the region, including the Welshpool and Walton monument groups in Wales (Gibson 1994, 1999), the Aston monument complex in the middle Trent valley, Leicestershire (Loveday 2004) and the Dorchester-on-Thames complex in the upper Thames valley (Loveday 1999). Although the Catholme/Whitemoor Haye and the Wasperton/Charlecote monument groups, in the Trent and Avon valleys respectively, have monument concentrations comparable with those outside the region, they do not include especially large or elaborate monuments. In this context, the west midlands as a 'cultural region' seems to be distinguished by the rarity of Middle Neolithic and especially Late Neolithic monuments, and by the development of relatively small-scale ceremonial centres.

### 2.6.3. Research agenda and specific research questions

#### Social and economic change

Although there appears to have been an expansion of clearance, settlement activity and monument building in the west midlands in this period, in common with many other parts of southern Britain (eg Knight and Howard 2004, 70; Thomas 1999, 188), there has been very little fine-grained analysis of Middle and Late Neolithic landscapes on which to base specific interpretations of social and economic change. The relative rarity of monument groups and the limited evidence for large-scale construction events raise important questions concerning the extent to which monument building became more complex or larger in social scale over time. If such 'complexity' is seen as an index of relative social organisational complexity (or hierarchy), it is apparent that this seems to have developed to a lesser extent in the west midlands in comparison with parts of southern Britain where very dense concentrations of large and/or elaborate monuments can be found. Late Neolithic Beaker burials with grave goods, which are sometimes used to suggest prestige goods exchange and hierarchy, are also exceptionally rare in the region. The west midlands evidence, therefore, has considerable potential for investigating regional variation in the character and direction of social change, and forms of social organisation different to those suggested for other regions such as Wessex.

#### Monuments and landscape

There is a clear need in the west midlands to enhance our understanding of ceremonial monuments, their spatial arrangement and aggregation as extensive 'ceremonial landscapes', and the sequences and tempos of constructional and depositional events (Ray 2007, 54-6). There have been some significant recent developments in this area of study, especially in relation to the spatial organisation and long-term development of large monument complexes such as Catholme/Whitemoor Haye, Barford, and Wasperton (Woodward 2007; Buteux and Champman forthcoming; Bain et al 2005, Coates 2002; Loveday 1989; Hughes and Crawford 1995). Other monument groups, however, have received far less attention, notably the cluster of megalithic monuments in western Shropshire. There is, above all, a need for more intensive landscape projects, especially in areas that have been subject to little concerted investigation such as the upper Trent valley west of Catholme.

At a larger scale, an interpretative synthesis of the evidence from the Avon valley in Warwickshire and Worcestershire is a clear research priority. This is the only part of the region that has significant numbers of Middle and Late Neolithic monuments with several distinct ceremonial foci. It is also the only area that has been subject to extensive survey and large-scale excavations of monuments and other sites. Comparisons with river valleys elsewhere in southern Britain such as the upper Thames and Great Ouse suggest some broad similarities in terms of site densities, spatial patterns and change over time, with similar potential for investigating ceremonial complexes, territoriality, and social and economic practices. Even so, the spacing of monument groups *c* 5-8km apart along the Great Ouse (Malim 2000), and cursuses at 5-10km intervals along the Thames and its tributaries south of Oxford (Barclay and Hey 1999, 68), contrasts with the wider spacing of monument groups *c* 20km apart along the Avon between King's Newnham/ Church Lawford, Barford/Wasperton/Charlecote and Cropthorne/Fladbury (although the spacing of cursuses *within* the Barford/Wasperton/Charlecote group (Ford 2003, fig 1) is more in line with the upper Thames and Great Ouse pattern). If not a reflection of uneven fieldwork, the Avon evidence suggests differences in the structuring of cultural landscapes from one part of southern Britain to another, with significant implications for future research and fieldwork projects.

Specific monument categories also deserve particular attention in regional research terms. A key aim, for example, must be to gain a fuller picture of the distribution, scale and use of Middle Neolithic monuments such as cursuses, pit rings, ring ditches and 'mortuary enclosures'. At present, these sites seem to be concentrated only in parts of the west midlands and very little is known about how they were used, the spatial organisation of monument groups or their relationships with contemporary settlements. The presence of cursus monuments in the Severn valley at Welshpool, Montgomeryshire (Gibson 1994), and in the Lugg valley at Walton, Radnorshire (Gibson 1999), suggests that such monuments may also be found along the river valleys in the western part of the region. Similarly, the Trent valley sites at Catholme, and the major cursus monument further downstream at Aston, Leicestershire (Loveday 2004), show the potential for future discoveries of Middle Neolithic monuments in the Trent valley.

The almost complete absence of henges, and the great rarity of 'hengiform' sites, ring ditches and pit circles in the region (Barber 2007, 90-2; Ray 2007, 64-8), is especially surprising given the presence of Middle Neolithic monuments which in other parts of Britain were often foci for the development of Late Neolithic ceremonial complexes (eg at Dorchester-on-Thames; Loveday 1999). The lack of henges and related sites in the Avon valley is especially striking as this is not only the most intensively investigated part of the region, with numerous Middle Neolithic monuments, but is also an area in which air photographic survey has been especially effective. It is also noticeable that where probable Late Neolithic enclosures *have* been identified in the region (eg in recent excavations at Stapleton, Herefordshire, Bredon's Norton, Worcestershire and Catholme, Staffordshire), they are very small in scale and found in river valley locations.

At present, therefore, it does appear that Late Neolithic ceremonial sites in the west midlands were rare, mostly small and architecturally unambitious. This may suggest smaller populations, less centralised social and religious institutions and/or less concern with collective ceremonial practices in comparison with areas such as Wessex (cf Harding 1995, 131). However, as so few crop mark sites have been investigated and many areas are not conducive to aerial photography, it is certainly too soon to assume this to be the case. More extensive, research-driven aerial survey and targeted investigation of possible Late Neolithic enclosures are clear research priorities (Barber 2007, 90-4). The presence of timber circles and palisade enclosures within and just outside the region at Catholme (Woodward 2007, 189; Bain et al 2005), Sarn-y-Bryn Caled (Gibson 1994), and Walton (Gibson 1999, Gibson et al 2001), suggest that there is potential for new discoveries of similar sites in the west midlands (cf Barber 2007, 94; Ray 2007, 64-7).

The rarity of early Beaker burials and monuments, and early Beaker ceramics in general, also deserves more attention. The south-western distribution of early Beaker burials in the region may suggest local variation in the ways that 'single grave' funerary practices (and their symbolic associations) were culturally valued and the extent to which they were adopted or rejected. It is especially noticeable that early Beaker graves are all located in areas that appear locally to lack Middle and Late Neolithic ceremonial monuments, which may indicate avoidance of these areas by communities adopting new practices and new kinds of cultural representation in the later 3rd millennium BC, or perhaps the exclusion of Beaker-associated practices from existing monument complexes by those with interests in 'orthodox' religious traditions (cf Thorpe and Richards 1984, 75-80).

*Settlement and landscape*
Research questions relating to the nature of settlement in Middle and Late Neolithic archaeology are in many respects similar to those in British Early Neolithic studies. These focus on residential mobility, the relative permanence and scale of occupation sites, the relationship between ceremonial sites and settlements, and social organisation. There is clearly considerable scope in the west midlands for investigating the character of settlement in areas with ceremonial monuments, and to compare these with areas in which durable and/or prominent architectural structures are absent. Recent work in many

parts of southern Britain has also highlighted the importance of riverside occupation sites and the enormous but under-explored potential of these for investigating Neolithic settlement in general (eg Allen et al 2004, Knight and Howard 2004, French and Pryor 2005). The long-term project at Wellington serves to illustrate the importance of such locales in the Neolithic landscape, their exceptional research potential, and also the considerable practical challenges involved in investigating them (Jackson 2007).

There is very little evidence for Middle and Late Neolithic settlement architecture or long-lived occupation sites anywhere in the west midlands. To a large extent this can be explained by the insubstantial nature of house structures (Darvill 1996, Gibson 2003), dispersed settlement patterns, residential mobility and low discard rates of inorganic cultural material (Thomas 1996, Whittle 1996), giving rise to thinly-stratified and spatially discontinuous occupation sites that are especially vulnerable to destruction by ploughing and natural erosion processes. In favourable preservation conditions, however, it is possible for settlement evidence of this kind to survive (as at Barford). The Late Neolithic buildings discovered just outside the region at Trelystan, Montgomeryshire (Britnell 1982, Gibson 1996), and Upper Ninepence, Radnorshire (Structure 1: Gibson 1999, 36-7), in both cases protected by later barrow mounds, and at Willington in the Trent valley (Darvill 1996, 102), highlight the potential for similar sites to exist in the west midlands. The investigation of well-preserved Middle and Late Neolithic settlements, especially where these have been buried beneath later monuments or sealed by colluvial or alluvial deposits, should clearly be a research priority.

In the absence of architectural remains, Middle and Late Neolithic 'settlement' evidence is usually ephemeral and ambiguous. The interpretation of isolated pits and pit groups as settlement sites is especially problematic (cf Thomas 1999, 62-74). In some cases these may be the outcomes of ordinary daily routines and tasks that took place within or around short-lived occupation sites. Yet the deliberate and selective nature of many pit deposits suggests that these resulted from the deliberate placement of objects and materials as part of more formal social practices (ibid). Indeed, these depositional events may have been significant not only as cultural media in themselves but may have taken place at 'special' locales. The complexity and diversity of these practices are especially well represented by the pit groups excavated recently at Church Lawford and King's Newnham, Warwickshire (Palmer 2007), which suggest repeated, structured depositional events spanning the entire Neolithic and Early Bronze Age. At present, however, it is not possible to discern the duration and frequency of these practices at a scale of less than half millennia, nor accurately define their spatial extent and organisation (ibid). Without some understanding of the temporal and spatial conditions of the evidence, it is very difficult to suggest specific interpretations of the kinds of social agency and signification embodied in pit deposits or changes in these over time.

Middle and Late Neolithic pit groups excavated in the west midlands are directly comparable with those in other parts of Britain in terms of their complexity, diversity and the material assemblages they contain. They are clearly important in research terms, especially as they often provide the *only* evidence for both settlement-related and non-routine activities across great swathes of the British landscape. Yet the nature of the social practices and the cultural meanings represented in pit-digging and deposition remain little understood. In the west midlands case, Ray (2007, 71-2) has suggested that in the absence of a monumental focus in many areas, pits are perhaps *the* defining feature of the Neolithic: detailed contextual and comparative analyses of pits and their landscape settings should therefore be undertaken with great care wherever such evidence is encountered, and at the most extensive spatial scales possible.

Other site categories that seem to represent residential or specialised economic and social activities are little represented in the region. Midden deposits, for example, which are now recognised as a significant component of Neolithic occupation practices (Pollard 1999, 2000, 2005) have been recorded only at Wellington and Staunton-on Arrow, Herefordshire (Ray 2007, 68), in both cases as linear deposits adjacent to former stream courses. The rarity of middens may be due in part to destruction by modern ploughing, but it is likely that some will survive beneath later sediments and in areas of pasture. In addition, while most of the burnt mound sites investigated in the west midlands are Middle Bronze Age in date (Ehrenburg 1991, Hodder 1990), the presence of Late Neolithic burnt mounds in the lower Trent valley (Knight and Howard 2004, 57) and possibly at Harborne, Birmingham (Hodder 1990, 108), suggest that Neolithic burnt mounds may also be encountered more widely across the region in the future.

The relationship between occupation sites and monuments is of central importance in research terms, especially with regard to the supposed distinction between 'sacred' and 'secular' landscapes (cf Gibson et al 2001, 108-9). Whilst there is broad agreement that occupation sites existed within and/or around monument groups, it is far less clear whether such inhabitation was continuous or discontinuous, and whether it differed in character from occupation in areas without monuments. Indeed, very little is known about how occupation sites of any kind were organised, either in terms of the spatial arrangement and scale of settlement, or in terms of the temporal rhythms and durations of occupation episodes. In the Walton Basin, settlement sites and monuments were situated in close proximity but may have occupied different parts of the landscape, with settlements on higher ground overlooking the monument complex to the south (ibid). A similar spatial pattern may be apparent around Avebury, with repeated occupation of hillside locations overlooking major monuments (Pollard 2005, 109-10; Holgate 1988, 91-7), although both here and at Stonehenge it is evident that some occupation areas were interspersed among the monuments (Thomas 1999, 174-77).

It is also possible that the organisation of the later Neolithic landscape was more variable or changed more radically over time in areas where monuments were dispersed rather than concentrated. In the upper Thames valley, for example, it has been suggested that settlements and monuments at Stanton Harcourt were closely integrated (Barclay et al 1995, 112), yet not far away at Yarnton it is argued that distinct ceremonial, funerary and occupation areas were maintained over a long period (Thomas 1999, 190; cf Hey 1997). To some extent these contrasts may be less pronounced, or may be interpreted rather differently if landscapes are studied at a larger scale: in the Abingdon to Dorchester-on-Thames area, for example, changes in the nature and intensity of activity at one monument group may have been complemented by changes at others (Garwood 1999a, 292-98; Thomas 1999, 195). This suggests that occupation practices may be best understood at a very large spatial scale, and that 'separate' monument groups and settlement foci were in fact closely interrelated within extensive social and economic landscapes (cf Whittle 1997a). These themes have barely been addressed in the west midlands, although the potential for investigating the spatial structuring of activity areas within monumentalised landscapes is apparent in recent studies of the Barford, Wasperton and Catholme/Whitemoor Haye ceremonial complexes (Woodward 2007).

The distribution of lithic artefacts perhaps provides some idea of wider settlement patterns in the west midlands, although programmes of systematic surface artefact collection in the region have been rare and localised in comparison with much larger-scale surveys in areas such as the Thames valley (eg Holgate 1988). Even so, the presence of exceptionally dense, extensive concentrations of lithic artefacts in parts of the region (Barfield 2007, 99-103), mostly in areas *without* major Middle and Late Neolithic monuments, raises important research questions concerning the character and overall spatial patterning of settlement, as well as particular problems of social interpretation (ibid). There is a clear need to re-assess these lithic assemblages, and to investigate the socio-political, economic and/or cultural significance of the locales in which they have been found.

### Material culture

Many of the research priorities in Middle and Late Neolithic material culture studies are the same as those identified for the Early Neolithic. There is a need to produce more reliable artefact chronologies, identify functional and technological aspects of tool use, and investigate the sourcing, production, exchange and deposition of specific artefact types (Barfield 2007, 106; Ray 2007, 74). There are especially important research questions concerning the scales and forms of technology-reproducing social groups, including the organisation of stone extraction and tool manufacturing in relation to Group XII and Group XIV stone sources, and the social relationships realised in exchanges marked by the widespread use of flint derived from primary flint sources outside the region (Barfield 2003; 2007, 106). Another key research issue is the extent to which widespread trans-regional artefact categories such as Grooved Ware styles and early Beaker types were produced locally or were accumulated through exchanges and/or 'collecting' practices in the course of residential movements or special journeys (eg pilgrimages to cult centres; cf Loveday 1999). At regional and inter-regional scales of study, there is clearly a need for more detailed analyses of raw material sourcing (including pottery clays and tempers), production technologies and artefact 'biographies'.

### Spatial patterns and regionality

The key research issue at a regional scale is the extent to which the known distribution of monuments is a real reflection of occupation and monument building practices or a consequence of previous research limitations (Barber 2007; Ray 2007, 52-3, 72-3). If monument building really was as rare in the west midlands as the present evidence suggests, then this raises fundamental questions about *why* settlement patterns and social organisations in the region were so different from those in areas where monuments and other sites were more densely clustered (ibid; Garwood 2007c). There is clearly also a need to gain a far more detailed understanding of the few areas with relatively greater evidence for monument building and the development of distinct ceremonial landscapes (notably at Catholme/Whitemoor Haye and along the Avon valley), and to compare these with other monumentalised landscapes in southern Britain. In these cases there is potential for discussions of political and territorial organisation (eg in relation to the spacing of monument groups along the Avon valley) and interactions between what appear to be distinct communities (eg the groups using the Catholme/Whitemoor Haye ceremonial centre and their neighbours just to the north in the Peak District).

The west midlands may also be an especially suitable regional context for considering the nature of regional cultural diversity in the Middle and Late Neolithic (cf Harding 1995, Barclay 2000). This is not because of any kind of intrinsic or coherent cultural identity, but because of the *lack* of such an identity, and the evidence instead for considerable variation in cultural practices (Ray 2007, 72; Garwood 2007c, 194-5). The central part of the region seems to have been thinly occupied and certainly lacks monuments, while the diversity of the cultural forms, practices and local sequences of change around the periphery relates to the cultural repertoires and activities of social groups that lived mainly *outside* the region. The 'west midlands' is thus an arbitrary unit of study in cultural terms, but embraces parts of what in the Neolithic were many culturally distinct areas that can be studied both comparatively and in terms of the cultural and economic interactions that took place between them. At a larger scale, the region is geographically central to, and traversed by, a multiplicity of routes across southern Britain: between the Welsh mountains and east midlands' plains, between the south-west peninsular and the Yorkshire Wolds and Moors, and between the chalk and limestone hills and river valleys of southern England and the Pennine and Cumbrian uplands. The distribution of sourced stone axes in the west midlands, and across southern Britain as a whole, is striking testimony to the scale and complexity of the networks of exchange and cultural interaction that reached or extended across the west midlands in the Middle and Late Neolithic (eg see Clough and Cummins 1988, maps 1-23; Shotton 1988).

### 2.6.4. Research aims and methods

The research agenda and key research questions outlined above have important implications for methods of resource assessment, curatorial practices, fieldwork methods, and networks of communication and data gathering in the region. In many respects, the methodological and practical requirements of research-led archaeological work already identified for Early Neolithic studies are also applicable to the Middle and Late Neolithic: these are summarised below, with additional points where relevant.

- There is an urgent need for significant enhancement of HER resources in the west midlands, especially in relation to the description, dating and full listing of sites and finds (Barfield 2007, 97-9, 106).

- Reassessment of the existing air photographic record and further aerial survey work (especially in major river valleys, areas which have received less attention in the past, and areas where crop marks are rarely seen) is needed in all parts of the region (Barber 2007, 94). Sample excavations of crop mark sites should be a high priority (ibid).

- The identification and investigation of Middle and Late Neolithic monuments, especially cursuses, pit circles, henges and palisade enclosures, is a clear research priority in west midlands archaeology. There is a particular need to recover evidence relating to architectural design, artefact deposition and chronology. Opportunities for investigating possible Middle and Late Neolithic monuments in development archaeology contexts should be grasped immediately and arrangements made for full resourcing of excavation and post-excavation work (ibid; Ray 2007, 73-4).

- The dispersed character of social activity in the Middle and Late Neolithic, and the structured organisation of social practices at large spatial scales (Darvill 1997b; Pollard 2002), must be recognised in preparing fieldwork designs.

- Fieldwork methods should be appropriate to the study of Middle and Late Neolithic landscapes. In particular, site identification methods such as surface collection and test pit survey require narrow transect intervals, and site evaluation methods should operate at 6-10% sampling levels (Hey and Lacey 2001).

- The development of effective predictive modelling and site prospection methods in sub-alluvial and sub-colluvial contexts offers new opportunities for studying prehistoric settlement areas that cannot be investigated using surface survey and shallow excavation techniques (Jackson 2007, 120-1; cf Challis and Howard 2003).

- Extensive open-area excavation is essential for investigating the wider culturally-ordered spatial contexts of particular social practices. The 'strip, map and sample' process (Hey and Lacey 2001, 55-7) seems to be the most effective method for initial investigation of prehistoric sites and for planning effective excavation strategies.

- Where well-defined Middle and Late Neolithic sites are identified, it is important that they are totally excavated at least within the areas to be affected by development, to identify overall spatial designs, constructional features, and the structuring of depositional practices, artefacts and materials (using 100% artefact recovery and three-dimensional recording methods). The recovery of dating evidence, especially radiocarbon sample materials, is a research priority.

- A key area of concern in Middle and Late Neolithic archaeology is recognition and interpretation of the structured, purposeful deposition of artefacts and other materials. It is worth noting that this approach to British prehistoric material culture was developed initially in Late Neolithic studies, as a means of analysing and explaining the distinctive nature of artefact deposits at henges and other sites (eg Richards and Thomas 1984; Pollard 1995; Thomas 1999, 62-88). In fieldwork terms, this demands context-sensitive and precise recording methods, 100% recovery of artefacts and other materials from single depositional contexts, and rejection of inappropriate practices such as 50% sampling (eg half-sectioning) of pits and other features.

- Middle and Late Neolithic material culture studies in the west midlands need significant attention, especially in relation to chronology (which requires radiocarbon dating programmes and typo-chronological study), function (there is a need for residue and microwear analyses), raw material sourcing and the social organisation of production (Ray 2007, 74; Barfield 2007, 106; cf Lithic Studies Society 2004).

- A major weakness in Neolithic material culture studies in the region is the extreme scarcity of specialists to undertake artefact analyses and related research work. There is an urgent need to develop systems of training and support for new specialists in artefact studies, especially within field archaeology organisations (Ray 2007, 74).

- It is important to emphasise that recognition of the potential of Middle and Late Neolithic sites depends on the familiarity of curatorial and field archaeologists with the material evidence, current interpretative frameworks and research priorities. Ray (2007) has suggested that there is a need to develop expertise in these areas, and to encourage a more dynamic and interactive research culture among the archaeologists working in the region.

### 2.6.5. Conclusion

Of the earlier prehistoric periods in the west midlands, the Middle and Late Neolithic has perhaps attracted the most visible and consistent attention in both regional and national research literature. This in part reflects the distinct and relatively substantial nature of the material evidence, and in part the especially prominent research profile that Middle and Late Neolithic studies have had in recent prehistoric archaeology in Britain. On closer inspection, however, much of this attention in the west midlands has focused on a very small number of sites and landscape areas, above all the cursuses, ring ditches and long enclosures at Barford, Wasperton and Charlecote in the Avon valley. In contrast, other significant sites and sources of evidence have either been neglected (such as the important monuments and lithic concentrations in western parts of the region, including Stapeley Hill and Clun in Shropshire), or have yet to reach a wider audience (especially recent work at Church Lawford in Warwickshire, and Catholme and Whitemoor Haye in Staffordshire).

In many respects, Middle and Late Neolithic monuments, ceremonial complexes and landscapes in the west midlands are similar to those in other regions, and are directly comparable in terms of their research significance and potential. Nonetheless, the relative rarity of monument groups, their wider spacing in the landscape, limited evidence for large-scale construction events and the lack of evidence for continuing development of ceremonial centres during the Late Neolithic, raise important questions concerning the relative scale and complexity of social and political communities and the nature of social change in the region. Evidence for economic practices and settlement (in the broadest sense) is also similar to that found in other regions, with very much the same research potential. Given the general absence of architectural remains, the investigation of pit deposits is especially important, whether these were the outcomes of routine daily tasks around occupation sites or more formal social practices at 'special' locales in the landscape. At the same time, there is clearly considerable potential in the west midlands for pursuing research questions that focus on the relationships between monuments, settlements and economic activities, especially through landscape-scale studies.

## 2.7. Early Bronze Age

### 2.7.1. Introduction

*The Early Bronze Age in the west midlands: previous research*

The Early Bronze Age, defined here as the period *c* 2100-1500 BC (see below), is represented in the archaeological record predominantly by large numbers of round barrows and burials, together with a range of new artefact categories including ceramics such as Food Vessels and Collared Urns, and bronze items such as flat and flanged axes and riveted daggers. The clustering of round barrows in large groups marks the development of ceremonial centres and distinctive 'sacred landscapes' very different to those of the Late Neolithic. Settlement sites, in contrast, are exceptionally rare and materially ephemeral, and relatively little is known about economic practices or other aspects of everyday social life. This still holds true despite new discoveries and increasingly subtle interpretations of settlement evidence (eg Brück 1999b; cf Brück 2000) and metal production and exchange (eg Needham 1988; Barber 2001, 2003).

There has been little research work devoted specifically to the Early Bronze Age of the west midlands. Summaries of round barrow and material culture evidence at a county scale, with the exception of Grinsell's (1993) survey of Herefordshire barrows, are mostly out of date (eg Smith 1957; Gunstone 1965) or lack detailed assessment of the evidence (eg Hingley 1996). Vine's larger-scale study of the middle and upper Trent basin (1982) remains a useful survey of the Early Bronze Age evidence known at the time of publication, but this is also now dated, while Mullin's (2003) more recent outline of the Bronze Age in the north-west English midlands embraces only a small part of the region (north Shropshire and west Staffordshire). There has, however, been a large number of investigations of round barrows and ring ditch sites in the region, including work by Bateman (1848 and 1861) and others in the Staffordshire Peak District in the 19th century, and significant recent excavations of groups of barrows at Catholme and Whitemoor Haye, Staffordshire, Wolvey, and King's Newnham, Warwickshire, Bromfield, Shropshire, and Holt, Worcestershire (see below).

*Current research agenda in Early Bronze Age archaeology*

The definition of research agenda in Early Bronze Age studies is complicated by the lack of consensus concerning temporal boundaries and the extent to which these relate to cultural, social and economic changes. The period *c* 2500-2000 BC has been particularly prone to terminological confusion, especially as the presence of both metal artefacts in Britain from *c* 2700 BC and Beaker burials from *c* 2500 BC are sometimes used as chronological markers for the beginning of the Bronze Age, despite the dating of several 'classic' Late Neolithic site and artefact categories to the late 3rd millennium BC (discussed in the previous section). There are, in fact, several chronological frameworks available, ranging from artefact typo-chronologies (eg Gerloff 1975) to general periodisations (eg Bradley 1984a; Burgess 1980, 1986; Needham 1996). The most reliable general scheme in current use, Needham's phasing of the British Bronze Age into seven distinct 'Periods' (1996, revised 2005), provides a synthesis of available dating evidence, although the period division has not been universally adopted for descriptive or interpretative purposes.

For the purposes of this review, the chronological boundary for the start of the Early Bronze Age is placed at 2100 BC. This date marks some widespread changes in both material culture and social practices. In particular, several long-lived architectural traditions associated with henges, massive timber circles and stone circles came to an end, construction events at most existing ceremonial monuments ceased and depositional practices at these places were generally discontinued, especially those associated with Grooved Ware (Garwood 1999b). This corresponds with significant changes in funerary practices. Beaker ceramics and burial assemblages, for example, changed from low-carinated vessels with a 'primary package' of artefact associations, to a diversified range of vessel types associated with several 'emergent' artefact sets (Needham 2005). This parallels changes in funerary practices and monuments: from rare, small, single phase round barrows usually with single event central burials, to more complex monuments, more frequent mound construction events, successive mound elaboration episodes, free-standing timber structures, successive burials and an increasingly diverse range of funerary artefacts (Garwood 2007a). Finally, it is important to note that the period *c* 2200-2100 BC saw the transition in Britain (very early in European terms) from predominantly copper to predominantly bronze production (Pare 2000; cf Needham 2005, fig 13), marking the *floruit* – at least in metallurgical terms - of the 'full' Early Bronze Age.

The chronological boundary at the end of the Early Bronze Age, *c* 1500 BC, is associated with far-reaching cultural, social and economic changes (Bradley 1991; Barrett 1994, 146-53; Brück 2000) marked by the widespread appearance of substantial and durable Middle Bronze Age settlement architecture, fortified enclosures, land boundaries and field systems, intensive farming practices, cremation cemeteries and new types and greater quantities of bronze metalwork (such as rapiers, spearheads and palstaves).

In the west midlands, the boundary between the 'Late Neolithic' and the 'Early Bronze Age' is reasonably well defined. Although it is not possible to point to the cessation of henge construction as a temporal threshold (as these monuments are largely absent from the region), nevertheless a major change *is* evident from *c* 1900 BC when round barrow construction increased very rapidly, with dense concentrations around the periphery of the region and monument construction in central areas such as the lower Severn valley for the first time (Garwood 2007b, 148, 154). This is associated with the appearance of new Early Bronze Age material culture types and evidence for wider woodland clearance and agriculture. The end of the Early Bronze Age, perhaps surprisingly, is less evident in material terms: round barrow construction continued after 1500 BC and there are very few well-dated Middle Bronze Age settlements or field systems in the region. Even so, Middle Bronze Age metalwork hoards and stray finds, burnt mounds and occasional cremation cemeteries point to some significant cultural changes in the mid 2nd millennium BC.

Although there is presently no agreement about research priorities in Early Bronze Age archaeology, key themes are highlighted in several recent books (especially Barrett 1994, Barber 2003, Harding 2000, Woodward 2000, Brück 2001; Bradley 2007) and a large number of interpretative studies that raise research questions relevant to the west midlands:

1.  *Social and cultural change.* The nature of Early Bronze Age society has become a neglected area of study, especially since all-embracing evolutionary frameworks and chiefdom models have been widely questioned, if not rejected (eg Barrett 1994, Richards 1998; cf Pluciennik 2005). Even so, descriptions of Bronze Age society remain wedded to models of hierarchical social forms, and social change is usually seen in terms of increasing complexity and centralisation, shifts in economic and political principles underlying different kinds of chiefdoms, and/or changes in the representation of structures of authority (eg Renfrew 1973, Shennan 1982, Braithwaite 1984, Whittle 1997b, Fleming 2004: cf Chapman 2003; Earle 2002; Harding 2000, 386-413; Kristiansen and Larsson 2005). A key research issue, in this context, is how well these abstract 'top-down' models explain the diversity and particular characteristics of social life in this period. This is clearly best addressed by investigating social practices at regional, local, site and 'event' levels of analysis. Renewed interest in social change *during* the Early Bronze Age is also long overdue, especially now that it is possible to recognise major changes in monumental architecture and funerary practices within the period (Garwood 2007a). Another, currently undervalued, approach to understanding Bronze Age society concerns the large-scale structuring of economic and political systems, cultural interactions and trade, exemplified by Sherratt's work on 'world systems' (1993, 1994; cf Harding 2000, 414-22; Kristiansen and Larsson 2005). From this perspective, social

structures and cultural change during the British Early Bronze Age are partly explicable with reference to transformations at a European scale (see also Gerloff 1975; Tomalin 1988; Needham 1996, 2000, 2005), the regional implications of which are rarely explored.

2. *Environmental change and agriculture.* Recent studies of Holocene environments in north-west Europe suggest a period of relatively unstable, 'poorer' climate in the late 3rd/early 2nd millennia BC, possibly resulting in landscape change and more difficult conditions for agrarian farming (Bell and Walker 2005; Tipping and Tisdall 2004, 76-7). There is, however, also evidence for more widespread and sustained clearance, the continuing development of extensive pastureland and the increasing importance of cereal cultivation (Richmond 1999). The development of field systems in this context is poorly understood: despite occasional claims for origins in the Neolithic or Early Bronze Age (eg Pryor 1998, 89) there is no strong evidence from southern Britain for the creation of large field systems before the mid 2nd millennium BC (cf Johnston 2001). Key research themes, therefore, include: (i) climate change and its impact on local environmental conditions and farming practices; (ii) the nature of Early Bronze Age agricultural economies; and (iii) the architectural and socio-economic transformation of the Bronze Age landscape.

3. *Monuments.* Although the evidence from round barrows is still central to interpretations of Early Bronze Age society, the only recent general study of these monuments is Ann Woodward's *British Barrows* (2000) which provides an excellent introduction to Wessex burials and round barrows in the landscape (replacing Ashbee's *The Bronze Age Barrow in Britain* (1960) as the main overview of the nature of the evidence). Research themes in current round barrow studies include: (i) the social significance of funerary practices and mound building (Bradley 1984a, 68-84; Garwood 1991; Barrett 1990, 1994, 112-31; Last 2007); (ii) the spatial organisation of barrow groups (Exon et al 2000; Garwood 1991, 1999a, 2003, 2007a); (iii) the chronology and cultural significance of changes in mound architecture and ritual practices (Garwood 1991, 2007a); and (iv) the role of round barrows as media for remembrance and historical and cosmological representation (eg Last 1998; Owoc 2000, 2001; Garwood 2003; cf Bradley 2002). These themes are prominent in several important publications of round barrow excavations, including groups of sites at Radley Barrow Hills, Oxfordshire (Barclay and Halpin 1999), Raunds, Northamptonshire (Healy and Harding 2007), and Brenig, Clwyd (Lynch 1993).

4. *Burials.* The diverse interpretative approaches in studies of Beaker graves (eg Thomas 1991; 1999, 156-62; Mizoguchi 1993; Last 1998; Healy and Harding 2004; Needham 2005) are broadly relevant to Early Bronze Age inhumation burials (and to some extent cremations; cf Barrett 1994, 119-23), but until recently there have been relatively few specific interpretations of Early Bronze Age funerary practices (notably: Bradley 1984a, 73-89; Clarke et al 1985; Barrett 1988; 1994, 113-31). Renewed research interest in the last decade has focused on the representation of social and cultural identities (eg Brück 2004a, 2004b; Jones 2004; Sørensen 2004), the social significance of 'rich graves' (eg Woodward 2000, 101-22; Needham 2000; Sørensen 2004), and the role of funerary artefacts as symbolic media (ibid; see also Woodward 2002a).

5. *Ceremonial landscapes.* The research themes and interpretative approaches found in recent studies of Middle and Late Neolithic ceremonial landscapes are also relevant to the Early Bronze Age. Inevitably, however, attention in Early Bronze Age studies has focused mainly on the large-scale spatial organisation of round barrows, cosmography and the creation of 'sacred landscapes', especially in relation to earlier monuments, natural landforms and celestial phenomena (eg see Field 1998; Parker Pearson and Ramilisonina 1998; Garwood 2003, 2007a; Tilley 1998, 177-238; Woodward and Woodward 1996).

6. *Settlement.* The dearth of Early Bronze Age settlement evidence at a national scale, despite some important recent discoveries (eg Garner 2001, Hey 2001, McCullagh and Tipping 1998) remains a major barrier to social interpretation (see Brück 1999b for a recent assessment of the evidence). Settlement studies have tended to focus on large-scale socio-economic organisations (eg Barnatt 2000, Fleming 1998, Johnston 2001), residential mobility, and systems of tenure and territoriality (eg Whittle 1997a, Brück 1999b, Kitchen 2001). These include very diverse approaches to the relationship between monument groups and settlement, which are believed either to have been broadly congruent (eg Barnatt 1999; Barnatt and Collis 1996; Malim 2000), or to have occupied largely separate areas (ie 'sacred' and 'secular' landscapes; eg Fleming 1971, Field 1998). Although the sacred:secular dichotomy has been widely questioned as a classificatory scheme in prehistory (cf Barrett 1994, Brück 1999a, Bradley 2005, Fleming 1998), it still has a strong presence in interpretations of Early Bronze Age landscapes.

7. *Material culture.* The study of Early Bronze Age artefacts is marked by a high degree of specialisation, due in part to the wide range of material categories and the scale of artefact *corpora*. The only significant area of collaborative work concerns rich grave assemblages (see: Clarke et al 1985, Woodward 2000, 2002a; Woodward et al 2005). The principal artefact types have been catalogued at national or regional scales within the last 40 years (eg see: Beck and Shennan 1991; Burgess 1980, 62-115; Clarke 1970; Eogan 1994; Edmonds 1995, 122-83; Gerloff 1975; Gibson 2002a; Kinnes and Varndell 1995; Longworth 1984; Needham 1996; Needham et al 1997; Sheridan and Shortland 2004). Questions of chronology, typology and technology continue to be important, but there has been a shift of research emphasis to focus on the cultural significance of objects and depositional practices, social relations of production, exchange and consumption, and value systems (eg Barrett and Needham 1988, Bradley 1990, Sherratt 1994, Barber 2003).

8. *Regionality and cultural diversity.* The recent interest in regional cultural identities in the Neolithic has not been paralleled in Early Bronze Age studies. To some extent this reflects the relatively consistent character of monument building and burial practices across the British Isles, which suggests weak or fluid regional ethno-cultural identities. Moreover, recent research emphasis on cultural interactions at a European scale, multiple or fractal rather than 'individual' identities (eg Brück 2004a, 2004b; Jones 2004), and social practices at a local scale, have all marginalised discussion of exclusive 'group' identities. The consistency of funerary traditions may, however, be overemphasised (there is, in fact, considerable variation in funerary practices and artefact associations from one area to another), while recent work on identity and ethnicity (eg see Diaz-Andreu et al 2005) point to potential new lines of enquiry.

## 2.7.2. Research assessment: current knowledge and understanding of the evidence

### Environmental data

Early Bronze Age environments in the west midlands are not well understood. There is very little botanical or faunal evidence and there are few pollen diagrams relating to this period (Greig 2007, 46). Extensive woodland clearance phases have been identified at Wellington, Herefordshire, *c* 2200/1900 BC (lime and elm) and *c* 1950/1750 BC (oak), and at Cookley, Worcestershire, *c* 1900/1600 BC. More localised and sporadic clearance episodes have been suggested around the wetland areas of mid Shropshire (Leah et al 1998, 53). In the lower Severn valley, pollen and other evidence suggests that extensive clearance and arable farming on the gravel terraces began no earlier than the early/mid 2nd millennium BC (Brown 1982), which is consistent with the evidence for a fairly

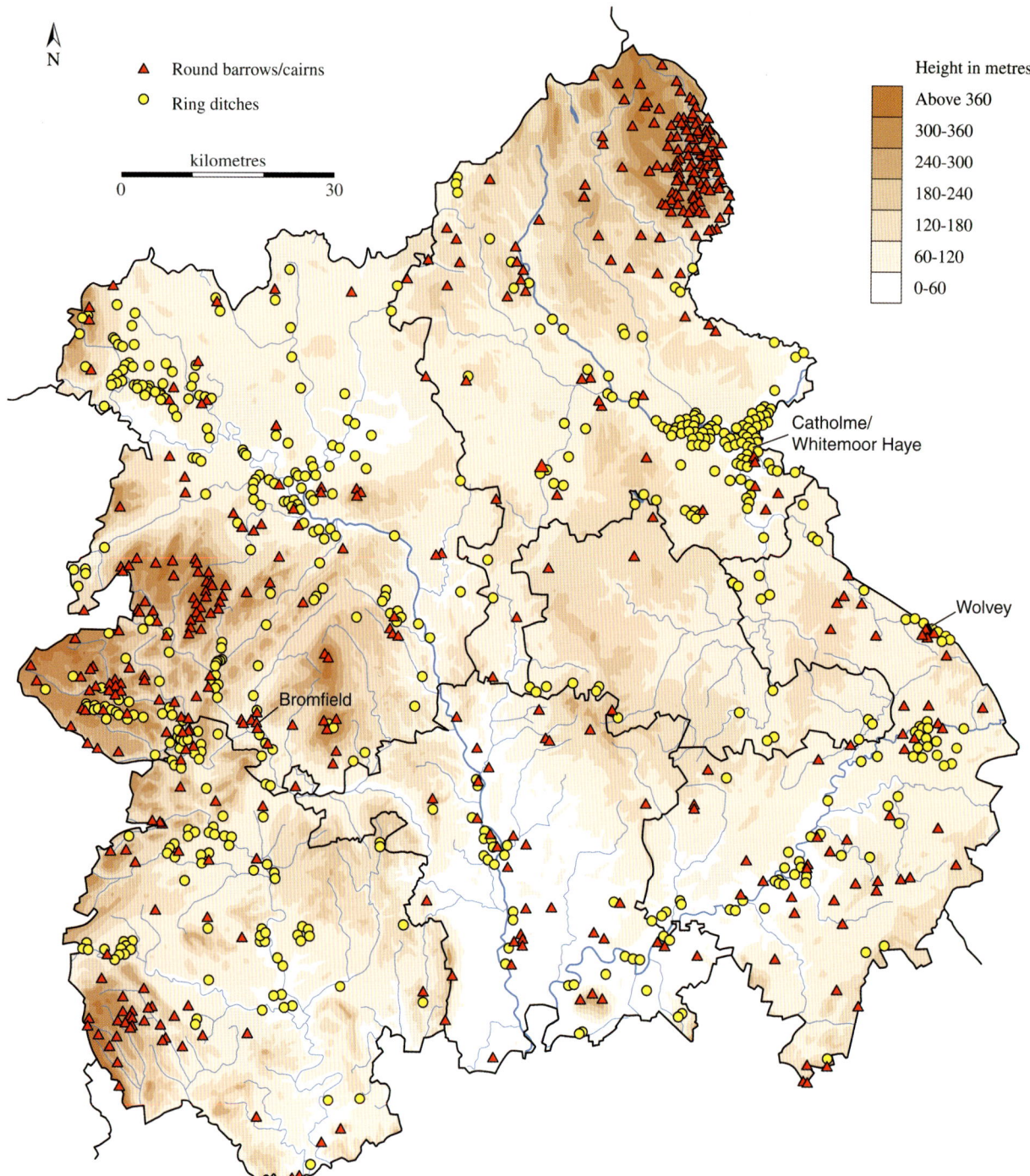

**Fig 2.12** Early Bronze Age round barrows and ring ditches in the west midlands (after Garwood 2007b, fig.1)

open landscape in the environs of the Perdiswell enclosure at Worcester in the mid 2nd millennium BC (Griffin et al 2002, 20), and around the barrows at Holt on the other side of the Severn in the early 2nd millennium BC. There is, however, minimal direct evidence either for agriculture or exploitation of wild resources in the region, other than occasional finds of cultivated cereal grains and hazelnut shells: for example at Church Lawford (Area D; Palmer 2007, 128) and Boteler's Castle, Warwickshire; Kemerton, Worcestershire (L, Moffett, pers comm); and Bromfield B9, Shropshire (Hughes et al 1995).

### Monuments

The Early Bronze Age round barrow evidence in the west midlands is considerable, diverse, and occasionally richly detailed (Garwood 2007b). Over 900 round barrows and ring ditches have been recorded, roughly half with surviving or recorded mound structures (Fig 2.12). Although some of these are undoubtedly Neolithic in date, and a

few Middle Bronze Age or later, the available dating evidence suggests that most round barrows in the region were built in the period c 2100-1500 BC. These monuments are so numerous and widely distributed that it is possible to make some general statements about spatial patterns and processes of site preservation and destruction.

**Fig 2.13** Cairn on Stiperstones, Shropshire (copyright Paul Garwood)

The spatial distribution of round barrows and ring ditches in the west midlands is closely related to the geographical and historical incidence of arable farming. Most surviving earthen mounds and cairns are located in areas used for pasture or in marginal upland landscapes (Fig 2.13), with major concentrations in the Staffordshire Peak District and south-west Shropshire, and smaller groups in north Warwickshire and south-west Herefordshire. Ring ditches, in contrast, occur mostly in areas subject to long-term arable farming, especially in river terrace locations where round barrows rarely survive as standing monuments. There are large concentrations of ring ditches in the upper Severn, upper Teme and tributary valleys of the Severn in Shropshire, the Warwickshire Avon, and the Trent and Teme in Staffordshire. Few sites are known along the middle and lower Severn in south Shropshire and Worcestershire, or the Wye in Herefordshire (ibid).

Agricultural destruction of round barrows in the region has been extensive, in some places beginning as early as the Iron Age (eg at Sharpstones Hill A1, Shropshire; Barker et al 1991). It is difficult, however, to generalise about the process of destruction given the local diversity of farming regimes and changes in these over time. Animal husbandry of various kinds has been prevalent in the region, and only in the light soil areas of south Staffordshire and south Warwickshire has there been sustained arable farming since the Middle Ages (Rowlands 1989). Elsewhere, it is likely that monuments were levelled during short-lived cultivation episodes in areas otherwise mainly pastoral in character. It is certain, however, that monument destruction accelerated from the late 17th century as new agricultural systems led to an expansion of arable farming and the improvement of grasslands (ibid, 177): by 1900 the majority of barrows in lowland parts of the region were severely eroded or truncated. Mechanised agricultural practices have continued the process of destruction at an even more extensive scale.

Quarrying has also led to widespread if localised destruction of round barrows. Salvage recording of sites in advance of gravel extraction in the 1960s and 1970s sometimes produced valuable results (eg at Holt, Worcestershire, excavated 1970-75; Hunt et al 1986), but only since the advent of PPG16 have major programmes of fieldwork taken place in river terrace locations. These are now beginning to produce impressive results: eg at Wellington, Herefordshire (Dinn and Roseff 1992; Jackson 2007), and Catholme and Whitemoor Haye, Staffordshire (Coates 2002; Woodward 2007, 182, 189-92; Buteux and Chapman forthcomingh).

The extent of destruction caused by urban growth and industrial activity is more difficult to assess. Recent air photographic survey (eg Watson 1991) and excavation of ring ditches (eg at Meole Brace: Hughes and Woodward 1995) suggest that monuments may have existed in areas now covered by urban development. Yet documentary and early map sources provide little evidence for the presence of round barrows in these areas, and there are very few accounts of discoveries of prehistoric sites or finds during the growth of cities and towns in the region in the 18th to 20th centuries (Garwood 2007b, 139). None of the possible 'round barrows' destroyed by urban and industrial development in places such as Dudley, Walsall and Wolverhampton produced a single artefact or burial deposit, or any evidence for distinctive constructional features. Although it is possible that evidence was missed (Mike Hodder, pers comm), it is most likely that these were natural mounds or spoil heaps derived from building work and industrial practices (Garwood 2007b, 136-7). This does not negate the possibility that round barrows and ring ditches may yet be found in areas like Birmingham, Wolverhampton and Coventry (indeed, their identification and investigation should be a high priority in future evaluation work), but at present there is no indication that they were common in these areas in prehistory.

Processes of site obscuration may also have had an impact on site distributions. The rarity of ring ditches in the lower Severn valley in Worcestershire and south Shropshire contrasts with clusters of ring ditches in the upper Severn and Avon (Watson 1991). This suggests that round barrows in the lower Severn were either relatively sparse or that mounds in low-lying situations were eroded in antiquity and have since been concealed by alluviation (eg as at Wellington Quarry, Herefordshire; Dinn and Roseff 1992; Jackson 2007, 115-6). It is also important to note that a large part of the west midlands landscape is defined broadly as wood pasture (Dyer 2000, 98), with patchy if still extensive woodland that may have obscured the presence of mounds at a local level.

There has been considerable investigation of round barrows in the west midlands, with information of varying quality from over 250 sites. Of these, 64 sites have been excavated since 1960, in some cases providing significant constructional, funerary, artefactual and/or chronological evidence, including sites at: Bromfield (Stanford 1982; Hughes et al 1995), Meole Brace (Hughes and Woodward 1995; Barfield and Hughes 1997, 1998) and Sharpstones Hill, Shropshire (Barker et al 1991); Low Bent, Low Farm (Wilson and Cleverdon 1987), King's Low (Lock and Spicer 1986, 1987), and Tucklesholme Farm, Staffordshire (Martin and Allen 2001); Wolvey (Garwood in prep), King's Newnham (Simpson 1969; Palmer 2003) and Wasperton, Warwickshire (Hughes and Crawford 1995); and Holt, Worcestershire (Hunt et al 1986). Records are also available for a further 191 sites (104 located precisely) investigated mainly in the 19th century, the majority in the Peak District (Garwood 2007b, 134-40, App 1).

A wide range of monument types can be identified, including single-phase and multi-phase mounds, platform mounds, ring barrows, cairns, and possible bell and disc barrows, and there are a few examples of timber settings (although no complex structures such as concentric stake circles; Garwood 2007b, 142-3). Unfortunately, there is very little reliable dating evidence of any kind from round barrows in the region: most of those excavated recently were ring ditch sites with few surviving constructional features, and more than half lack *in situ* burial deposits (see below). Although artefacts have been recovered from more than 70 sites, only in 23 cases (16 in the Peak District) are these in primary contexts related stratigraphically to mound structures, or located centrally to ring ditches (ibid). Absolute dating has also contributed little to our understanding of round barrow chronologies in the region: although there are 27 radiocarbon dates available from 15 sites (ibid), only in four cases do these provide precise and stratigraphically relevant

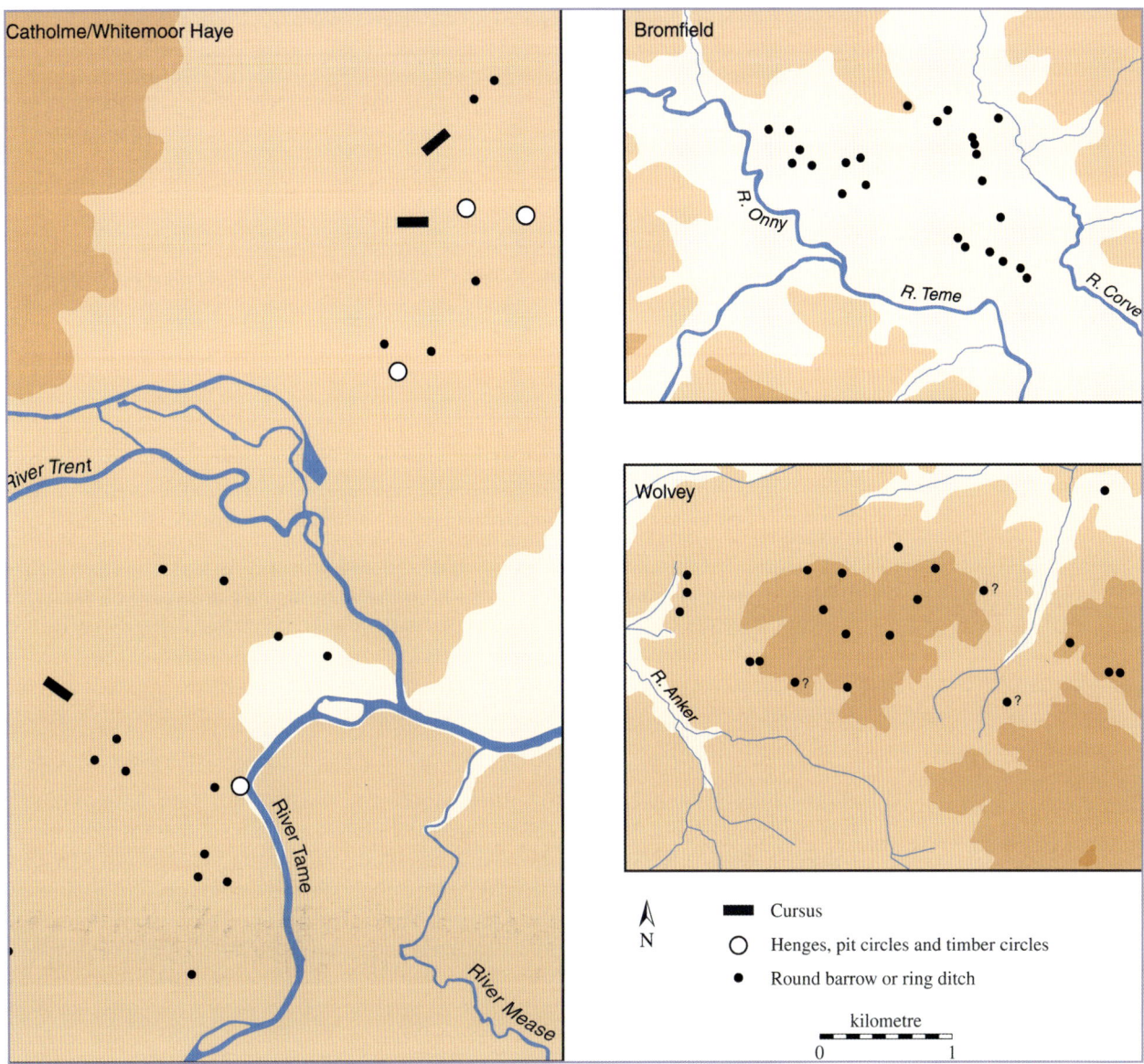

**Fig 2.14** Dispersed barrow groups in the west midlands: Catholme/ Whitemoor Haye, Staffordshire; Bromfield, Shropshire; Wolvey, Warwickshire (after Garwood 2007b, figs 6, 7; Woodward 2007, fig. 6

information for dating constructional events or features (Bromfield B15, Shropshire; Low Bent and King's Low, Staffordshire; and the Perdiswell enclosure, Worcester).

The spatial organisation of round barrow groups in the west midlands is distinctive. Large linear barrow cemeteries of the kind found in Wessex have not been identified anywhere in the region and the very few known linear barrow groups consist of just three or four mounds (eg at King's Newnham, Warwickshire; Palmer 2007, 123-6). This suggests that attempts to express lines of descent, succession and social or political continuity within barrow groups could not be sustained for long periods of time. Instead, most 'groups' of barrows consist of dispersed clusters of mounds or ring ditches, sometimes forming aggregations of 20-30 monuments, situated along ridges or river terraces.

### Burials

A wide range of Early Bronze Age burial practices are represented in the west midlands, with the notable exception of 'rich' graves (Garwood 2007b, 144-8). Well-recorded in situ burial deposits, however, are rare, not all of them are definitely associated with mounds and most are concentrated in the Peak District. Few of these burials can be dated precisely and the majority lack reliable contextual information. Of more than 100 Staffordshire barrow sites described by Bateman (1861), for example, there is a site plan for only one and there are few details of burial orientations, spatial relationships or sequences. In fact, in the whole of the west midlands, only ten inhumation graves of broadly Late Neolithic/Early Bronze Age date can be reconstructed to show body posture and the layout of burial assemblages (Garwood 2007b, 144, fig 10.3). Similarly, there are only nine sites in the region with well-documented cremation burials (ibid, 147).

The architectural contexts and temporal ordering of funerary practices vary enormously, with particular contrasts between 'open' arenas for repeated funerary events and 'closed' burial settings immediately sealed by mounds, and between burials 'housed' in containers (such as stone cists, pits and pottery vessels) and those 'exposed' on the ground surface and in pits open to view prior to mound construction. These practices were not mutually exclusive, but in general terms there seems to have been a trend from accessible arenas in the Late Neolithic to 'closed' mounds with sealed burial deposits in the Bronze Age (cf Bradley 1998, 139-46).

Open access to both ceremonial arenas and burial deposits can be recognised at several sites in the Staffordshire Peak District (eg Top Low and Mare Hill; Bateman 1861, 133-8). In contrast, identification of sites with 'open' arenas but sealed burial deposits is difficult because of uncertainties about the 'accessibility' of pits or stone-built cists (as at Arbor Hill, ibid 112-3) and their relationship to mound building events. This problem is exacerbated where sites have been heavily eroded or truncated (eg at Bromfield B15, Shropshire). The time elapsed between burial and monument construction events is also difficult to estimate, though it is sometimes possible to identify examples of 'exposed' funerary deposits that were covered by mounds immediately after deposition (eg the heaped cremated bone deposits at Throwley, Staffordshire; cf Garwood 2007b, 147).

The most surprising aspect of the burial evidence from the west midlands, given conventional expectations concerning funerary practices at round barrow sites, is that there are so few well documented cases of single-event enclosed or 'housed' burials sealed immediately by mound structures. There is one convincing example at Thorncliff Low, Staffordshire, where a deep pit containing an inhumation with a dagger was covered by a large mound (Bateman 1861, 118-9; Gerloff 1975, 50), and another possible example of a late Beaker burial sealed by a mound at Castern (Bateman 1848, 87-8). Ring ditch sites are especially difficult to interpret in these terms because of the truncation of mound structures, although Sharpstones Hill A1 and A2, Shropshire, both with central cremation burials beneath inverted ceramic vessels, may be sites of this kind (Barker et al 1991).

Recent excavations have tended to reinforce the long-held impression that Early Bronze Age burial assemblages were relatively 'impoverished' in the west midlands. The rarity of artefacts, particularly finer objects, does appear to be characteristic of this period in the region, and there are numerous examples of burials with no grave goods at all (especially in the Severn valley: Buteux and Hughes 1995, 161). Even in the Peak District, which has by far the greatest concentration of grave finds, there are no 'rich' burials (Barnatt and Collis 1996, 56), and very few burials associated with more than one artefact. In this context, the dating of Early Bronze Age mortuary practices is weak in relative terms, and there are only 12 reliable radiocarbon dates from the entire region from burial contexts. These are from 11 burials, all cremations, at nine sites (Garwood 2007b, 47), only one of which is associated with an artefact (a Collared Urn, at King's Low, Staffordshire).

### Ceremonial landscapes

In some parts of the region it is possible to recognise landscape areas with extensive aggregations of round barrows and ring ditches, although it is arguable whether these landscapes had 'special' ceremonial significance separate from settlement areas. In some places these monument clusters are close to Neolithic monuments but they may also form dispersed groups in areas without pre-existing monuments (Garwood 2007b, 148-52). Notable monument concentrations of these kinds exist along the Avon, Trent, Tame and upper Severn valleys, and in upland areas around the fringes of the west midlands, especially in the Peak District.

Linear barrow groups with closely spaced mounds are extremely rare and most barrows in the region are instead found in dispersed clusters along ridges or river terraces, with occasional examples of two or three close-set barrows among them (ibid). Especially large groups (Fig 2.14) have been recorded at Catholme/Whitemoor Haye, Staffordshire (to the north and south of the Trent-Tame confluence; Woodward 2007, 189-90), Bromfield, Shropshire (between the rivers Teme and Corve), and Wolvey, Warwickshire (on low ridges near the river Anker; Garwood 2007b, 150, fig 10.7).

These barrow groups, and the smaller monument clusters in the upper Severn valley (distributed at fairly regular 5-10km intervals), may perhaps be interpreted as 'focal points' for gatherings of interrelated communities whose settlements were scattered and transient (Buteux and Hughes 1995, 161-2; Garwood 2007b, 151-4). Periodic construction events, ceremonies and exchanges that took place at these foci may have been media for expressions of social solidarity and identity within small corporate or descent groups, while larger monument aggregations represent cumulative outcomes of these practices by several groups who recognised shared kinship, political and/or cultural affinities (ibid).

### Settlement and occupation sites

There is virtually no direct evidence relating to Early Bronze Age settlement in the west midlands. This is consistent with the wider pattern of rare and insubstantial settlement in Britain in this period (cf Brück 1999b; Halsted 2005, 16-25). Occasional finds of hearths or pits with late Beaker ceramics (c 2100-1750 BC) suggest short-term occupation events, but evidence for buildings is lacking and these sites are open to alternative interpretations. Examples include a hearth at Rock Green, Ludlow, Shropshire (Carver and Hummler 1991), and isolated pits at Whitemoor Haye Area R (F167; Coates 2002, 9), and Area P (Pit F122; Ann Woodward pers comm) and the National Memorial Arboretum site (Coates 2002, 9-13). These deposits are difficult to interpret but do not seem to represent routine everyday activities. Recent finds of Beaker middens adjacent to former stream courses at Wellington and Staunton-on Arrow, Herefordshire (Ray 2007, 68), highlight the possibility that many occupation sites were situated close to rivers (and since vulnerable to river erosion). Activity close to water sources is also evident in the case of burnt mounds, the purpose of which remains uncertain (cf. Halsted 2005, 39-41). Although most of the examples investigated in the west midlands are Middle Bronze Age or later in date (Ehrenburg 1991, Hodder 1990; cf Powell et al 2008), a few may be Late Neolithic or Early Bronze Age (eg at Harborne, Birmingham; Hodder 1990, 108). More generally, there is an almost complete lack of 'domestic' Food Vessel, Collared Urn and Biconical Urn ceramic assemblages in the region, which elsewhere provide evidence for occupation sites and practices during the early 2nd millennium BC (especially in East Anglia; Healy 1995).

In the absence of direct settlement evidence, interpretations of settlement patterns and economic practices rely instead on the distribution of round barrows, lithic artefact scatters and finds of Early Bronze Age stone and metal artefacts. This evidence allows for some general claims to be made about the presence of farming communities and their exploitation of the landscape (eg Garwood 2007b, 152-4; Halsted 2005, 30-2; 2007). It is evident, for example, that settlement areas marked by *monuments* were very unevenly distributed, with especially low levels of activity in the central part of the region. This need not imply, however, that this area was an uninhabited wilderness (Buteux and Hughes 1995). The large numbers of ring ditches recorded in the upper Severn valley, for example, may indicate considerable intensity and longevity of occupation, while the sparse occurrence of artefacts may reflect local traditions of settlement mobility and use of organic materials. Round barrows in this area, it is suggested, served to formalise long-established, if materially ephemeral attachments, of particular communities to specific residential and/or sacred areas within the landscape (ibid).

The only part of the region that has attracted sustained discussion of the relationship between monuments and settlement is north Staffordshire, in the context of wider interpretations of the Peak District evidence (see: Barnatt 1998, 1999, 2000; Barnatt and Collis 1996; Kitchen 2001). Round barrows in this area occur singly or in small clusters in two main topographical/land use settings: around localised 'cultivation zones' on

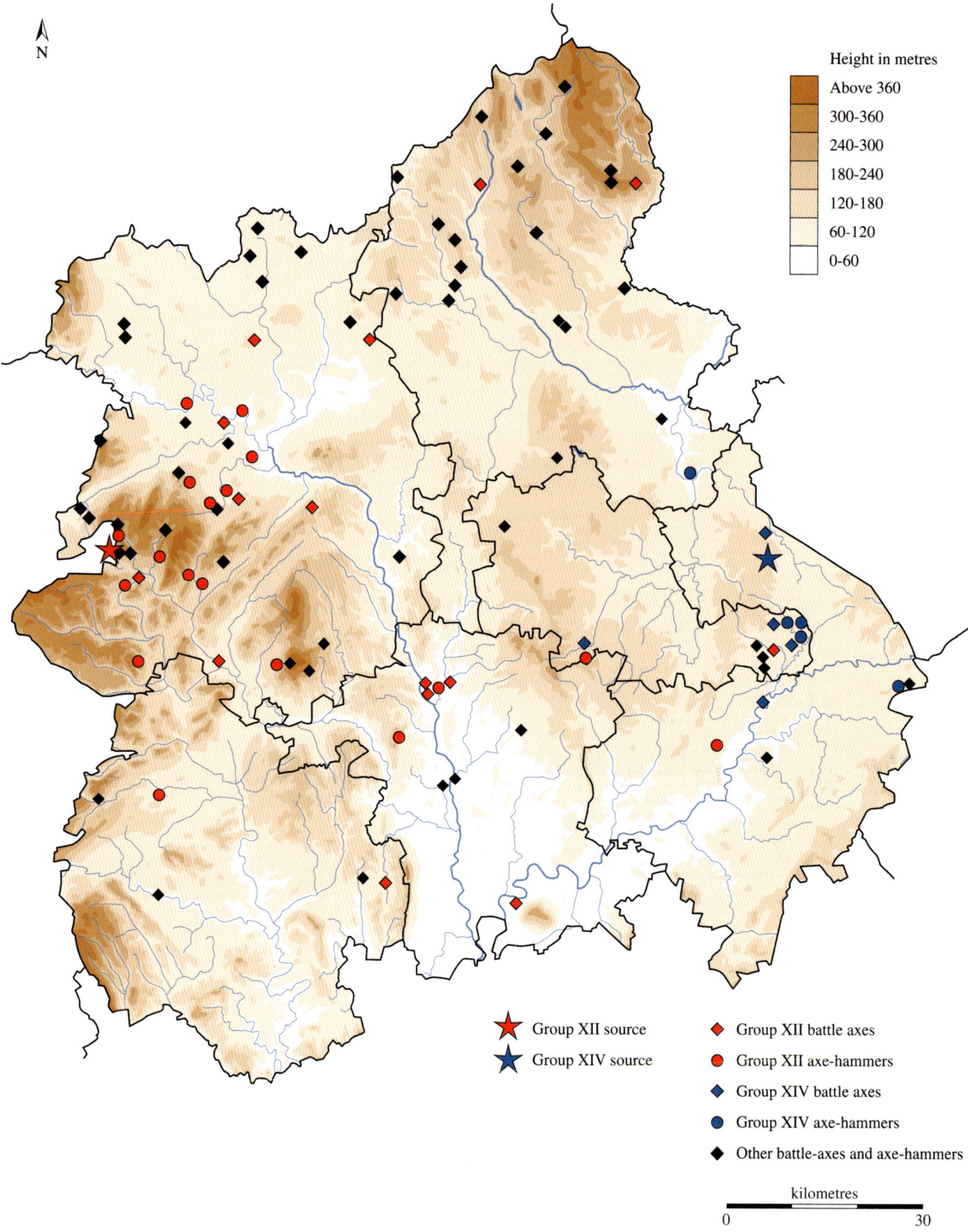

**Fig 2.15** Early Bronze Age perforated stone battle axes and axe-hammers in the west midlands in relation to stone sources within the region (Group XII Picrite, from the Hyssington area; Group XIV Camptonite, from the Nuneaton area) (information from: Woodward 2007, fig 12.3; Roe 1979)

relatively fertile limestone shelves between the upland moors and steep-sided valleys; and in ridge- or hill-top locations overlooking upland pasture (Barnatt and Collis 1996, 3, 69, figs 1.17, 1.18). Mounds built in these contrasting locations may have served different purposes: those around cultivation zones belonging to land holding farming communities; those in upland settings marking claims by several groups to limited areas of grazing land (ibid). Although this interpretation cannot simply be extended to other parts of the west midlands, it is possible that ring ditches in river terrace locations were sited close to occupation sites or on marginal land bordering settlement areas (patterns of this kind have been suggested in the east midlands; Malim 2000, 81-2), while barrows in less well-watered plateau and ridge locations may reflect repeated short-term occupation of places on routes traversed through the landscape as part of transhumance regimes.

Surface artefact finds add little to our understanding of Early Bronze Age occupation sites in the west midlands, except in terms of the overall distribution and density of activity at a regional scale (see below). In any case, the relationship between artefact distributions and settlement is open to question. It is important to note, for example, that many Early Bronze Age objects are found in hilltop or wetland contexts, which suggests they were deliberate deposits in settings some distance from residential sites (Halsted 2005; 2007, 171-3). The wider significance of this observation, however, is difficult to assess as early metal finds in the region have not been the subject of any kind of recent survey (there was no contribution to the framework process, for example). There are also problems with dating: lithic scatters, for example, are notoriously difficult to assign to different parts of the late 3rd and early 2nd millennia BC, and may be the result of multiple depositional events over long periods of time (Barfield 2007, 105), while some artefact types such as barbed-and-tanged arrowheads span the entire Late Neolithic and Early Bronze Age.

### Regionality and cultural diversity

The distribution of monuments within the west midlands suggests concentrations of funerary activity, and therefore perhaps settlement, in the Avon, middle Trent and upper Severn valleys, north-east Warwickshire, and the uplands of north Staffordshire, west Herefordshire and west Shropshire (see Fig 2.12; Garwood 2007b, 134-7, 153-4). In contrast, very few monuments have been recorded in the central part of the region. The distribution of lithic and metal artefacts largely reinforces this pattern. There are concentrations of barbed-and-tanged arrowheads, for example, in south Herefordshire, south-west Shropshire, north Staffordshire and east Warwickshire, while finds in the central part of the region are rare, especially in east Shropshire, south Staffordshire and Birmingham (Barfield 2007, 105, fig 7.4; cf Hodder 2004, 25-6). Similarly, there are concentrations of perforated stone implements in west Shropshire, north Staffordshire and around Coventry (Fig 2.15) but few recorded in more central areas. The spatial distribution of battle-axes and axe-hammers made from stone sources located within the region (Group XII, on the Shropshire-Montgomeryshire border; and Group XIV, near Nuneaton, Warwickshire) is especially striking, with clear concentrations close to the source areas and almost exclusive distributional zones, suggesting separate exchange and alliance networks or perhaps ethno-cultural distinctions (cf Woodward 2007, 184-7; Roe 1978; Shotton 1959, 1988). Finally, most of the Early Bronze Age metal objects found in the west midlands, whether in graves, hoards or surface contexts are again distributed around the fringes of the region. They are almost completely absent from central areas (which contrasts significantly with the distribution of Middle Bronze Age metal artefacts; Vine 1982, 95, 98, maps Y, Z).

In this context, there is little to indicate a distinct regional cultural identity specific to the west midlands in the Early Bronze Age, except perhaps in terms of relatively low intensity social and economic practices that had little lasting material impact on the landscape (Buteux and Hughes 1995). The occurrence of simple mound structures with infrequent, modest funerary deposits in areas such as the Severn valley, for example, may represent local strategies for laying claim to land within thinly occupied and territorially amorphous woodland landscapes (ibid; Garwood 2007b, 154). The distributions of some portable material categories, such as perforated stone implements, may also suggest the existence of exclusive local or regional social networks, and even spatially articulated cultural distinctions, rather than a shared cultural identity. In other respects, regional interpretations of the Early Bronze Age evidence require a larger geographical frame of reference. The major groups of round barrows within the west midlands, for example, can again be seen as extensions of monument concentrations *outside* the region, especially in eastern Wales, the Peak District and the Cotswolds (Garwood 2007c, 201-2). Unlike the Neolithic, however, there appears to be little differentiation between these areas in terms of monument types, funerary practices or material culture, which is consistent with the view that funerary traditions and monument building practices in the Early Bronze Age largely transcended local and regional cultural distinctions (eg Gibbs 1990, 172).

### 2.7.3. Research agenda and specific research questions

*Social and economic change*

Interpretations of social change *during* the Early Bronze Age in Britain are exceptionally rare. All too often the period is treated as a continuation of the Neolithic by slightly different means (ie individual funerary monuments rather than communal ceremonial monuments) or a transitional phase between the Neolithic and the Middle Bronze Age (when durable settlements and land division become visible in the material record). This view is misleading, as recent studies of rapid and far-reaching changes in monumental architecture, funerary practices and cultural landscapes *during* the Early Bronze Age demonstrate (eg Garwood 2007a; Needham 2005; Owoc 2001).

In the west midlands, there is evidence for an expansion of settlement, woodland clearance and agriculture, but most striking is the construction of round barrows in very large numbers throughout the region, leading to the creation of landscapes dominated by funerary monuments. This could be seen as an outcome of successful political and economic strategies among elite social groups and the development of increasingly hierarchical social organisations, in ways very similar – in terms of the scale and density of monument building – to the pattern evident in other parts of southern Britain. Yet the predominance of dispersed monument groups, the absence of rich graves, the contrasting spatial distributions of monuments between central and outer parts of the region, and the evidence for mound construction after *c* 1900 BC in areas where earlier monuments are absent, suggest rather different forms of social organisation and processes of change in comparison with regions such as Wessex. There is thus considerable potential in the west midlands for investigating *distinctive* Early Bronze Age societies and their cultural landscapes, and how these changed during the late 3rd and early 2nd millennia BC.

*Monuments, burials and landscape*

The existence of large numbers of round barrows and ring ditches in the west midlands is significant in national research terms. In some places these sites are sufficiently well preserved and numerous to allow for extremely detailed studies of the Early Bronze Age cultural landscape. Moreover, the results of air photographic survey and excavation projects over the last 30 years show that there is potential for significant new discoveries of ring ditch sites (Garwood 2007b, 137, 140). In this context, developer-funded fieldwork will have a prominent role in the future for enhancing our knowledge of round barrow distributions and monument types, but there is also a fundamental need for research-led excavations of well-preserved round barrows and groups of monuments within wider landscape projects.

In general research terms, there is a need to investigate the monumental architecture of round barrows and ring ditch sites in the region and to recover detailed evidence relating to funerary and other practices. This requires both site-focused and landscape-scale projects involving: (i) total excavation of monuments and associated funerary and other deposits; (ii) investigation of the areas around and between monuments (involving air photographic survey, remote sensing, surface collection work and excavation); (iii) comprehensive radiocarbon dating programmes (it is worth emphasising again that there are only four sites in the whole of the west midlands with reliable radiocarbon dates for construction events, and only one for a burial deposit associated with artefacts); and (iv) detailed palaeo-environmental study of the landscape contexts of Early Bronze Age monuments (at present there is virtually no detailed environmental evidence from any round barrow or ring ditch site in the region). It is essential that future fieldwork takes full account of current research themes, such as the role of memory and the referencing of mythical and historical pasts in the spatial relationships between monuments and in the deposition of ancient materials (eg Bradley 2002; Edmonds and Seaborne 2001, 140-2; Garwood 1999a, 2003; Woodward 2002a).

An especially important research theme concerns the spatial development of round barrow groups and their place within Early Bronze Age landscapes. Current interpretations, based mainly on evidence from southern England (eg Field 1998, Garwood 2003), may not be appropriate for understanding round barrows in other parts of Britain, where large barrow cemeteries are extremely rare and barrow groups instead consist mainly of dispersed clusters of mounds or ring ditches. Only two barrow groups of this kind have been extensively investigated in Britain in recent times: at Brenig, Denbighshire (Lynch 1993), and Raunds, Northamptonshire (Healy and Harding 2007). Although the longevity and diversity of monument-building and ritual-funerary practices in these cases is striking, sequences and tempos of construction and depositional events, and the spatial organisation of dispersed monument groups, remain little understood (Garwood 2007a, 48-9). There is a particular need, in this context, for reliable dating evidence from groups of sites, especially given the rapidity of change in monument building and funerary practices (ibid). There is considerable potential in the west midlands to address these research agenda, as demonstrated by recent work on large dispersed round barrow groups at Wolvey in Warwickshire (Garwood in prep) and in the Catholme/Whitemoor Haye area in Staffordshire (cf Woodward 2007, 189-91;Buteux and Chapman forthcoming).

The predominance of dispersed barrow groups and the rarity of Neolithic monument complexes with round barrows clustered around them, does not necessarily preclude the creation of Early Bronze Age 'sacred landscapes' in the west midlands, but they may be less easy to recognise as organised spatial forms. It is also possible that sacred landscapes structured at very large spatial scales have gone unrecognised in local studies (cf Field 1998, 2004). With the exception of fieldwork around Catholme/Whitemoor Haye, Staffordshire (Woodward 2007, 182, 189-92), and Wasperton (ibid, 187-8) and King's Newnham/Church Lawton in Warwickshire (Palmer 2003, 2007), there has been very little recent study of ceremonial landscapes of this period in the region. Large-scale landscape projects that draw together existing data and new research to investigate the spatial organisation of monuments and ceremonial practices are clearly a research priority.

### Settlement and landscape

Interpretations of Early Bronze Age settlement are weakened by the limited evidence from occupation sites, a lack of agreement about appropriate spatial scales of analysis and imprecise chronologies. This is especially apparent in discussions of the social significance and organisation of sedentary as opposed to mobile residence patterns. In the Peak District's case, for example, the same bodies of evidence have been used to support arguments for mobility and diversity in residence patterns (with only a minor sedentary element in the farming landscape) (Kitchen 2001) *and* for a close relationship between permanent settlement, arable land and monuments (with only limited short-term mobility in transhumance practices) (Barnatt and Collis 1996, 67-80; Barnatt 2000, 4-7). Neither of these interpretations takes account of possible changes in economic practices and funerary customs over time, and there is no supporting evidence either way from actual occupation sites (Garwood 2007b, 151-53). There is clearly a need throughout the region to identify and investigate well-preserved settlements to recover information about the relative permanence and scale of occupation, spatial organisation, economic practices and everyday social life (Halsted 2007, 178). Similarly, very little is known at present about the nature of subsistence economies, manufacturing technologies, the social organisation of production, or exchange practices. In this context, an obvious research priority is to identify Group XII and Group XIV stone implement production sites (cf Shotton 1959; 1988, 51).

The relationships between monuments, residence patterns and economic practices are also central to current debates in Early Bronze Age archaeology (Halsted 2005, 19-32; 2007). There is particular scope in the west midlands for investigating the character of settlement both in areas with funerary monuments and in areas where monuments are absent. A key question is how these areas differed economically, socially and culturally: eg in terms of economic strategies, funerary traditions, social complexity, demographic patterns, political histories and territorial or ethno-cultural identities. There is a need here for comparative studies of settlement and landscape organisation in different environmental and topographic zones: to establish the presence/absence of Early Bronze Age activity, and to investigate diverse settlement, resource exploitation and production systems in different parts of the region and in different landscape settings (cf Halsted 2007, 168). It is notable that the Early Bronze Age is highlighted as a relatively 'neglected' or poorly represented period in recent English Heritage appraisals of the environmental archaeology of the English midlands (eg Murphy 2001, 12-13; Robinson 2003, 115). In this light, recovery of environmental evidence for reconstructing Early Bronze Age landscapes, subsistence economies and settlement is a research priority. There is a particular need for well-dated pollen sequences from different landscape contexts in all parts of the west midlands, including urban areas. The pollen evidence recovered recently from alluvial deposits beside the River Tame in Perry Barr, Birmingham (Mike Hodder, pers comm), clearly demonstrates the considerable potential for recovering environmental data from present urban contexts.

### Spatial patterns and regionality

There are several possible explanations for the apparent absence of Early Bronze Age evidence from the central part of the region, none being necessarily exclusive of the others. A long-held view is that the absence of evidence simply reflects sparse and/or low intensity occupation in prehistory (eg Seaby 1949). Alternatively, it has been argued that social practices in the region involved relatively little use of durable ceramic, metal and lithic artefacts (Buteux and Hughes 1995). It is also commonly assumed that uneven and low levels of previous fieldwork and geo-environmental conditions (eg soils unfavourable to air photographic survey and alluviation in river valleys) have strongly biased recorded distributions of Early Bronze Age sites and finds (ibid; cf Barber 2007, 81-2). Yet the persistence of the overall distribution pattern over the last 50 years – despite extensive fieldwork and air photographic survey – suggests that real contrasts in the character and intensity of occupation *did* exist between the central and outer parts of the west midlands during the Early Bronze Age (Garwood 2007b, 153). In many respects, this can be seen as a continuation of the pattern recognised throughout the Neolithic, with some changes during the early 2nd millennium BC as monument building expanded into the middle Severn valley (but still not into the central uplands) (ibid; cf Buteux and Hughes 1995).

The west midlands thus provides significant opportunities for investigating variation in the social and economic character of Early Bronze Age landscapes. Extensive monument groups found in upland areas, for example, can be contrasted with the beaded distribution of small monument clusters along river valleys. It is possible that these contrasts relate to differences in the way that political and cultural communities were organised: in some areas as relatively large-scale polities associated with large round barrow concentrations (eg the Peak District); in other areas taking the form of more numerous smaller-scale socio-political entities with their own local monument groups (eg along the Avon valley). There may also be contrasts in expressions of 'historicity' and reference to the past (cf Garwood 1991). In the Peak District and the Avon valley a considerable time depth to monument groups is evident, with round barrows often clustered close to Neolithic monuments. In contrast, in the middle and lower Severn valley, round barrows were built in landscapes with little evidence for earlier occupation (Buteux and Hughes 1995; Garwood 2007b, 152-4). In these areas, mound building and burial events may have been intended specifically to legitimise claims to land. The limited development of linear barrow groups in the region may also relate to the organisation of mound-building groups. In particular, the expansion of settlement during the Early Bronze Age into relatively unsettled landscapes allowed for a degree of social mobility. In this context, elite groups may not have been able to sustain their dynastic pre-eminence, marked by successive monument-building events, for more than a few generations (ibid).

These observations highlight the diverse character of mound building and burial events during the Early Bronze Age (cf Garwood 2007a), and differences in their local political and cultural significance from one part of the region to another and over time. In this context, simplistic treatment of all round barrows as if they represent the 'same' set of social concerns and practices is clearly misleading.

## 2.7.4. Research aims and methods

Recommendations for appropriate methodologies and practices in Early Bronze Age archaeology in the west midlands to some extent parallel those suggested for work on Neolithic sites. The nature of the Early Bronze Age evidence, however, points to several issues that require particular attention (especially in relation to funerary sites).

- County-based assessments of round barrows and ring ditches are required to establish the scale and nature of the archaeological resource, and as a means of developing predictive modelling techniques for site location and distributional studies. This should include GIS-based evaluations of processes of site destruction and obscuration.

- In wider curatorial terms there is an urgent need for significant enhancement of local authority HERs (Barfield 2007, 97-100, 106). Information concerning Early Bronze Age artefacts is especially weak.

- There is a need to determine whether the regional distribution of monuments and settlement accurately represents the overall distribution and nature of activity, or low levels of previous research and/or geo-environmental conditions. Survey and test excavation of possible sites is needed in areas where monuments are rare or absent.

- Opportunities for investigating round barrows, ring ditches and other site categories in development archaeology contexts should be pursued without hesitation and arrangements made for full resourcing of excavation and post-excavation work (Garwood 2007, 155). Methods for identifying and recording Early Bronze Age evidence should be included in specifications for excavations in urban areas.

- Studies of round barrows and ring ditches in the region potentially have a major contribution to make to Early Bronze Age research at a national scale. A key aim is to determine constructional and depositional sequences and spatial relationships among *groups* of monuments. The complex multi-phase nature of activity at many round barrow sites demands especially thorough stratigraphic and chronological analysis (ibid).

- There is a need for research-led excavations of well-preserved round barrows as an essential source of both primary and comparative data for the study of monuments and funerary practices in the region (ibid).

- The development of fieldwork programmes to identify and investigate Early Bronze Age sites in all kinds of landscape contexts is a high priority (Halsted 2007, 168). The methodological and technical requirements involved are similar to those identified for dealing with Neolithic evidence, especially in relation to sampling levels, site prospection techniques and extensive survey and open-area excavation methods.

- Funerary sites and pit groups should be totally excavated as this is the only way to make sense of architectural forms and the spatial patterning of depositional practices (Garwood 2007, 155). If possible, this should be achieved even where sites are only partly located within development areas (eg by negotiating access to adjacent land to complete full excavation in collaboration with university-based archaeologists or skilled amateurs).

- Excavation of areas around and between monuments is essential, as round barrows were not isolated and finite memorials but foci for repeated ceremonial activities that extended beyond the physical limits of monuments and sometimes linked several monuments together (see Garwood 1999a; 2003).

- Careful attention needs to be paid to the recovery of dating evidence from all Early Bronze Age sites, especially radiocarbon sample materials. The chronologies of monument forms and burial categories and sequences remain imprecise, while dating evidence for occupation practices, pit deposits and built structures is rare nationally (Garwood 2007a, 48-9).

- Early Bronze Age material culture in the region deserves more synthetic and detailed study, focusing on: (i) the creation of artefact chronologies based on radiocarbon dating evidence; (ii) studies of artefact 'biographies', including residue and microwear analyses; and (iii) studies of raw material sourcing, production sites, finds distributions and depositional contexts, especially of stone shaft-hole implements and metalwork.

- Finally, recognition of the significance and potential of Early Bronze Age sites in the west midlands depends on the familiarity of curatorial and field archaeologists with the material evidence and current research agenda. There is a need to develop expertise in these areas, and to encourage a more dynamic and interactive research culture among archaeologists working in the region.

### 2.7.5. Conclusion

The Early Bronze Age in the west midlands is materially the most represented and the most widely investigated of earlier prehistoric periods in the region. Hundreds of monuments are listed in local authority HERs, together with hundreds more finds of lithic and metal artefacts and other remains. Over 230 monuments have been investigated, and many more non-monumental sites have produced evidence of this period. Overall, our knowledge of the Early Bronze Age in the west midlands easily bears comparison – in terms of the number and diversity of excavated sites of all kinds, the richness and complexity of the artefactual evidence, and wider spatial patterns and landscape contexts – with other English regions. Yet this period has attracted little attention within the region until recently and the west midlands has a low profile in Early Bronze Age research nationally. One reason for this is separate treatment of the Peak District evidence: work on this area tends to focus on the limestone uplands in geographical isolation and to look to north-east England and Wessex for comparanda and interpretative themes rather than closer regional contexts. Although the Peak District evidence is clearly important, in other respects it gives a misleading impression of the nature and significance of the west midlands evidence, and is certainly not representative of the wider spatial distribution of barrows or the funerary record in the region.

In current research terms there is no question about the relevance of the west midlands evidence to interpretative themes and debates at regional, national and European scales of enquiry. Above all, investigation of the nature and development of round barrow groups, and the wider character of settlement and ceremony in the prehistoric landscape, are key themes in current research agenda. Study of the Early Bronze Age in the west midlands has a significant contribution to make to our understanding of the unique cultural worlds that existed in Britain in the late 3rd and early 2nd millennia BC.

## Bibliography

Allen, M, 1997   Environment and land-use: the economic development of the communities who built Stonehenge an economy to support the stones, in *Science and Stonehenge* (eds B Cunliffe, and C Renfrew), Proc Brit Acad 92, Oxford, 115-44

Allen, T, Barclay, A, and Lamdin-Whymark, H, 2004   Opening the wood, making the land: the study of a Neolithic landscape in the Dorney area of the Middle Thames valley, in *Towards a New Stone Age: aspects of the Neolithic in south-east England* (eds J Cotton and D Field), CBA Res Rep 137, London, 82-98

Armit, I, Murphy, E, Nelis, E, and Simpson, D (eds), 2003   *Neolithic Settlement in Ireland and Western Britain*, Oxford

Ashbee, P, 1960   *The Bronze Age Round Barrow in Britain*, London

Ashton, N M, Cook, J, Lewis, S G, and Rose, J, 1992   *High Lodge: excavations by G de G Sieveking 1962-8 and J Cook 1988*, London

Ashton, N M, Healy, F, and Pettitt, P (eds), 2002   *Stone Age Archaeology: essays in honour of John Wymer*, Oxbow Monogr 102, Lithic Studies Soc Occ Papers 6, Oxford

Ashton, N M, and Lewis, S G, 2002   Deserted Britain: declining populations in the British Late Middle Pleistocene, *Antiquity* 76, 388-96

Austin, P, 2000   The emperor's new garden: woodland, trees, and people in the Neolithic of southern Britain, in *Plants in Neolithic Britain and Beyond* (ed A Fairbairn), Neolithic Stud Grp Sem Papers 4, Oxford, 65-78

Bain, K, Buteux, S, Hancox, E, Hewson, M, Jordan, D, Hounslow, M, Karlokovsky, V, and Watters, M, 2005   *Catholme Ritual Landscape Ground Truthing Project, 2004*, Report 1: Post-excavation assessment and updated project design, Unpub report project 1214, Birmingham Archaeology

Barber, K E, and Twigger, S N, 1987   Late Quaternary palaeoecology of the Severn Basin, in *Palaeohydrology in Practice* (eds K J Gregory, J Lewin and B Thornes), Chichester, 217-46

Barber, M, 2001   A time and a place for bronze, in *Bronze Age Landscapes: tradition and transformation* (ed J, Brück), Oxford, 161-69

Barber, M, 2003   *Bronze and the Bronze Age: metalwork and society in Britain c 2500-800 BC*, Stroud

Barber, M, 2007   The blank country? Neolithic enclosures and landscapes in the West Midlands, in *The Undiscovered Country: the earlier prehistory of the West Midlands* (ed P Garwood), Oxford, 79-96

Barber, M, Field, D, and Topping, P, 1999   *The Neolithic Flint Mines of England*, Swindon

Barclay, A, Grey, M, and Lambrick, G, 1995   *Excavations at the Devil's Quoits, Stanton Harcourt, Oxfordshire, 1972-3 and 1988*, Thames Valley Landscapes: the Windrush Valley, Vol 3, Oxford

Barclay, A, and Halpin, C (eds), 1999   *Excavations at Barrow Hills, Radley, Oxfordshire, Vol I: The Neolithic and Bronze Age monument complex*, Thames Valley Landscapes Monogr 1, Oxford

Barclay, A, and Harding, J (eds), 1999   *Pathways and Ceremonies: the cursus monuments of Britain and Ireland*, Neolithic Stud Grp Sem Papers 4, Oxford

Barclay, G, 2000   Between Orkney and Wessex: the search for the regional Neolithics of Britain, in *Orkney in its European Context* (ed A Ritchie), McDonald Institute Monogr, Cambridge, 275-85

Barclay, G, and Hey, G, 1999  Cattle, cursus monuments and the river: the development of ritual and domestic landscapes in the Upper Thames Valley, in *Pathways and Ceremonies: the cursus monuments of Britain and Ireland* (eds A Barclay and J Harding), Neolithic Stud Grp Sem Papers 4, Oxford, 67-76

Barfield, L, 2003  Flint and stone: the significance of Clun and the Clun-Clee Ridgeway, *J South-West Shropshire Hist Archaeol Soc* 14, 17-21

Barfield, L, 2007  Later lithics in the West Midlands counties, in *The Undiscovered Country: the earlier prehistory of the West Midlands* (ed P Garwood), Oxford, 97-108

Barfield, L, and Hughes, G, 1997  The excavation of a double ring ditch at Meole Brace, Shrewsbury, Shropshire, *Ann Rev Dept Ancient History and Archaeology, Univ Birmingham* 1997, 43-4

Barfield, L, and Hughes, G, 1998  Meole Brace excavations, *Ann Rev Dept Ancient History and Archaeology, Univ Birmingham* 1998, 47-8

Barker, P, Haldon, R, and Jenks, W, 1991  Excavations on Sharpstones Hill near Shrewsbury, 1965-71, *Trans Shropshire Archaeol Hist Soc* 67, 15-57

Barnatt, J, 1996  Moving beyond the monuments: paths and people in the Neolithic landscapes of the Peak District, *Northern Archaeology* 13/14, 45-59

Barnatt, J, 1998  Monuments in the landscape: thoughts from the Peak, in *Prehistoric Ritual and Religion*, (eds A Gibson and D D A Simpson), Stroud, 92-105

Barnatt, J, 1999  Taming the land: Peak District farming and ritual in the Bronze Age, *Derbyshire Archaeol J* 119, 19-78

Barnatt, J, 2000  To each their own: later prehistoric farming communities and their monuments in the Peak, *Derbyshire Archaeol J* 120, 1-86

Barnatt, J, and Collis, J, 1996  *Barrows in the Peak District: recent research*, Sheffield

Barrett, J, 1988  The living, the dead and the ancestors: Neolithic and early Bronze Age mortuary practices, in *The Archaeology of Context in the Neolithic and Bronze Age: recent trends* (eds J Barrett and I Kinnes), Sheffield, 30-41

Barrett, J, 1990  The monumentality of death: the character of Early Bronze Age mortuary mounds in southern England, *World Archaeol* 22, 179-89

Barrett, J, 1994  *Fragments from Antiquity*, Oxford

Barrett, J, and Needham, S, 1988  Production, accumulation and exchange: problems in the interpretation of Bronze Age bronzework, in *The Archaeology of Context in the Neolithic and Bronze Age: recent trends* (eds J Barrett and I Kinnes), Sheffield, 127-40

Bartley, D D, and Morgan, A, 1990  The palynological record of the King's Pool, Stafford, *New Phytologist* 116, 117-94

Barton, R N E, 1991  Technological innovation and continuity at the end of the Pleistocene in Britain, in *The Late Glacial in North-West Europe: human adaptation and environmental change at the end of the Pleistocene* (eds R N E Barton, A J Roberts and D A Roe), CBA Res Rep 77, London, 234-45

Barton, R, N, E, 1999  The Lateglacial or Late and Final Upper Palaeolithic colonization of Britain, in *The Archaeology of Britain: an introduction from the Upper Palaeolithic to the Industrial Revolution* (eds J Hunter and I Ralston), London, 13-34

Barton, R N E, 2005  *Ice Age Britain*, London

Barton, R N E, Roberts, A J, and Roe, D A (eds), 1991  *The Late Glacial in North-West Europe: human adaptation and environmental change at the end of the Pleistocene*, CBA Res Rep 77, London

Bateman, T, 1848 *Vestiges of the Antiquities of Derbyshire*, London

Bateman, T, 1861 *Ten Years Diggings in Celtic and Saxon Grave Hills in the Counties of Derby, Stafford and York*, London and Derby

Beales, P W, 1980 The late Devensian and Flandrian vegetation history of Crose Mere, Shropshire, *New Phytologist* 85, 133-61

Beck, C, and Shennan, S, 1991 *Amber in Prehistoric Britain*, Oxbow Monogr 8, Oxford

Bell, M, and Walker, M J C, 2005 *Late Quaternary Environmental Change: physical and human perspectives*, 2nd edn, Harlow

Bergsvik, K A, 2003 Mesolithic ethnicity – too hard to handle? in *Mesolithic on the Move* (eds L Larsen, H Kindgren, K Knutsson, D Loeffler and A Åkelund), Oxford, 290-301

Bevan, L, 1995 *Later Mesolithic Settlement in the West Midlands: the analysis of worked flint from surface collections near Kinver Edge and excavated assemblages from the Trimpley-Blackstone aqueduct*, Unpub MPhil thesis, University of Birmingham

Bevan, L, and Moore, J (eds), 2003 *Peopling the Mesolithic in a Northern Environment*, Oxford, BAR International Series 1157

Boast, R, 1998 Patterns by design: changing perspectives of Beaker variation, in *Understanding the Neolithic of North-west Europe* (eds M, Edmonds and C, Richards), Glasgow, 385-406

Bradley, R, 1984a *The Social Foundations of Prehistoric Britain*, London

Bradley, R, 1984b Regional systems in Neolithic Britain, in *Neolithic Studies: a review of some recent research* (eds R Bradley and J Gardiner), 5-14, Oxford, BAR British Series 133

Bradley, R, 1990 *The Passage of Arms: an archaeological analysis of hoards and votive deposits*, Cambridge

Bradley, R, 1991 The pattern of change in British prehistory, in *Chiefdoms: power, economy and ideology* (ed T Earle), Cambridge, 44-70

Bradley, R, 1998 *The Significance of Monuments*, London

Bradley, R, 2000 *An Archaeology of Natural Places*, London

Bradley, R, 2002 *The Past in Prehistoric Societies*, London

Bradley, R, 2003 Neolithic expectations, in *Neolithic Settlement in Ireland and Western Britain* (eds I, Armit, E Murphy, E Nelis and D Simpson), Oxford, 218-22

Bradley, R, 2003 *The Prehistory of Britain and Ireland*, Cambridge

Bradley, R, 2004 Domestication, sedentism, property and time: materiality and the beginnings of agriculture in northern Europe, in *Rethinking Materiality* (eds E DeMarrais, C Gosden and C Renfrew), McDonald Institute Monogr, Cambridge, 107-15

Bradley, R, 2005 *Ritual and Domestic Life in Prehistoric Europe*, London

Bradley, R, and Edmonds, M, 1993 *Interpreting the Axe Trade: production and exchange in Neolithic Britain*, Cambridge

Braithwaite, M, 1984 Ritual and prestige in the prehistory of Wessex, c 2200-1400 BC: a new dimension to the archaeological evidence, in *Ideology, Power and Prehistory* (eds D Miller and C Tilley), Cambridge, 93-110

Bridgland, D, 2000 River-terrace systems in north-west Europe: an archive of environmental change, uplift and early human occupation, *Quaternary Science Reviews* 19, 1293-1303

Britnell, W J, 1982   The excavation of two round barrows at Trelystan, Powys, *Proc Prehist Soc* 48, 133-201

Brown, A G, 1982   Human impact on the former floodplain woodlands of the Severn, in *Archaeological Aspects of Woodland Ecology* (eds M Bell and S Limbrey), BAR International Series 146, Oxford, 93-105

Brown, A G, 1988   The palaeoecology of Alnus and the postglacial history of floodplain vegetation, *New Phytologist* 110, 425-36

Brown, A G, 2000   Floodplain vegetation history: changes in potential ritual spaces, in *Plants in Neolithic Britain and Beyond* (ed A Fairbairn), Neolithic Stud Grp Sem Papers 4, Oxford, 49-62

Brück, J, 1999a   Ritual and rationality: some problems of interpretation in European archaeology, *European J Archaeol* 23, 313-44

Brück, J, 1999b   What's in a settlement? Domestic practice and residential mobility in Early Bronze Age southern England, in *Making Places in the Prehistoric World: themes in settlement archaeology* (eds J Brück and M Goodman), London, 52-75

Brück, J, 2000   Settlement, landscape and social identity: the Early-Middle Bronze Age transition in Wessex, Sussex and the Thames valley, *Oxford J Archaeol* 19, 273-300

Brück, J (ed), 2001   *Bronze Age Landscapes: tradition and transformation*, Oxford

Brück, J, 2004a   Early Bronze Age burial practices in Scotland and beyond: differences and similarities, in *Scotland in Ancient Europe* (eds I A G Shepherd and G J Barclay), Soc Antiq Scotland, Edinburgh, 179-88

Brück, J, 2004b   Material metaphors: the relational construction of identity in early Bronze Age burials in Ireland and Britain, *J Social Archaeology* 43, 307-33

Burgess, C, 1980   *The Age of Stonehenge*, London

Burgess, C, 1986   'Urnes of no small variety', Collared urns reviewed, *Proc Prehist Soc* 52, 339-51

Burl, A, 1976   *The Stone Circles of the British Isles*, New Haven and London

Buteux, S and Chapman, H forthcoming Where Rivers Meet: the archaeology of Catholme and the Trent-Tame confluence

Buteux, S, and Hughes, G, 1995   Reclaiming a wilderness: the prehistory of lowland Shropshire, *Trans Shropshire Archaeol Hist Soc* 70, 157-64

Campbell, J B, 1977   *The Upper Palaeolithic of Britain: a study of man and nature in the Late Ice Age*, Oxford

Carver, M, 1991   A strategy for lowland Shropshire, *Trans Shropshire Archaeol Hist Soc* 67, 1-8

Carver, M, and Hummler, M, 1991   Excavations at Rock Green, Ludlow, 1975, *Trans Shropshire Archaeol Hist Soc* 67, 84-97

Case, H, 1993   Beakers: deconstruction and after, *Proc Prehist Soc* 59, 241-68

Case, H, 1995   Beakers: loosening a stereotype, in *'Unbaked Urns of Rudely Shape': essays on British and Irish pottery for Ian Longworth* (eds I Kinnes and G Varndell), Oxbow Monogr 55, Oxford, 55-67

Case, H, 2001   The Beaker culture in Britain and Ireland: groups, European contacts and chronology, in *Bell Beakers Today: pottery, people, culture, symbols in prehistoric Europe* (ed F Nicolis), Trento, 361-77

Challis, K, and Howard, A, 2003   GIS based modelling of sub-surface deposits for archaeological prospection in alluvial landscapes, in *Alluvial Archaeology in Europe* (eds A J Howard, M M G Macklin and D G Passmore), Rotterdam, 263-75

Chapman, R, 2003   *Archaeologies of Complexity*, London

Chitty, L, 1963   The Clun-Clee ridgeway: a prehistoric trackway across south Shropshire, in *Culture and Environment: essays in honour of Sir Cyril Fox* (eds I Foster and L Alcock), London, 171-92

Clarke, D L, 1970   *Beaker Pottery of Great Britain and Ireland*, Cambridge

Clarke, D V, Cowie, T, and Foxon, A, 1985   *Symbols of Power at the Time of Stonehenge*, Edinburgh

Cleal, R M J, 1992   Significant form: ceramic styles in the earlier Neolithic of southern England, in *Vessels for the Ancestors* (eds N Sharples and A Sheridan), Edinburgh, 286-306

Cleal, R M J, and MacSween, A (eds), 1999   *Grooved Ware in Britain and Ireland*, Neolithic Stud Grp Sem Papers 3, Oxford

Cleal, R M J, Walker, K, and Montague, R, 1995   *Stonehenge in its Landscape*, English Heritage Arch Rep 10, London

Clough, T H McK, and Cummins, W A (eds), 1988   *Stone Axe Studies, Volume 2: the petrology of prehistoric stone implements from the British Isles*, CBA Res Rep 67, London

Coates, G, 2002   *A Prehistoric and Romano-British Landscape: excavations at Whitemoor Haye Quarry, Staffordshire, 1997-1999*, BAR British Series 340, Oxford

Conneller, C, 2006   Death, in *Mesolithic Britain and Ireland: new approaches* (eds C, Conneller and C, Warren), Stroud, 139-64

Conneller, C, and Warren, G (eds), 2006   *Mesolithic Britain and Ireland: new approaches*, Stroud

Cooney, G, 2000a   *Landscapes of Neolithic Ireland*, London

Cooney, G, 2000b   Recognising regionality in the Irish Neolithic, in *New Agendas in Irish Prehistory* (eds A Desmond, G Johnson, M McCarthy, I Sheehan and E Shee Twohig), Bray, 49-65

Cooper, L, 2006   Launde, a terminal Palaeolithic camp-site in the English midlands and its north European context, *Proc Prehist Soc* 72, 53-93

Cracknell, S, and Bishop, M, 1992   Excavations at 25-33 Brook Street, Warwick, *Trans Birmingham Warwickshire Archaeol Soc* 97, 1-40

Cummings, V, and Whittle, A, 2003a   *Places of Special Virtue: megaliths in the Neolithic landscapes of Wales*, Oxford

Cummings, V, and Whittle, A, 2003b   Tombs with a view: landscape, monuments and trees, *Antiquity* 77, 255-66

Darvill, T, 1996   Neolithic buildings in England, Wales and the Isle of Man, in Davill, T, and Thomas, J (eds), *Neolithic Houses in Northwest Europe and Beyond*, Oxbow Monogr 57, Oxford, 77-112

Darvill, T, 1997a   Ever increasing circles: the sacred geographies of Stonehenge in its landscape, in *Science and Stonehenge* (eds B Cunliffe and C Renfrew), Proc Brit Acad 92, Oxford, 167-202

Darvill, T, 1997b   Neolithic landscapes: identity and definition, in *Neolithic Landscapes* (ed P Topping), Oxbow Monogr 86, Oxford, 1-13

Darvill, T, 2003   Analytical scale, populations and the Mesolithic-Neolithic transition in the far northwest of Europe, in *Peopling the Mesolithic in a Northern Environment* (eds L Bevan and J Moore), BAR International Series 1157, Oxford, 95-102

Darvill, T, 2004   *Long Barrows of the Cotswolds and Surrounding Areas*, Stroud

Darvill, T, and Russell, B, 2002   *Archaeology After PPG16: archaeological investigations in England 1990–1999*, Univ Bournemouth School Conserv Sci Res Rep 10, Poole

Denison, S, 2002   Dig in West Midlands reveals empty landscape, *British Archaeology* 65, 5

Díaz-Andreu, M, Lucy, S, Babić, S, and Edwards, D N, 2005   *The Archaeology of Identity: approaches to gender, age status, ethnicity and religion*, London

Dinn, J, and Evans, J, 1990   Aston Farm, Kemerton: excavation of a ring ditch, Middle Iron Age enclosures and a *grubenhaus*, *Trans Worcestershire Archaeol Soc* 12, 5-66

Dinn, J, and Hemingway, J, 1992   Archaeology on the Blackstone to Astley aqueduct, *Trans Worcestershire Archaeol Soc* 14, 105-19

Dinn, J, and Roseff, R, 1992   Alluvium and archaeology in the Herefordshire valleys, in *Alluvial Archaeology in Britain* (eds S Needham and M Macklin), Oxbow Monogr 27, Oxford, 141-51

Drewett, P, Rudling, D, and Gardiner, M, 1988   *The South-East to AD 1000*, London

Dyer, C, 2000   Woodlands and wood pasture in western England, in *Rural England, An illustrated history of the landscape* (ed J Thirsk), Oxford, 97-121

Earle, T, 2002   *Bronze Age Economics: the beginnings of political economies*, Oxford

Edmonds, M, 1995   *Stone Tools and Society: working stone in Neolithic and Bronze Age Britain*, London

Edmonds, M, and Seaborne, T, 2001   *Prehistory in the Peak*, Stroud

Ehrenberg, M, 1991   Some aspects of the distribution of burnt mounds, in *Burnt Mounds and Hot Stone Technology* (eds M Hodder and L Barfield), Sandwell, 41-58

English Heritage 1998   *Identifying and protecting Palaeolithic remains: archaeological guidance for planning authorities and developers*, London

English Heritage 2000   *Managing Lithic Scatters: archaeological guidance for planning authorities and developers*, London

Entwistle, R, and Grant, A, 1989   The evidence for cereal cultivation and animal husbandry in the southern British Neolithic and Early Bronze Age, in *The Beginnings of Agriculture* (eds A Milles, D Williams and N Gardner), BAR International Series 496, Oxford, 203-15

Eogan, G, 1994   *The Accomplished Art: gold and gold-working in Britain and Ireland during the Bronze Age*, Oxbow Monogr 42, Oxford

Evans, C, Pollard, J, and Knight, M, 1999   Life in woods: tree-throws, 'settlement' and forest cognition, *Oxford J Archaeol* 18, 241-54

Exon, S, Gaffney, V, Woodward, A and Yorston, R, 2000   *Stonehenge Landscapes: journeys through real-and-imagined worlds*, Oxford

Fairbairn, A, 2000   On the spread of crops across Neolithic Britain, with special reference to southern England, in *Plants in Neolithic Britain and Beyond*, (ed A Fairbairn), Neolithic Stud Grp Sem Papers 4, Oxford, 107-21

Field, D, 1998   Round barrows and the harmonious landscape: placing Early Bronze Age burial monuments in south-east England, *Oxford J Archaeol* 17, 309-26

Field, D, 2004   Sacred geographies in the Neolithic of south-east England, in *Towards a New Stone Age: aspects of the Neolithic in south-east England* (eds J Cotton and D Field), CBA Res Rep 137, London, 153-63

Field, D, 2006   *Earthen Long Barrows: the earliest monuments in the British Isles*, Stroud

Fleming, A, 1971   Territorial patterns in Bronze Age Wessex, *Proc Prehist Soc* 37, 352-81

Fleming, A, 1998   Prehistoric landscapes and the quest for territorial pattern, in *The Archaeology of Landscape: studies presented to Christopher Taylor* (eds P Everson and T Williamson), Manchester, 42-66

Fleming, A, 2004   Hail to the Chiefdom? The quest for social archaeology, in *Explaining Social Change: studies in honour of Colin Renfrew* (eds J Cherry, C Scarre and S Shennan), McDonald Institute Monogr, Cambridge, 141-47

Ford, W J, 2003   The Neolithic complex at Charlecote, Warwickshire, *Trans Birmingham Warwickshire Archaeol Soc* 107, 1-39

French, C, and Pryor, F, 2005   *Archaeology and Environment of the Etton Landscape*, East Anglian Archaeol Rep 109, Peterborough

Gamble, C S, 1996   Hominid behaviour in the Middle Pleistocene: an English perspective, in *The English Palaeolithic Reviewed* (eds C S Gamble and A J Lawson), Salisbury, 63-71

Gamble, C S, 1999   *The Palaeolithic Societies of Europe*, Cambridge

Gamble, C S, and Lawson, A J (ed), 1996   *The English Palaeolithic Reviewed*, Salisbury

Gardiner, P, Haldon, R, and Malam, J, 1980   Prehistoric, Roman and Medieval settlement at Stretton-on–Fosse: excavations and salvage 1971-76, *Trans Birmingham Warwickshire Archaeol Soc* 90, 1-35

Garner, D, 2001   The Bronze Age of Manchester Airport: Runway 2, in *Bronze Age Landscapes: tradition and transformation* (ed J Brück), Oxford, 41-56

Garwood, P, 1991   Ritual tradition and the reconstitution of society, in *Sacred and Profane: archaeology, ritual and religion* (eds P Garwood, D Jennings, R Skeates, R and J, Toms), Oxford Univ Comm Archaeol Monogr 32, Oxford, 10-32

Garwood, P, 1999a   The chronology of depositional contexts and monuments with contributions by A, Barclay, in *Excavations at Barrow Hills, Radley, Oxfordshire, Vol I: The Neolithic and Bronze Age monument complex* (eds A Barclay and C Halpin), Thames Valley Landscapes Monogr 1, Oxford, 275-93

Garwood, P, 1999b   Grooved Ware in southern Britain: chronology and interpretation, in *Grooved Ware* (eds R Cleal and A MacSween), Neolithic Stud Grp Sem Papers 3, Oxford, 145-76

Garwood, P, 2003   Round barrows and funerary traditions in Late Neolithic and Bronze Age Sussex, in *The Archaeology of Sussex to AD 2000* (ed D Rudling), Great Dunham, 47-68

Garwood, P, 2007a   Before the hills in order stood: chronology, time and history in the interpretation of early Bronze Age round barrows, in *Beyond the Grave: new perspectives on round barrows* (ed J Last), Oxford, 30-52

Garwood, P, 2007b   Late Neolithic and Early Bronze Age funerary monuments and burial traditions in the West Midlands, in *The Undiscovered Country: the earlier prehistory of the West Midlands* (ed P Garwood), Oxford, 134-65

Garwood, P, 2007c   Regions, cultural identity and social change, 4500-1500 BC: the West Midlands in context, in *The Undiscovered Country: the earlier prehistory of the West Midlands* (ed P Garwood), Oxford, 194-215

Garwood, P (ed), 2007d   *The Undiscovered Country: the earlier prehistory of the West Midlands*, Oxford

Garwood, P, in prep   *Prehistoric Monuments in Central England: the Wolvey landscape project*

Gerloff, S, 1975   *The Early Bronze Age Daggers of Great Britain and a Reconsideration of the Wessex Culture*, Prahistorische Bronzefunde Abt VI, B2, Munich

Gibbs, A V, 1990   *Sex, Gender and Material Culture Patterning in Later Neolithic and Early Bronze Age England*, Unpub PhD thesis, Univ of Cambridge

Gibson, A (ed), 1989   *Midlands Prehistory: some recent and current researches into the prehistory of central England*, BAR British Series 204, Oxford

Gibson, A, 1994   Excavations at the Sarn-y-bryn-caled cursus complex, Welshpool, Powys, and the timber circles of Great Britain and Ireland, *Proc Prehist Soc* 60, 143-223

Gibson, A, 1996   The later Neolithic structures at Trelystan, Powys, Wales: ten years on, in *Neolithic Houses in Northwest Europe and Beyond* (eds T Darvill and J Thomas), Oxbow Monogr 57, Oxford, 133-41

Gibson, A, 1998   *Stonehenge and Timber Circles*, Stroud

Gibson, A, 1999   *The Walton Basin Project: excavation and survey in a prehistoric landscape 1993-7*, CBA Res Rep 118, York

Gibson, A, 2002a   *Prehistoric Pottery in Britain and Ireland*, Stroud

Gibson, A, 2002b   The later Neolithic palisaded enclosures of the United Kingdom, in *Behind Wooden Walls: Neolithic palisaded enclosures in Europe* (ed A Gibson), BAR International Series 1013, Oxford, 5-23

Gibson, A, 2003   What do we mean by Neolithic settlement? Some approaches, 10 years on, in *Neolithic Settlement in Ireland and Western Britain* (eds I Armit, E Murphy, E Nelis and D Simpson), Oxford, 135-45

Gibson, A, 2006   Excavations at a Neolithic Enclosure at Lower Luggy near Welshpool, Powys, Wales, *Proc Prehist Soc* 71, 163-91

Gibson, A, Becker, H, Grogan, E, Jones, N, and Masterson, B, 2001   Survey at Hindwell enclosure, Walton, Powys, Wales, in *Neolithic Enclosures in Atlantic Northwest Europe* (eds T Darvill and J Thomas), Neolithic Stud Grp Sem Papers 6, Oxford, 101-10

Gibson, A, and Kinnes, I, 1997   On the urns of a dilemma: radiocarbon and the Peterborough problem, *Oxford J Archaeol* 16, 65-72

Green, C, and Rollo-Smith, S 1984   The excavation of eighteen round barrows near Shrewton, Wiltshire, *Proc Prehist Soc* 50, 255-318

Greig, J, 2007   Priorities in Mesolithic, Neolithic and Bronze Age environmental archaeology in the West Midlands, in *The Undiscovered Country: the earlier prehistory of the West Midlands* (ed P Garwood), Oxford, 39-50

Griffin, S, Dalwood, H, Hurst, D, and Pearson, E, 2002   Excavation at Perdiswell park and ride, Droitwich Road, Worcester, *Trans Worcestershire Archaeol Soc* 18, 1-24

Grinsell, L, 1993   Herefordshire barrows, *Trans Woolhope Natur Field Club* 47, 299-317

Grogan, E, 2002   Neolithic houses in Ireland: a broader perspective, *Antiquity* 76, 517-25

Grøn, O, 2001   Mesolithic dwelling places in south Scandinavia: their definition and social interpretation, *Antiquity* 77, 685-708

Gunstone, A, 1964   An archaeological gazeteer of Staffordshire, Part I: Chance finds and sites, excluding barrows and their contents, *North Staffordshire J Field Stud* 4, 11-45

Gunstone, A, 1965   An archaeological gazeteer of Staffordshire, Part II: The barrows, *North Staffordshire J Field Stud* 5, 20-63

Halsted, J, 2005   *Bronze Age Settlement in the Welsh Marches*, BAR British Series 384, Oxford

Halsted, J, 2007   Bronze Age settlement in Shropshire: research potential and frameworks for settlement studies in the West Midlands, in *The Undiscovered Country: the earlier prehistory of the West Midlands* (ed P Garwood), Oxford, 166-81

Hamilton, S, 2002   Between ritual and routine: interpreting British prehistoric pottery production and distribution, in *Prehistoric Britain: the ceramic basis* (eds A, Woodward and J D, Hill), Oxford, 38-53

Hardaker, T, and MacRae, R J, 2000   A lost river and some Palaeolithic surprises: new quartzite finds from Norfolk and Oxfordshire, *Lithics* 21, 52-9

Harding, A, 2000   *European Societies in the Bronze Age*, Cambridge

Harding, J, 1995   Social histories and regional perspectives in the Neolithic of lowland England, *Proc Prehist Soc* 61, 117-36

Harding, J, 2003   *Henge Monuments of the British Isles*, Stroud

Harrison, R J, Jackson, R, and Napthan, M, 1999   A rich bell Beaker burial from Wellington Quarry, Marden, Herefordshire, *Oxford J Archaeol* 18, 1-16

Healy, F, 1995   Pots, pits and peat: ceramics and settlement in East Anglia, in '*Unbaked Urns of Rudely Shape': essays on British and Irish pottery for Ian Longworth* (eds I Kinnes and G Varndell), Oxbow Monogr 55, Oxford, 173-84

Healy, F, 1997   Site 3, Flagstones, in *Excavations Along the Route of the Dorchester By-Pass, Dorset, 1986-8* (R J C Smith, F Healy, M Allen, E Morris, I Barnes, and P Woodward), Wessex Archaeol Rep 11, Salisbury, 27-47

Healy, F, and Harding, J, 2004   Reading a burial: the legacy of Overton Hill, in *From Sickles to Circles: Britain and Ireland at the time of Stonehenge* (eds A Gibson and A Sheridan), Stroud, 176-93

Healy, F, and Harding, J, 2007   *The Raunds Area Project: a Neolithic and Bronze Age landscapes, Northamptonshire*, Swindon

Hey, G, 1997   Neolithic settlement at Yarnton, Oxfordshire, in *Neolithic Landscapes* (ed P, Topping), Oxbow Monogr 86, Oxford, 99-112

Hey, G, 1998   The Yarnton-Cassington project: evaluating a floodplain landscape, *Lithics* 19, 47-60

Hey, G, 2001   Yarnton, *Current Archaeology* 173, 216-25

Hey, G, and Lacey, M, 2001   *Evaluation of Archaeological Decision-making Processes and Sampling Strategies*, Oxford

Hill, J D, 1995   *Ritual and Rubbish in the Iron Age of Wessex*, BAR British Series 242, Oxford

Hingley, R, 1996   Prehistoric Warwickshire: a review of the evidence, *Trans Birmingham Warwickshire Archaeol Soc* 100, 1-24

Hobley, B, 1971   Neolithic storage hollows and an undated ring ditch at Baginton, Warwickshire, *Trans Birmingham Warwickshire Archaeol Soc* 84, 1-6

Hodder, M, 1990   Burnt mounds in the English West Midlands, in *Burnt Offerings: international contributions to burnt mound archaeology* (ed V Buckley), Dublin, 106-11

Hodder, M, 1991   Excavations at Sandwell Priory and Hall, 1982-88: a mesolithic settlement, medieval monastery and post-medieval country house in West Bromwich, *Trans South Staffordshire Archaeol Hist Soc* 31

Hodder, M, 2004   *Birmingham: the hidden history*, Stroud

Holgate, R, 1988   *Neolithic Settlement of the Thames Basin*, BAR British Series 194, Oxford

Housley, R A, Gamble, C S, Street, M J, and Pettitt, P, 1997   Radiocarbon evidence for the Lateglacial recolonisation of northern Europe, *Proc Prehist Soc* 63, 25-54

Hughes, G, and Crawford, G, 1995   Excavations at Wasperton, Warwickshire: Part 1, *Trans Birmingham Warwickshire Archaeol Soc* 99, 9-47

Hughes, G, Leach, P, and Stanford, S, 1995   Excavations at Bromfield, Shropshire 1981-1991, *Trans Shropshire Archaeol Hist Soc* 99, 9-45

Hughes, G, and Woodward, A, 1995   A ring ditch and Neolithic pit complex at Meole Brace, Shrewsbury, *Trans Shropshire Archaeol Hist Soc* 70, 1-21

Hunt, A, 1982   Archaeology in the Avon and Severn valleys – a review, *West Midlands Archaeology* 25, 1-24

Hunt, A, Shotliff, A, and Woodhouse, J, 1986   A Bronze Age barrow cemetery and Iron Age enclosure at Holt, *Trans Worcestershire Archaeol Soc* 3, 7-36

Jackson, R, 2007   Pits, pots, places and people: approaching the Neolithic at Wellington Quarry, in *The Undiscovered Country: the earlier prehistory of the West Midlands* (ed P Garwood), Oxford, 109-22

Jackson, R, Bevan, L, Hurst, D, and de Rouffignac, C, 1996   Archaeology on the Trimpley to Blackstone Aqueduct, *Trans Worcestershire Archaeol Soc* 15, 93-126

Jacobi, R, 1976   Britain inside and outside Mesolithic Europe, *Proc Prehist Soc* 42, 67-84

Johnston, R, 2001   'Breaking new ground': land tenure and fieldstone clearance during the Bronze Age, in *Bronze Age Landscapes: tradition and transformation* (ed J Brück), Oxford, 98-109

Jones, G, 2000   Evaluating the importance of cultivation and collecting in Neolithic Britain, in *Plants in Neolithic Britain and Beyond* (ed A Fairbairn), Neolithic Stud Grp Sem Papers 4, Oxford, 79-84

Jones, A, 2004   Matter and memory: colour, remembrance and the Neolithic/Bronze Age transition, in *Rethinking Materiality* (eds E DeMarrais, C Gosden and C Renfrew), Macdonald Institute Monogr, Cambridge, 167-78

King, M P, 2003   *Unparalleled Behaviour: Britain and Ireland during the 'Mesolithic' and 'Neolithic'*, BAR British Series 355, Oxford

Kinnes, I, 1979   *Round Barrows and Ring-ditches in the British Neolithic*, Brit Mus Occ Paper 7, London

Kinnes, I, 1988   The Cattleship Potemkin: reflections on the First Neolithic in Britain, in *The Archaeology of Context in the Neolithic and Bronze Age: recent trends* (eds J Barrett and I Kinnes), Sheffield, 2-8

Kinnes, I, 1992  *Non-megalithic Long Barrows and Allied Structures in the British Neolithic,* Brit Mus Occ Paper 52, London

Kinnes, I, 1994  The Neolithic, in *Building on the Past* (ed B Vyner), Royal Archaeological Institute, London, 90-102

Kinnes, I, and Varndell, G (eds), 1995  *'Unbaked Urns of Rudely Shape': essays on British and Irish pottery for Ian Longworth,* Oxbow Monogr 55, Oxford

Kinnes, I, Gibson, A, Ambers, J, Bowman, S, Leese, M, and Boast, R, 1991  Radiocarbon dating and British Beakers: the British Museum programme, *Scottish Archaeol Rev* 8, 35-68

Kitchen, W, 2001  Tenure and territoriality in the British Bronze Age: a question of varying social and geographic scales? in *Bronze Age Landscapes: tradition and transformation* (ed J Brück), Oxford, 110-20

Knight, D, and Howard, A, 2004  From Neolithic to Early Bronze Age: the first agricultural landscapes, in *Trent Valley Landscapes* (eds D Knight and A Howard), Great Dunham, 47-77

Kristiansen, K, and Larsson, T B, 2005  *The Rise of Bronze Age Society: travels, transmissions and transformation*s, Cambridge

Lambrick, G, 1988  *The Rollright Stones: megaliths, monuments and settlement in the prehistoric landscape,* English Heritage Arch Rep 6, London

Lang, A T O, and Keen, D H, 2005  Hominid colonization and the Lower and Middle Palaeolithic of the West Midlands, *Proc Prehist Soc* 71, 63-83

Lang, A T O, and Buteux, S T E, 2007  Lost but not forgotten: the Lower and Middle Palaeolithic occupation of the West Midlands, in *The Undiscovered Country: the earlier prehistory of the West Midlands* (ed P Garwood), Oxford, 6-22

Larsen, L, Kindgren, H, Knutsson, K, Loeffler, D, and Åkelund, A (eds), 2003  *Mesolithic on the Move,* Oxford

Last, J, 1998  Books of life: biography and memory in a Bronze Age barrow, *Oxford J Archaeol* 17, 43-53

Last, J (ed), 2007  *Beyond the Grave: new perspectives on round barrows,* Oxford

Leah, M, Wells, C, Stamper, P, Huckerby, E, and Welch, C 1998  *The Wetlands of Shropshire and Staffordshire,* North Wetlands Survey 5, Lancaster

Legge, A J, 1989  Milking the evidence: a reply to Entwistle and Grant, in *The Beginnings of Agriculture* (eds A Milles, D Williams and N Gardner), BAR International Series 496, Oxford, 217-42

Lithic Studies Society 2004  *Research Frameworks for Holocene Lithics in Britain,* Lithic Studies Society

Lock, G, and Spicer, D, 1986  Tixall, King's Low, *West Midlands Archaeology* 29, 42-5

Lock, G, and Spicer, D, 1987  Tixall, King's Low, *West Midlands Archaeology* 30, 38-9

Longworth, I, 1984  *Collared Urns of the Bronze Age in Great Britain and Ireland,* Cambridge

Losco-Bradley, S, 1984  Fatholme, Barton under-Needwood, Staffordshire, *Proc Prehist Soc* 50, 402

Loveday, R, 1989  The Barford ritual complex: further excavations 1972 and a regional perspective, in *Midlands Prehistory* (ed A Gibson), BAR British Series 204, Oxford, 51-84

Loveday, R, 1999   Dorchester-on-Thames – ritual complex or ritual landscape, in *Pathways and Ceremonies: the cursus monuments of Britain and Ireland* (eds A Barclay and J Harding), Neolithic Stud Grp Sem Papers 4, Oxford, 49-63

Loveday, R, 2003   Appendix: Charlecote 71: An evaluation in the light of recent research, in The Neolithic complex at Charlecote, Warwickshire (W J Ford), *Trans Birmingham Warwickshire Archaeol Soc* 107, 1-39 (30-9)

Loveday, R, 2004   Contextualising monuments: the exceptional potential of the Middle Trent Valley, *Derbyshire Archaeol J* 124, 1-12

Loveday, R, 2006   *Inscribed Across the Landscape: the cursus enigma*, Stroud

Loveday, R, and Petchey, M, 1982   Oblong ditches: a discussion and some new evidence, *Aerial Archaeology* 8, 17-24

Lynch, F 1993   *Excavations in the Brenig Valley: a Mesolithic and Bronze Age landscape in north Wales*, Cambrian Archaeology Monogr 5, Bangor

McAvoy, F, 2000   The development of a Neolithic monument complex at Godmanchester, Cambridgeshire, in *Prehistoric, Roman, and Post-Roman Landscapes of the Great Ouse Valley* (ed M Dawson), CBA Res Rep 119, London, 51-6

McCullagh, R, and Tipping, R (eds), 1998   *The Lairg Project 1988-1996: the evolution of an archaeological landscape in northern Scotland*, Scot Trust Archaeol Res Monogr 3, Edinburgh

McFadyen, L, 2006   Landscape, in *Mesolithic Britain and Ireland: new approaches* (eds C Conneller and C Warren), Stroud, 121-38

McNabb, J, 2006   The Palaeolithic, in *The Archaeology of the East Midlands: an archaeological resource assessment and research agenda* (ed N J Cooper), Leicester Archaeol Monogr 11, Leicester, 11-49

Maddy, D, 1999   The English Midlands, in *A Revised Correlation of Quaternary Deposits in the British Isles* (ed D Q Bowen), Geol Soc London Spec Rep 23, Bath, 28-44

Malim, T, 2000   The ritual landscape of the Neolithic and Bronze Age along the middle and lower Ouse valley, in *Prehistoric, Roman, and Post-Roman Landscapes of the Great Ouse Valley* (ed M Dawson), CBA Res Rep 119, London, 57-88

Marshall, G, 1932   Report on the discovery of two Bronze Age cists in the Olchon valley, Herefordshire, *Trans Woolhope Natur Field Club* 1930-32, 147-53

Martin, A, and Allen, C, 2001   Two prehistoric ring ditches and associated Bronze Age cremation cemetery at Tuckleshome Farm, Barton-under-Needwood, Staffordshire, *Trans Staffordshire Archaeol Hist Soc* 39, 1-15

Milner, N, 2006   Subsistence, in *Mesolithic Britain and Ireland: new approaches* (eds C Conneller and C Warren), Stroud, 61-82

Mithen, S, 1996   Domain-specific intelligence and the Neanderthal mind, in *Modelling the Early Human Mind* (eds P Mellars and K Gibson), McDonald Institute Monogr, Cambridge, 217-29

Mithen, S, 1999   Hunter-gatherers of the Mesolithic, in *The Archaeology of Britain: an introduction from the Upper Palaeolithic to the Industrial Revolution* (eds J Hunter and I Ralston), London, 35-57

Mizoguchi, K, 1993   Time in the reproduction of mortuary practices, *World Archaeol* 25, 223-35

Moffett, L, 1999   The Arrow valley landscape; the environmental evidence through time, in, Archaeological excavations in the Arrow Valley, Warwickshire (S C Palmer), *Trans Birmingham Warwickshire Archaeol Soc* 103, 1-231 (211-16)

Moffett, L, Robinson, M A, and Straker, V, 1989   Cereals, fruits and nuts: charred plant remains from Neolithic sites in England and Wales and the Neolithic economy, in *The Beginnings of Agriculture* (eds A Milles, D Williams and N Gardner), BAR International Series 496, Oxford, 243-61

Moore, J, 2003   Enculturation through fire: beyond hazelnuts and into the forest, in *Mesolithic on the Move* (eds L Larsen, H Kindgren, K Knutsson, D Loeffler and A Åkelund), Oxford, 139-44

Mullin, D, 2003   *The Bronze Age Landscape of the Northern British Midlands*, BAR British Series 351, Oxford

Murphy, P, 2001   *Review of Wood and Macroscopic Wood Charcoal from Archaeological Sites in the West & East Midlands Regions and the East of England*, English Heritage Centre Archaeol Rep 23/2001, London

Myers, A M, 2006   The Mesolithic, in *Archaeology of the East Midlands: an archaeological resource assessment and research agenda* (ed N Cooper), Leicester Archaeol Monogr 12, Leicester, 51-68

Myers, A M, 2007   The Upper Palaeolithic and Mesolithic archaeology of the West Midlands region, in *The Undiscovered Country: the earlier prehistory of the West Midlands* (ed P Garwood), Oxford, 23-38

Nash, G, 2002   A Neolithic monument in interpretative transition: a re-evaluation of Arthur's Stone, Dorstone, Herefordshire, *Trans Woolhope Natur Field Club* 50(3), 37-50

Needham, S, 1988   Selective deposition in the British Early Bronze Age, *World Archaeol* 20, 229-48

Needham, S, 1996   Chronology and periodisation in the British Bronze Age, in Randsborg, K (ed), Absolute Chronology: Archaeological Europe 2500-500 BC, *Acta Archaeologica* (Copenhagen) 67, 121-40

Needham, S, 2000   Power pulses across a cultural divide: cosmologically driven acquisition between Armorica and Wessex, *Proc Prehist Soc* 66, 151-207

Needham, S, 2005   Transforming Beaker culture in north-west Europe: processes of fusion and fission, *Proc Prehist Soc* 71, 159-70

Needham, S, Bronk Ramsay, C, Coombs, D, Cartwright, C, and Pettitt, P, 1997   An independent chronology for British Bronze Age metalwork: the results of the Oxford Radiocarbon Accelerator programme, *Archaeol J* 154, 55-107

Oswald, A, 1969   Excavations for the Avon/Severn Research Committee at Barford, Warwickshire, *Trans Birmingham Archaeol Soc* 83, 1-64

Oswald, A, Dyer, C, and Barber, M, 2001   *The Creation of Monuments, Neolithic causewayed enclosures in the British Isles*, Swindon

Owoc, M A, 2000   The times, they are a changin': experiencing continuity and development in the early Bronze Age rituals of southwestern Britain, in *Bronze Age Landscapes: tradition and transformation* (ed J Brück), Oxford, 193-206

Owoc, M A, 2001   Bronze Age cosmologies: the construction of time and space in south-western funerary/ritual monuments, in *Holy Ground: theoretical issues relating to the landscape and material culture of ritual space objects* (eds A T Smith and A Brookes), BAR International Series 956, Oxford, 27-38

Palmer, S C, 1999   Archaeological excavations in the Arrow valley, Warwickshire, *Trans Birmingham Warwickshire Archaeol Soc* 103

Palmer, S C, 2003   King's Newnham, Warwickshire: Neolithic, Bronze Age and Iron Age excavations along a gas pipeline in 1990, *Trans Birmingham Warwickshire Archaeol Soc* 107, 41-74

Palmer, S C, 2007  Recent work on the Neolithic and Bronze Age in Warwickshire, in *The Undiscovered Country: the earlier prehistory of the West Midlands* (ed P, Garwood), Oxford, 123-33

Panter-Brick, C, Layton, R H, and Rowley-Conwy, P (eds), 2001  *Hunter-gatherers: an interdisciplinary perspective*, Cambridge

Pare, C F E, 2000  Bronze and the Bronze Age, in *Metals Make the World Go Round: the supply and circulation of metals in Bronze Age Europe* (ed C F E Pare), Oxford, 1-38

Parfitt, S A, Barendregt, R W, Breda, M, Candy, I, Collins, M J, Coope, G R, Durbridge, P, Field, M H, Lee, J R, Lister, A M, Mutch, R, Penkman, K E H, Prece, R C, Rose, J, Stringer, C B, Symmons, R, Whittaker, J E, Wymer, J J, and Stuart, A J, 2005  The earliest record of human activity in northern Europe, *Nature* 438, 1008-12

Parker Pearson, M, 1999  The earlier Bronze Age, in *The Archaeology of Britain: an introduction from the Upper Palaeolithic to the Industrial Revolution* (eds J, Hunter and I, Ralston), London, 77-94

Parker Pearson, M, and Ramilisonina, 1998  Stonehenge for the ancestors: the stones pass on the message, *Antiquity* 72, 308-26

Piggott, S, 1954  *Neolithic Cultures of the British Isles*, Cambridge

Pitts, M, 1996  The stone axe in Neolithic Britain, *Proc Prehist Soc* 62, 311-71

Planas, M, and Wilson, M, 2006  Redefining the earthwork enclosure at Pile Coppice, Binley, Warwickshire, *West Midlands Archaeology* 48, 15-19

Pluciennik, M, 2005  *Social Evolution*, London

Pollard, J, 1995  inscribing space: formal deposition at the later Neolithic monument of Woodhenge, Wiltshire, *Proc Prehist Soc* 61, 137-56

Pollard, J, 1998  Prehistoric settlement and non-settlement in two southern Cambridgeshire river valleys: the lithic dimension and interpretative dilemmas, *Lithics* 19, 61-71

Pollard, J, 1999  'These places have their moments': thoughts on occupation practices in the British Neolithic, in *Making Places in the Prehistoric World: themes in settlement archaeology* (eds J Brück and M Goodman), London, 76-93

Pollard, J, 2000  Neolithic occupation practices and social ecologies from Rinyo to Clacton, in *Orkney in its European Context* (ed A Ritchie), McDonald Institute Monogr, Cambridge, 363-9

Pollard, J, 2002  The nature of archaeological deposits and finds assemblages, in *Prehistoric Britain: the ceramic basis* (eds A Woodward and J D Hill), Oxford, 22-37

Pollard, J, 2004  'A movement of becoming': realms of existence in the Early Neolithic of southern Britain, in *Stories From the Landscape: archaeologies of inhabitation* (ed A, Chadwick), BAR International Series 1238, Oxford, 55-69

Pollard, J, 2005  Memory, monuments or middens in the Avebury landscape, in *The Avebury Landscape: aspects of the field archaeology of the Marlborough Downs* (eds G Brown, D Field and D McOmish), Oxford, 103-14

Powell, A B, Booth, P, Fitzpatrick, A P, and Crockett, A D 2008 *The Archaeology of the M6 Toll, 2000-2003*, Salisbury

Prehistoric Society 1984  *Prehistory, Priorities and Society: the way forward*, Leeds

Prehistoric Society 1988  *Saving our Prehistoric Heritage: landscapes under threat*, Leeds

Prehistoric Society 1999   *Research Frameworks for the Palaeolithic and Mesolithic of Britain and Ireland*, Salisbury

Pryor, F, 1998   *Farmers in Prehistoric Britain*, Stroud

Rackham, O, 1980   *Ancient Woodland*, London

Ray, K, 2001   Early enclosures in southeast Cornwall, in *Neolithic Enclosures in Atlantic Northwest Europe* (eds T Darvill and J Thomas), Neolithic Stud Grp Sem Papers 6, Oxford, 50-65

Ray, K, 2007   The Neolithic in the West Midlands: an overview, in *The Undiscovered Country: the earlier prehistory of the West Midlands* (ed P Garwood), Oxford, 51-78

Renfrew, C, 1973   Monuments, mobilisation and social organisation in Neolithic Wessex, in *The Explanation of Culture Change* (ed C Renfrew), London, 539-58

Reynier, M J, 1998   Early Mesolithic settlement in England and Wales: some preliminary observations, in *Stone Age Archaeology: essays in honour of John Wymer* (eds N, Ashton, F Healy and P Pettitt), Oxbow Monogr 102, Oxford, 174-84

Richards, C, 1996   Monuments as landscape: creating the centre of the world in late Neolithic Orkney, *World Archaeol* 28, 190-208

Richards, C, 1998   Centralising tendencies? A re-examination of social evolution in Late Neolithic Orkney, in *Understanding the Neolithic of North-west Europe* (eds M Edmonds and C Richards), Glasgow, 516-32

Richards, C, and Thomas, J, 1984   Ritual activity and structured deposition in Neolithic Wessex, in *Neolithic Studies: a review of some recent research* (eds R Bradley and J Gardiner), BAR British Series 133, Oxford, 189-218

Richards, M P, and Hedges, R, 1999   A Neolithic revolution? New evidence of diet in the British Neolithic, *Antiquity* 73, 891-97

Richards, M P, and Schulting, R J, 2003   Characterising subsistence in Mesolithic Britain using stable isotope analysis, in *Peopling the Mesolithic in a Northern Environment* (eds L, Bevan and J, Moore), BAR International Series 1157, Oxford, 119-28

Richmond, A, 1999   *Preferred Economies: the nature of the subsistence base throughout mainland Britain during prehistory*, BAR British Series 290, Oxford

Ripoll, S, Muñoz, F, Bahn, P, and Pettitt, P, 2004   Paleolithic cave engravings at Creswell Crags, England, *Proc Prehist Soc* 70, 93-106

Roberts, M B, and Parfitt, S A, 1999   *Boxgrove: a Middle Pleistocene hominid site at Eartham Quarry, Boxgrove, West Sussex*, English Heritage Res Rep 17, London

Robinson, M, 2000   Further considerations of Neolithic charred cereals, fruit and nuts, in *Plants in Neolithic Britain and Beyond* (ed A Fairbairn), Neolithic Stud Grp Sem Papers 4, Oxford, 85-90

Robinson, M, 2003   *English Heritage Reviews of Environmental Archaeology: Midlands regions and insects*, English Heritage Centre Archaeol Rep 9/2003, London

Roe, F S S, 1978   Typology of stone implements with shaftholes, in *Stone Axe Studies* (eds T H McK Clough and W A Cummins), CBA Res Rep 23, London, 23-48

Rose, J, 1989   Tracing the Baginton-Lillington Sands and Gravels from the West Midlands to East Anglia, in *The Pleistocene of the West Midlands: Field Guide* (ed D H Keen), Quaternary Res Assoc, Cambridge, 102-10

Rose, J, 1994   Major river systems of central and southern Britain, *Terra Nova* 6, 435-43

Rowlands, M, 1989   *The West Midlands from AD 1000*, London

Rowley-Conwy, P, 2003  No fixed abode? Nomadism in the northwest European Neolithic, in *Stones and Bones: formal disposal of the dead in Atlantic Europe during the Mesolithic-Neolithic interface 6000-3000 BC* (ed G Burenhult), BAR International Series 1201, Oxford, 115-43

Saville, A, 1972-3  A reconsideration of the prehistoric flint assemblage from Bourne Pool, Aldridge, Staffs, *Trans South Staffordshire Archaeol Hist Soc* 14, 6-28

Saville, A, 1981  Mesolithic industries in central England: an exploratory investigation using microlith typology, *Archaeol J* 138, 49-71

Saville, A, 1988  The Waite Collection of Palaeolithic quartzites from the Nuneaton area of Warwickshire, in *Non-Flint Stone Tools and the Palaeolithic Occupation of Britain* (eds R J MacRae and N Moloney), BAR British Series 189, Oxford, 67-88

Saville, A, 2003  indications of regionalization in Mesolithic Scotland, in *Mesolithic on the Move* (eds L Larsen, H Kindgren, K Knutsson, D Loeffler and A Åkelund), Oxford, 340-50

Scarre, C, 2001  Modeling prehistoric populations: the case of Neolithic Brittany, *J Anthrop Archaeol* 20, 285-313

Schulting, R, 2000  New AMS dates from the Lambourn long barrow and the question of the earliest Neolithic in southern Britain: repacking the Neolithic package? *Oxford J Archaeol* 19, 25-35

Seaby W A, 1949  Archaeology of the Birmingham plateau and its margins, *Archaeol News Letter* 26, 85-90

Shennan, S, 1982  Ideology, change and the European Early Bronze Age, in *Symbolic and Structural Archaeology* (ed I Hodder), Cambridge, 155-61

Sheridan, A, and Shortland, A, 2004  '...beads which have given rise to so much dogmatism, controversy and rash speculation': faience in Early Bronze Age Britain and Ireland, in *Scotland in Ancient Europe* (eds I A G Shepherd and G J Barclay), Soc Antiq Scotland, Edinburgh, 263-79

Sherratt, A, 1981  Plough and pastoralism: aspects of the secondary products revolution, in *Pattern of the Past* (eds I Hodder, G Isaac and N Hammond), Cambridge, 261-305

Sherratt, A, 1993  What would a Bronze Age world system look like? Relations between temperate Europe and the Mediterranean in later prehistory, *J European Archaeol* 1, 1-59

Sherratt, A, 1994  Core, periphery and margin: perspectives on the Bronze Age, in *Development and Decline in the Mediterranean Bronze Age* (eds C Mathers and S Stoddart), Sheffield Archaeol Monogr 8, Sheffield, 335-45

Shotton, F W, 1959  New petrological groups based on axes from the West Midlands, *Proc Prehist Soc* 25, 135-53

Shotton, F W, 1978  Archaeological inferences from the study of alluvium in the lower Severn-Avon valleys, in *The Effect of Man on the Landscape: the lowland zone* (eds S Limbrey and J G Evans), CBA Res Rep 21, London, 27-32

Shotton, F W, 1988  The petrological identification of stone implements from the west Midlands: third report, in *Stone Axe Studies, Volume 2: the petrology of prehistoric stone implements from the British Isles* (eds T H McK Clough and W A Cummins), CBA Res Rep 67, London, 49-51

Shotton, F W, and Wymer, J J, 1989  Handaxes of Andesitic Tuff from beneath the standard Wolston Succession in Warwickshire, *Lithics* 10, 1-7

Shotton, F W, Keen, D H, Coope, G R, Currant, A P, Gibbard, P C, Aalto, M, Peglar, S M, and Robinson, J K, 1993  Pleistocene deposits at Waverley Wood Farm Pit, Warwickshire, England, *J Quaternary Science* 8, 293-325

Simpson, D, 1969  Kings Newnham, Site No 104, *Avon-Severn Valley Res Proj Rep* 5, 15-18

Smith, C N, 1957  A catalogue of the prehistoric finds from Worcestershire, *Trans Worcestershire Archaeol Soc* 34, 1-27

Smith, C, 1992  *Late Stone Age Hunters of the British Isles*, London

Smith, C, and Openshaw, S, 1990  Mapping the Mesolithic, in *Contributions to the Mesolithic in Europe* (eds P Vermeersch and P van Peer), Leuven, 17-22

Smith, R, 1984  The ecology of Neolithic farming systems as exemplified by the Avebury region of Wiltshire, *Proc Prehist Soc* 50, 99-120

Sørenson, M L S, 2004  Stating identities: the use of objects in rich Bronze Age graves, in *Explaining Social Change: studies in honour of Colin Renfrew* (eds J Cherry, C Scarre and S Shennan), Macdonald Institute Monogr, Cambridge, 167-76

Spikens, P, 2000  Ethno-facts or ethno-fiction? Searching for the structure of settlement patterns, in *Mesolithic Lifeways: current research from Britain and Ireland* (ed R Young), Leicester Archaeol Monogr 7, Leicester, 105-18

Stanford, S C, 1980  *The Archaeology of the Welsh Marches*, London

Stanford, S C, 1982  Bromfield, Shropshire – Neolithic, Beaker and Bronze Age sites, 1966-79, *Proc Prehist Soc* 48, 279-320

Stringer, C, and Gamble, C, 1993  *In Search of the Neanderthals*, London

Thomas, J, 1984  A tale of two polities, in *Neolithic Studies: a review of some recent research* (eds R Bradley and J Gardiner), BAR British Series 133, Oxford, 161-76

Thomas, J, 1991  Reading the body: Beaker funerary practice in Britain, in *Sacred and Profane: archaeology, ritual and religion* (eds P Garwood, D Jennings, R Skeates and J Toms), Oxford Univ Comm Archaeol Monogr 32, Oxford, 33-42

Thomas, J, 1993  Discourse, totalization and the 'Neolithic', in *Interpretative Archaeology* (ed C Tilley), Oxford, 357-94

Thomas, J, 1996  Neolithic houses in mainland Britain and Ireland - a sceptical view, in *Neolithic Houses in Northwest Europe and Beyond* (eds T Darvill and J Thomas), Oxbow Monogr 57, Oxford, 1-12

Thomas, J, 1998  Towards a regional geography of the Neolithic, in *Understanding the Neolithic of North-west Europe* (eds M Edmonds and C Richards), Glasgow, 37-60

Thomas, J, 1999  *Understanding the Neolithic*, London

Thomas, J, 2003  Thoughts on the 'repacked' Neolithic revolution, *Antiquity* 77, 67-74

Thomas, N, 1965  A double Beaker burial on Bredon Hill, Worcestershire, *Trans Birmingham Archaeol Soc* 82, 58-76

Thorpe, I J, and Richards, C, 1984  The decline of ritual authority and the introduction of Beakers into Britain, in *Neolithic Studies: a review of some recent research* (eds R Bradley and J Gardiner), BAR British Series 133, Oxford, 67-84

Tilley, C, 1994  *A Phenomenology of Landscape*, Oxford

Tilley, C, 1998  *Material Culture and Metaphor*, Oxford, 177-238

Tipping, R, and Tisdall, E, 2004  Continuity, crisis and climate change in the Neolithic and Early Bronze Age periods of north-west Europe, in *Scotland in Ancient Europe* (eds I A G Shepherd and G J Barclay), Soc of Antiq Scotland, Edinburgh, 71-81

Tolan-Smith, C, 2003a   Colonisation – event or process, in *Mesolithic on the Move* (eds L Larsen, H Kindgren, K Knutsson, D Loeffler and A Åkelund), Oxford, 52-6

Tolan-Smith, C, 2003b   Social interaction and settlement patterns in hunter-gatherer societies – applications of the 'amity-enmity' model, in *Peopling the Mesolithic in a Northern Environment* (eds L Bevan and J Moore), BAR International Series 1157, Oxford, 113-18

Tomalin, D, 1988   Armorican *vases á anses* and their occurrence in southern Britain, *Proc Prehist Soc* 54, 203-21

Vine, P, 1982   *The Neolithic and Bronze Age Cultures of the Middle and Upper Trent Basin*, BAR British Series 105, Oxford

Warren, G, 2006   Technology, in *Mesolithic Britain and Ireland: new approaches* (eds C Conneller and C Warren), Stroud, 13-34

Watson, M, 1991   Ring ditches of the Upper Severn valley, *Trans Shropshire Archaeol Hist Soc* 67, 9-14

Webster, G, and Hobley, B, 1964   Aerial reconnaissance over the Warwickshire Avon, *Archaeol J* 121, 1-22

Wessex Archaeology 1996   *The English Paleolithic Rivers Project – Regions 7 (Thames) and 10 (Warwickshire Avon): Report No 5, 1994-1995*, Salisbury

White, P, 2003   *The Arrow Valley, Herefordshire: Archaeology, Landscape Change and Conservation*, Herefordshire Stud Archaeol 2, Leominster

Whitelaw, T, 1994   Order without architecture: functional, social and symbolic dimensions of hunter-gatherer settlement organization, in *Architecture and Order: approaches to social space* (eds M Parker Pearson and C Richards), London, 217-43

Whittle, A, 1996   *Europe in the Neolithic: the creation of new worlds*, Cambridge

Whittle, A, 1997a   Moving on and moving around: Neolithic settlement mobility, in *Neolithic Landscapes* (ed P Topping), Oxbow Monogr 86, Oxford, 15-22

Whittle, A, 1997b   *Sacred Mound, Holy Rings: Silbury Hill and the West Kennet palisade enclosures: a later Neolithic complex in Wiltshire*, Oxford

Whittle, A, 2000   Bringing plants into the taskscape, in *Plants in Neolithic Britain and Beyond* (ed A Fairbairn), Neolithic Stud Grp Sem Papers 4, Oxford, 1-7

Whittle, A, 2007 The temporality of transformation: dating the early development of the southern British Neolithic in *Going Over: the Mesolithic–Neolithic transition in north–west Europe* (eds A Whittle and V Cummings), Proceedings of the British Academy 144, Oxford, 377-98

Whittle, A, Atkinson, R J C, Chambers, R, and Thomas, N, 1992   Excavations in the Neolithic and Bronze Age complex at Dorchester-on-Thames, Oxfordshire, 1947-52 and 1981, *Proc Prehist Soc* 58, 143-201

Whittle, A, and Pollard, J, 1999   The harmony of symbols: wider meanings, in *The Harmony of Symbols: the Windmill Hill causewayed enclosure* (A Whittle, J Pollard and C Grigson), Oxford, 381-90

Wilson, D, and Cleverdon, F, 1987   Excavation of two round barrows at Low Farm and Low Bent, Fawfieldhead, Longnor, Staffordshire, *Trans South Staffordshire Archaeol Hist Soc* 27, 1-26

Wise, P, 1990   The Warwickshire stone axe survey: recent work, *West Midlands Archaeology* 33, 30-3

Woodward, A, 2000   *British Barrows: a matter of life and death*, Stroud

Woodward, A, 2002a   Beads and beakers: heirlooms and relics in the British early Bronze Age, *Antiquity* 76, 1040-47

Woodward, A, 2002b   Inclusions, impressions and interpretations, in *Prehistoric Britain: the ceramic basis* (eds A Woodward and J D Hill), Oxford, 106-18

Woodward, A, 2002c   Sherds in space: pottery and the analysis of site organisation, in *Prehistoric Britain: the ceramic basis* (eds A Woodward and J D Hill), Oxford, 62-74

Woodward, A, 2007   Ceremonial landscapes and ritual deposits in the Neolithic and Early Bronze Age periods in the West Midlands, in *The Undiscovered Country: the earlier prehistory of the West Midlands* (ed P Garwood), Oxford, 182-93

Woodward, A, Hunter, J, Ixer, R, Maltby, M, Potts, P J, Webb, P C, Watson, J S, and Jones, M C, 2005   Ritual in some Early Bronze Age gravegoods, *Archaeol J* 162, 31-64

Woodward, A, and Woodward, P, 1996   The topography of some barrow cemeteries in Bronze Age Wessex, *Proc Prehist Soc* 62, 275-91

Wymer, J J, 1977   *Gazetteer of Mesolithic Sites in England and Wales, with a Gazetteer of Upper Palaeolithic Sites in England and Wales*, CBA Res Rep 20, London

Wymer, J J, 1999   *The Lower Palaeolithic Occupation of Britain*, Salisbury

Wymer, J J, 2001   Palaeoliths in a lost pre-Anglian landscape, in *A Very Remote Period Indeed: papers on the Palaeolithic presented to Derek Roe* (eds S Milliken and J Cook), Oxford, 174-9

Young, R (ed), 2000   *Mesolithic Lifeways: current research from Britain and Ireland*, Leicester Archaeol Monogr 7, Leicester

Zvelebil, M, 2003   Enculturation of Mesolithic landscapes, in *Mesolithic on the Move* (eds L Larsen, H Kindgren, K Knutsson, D Loeffler and A Åkelund), Oxford, 65-73

# 3. Middle Bronze Age to Iron Age: a research assessment overview and agenda

## Derek Hurst

With a contribution by Elizabeth Pearson

DHurst@worcestershire.gov.uk

## 3.1. Introduction

The west midlands does not constitute a readily identifiable region, since topographically it is very varied, including, as defined in the present survey, parts of two major river valleys, the Severn and the Trent. It is also characterised by a variable geology ranging from pre-Cambrian to Pleistocene, though the largest area is covered by Triassic Mercian Mudstone deposits. The terrain ranges from the peaks of Staffordshire in the north to the fertile vales of the Severn in the south, and the uplands of Herefordshire to the west. This encompasses a region which historically included frontier zones, such as the Welsh Marches, and in other periods included parts of distinct different political regions, such as during the Danelaw when this boundary stretched across Staffordshire separating north and south. The region also boasts an unusual resource, salt, as well as other minerals, and was not short of basic energy resources such as wood and coal. Such a diverse region offers greater challenges in characterisation as it is likely to contain considerable variation in cultural traits and life styles, reflecting the variable economic and environmental backgrounds of different parts of the region.

The general absence of large-scale research programmes that encompass large parts of this area has also tended to deprive it of any substance as a viable research area, in contrast with other more homogeneous parts of the country such as East Anglia and the Thames valley. Consequently, one of the main objectives of the research framework process, in addition to setting targets for research, should be to develop the concept of the west midlands more formally as a research context.

The papers forming the basis for this research assessment and agenda were delivered at the research audit presentation and seminar session of 2002-3, and are available on the Web (http://www.iaa.bham.ac.uk/research/projects/wmrrfa/index.shtml) with publication to follow in due course (Hurst in prep a). This assessment overview aims to address many of the same themes as were explored in *Understanding the British Iron Age: an agenda for action* (Haselgrove et al 2001).

## 3.2. Current knowledge

### 3.2.1. Chronology

Though the periods of Bronze Age and Iron Age are broadly distinguishable, there is less clear definition of development within these periods, and the transition from one period to another is also less well defined in the west midlands than some other areas. The problem with the latter is exacerbated by the difficulties with the calibration curve for *c* 800-400 BC, though multiple dates and the use of Bayesian statistics can overcome this to some degree (Haselgrove et al 2001, 5). There is a need consequently for more effort on this dating front rather than less as a result of this problem. The knock-on effect of relatively few radiocarbon dates has been that well-dated ceramic sequences covering this whole period are generally patchy, and so, in Worcestershire for instance, the Bronze Age component is only just coming into focus. This shortage of scientific dates, and the additional shortage of associated contemporary material culture (eg burnt mounds; Barfield and Hodder 1989), such as exists for other periods particularly from burial groups, has also served to weaken the characterisation of the late prehistoric period in the west midlands.

Finds are often few and far between, and in the case of the Bronze Age have most often been found as a result of casual or metal-detecting discoveries, and even where more Bronze Age finds are known (eg from Shropshire), they have come from antiquarian discoveries (A Wigley, pers comm) and so are without a context. This has naturally led to a dependence on assigned dates from other regions and, as such objects are isolated finds, they have no possibility of being part of a stratigraphic sequence that could provide more discrete evidence for regional stylistic development. This seems to be a general problem and even where sites are excavated they seem to give very flat stratigraphic development due to shallowness of deposits. This could be countered to some degree by very large-scale excavation strategies, where the tendency of settlements to shift and major alignments of boundaries to change, could be used to give a more extended stratigraphic sequence, though only if curatorial policies are developed to ensure that such opportunities are firmly grasped.

There can be too great a tendency to assign objects (including ceramics) to periods based on stylistic considerations alone, and this needs to be firmly grounded in an audit of scientific dates, and detailed long-term and systematic study of fabrics in the case of ceramics. At Kemerton in Worcestershire charred residues on pottery, for instance, have recently been accelerator mass spectrometry (AMS) radiocarbon dated and have provided the first comprehensive dating of Late Bronze Age pottery by scientific means for the region (R Jackson, pers comm). At the other end of the period under discussion in this paper there is a temptation to associate widespread change in cultural expression (ceramics etc) with the Roman conquest, but in the west midlands there is still little certainty how the evident trends towards Romanisation should actually be dated. This is a particularly long-established problem in this region, and yet has not been treated as the focus of research.

### 3.2.2. Settlement, landscapes and people

The varied topography of the west midlands must have given rise to many different ways of life in the past, and so far little progress has been made in getting beyond the site itself towards any wider appreciation of this. Fundamental questions remain such as, for instance, whether rivers primarily constituted barriers or acted as transport highways. It is possible that greater attention to ethnographic parallels would also enliven such issues.

#### Environmental perspective (by Elizabeth Pearson)

Environmental evidence usually has a major role in establishing the wider landscape context, but in the west midlands this approach has been inconsistent. In some counties the need for environmental sampling has routinely been included in archaeological briefs and hence carried out as part of archaeological projects at all levels of intervention. In other areas, its inclusion has been restricted mostly to larger excavations, or it is rarely included at all. In some areas, such as Shropshire and Staffordshire, very little palaeoenvironmental site-based study is generally being undertaken. Exceptionally in this region it has formed a primary aspect of a major regional project where the North West Wetlands Project covered parts of Shropshire (Leah et al 1998). Where environmental archaeology is normally an integral part of projects, the acceptance of using a broad range of scientific techniques has also increased over recent years. In particular, the use of palynology, geoarchaeology and radiocarbon dating on lowland floodplain sites has increased with a concomitant increase in landscape understanding. However, even

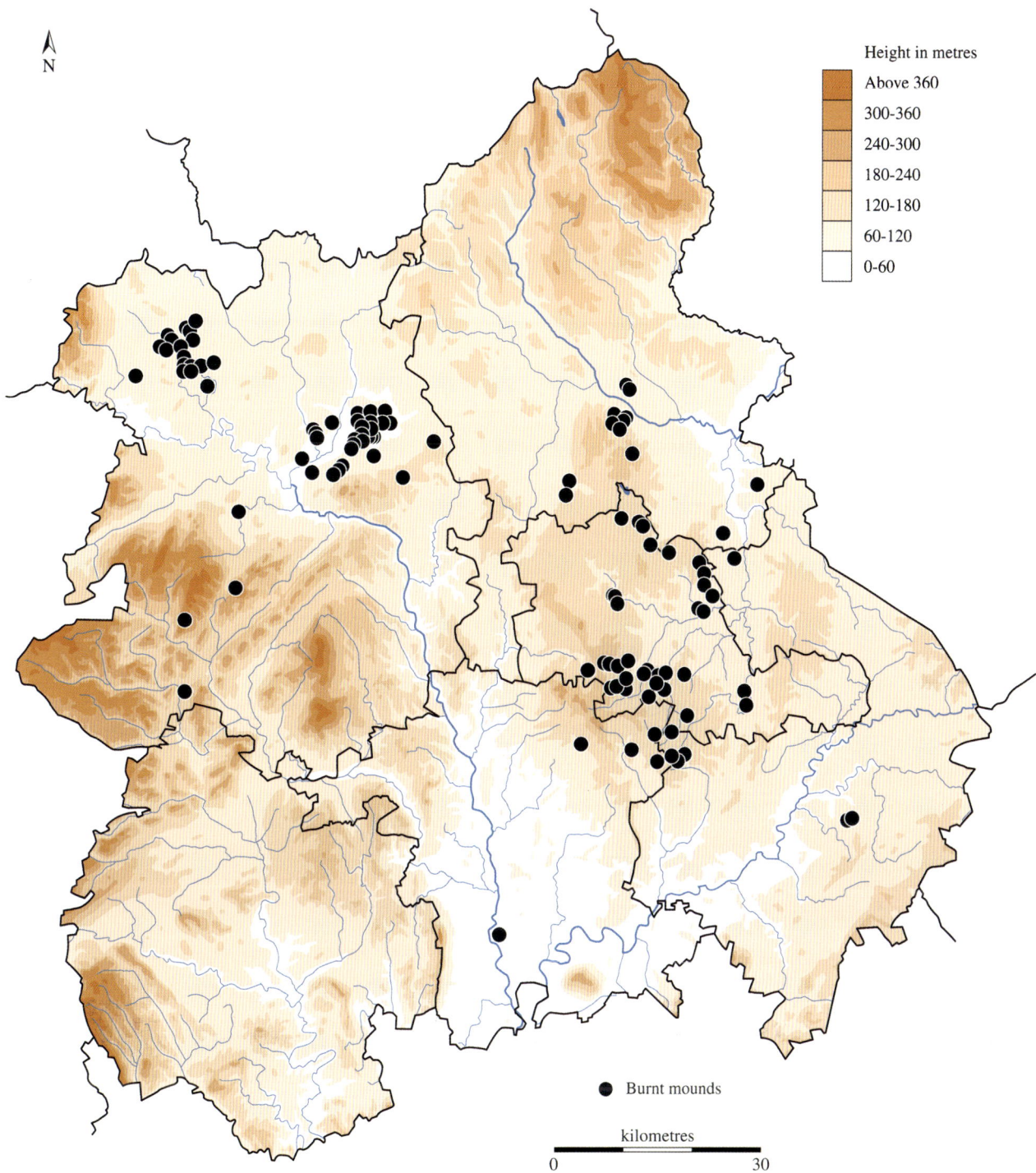

● Burnt mounds

kilometres

0                                  30

in areas where this aspect of work is prominent, the slow process of publication has hampered the dissemination of the results into the public domain.

Insect remains have generally been used in environmental analyses when encountered, although a lack of sampling opportunities has perhaps limited their use in some areas. The three main areas where such work has been undertaken are the Lugg valley in Herefordshire, for example Wellington Quarry, Moreton-on-Lugg and Mill Street, Leominster (Mann 2004, and Smith 2003, and 2004 respectively), the Trent valley in Staffordshire (Smith et al 2001), and the Avon valley in Warwickshire (eg Osborne 1994). In the much wider area of central England at large they have been found to be useful indicators of clearance of tree cover on the gravel terraces by the Late Bronze Age and increasing grassland at this location into the Iron Age (Robinson 2003). Waterlogged

**Fig 3.1** Bronze Age burnt mounds (based on HER plots dated 2003)

wood has also been an occasional find, although at Wellington Quarry near Hereford and at Mill Street in Leominster (Pearson 2004), it has been recovered in large quantities. Murphy (2001a) cites Fisherwick in Staffordshire as a site where positive evidence for hedging of Iron Age date was identified (Smith 1979).

Compared to earlier periods there have also been fewer molluscan studies generally for the Late Bronze Age to Iron Age periods, and no studies of this scale have yet occurred in the west midlands area (Murphy 2001b). This is the case because the survival of molluscs across the region is mostly poor, as the soil pH is slightly acidic and does not provide good conditions for preservation. Two exceptions to this are a large area of south-east Worcestershire where soils are developed on Lias clay or limestone of the Cotswolds scarp, and areas of boulder clay in eastern Warwickshire. This variation in survival of different types of biological remains is, therefore, a key curatorial issue, and to ensure further progress there should be greater clarity about where analysis should be a requirement for certain types of material (for example, animal bone and molluscs in south-east Worcestershire, and in parts of Herefordshire where animal bone has been well preserved eg at Croft Ambrey hillfort, and organic remains on the lowland floodplain). Some aspects of environmental archaeology have perhaps suffered because the region is not seen as an area where wetland landscapes are an important part of the topography, and yet at least four major rivers (the Trent, Severn, Avon, and Wye) and numerous minor rivers provide a large area of floodplain which acts as a sink for environmental evidence. Moreover, the increase in wetland restoration projects and flood alleviation schemes all impacts on deposits of importance for interpreting the past environment.

Parts of the west midlands, especially around Birmingham, are renowned for burnt mounds (Fig 3.1) which are potentially of great importance for the reconstruction of the palaeoenvironment, as they are usually associated with the survival of charcoal and other environmental indicators (see also below). Additionally they may preserve colluvial or alluvial deposits underneath and so provide an extended prehistoric sequence.

### Bronze Age
Bronze Age sites are most often represented by funerary monuments (Garwood this volume fig 2.12), of which many were dug in the 19th century (eg in Staffordshire; C Wardle, pers comm), and relatively few in more modern times (eg at Holt in Worcestershire, (Hunt et al 1986). In contrast settlement sites have so far generally proved elusive. Funerary barrows might be expected to be some way from any occupation sites due to their prominent location, and so provide little clue about the whereabouts of settlement. Some flat cemeteries of the period associated with cremations have been located (Fig 3.2), especially in Warwickshire (at Ryton-on-Dunsmore; Bateman 1976-7), and in Shropshire (at Bromfield; Stanford 1982), both being suggested to be Middle rather than Late Bronze Age by Brück (1995, 247). Sometimes Iron Age hillforts have seen prior occupation such as the Breiddin (Musson et al 1991), but on lowland sites there have been few traces of ordinary domestic settlement. Burnt mounds are a prominent feature of some parts of the region being so far recorded in Birmingham, Warwickshire, Staffordshire, and Shropshire (Fig 3.1). These perhaps provide one of the best chances of finding Bronze Age domestic settlement, as they may be located close by (Hodder in prep). Where Late Bronze Age sites have been excavated, so far they have often been unenclosed, as well as extensive, settlements (eg Sharpstone Hill Site A in Shropshire (Wigley in prep a), and Kemerton in Worcestershire (Jackson and Napthan 1998).

Ritual sites are not commonly known in the region. Ritual sites such as the Mitchell's Fold stone circle in Shropshire may have continued to hold a ritual significance but excavated remains of such sites are very rare, a possible recent example being the Perdiswell penannular ditch near Worcester which was interpreted as a palisaded enclosure for ceremonial use with associated dating of the mid 2nd millennium BC (Griffin et al 2002).

Some progress has been made with reconstructing the landscape of the lower Severn and Avon valleys in the Bronze Age, where extensive clearance of woodland had occurred by

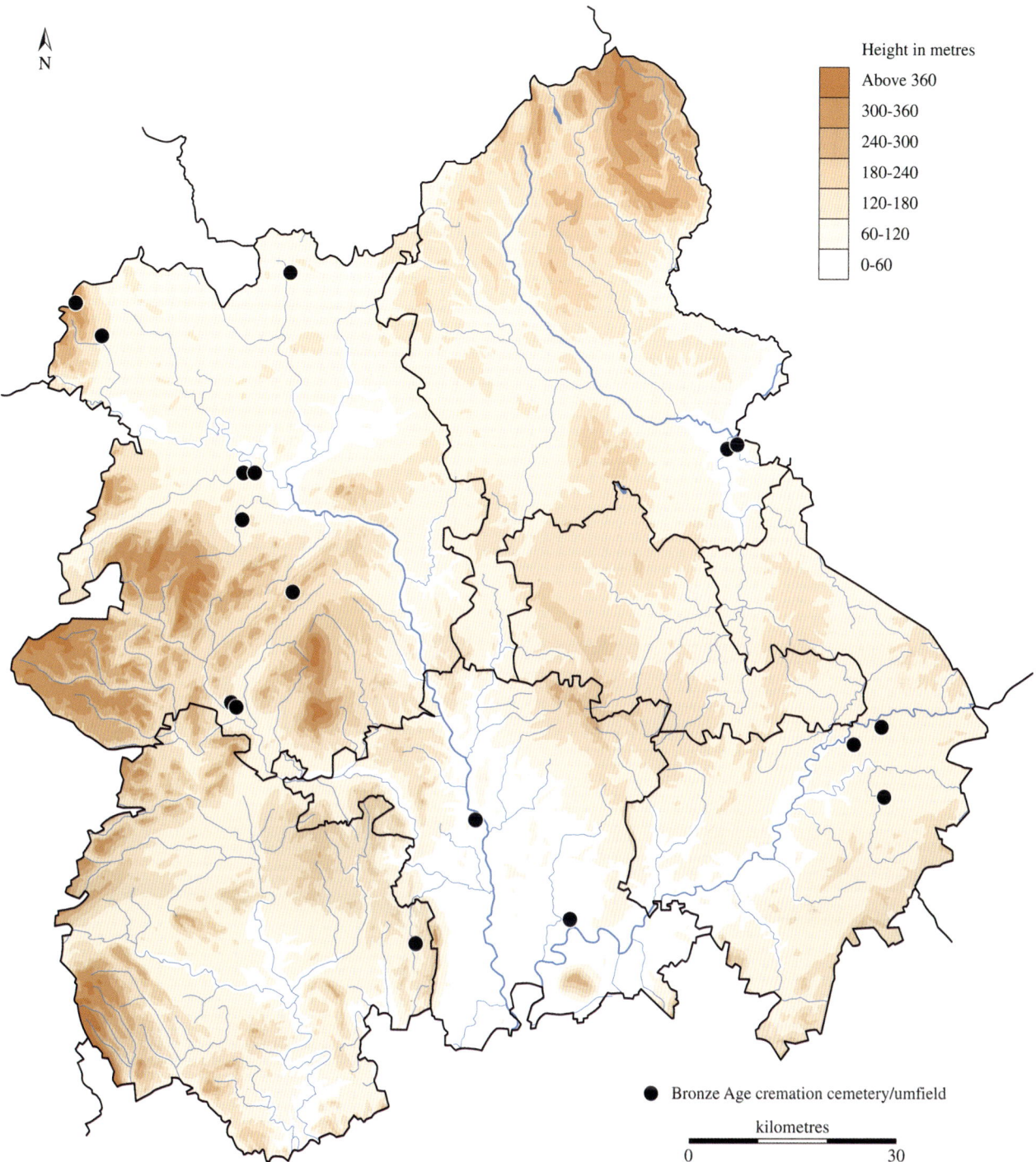

Height in metres

Above 360
300-360
240-300
180-240
120-180
60-120
0-60

● Bronze Age cremation cemetery/urnfield

kilometres

0                              30

the Middle Bronze Age on the terraces of the lower Severn valley, though clearance on the floodplain was generally much later, occurring during the Iron Age to Saxon period. This contrasts with the Avon valley (Worcestershire and Warwickshire) where the floodplain was cleared earlier (Brown 1982). Palaeoenvironmental research in the Severn estuary area (eg Rippon 2001) is also relevant to an understanding of the Severn valley in this period. Geoarchaeology also makes an important contribution but has been little used except for some pioneering studies, in particular by Shotton (1978), by Taylor and Lewin (1996) in the upper Severn valley, and more recently by Macklin et al (2003) in the Arrow valley of Herefordshire. In some cases it has been demonstrated that woodland clearance was followed by the development of heathland (as in Warwickshire; Palmer in prep). More, however, needs to be done on this front, not least in regard to understanding the impact of climatic deterioration in the first half of the 1st millennium BC (Pearson in prep), and current research at Wellington Quarry will make an important contribution through the study of sediments (Payne and Jordan 2004) and pollen (Greig 2004).

**Fig 3.2** Bronze Age cemeteries (based on HER plots dated 2003)

### Iron Age

In the Iron Age period settlement becomes more visible as it is often enclosed by ditches which show up clearly on aerial photographs, though at the same time funerary practice becomes even less evident. The general appearance is of a landscape being more intensively farmed and increasingly subdivided, including with new types of boundary represented by pits and posthole alignments (eg in Warwickshire; Palmer in prep), and with the use of natural boundaries.

By the Middle Iron Age, enclosures were in widespread use often associated with roundhouses (eg Fig 3.3), and this pattern remains consistent throughout the Late Iron Age as well. Lowland farmsteads have been located and also excavated (eg at Fisherwick in Staffordshire; Smith 1979). Though roundhouses can sometimes be seen to succeed each other the time span of individual sites is often unclear and so it remains uncertain whether or not there was a very long-lived stable community. Few sites of this period have generally been excavated in the region, but the evidence so far, for instance in Worcestershire (eg at Throckmorton; S Griffin, pers comm), suggests that once a lowland settlement was established there was relatively little radical change to its layout before final wholesale abandonment. This gives the impression that individual small settlements may have shifted to a new location rather than older sites being modified, though in the Welsh Marches there is more evidence of site refurbishment and continuity (A Wigley, pers comm). However, most data-sets from fieldwork on Iron Age settlement sites have been relatively limited, with only two exceptions which are at Beckford (Worcestershire) and at Wasperton (Warwickshire). In the case of the M6 toll-road fieldwork the scarcity of Iron Age settlement was indicated in the vicinity of Birmingham (M Hodder, pers comm), and other linear projects also seem to indicate that Iron Age features are not often encountered, where a number of these projects have criss-crossed the countryside, as for instance in Worcestershire. However, care should be taken that this is not necessarily interpreted as absence of activity, as there may be other explanations such as a greater dependence on stock rearing.

Hillforts of the west midlands (Fig 3.4) are a particularly prominent feature of the remnant Iron Age landscape (eg Fig 3.5), though little explored archaeologically, except

**Fig 3.3** A Middle Iron Age roundhouse at Beckford in south Worcestershire (copyright Archaeology Service, Worcestershire County Council)

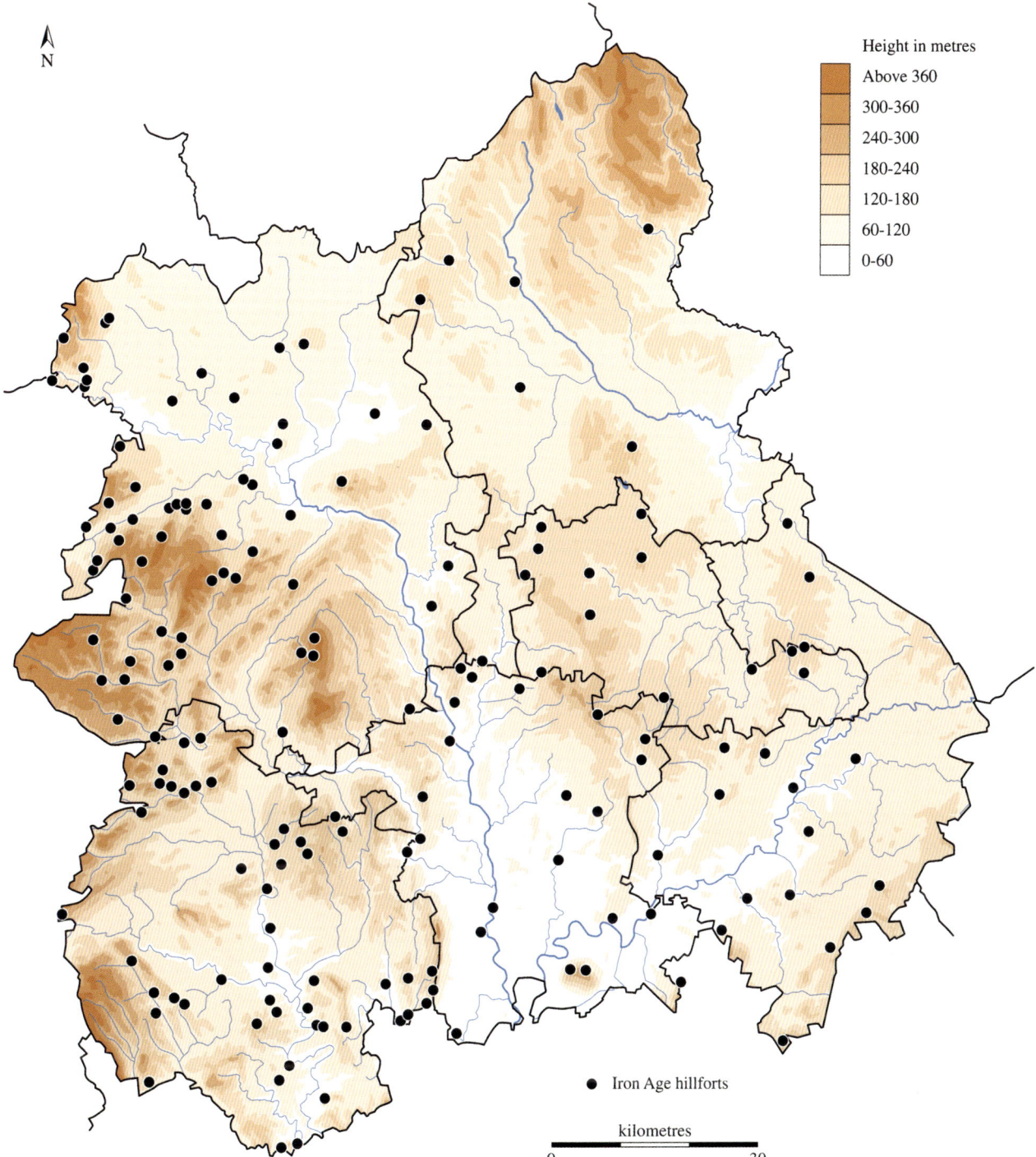

Fig 3.4 Iron Age hillforts (based on HER plots dated 2003)

for Stanford's major fieldwork in Shropshire and Herefordshire in the 1960s–1970s (eg Stanford 1974) and, more recently, the publication of the excavation at Conderton Camp on Bredon Hill (Thomas 2005), and of large-scale earthwork survey on the Malverns (Bowden 2005). This lack of investigation is especially the case in Staffordshire (C Wardle, pers comm). Where earlier fieldwork was undertaken prior to the current framework of pottery study being established from the 1980s onwards, there is now a need to re-examine earlier fieldwork critically, and to bring it up to date. Such sites for reconsideration should include the Bredon Hill excavations of Hencken (1938). And where counties contain large undeveloped upland tracts, as in Staffordshire, then it would be opportune to carry out extensive survey in order to identify wider landscape features potentially relating to hillforts (Wardle in prep).

So far there has been little detailed research carried out in a discrete region to see how sites compare, and to provide greater opportunity for understanding differing elements in the same wider landscape, as has been carried out at Danebury in Hampshire (Cunliffe 1984). The publication of a series of important sites in the vicinity of Bredon Hill (Worcestershire; Conderton and Bredon Hill hillforts, and Beckford), however, will move a long way towards presenting such a case-study of this type for part of the region. Early wider landscape features such as linear banks have been suggested by Historic Landscape Characterisation (HLC) analysis in Herefordshire, and these would be important new evidence, if proven (White in prep). Other such linear boundaries have also been suggested for elsewhere in the region, such as Hob Ditch Causeway in Solihull and Warwickshire (M Hodder, pers comm).

Overall there should be efforts to test blank areas where geology militates against the easier prospection techniques. In both Warwickshire (Palmer in prep) and Worcestershire (Hurst in prep b) some surprisingly extensive settlements have recently been discovered on less well-drained geologies. These may be the richer sites, and the gravel sites, where so much archaeological effort has been expended, may be marginal by comparison. The need to see the wider landscape remains paramount and, where sites are without environmental prospects, there should be some consideration of off-site sampling, in order to study the local environment of site settlement.

The intensification in arable farming during the Iron Age recognised in many areas of the country is difficult to reliably infer from plant macrofossil evidence. Widespread and relatively abundant charred cereal crop waste has been recorded on settlement sites, such as at Beckford in Worcestershire (Colledge 1990; Colledge undated), at Wasperton on the Warwickshire Avon (Bowker 1983), and on some hillfort sites, for example at Midsummer Hill (Colledge 1981). However, equally, crop residues are sparse and other evidence is suggestive of a more pastoral economy elsewhere, for example at Wyre Piddle and Throckmorton in the Vale of Evesham where large areas were sampled for this evidence (Pearson in prep). It is also possible that stock-rearing evidenced in the Romano-British period may have been a continuation of a widespread earlier practice (see Roman Chapter). It may be possible to carry out research into this aspect of landscape using regional pollen sequences. Some evidence has tentatively been interpreted as indicating an increase in arable activity, for example at Wellington Quarry (Greig 2004), although it is often difficult to detect arable indicators as they are frequently swamped by the grassland component on lowland floodplain sites (K Head, pers comm).

**Fig 3.5** British Camp hillfort on the Malverns (copyright Archaeology Service, Worcestershire County Council)

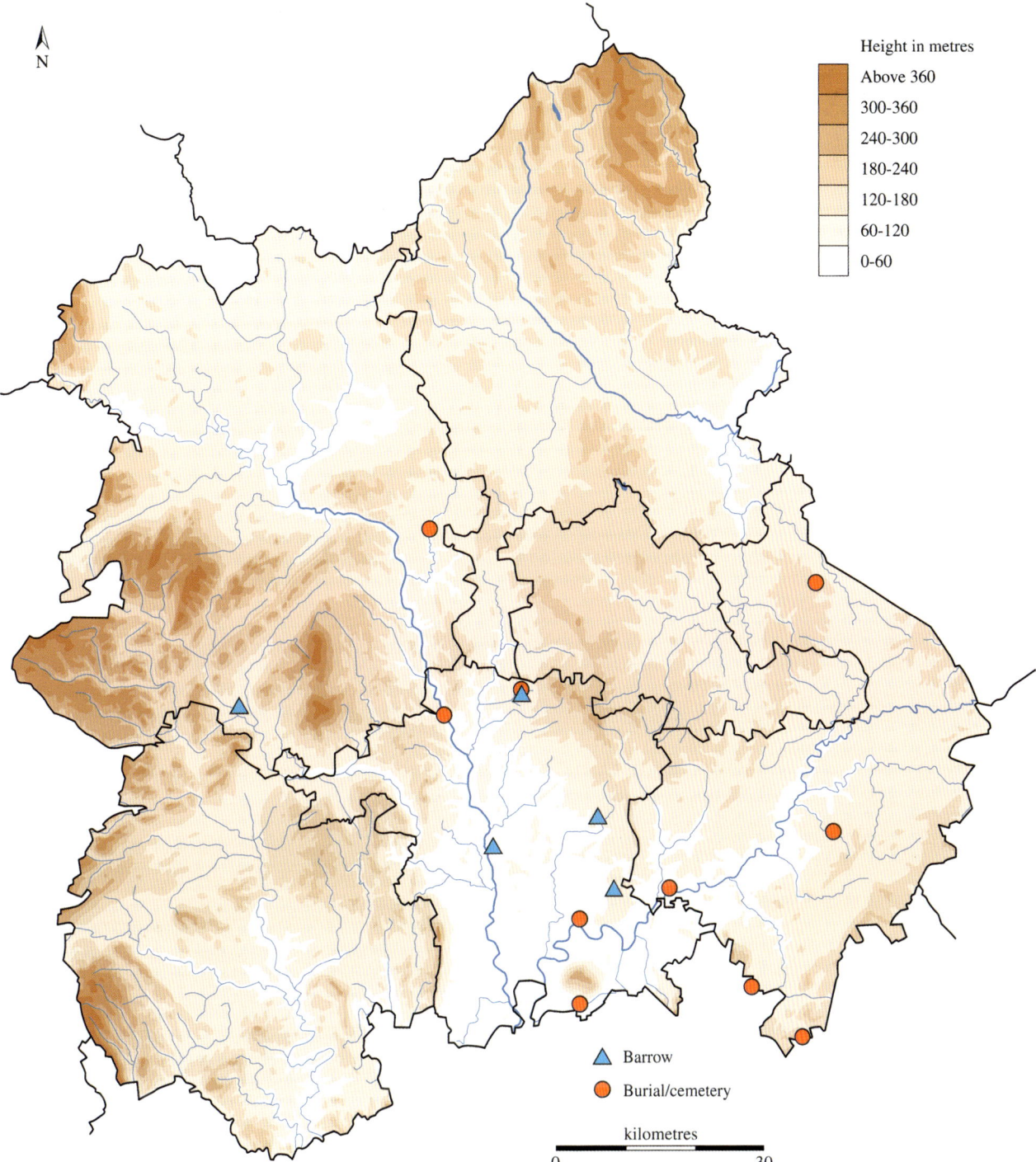

Height in metres

Above 360
300-360
240-300
180-240
120-180
60-120
0-60

▲ Barrow
● Burial/cemetery

kilometres

0                    30

Following the flat cremation burials of the Bronze Age the people themselves remain somewhat elusive (Brück 1995), as few human remains have been found in the region (Fig 3.6). A possible bog burial, normally assigned a Late Bronze Age date, occurred at Whixall Moss (Shropshire; Mullin 2003). Where assumptions have been questioned and unaccompanied inhumations (even in barrows) have been tested, these have sometimes turned out to be Iron Age in date (eg at Church Lench in Worcestershire; Griffin et al 2006). At Church Lawford in Warwickshire a mini ring ditch was also dated to the Late Iron Age (Palmer in prep), and an Iron Age inhumation probably set within an earlier ring ditch was found at Bromfield (A Wigley, pers comm). The discovery of odd human bones across settlement sites seems to be a feature which, as yet, has no explanation, though it tends to imply that bodies (or parts of) were not immediately buried. Comparing the date of these isolated bones with other associated finds would be useful to determine if these were likely to be items of ancestral significance. Though

**Fig 3.6** Iron Age human burial sites (based on HER plots dated 2003)

occasional individual inhumations and finds of human bone are the norm, sometimes at hillforts larger quantities have come to light as at Sutton Walls (Kenyon 1953) and at Bredon Hill (Hencken 1938).

Though more thought is now being given to the symbolic significance of the environment there are few clues to the landscape of the mind and of religious practice in the Iron Age. The best evidence of this is the practice of depositing objects in special places, including for instance objects which have been recovered from special pits and formerly wet locations in Warwickshire (Palmer in prep).

### 3.2.3. Material culture

#### Bronze Age

The material culture of the Bronze Age comprised a range of artefacts, including worked flint for everyday use and copper alloy metalwork finds, for instance of the Middle Bronze Age (cf Vine 1982), the latter providing a spectacular impression of the rarer and more valuable objects that some members of that society had access to, and in some cases giving us an insight into ritual practice. To some extent the latter is true of the Iron Age as well, though by this time there is a greater quantity of other material objects too. Where stratified finds have been recovered in association with burnt mounds there has been very little pottery, suggesting that on some types of site there may have been little use of pottery (Hodder in prep), which seems to confirm the specialised nature of this type of site. On the rare occasions where pottery has been relatively plentiful (ie at Kemerton in south Worcestershire) it was not found in the ploughsoil, which may be accounted for by the usual assumption that it had not survived here. However, the great majority of the material assemblage recovered during the Kemerton excavation had been deliberately deposited in the secondary fills of large features (R Jackson, pers comm), so that it is possible that few finds may ever have been available for incorporation into the ploughsoil. If so, these observations have important potential implications for our ability to identify the settlement sites of this period from the more conventional methods of fieldwork such as fieldwalking.

The extent to which Bronze Age objects were exchanged over distance is less clear, though the raw materials, for instance for metal working, were obviously available across the whole region from outside sources. At Bromfield in Shropshire (Stanford 1982) pottery from the nearby Clee Hills predominated, whereas at Kemerton (Worcestershire) a variety of different pottery fabrics, including from both local and non-local sources (from c30km away), suggested that the diverse Iron Age network of supply can be extended back into the Bronze Age (A Woodward, pers comm). In a similar vein stone axes (Group XII) produced from just over the Shropshire border into Wales, at Corndon Hill, are widely distributed into this region, but especially found west of the Severn (Shotton et al 1951).

Some Bronze Age sites have produced considerable quantities of pottery and, contrary to popular archaeological belief, sites have also been discovered through pottery and other artefacts being found during fieldwalking, occasionally in some profusion as at Whitchurch in Warwickshire (Hingley 1996, 12). It has, however, been suggested that chronologies of other parts of the country may not apply in the west midlands, as there is a possibility that Middle Bronze Age pottery continued to be used into the Late Bronze Age (Hingley 1996, 20), though recent evidence from Kemerton does not bear this out for south Worcestershire (R Jackson, pers comm).

#### Iron Age

The ceramic transition from the Late Bronze Age to the Early Iron Age is still a problematical area for the west midlands (Fig 3.7), mainly because of the sparsity of material of this date (Hancocks in prep). The picture changes radically in the Middle Iron Age, when the central and southern part of the region become associated with some distinctive regional pottery fabrics (Fig 3.8). The Malvern Hills of the Worcestershire/ Herefordshire border in particular became associated with pottery production, and

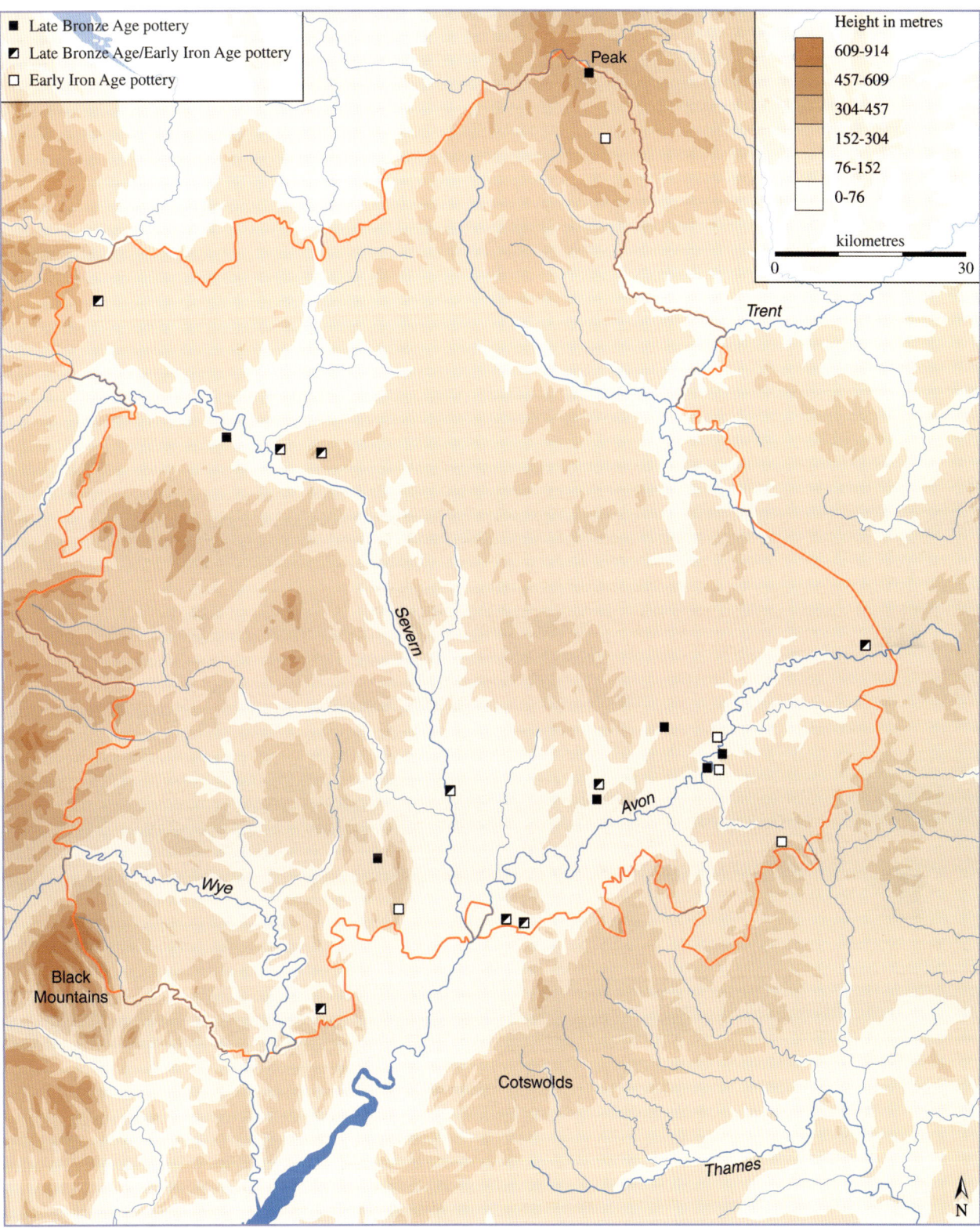

- ■ Late Bronze Age pottery
- ◪ Late Bronze Age/Early Iron Age pottery
- □ Early Iron Age pottery

Height in metres
| | |
|---|---|
| | 609-914 |
| | 457-609 |
| | 304-457 |
| | 152-304 |
| | 76-152 |
| | 0-76 |

kilometres
0        30

Peak

Trent

Severn

Avon

Wye

Black Mountains

Cotswolds

Thames

N

parts of either Gloucestershire or Herefordshire, depending on where the palaeozoic limestone tempered ware (Group B1) pottery originated (Peacock 1968; Morris 1982) continued into the Iron Age as ceramic sources. Several different ceramic producers seem to have emerged in a common ceramic tradition. Salt production also became an established industry at Droitwich at this time, and the salt-makers would have needed to have recourse to, or indeed develop, trade/exchange networks, as their product obviously needed access to a wide region to make larger scale production worthwhile. The common style of the pottery, and the broad correspondence of the Droitwich salt and *Dobunnic* coin distributions (cf Morris 1985, fig 6, and Allen 1961, fig 16 respectively

**Fig 3.7** Late Bronze Age/Early Iron Age pottery find spots (based on The Later Prehistoric Pottery Collections Register; Earl et al 2007)

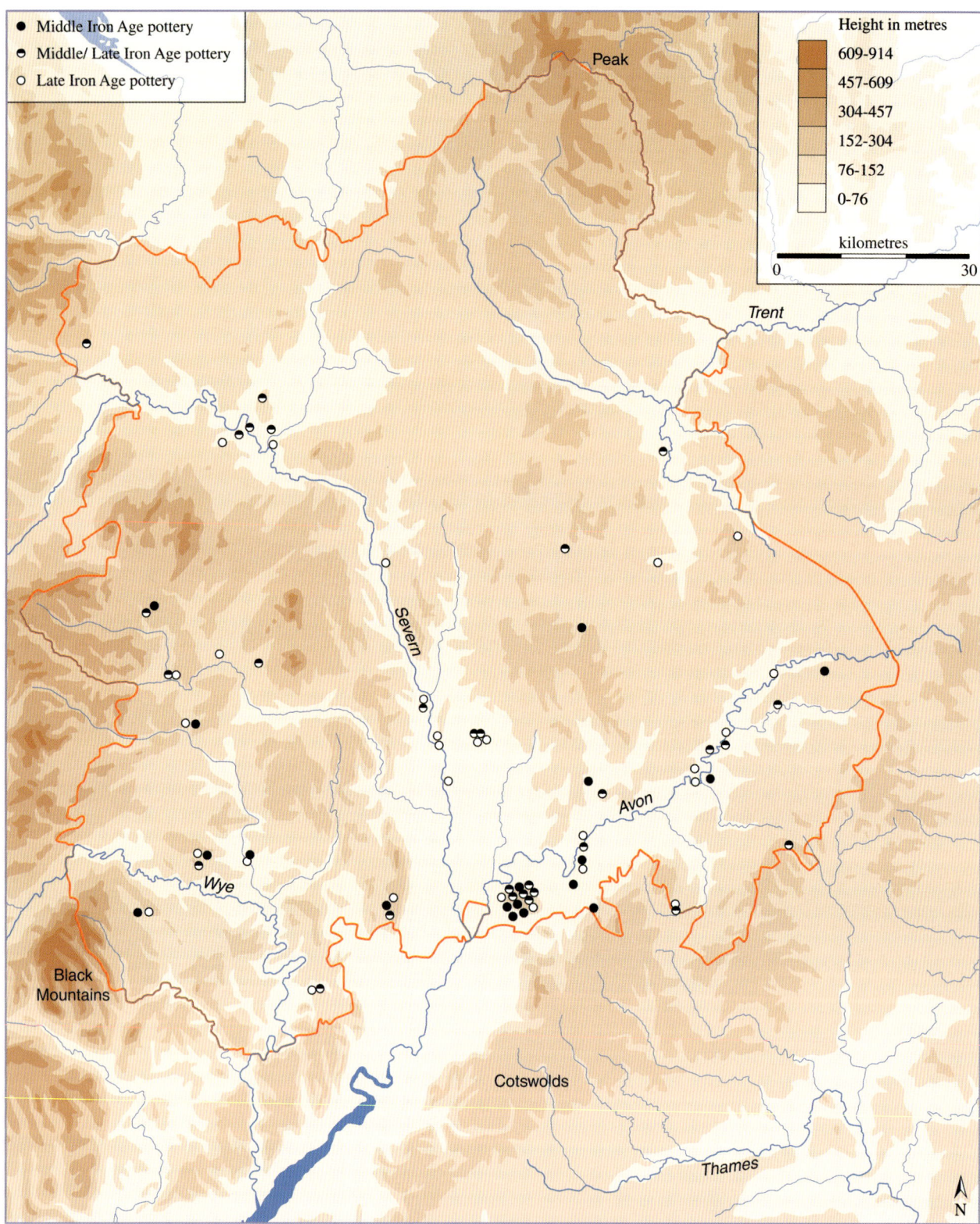

**Fig 3.8** Middle Iron Age and Late Iron Age pottery find spots (based on The Later Prehistoric Pottery Collections Register; Earl et al 2007)

and Fig 3.9), are of interest as they suggest some common cultural traits that may reflect a common political/tribal affiliation (Hurst 2001) across the southern part of the west midlands area.

The notable regional pottery studies of the 1960s saw some of the first definitions of fabrics using petrology in this country (Peacock 1965-7), including Iron Age fabrics (Peacock 1968), but this has not been followed up with fieldwork to locate the production areas in more detail. The largest assemblages of finds from the region still remain unpublished, in the case of Beckford in Worcestershire and Wasperton in Warwickshire, both excavated

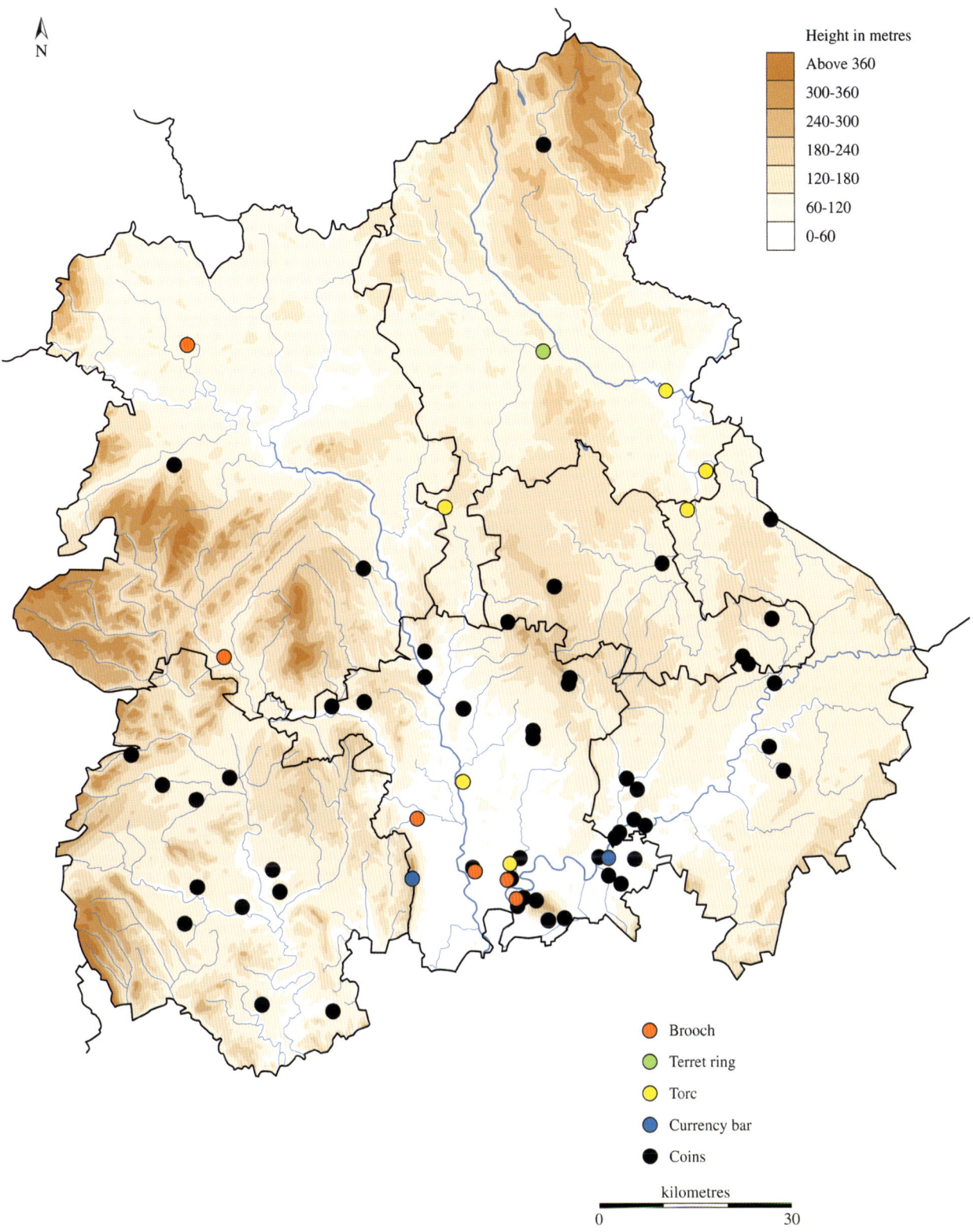

Height in metres
Above 360
300-360
240-300
180-240
120-180
60-120
0-60

Brooch

Terret ring

Torc

Currency bar

Coins

kilometres

0                    30

in the 1970s. This situation has, of course, severely disadvantaged research in this region, and is very unfortunate given the flying start given to the region by the work of David Peacock and Elaine Morris in the 1960s and 1970s respectively. The way forward is for the data from both these major sites to be computerised and additional dating of ceramics to be carried out using residues for AMS dating in view of the time that has passed since the original excavation of these sites, and in the case of Beckford this is currently under way. Other assemblages now in museum collections may form useful subjects for research in order to extract greater information where these still exist as viable archives (eg the 1935-7 Bredon hillfort excavation; Hurst and Jackson 2006).

**Fig 3.9** Iron Age select metalwork and coin find spots (based on HER plots dated 2003)

Other Iron Age artefact types are also characteristic of parts of this region and the distribution patterns of spit-shaped iron currency bars (Allen 1967; Fig 3.9) and of other artefacts tend to corroborate the idea of a cultural zone in the south-west section of the west midlands (Hurst 2001). In particular the distribution patterns of Late Iron Age coin findspots have been used to trace a similar region traditionally assigned to the *Dobunni* (Allen 1961; van Arsdell 1994), whose capitals have been reputed to have been at Minchinhampton and Bagendon in Gloucestershire. The other major tribe usually assigned to the study area is the *Cornovii*, who have normally been placed in Shropshire and west Staffordshire. Otherwise, the west midlands area of the present survey was largely peripheral to a number of other tribes, such as the *Corieltauvi* in eastern Staffordshire and north Warwickshire.

Overall, the impression is that material culture was sparse in artefactual terms and may have been measured more in terms of stock or stockpiles of livestock and crops, although

**Fig 3.10** Small selection of gold coins from the South Worcestershire Iron Age coin hoard discovered in 1993, at the time of its discovery the largest ever coin hoard of the period: modern penny shown as scale (copyright Archaeology Service, Worcestershire County Council)

iron currency bars are found in hoards and seem to corroborate Caesar's description of their use as wealth repositories. Where settlements have been excavated there has been little indication of any status variation based on material remains, despite occasional finds such as the mould for a bronze 'horn cap' (possibly a fitting for a chariot), which has been interpreted by some to signify higher status (Spratling 1972). Although a very large hoard of Iron Age coins (Fig 3.10) and a fragment of gold torc were discovered in 1995 in south Worcestershire, the site has not been further explored to establish its character, and at least one hoard was apparently from a Roman context (Hurst 2000). For such a major find the extent of the follow-up work seems wanting, as the site remains uncharacterised, except in the broadest sense as one of the largest area of complex geophysics results in the county.

The Portable Antiquities Scheme (PAS) will make a major contribution to the study of objects and will be an important resource for the future, as long as the data being collected are appropriately managed. The range of metalwork objects dated to the Iron Age (eg Figs 3.11-3.13), however, is completely different from the Bronze Age, indicating the considerable changes at work. Rich and elaborate objects have been recovered in the west midlands from both Bronze Age and Iron Age periods. For instance, several gold (eg Fig 3.11) and bronze torcs are known from Staffordshire (Wardle in prep; Fig 3.9). The recording of larger numbers of objects than before is allowing the west midlands to develop a distinctive character of its own, and in Staffordshire, for instance, such finds contradict the apparent material impoverishment of Iron Age culture (Wardle in prep). The number of Iron Age lynchpin terminals and pieces of horse-riding equipment coming to light has been the subject of interest (Bolton in prep; Fig 3.9), such objects often being elaborately decorated, and therefore indicative of display and high status.

**Fig 3.11** Gold torcs dating to the late 2nd century BC–early 1st century AD from Alrewas, Staffordshire (copyright The Potteries Museum & Art Gallery)

Perhaps because data is still insufficient there has, as yet, been little study of the economic potential of landholdings of individual settlements, such as that carried out for some Romano-British settlement, where models of consumption and productivity were constructed in order to gain a more basic economic appreciation of this period (eg Applebaum 1975). However, as more sites come to light, this type of analysis may become more feasible.

### 3.2.4. Regionality

Regionality is likely to have much to do with local geography and topography and the particular response that this entails. Clearly there was much variation. For instance, 'hillforts' are predictably common in some hilly areas such as Herefordshire, but interestingly are less common on the uplands of Staffordshire (Fig 3.4).

In the Middle and Late Bronze Age the Clee Hill dolerite-tempered pottery occurs west of the River Severn but does not reach sites such as Ryton-on-Dunsmore, suggesting

a fairly localised distribution (D Mullin, pers comm). Droitwich salt containers (Morris 1985; Morris 1994), Dobunnic coins and spit-shaped currency bars all coincide in much the same part of the region (Hurst 2001), though apparently produced in different parts of that region. In Shropshire briquetage is more common than pottery (ie White in prep), but this is not the case in Herefordshire or Worcestershire. Observations like these, based on the trade and exchange of artefacts, may lead eventually to the definition of specific sub-regions, and more localised areas.

Cropmarks are prolific in number, especially for the Iron Age, but studies of these, in an effort to characterise settlement types, are so far uncommon. Though there has been classification of cropmark sites in north Herefordshire and Shropshire (Whimster 1989), this has not been followed up systematically by excavation in these areas to characterise types of site by date and association. But such surveys remain crucial to the future as their wide geographical range and synthetic analysis provide data for comparison with other parts of the region, and beyond.

So far, therefore, it is difficult to define cultural differences in much detail as there has been too little concerted excavation. However, it is already possible to chart an inherent regionality of trade/exchange of some types of objects within the west midlands region in the Middle and later Iron Age, and this indicates a core area in south Worcestershire and north Gloucestershire with distinct 'frontiers', for instance to the north (beyond the Birmingham plateau); and to the east (the Thames valley). This suggests a cultural and/or economic region, which may in turn reflect political/tribal groupings of the Iron Age (Cunliffe 1991; Hurst 2001). The development of this cultural uniformity, despite a natural barrier such as the Cotswold scarp, makes it more likely that this has some real significance. In this context the definition of areas which are 'marginal' to other areas should be exercised with care in the light of the relatively low level of information available for regions such as the west midlands.

**Fig 3.12** Miniature shield from Alcester, Warwickshire (copper alloy; height 78.5mm) (copyright Birmingham City Council)

### 3.2.5. Processes of change

Over the period of the 1500 years from the Middle Bronze Age to the end of the Iron Age there must have been numerous changes in processes.

#### *Industry*

Raw metals for metal working are most likely to have been mainly imported from outside the region, though it has not yet been confirmed whether copper sources in Shropshire were significantly exploited at this early period (A Wigley, pers comm). The Roman importation of iron ore for smelting at Worcester may give pause for thought about whether this was a tradition with earlier roots. Ariconium (Weston under Penyard, south Herefordshire) was clearly engaged in Iron Age iron production and the number of finds of coins suggests that it also functioned as a centre for distribution (Van Arsdell 1994; Jackson 2000). Another industry indicating larger scale production than just for local consumption is represented by the Droitwich salt industry, and the pottery production centres of the Malverns and nearby areas. Though the salt containers (briquetage) are found on many sites from *c* 6th-5th centuries BC onwards (Morris 1985), none of the production at Droitwich has yet been dated to this early period. This may imply that the technology used for salt making by the later Iron Age, and which is now well known from several sites in Droitwich (eg Woodiwiss 1992), was not the same as that used in the earlier period. Though, of course, the other possibility is that it took place elsewhere in Droitwich and has not yet come to light.

Likewise there is a general lack of sites associated with pottery production despite the products being well known across much of the region for about 600 years at least. It is rare that ceramic production sites using open firing techniques can be evidenced in the archaeological record due to their superficial character, but given that this region is the centre for several prominent industries of this type it should be the focus of fieldwork when the occasion arises, as there may be special circumstances where remains could be attributed to pottery production with careful excavation and interpretation.

### Settlement and agriculture

Several areas have now produced good evidence of landscape organisation in the Bronze Age. At Kemerton this consisted of ditched trackways and fields (R Jackson, pers comm). Substantial linear boundaries of this date have also been noted on several sites, for instance, in south Worcestershire (Childswickham; Patrick and Hurst 2004), and in Warwickshire (Palmer in prep), and potentially under the earthworks of British Camp on the Malverns (Bowden 2005), and on the Long Mynd in Shropshire (D Mullin, pers comm). Recent research has shown that such landscapes follow a similar pattern to that seen in the Thames valley (Yates, pers comm). It is also possible that the cross-ridge dykes and numerous pit alignments in Shropshire date to this period (A Wigley, pers comm), and similar pit alignments datable to the Late Bronze Age or Early Iron Age have been recorded in Staffordshire at Whitemoor Haye (Coates 1997).

**Fig 3.13** Strap union from Warwickshire (copper alloy; scale in mm) (copyright Birmingham City Council)

Iron Age fields have been more elusive in this region, and there have been too few identifications. Where detailed surveying has been possible, for instance on the Malvern Hills, such fields have been lacking, indicating a long preference for pastoralism in this area (Bowden 2005). Although the overall picture may be somewhat unclear from the environmental evidence, the storage pits at Beckford, and the 4-post structures in the hillforts (usually interpreted as for grain storage), are isolated examples which may imply considerable change to the arable farming economy in the region.

## 3.3. Research agenda

The main research topics may be currently defined as follows:

### 3.3.1. Chronology

Rather than allowing the difficulties of radiocarbon dating to deter its use for dating in the Iron Age, on the contrary this technique should be used more often. It should be undertaken by the better laboratories, which are able to deliver the tightest dates, and so may require larger samples (high precision), or, if smaller samples are taken, AMS dating should be used. Ideally a series of dates from related stratigraphy should be obtained, with the possibility that Bayesian statistics might refine the dating.

There should not be an over-reliance on style in the study of ceramics, and any stylistic dating should be backed up by scientific dating, preferably by AMS dating of associated residues. Fabric descriptions should be given to the standard described by the Prehistoric Pottery Research Group (1995) and related wherever possible to regional fabric-type series.

Care should be taken to carry out other scientific dating, such as archaeo-magnetic dating of any ceramic ovens or kiln structures.

### 3.3.2. Settlement, landscapes and people

The broad pattern of landscape development is understood to mean an expansion of agricultural land-use from the Bronze Age into the Iron Age, though the dating and local character of this is still poorly understood due to limited evidence from sites and especially from environmental evidence. Where there is the potential for palaeoenvironmental investigation this should be followed up, and in some areas this may involve survey to locate local wetland sites (eg identifying smaller peat bogs) which have been largely overlooked, and where limited investigation so far has provided valuable landscape evidence (Hurst in prep b; Pearson in prep).

The location of Bronze Age settlement presents considerable difficulties, but burnt mounds (Fig 3.1) may present a good opportunity if the area around them was to be prioritised for prospection (Hodder in prep). Fieldwalking and geophysics may be appropriate techniques in these circumstances, as demonstrated in Warwickshire (Palmer in prep), in order to create a wider context.

There needs to be a clearer understanding of whether later prehistoric sites can be identified by other means than aerial photography, and in particular as to whether they are susceptible to discovery by fieldwalking (see Hingley 1996 for a positive account, now supported by the evidence of at least two sites in Worcestershire). Extensive settlements without major boundary ditches would be difficult to even locate by aerial photography, and so it is important to be clear about the most advantageous methods of site detection for this period. There is also some evidence that even where Bronze Age pottery was in general use it does not always get incorporated into surface deposits in any quantity but is instead found buried in the deeper features (ie at Kemerton in south Worcestershire). Therefore, in the case of new sites attention should be given to the ploughsoil to establish how far sites are detectable through fieldwalking and other field techniques. Assessment of the effectiveness of current field techniques will have important potential implications for our ability to identify the settlement sites of this period by more conventional methods such as fieldwalking rather than relying on techniques like aerial photography, which tend to reveal only certain types of site on certain geologies. For instance, the mapping and dating of Holocene terraces and palaeochannels in river valleys, as on the River Arrow in Herefordshire, will contribute to a better understanding of past land use and settlement development (C Moffett, pers comm).

Hillforts are a characteristic settlement type in the region (Fig 3.4), part of the 'hillfort zone' of western England and Wales (Cunliffe 1991). Their obvious nature has made them prone to passive management protection, tending to remove this resource from the research cycle, despite the success of modern non-invasive techniques (eg Bowden 2005). Since these sites are so important for both the Bronze Age and Iron Age in this region, with even basic aspects such as their chronology and function still in question, there should be an active research engagement to ensure that they continue to play their part in any developing understanding of the Iron Age. This situation should also give added impetus to the investigation of hillforts reputed to lie in some of the more urban areas (Hodder 2004, 45).

### 3.3.3. Material culture

There should be consistent recording of artefacts using recognised typologies and reference series. Where these have been maintained over many years, such as the stone axe and Celtic coin indexes, efforts should be made to continue these vitally important research resources. These specialist databases should be maintained with easy access for the submission of data and as a source of material for comparison and identification. The Portable Antiquities Scheme has a function in ensuring as much information as possible is incorporated in some of these specialist databases. Similarly more local reference series and databases such as the pottery fabric-type series of both Worcestershire and Warwickshire, for instance, should be supported as major contributors to research in the region. Such systems require expert curation in terms of the criteria for data creation and management, and should be recognised as an important part of the research equation, and so be supported where necessary.

Where finds from the Thames valley cross over into the Severn valley these will be of special significance for dating and cross-referencing the two regions, and the same will be true for between the Severn and Trent valleys. As an example, flint tempered pottery has recently been recovered from Late Iron Age levels of a site at Childswickham near Broadway (Timby 2004). Equally, pottery and salt containers from the middle Severn valley area were widely traded within the west midlands area, with some trickling into other regions such as the Thames valley (Morris 1985, 351), and such overlaps should be closely scrutinised as being of special interest for the cross-dating of the culture of disparate regions.

There may be occasions when reworking archived and published sites will make a further contribution, in the light of improved dating strategies and methods. The dating of carbonised residues from pots is a particularly promising approach.

### 3.3.4. Regionality

This is at the crux of research in that the region needs to develop its own typology of structures and refine its own sequences without the typological models of southern England being slavishly followed. The west midlands needs greater definition from synthesis, and there should be greater confidence in model building and greater awareness of the larger landscape context that can only come from more excavation (including publication of important unpublished excavations), a greater sense of building on data already accumulated (ie site discussion should be well informed – not particularly easy in a competitive tendering environment), and there should be an active effort to identify and use sites in the process of building local profiles of Middle Bronze Age to Iron Age development, rather than just publishing another site. For larger projects a reasonable level of synthesis should especially be built into briefs, as this in itself would be a desirable outcome of the archaeological intervention.

### 3.3.5. Processes of change

The processes of change are often poorly dated, with only broad date spans being possible. This needs to be addressed wherever possible with more and better scientific dates. Localised environmental evidence will be one of the best ways of charting change, and providing a physical context for human occupation, independent of the vagaries of site degradation, as well as providing detail about animal husbandry, farming practices, and general landscape management. However, for the latter to be effective there should be consistent methods of recording over a long period of research, which has not been the case to date in many of the more specialist areas of study.

### 3.3.6. Key research agenda points

1. There is a need for greater synthesis of data to provide an up-to-date context for current archaeological fieldwork. This should include an audit of existing data to establish the key deposits and sequences for dating in the region.

2. Historic Environment Records (HERs) present specific problems such as the consistency with which sites are recorded. Without increasingly consistent recording of data there will be little opportunity to use the

data held in HERs for regional research. A system such as OASIS, which is currently being introduced, may help with this direction, but other initiatives, such as providing indices to finds in the local authority HER also need to be developed to facilitate research. HERs should consult widely to ensure that the data they hold is made available to all users in the most useful ways possible, and that the problem of data compatibility across local authority boundaries is addressed as a significant issue.

3. Briefs for archaeological work presently follow no uniform standard and this may be an issue that requires professional scrutiny. Where briefs are drawn up for very large projects it would generally be sensible for these to have a staged approach, and on linear projects in particular negative results should not be accepted as necessarily conclusive without the conducting of a watching brief during groundworks at the outset of construction.

4. Curators might usefully use a checklist in an effort to establish baseline recording to facilitate comparability of data across modern administrative boundaries. This would be particularly useful to ensure that more specialised work such as palaeoenvironmental sampling and analysis are considered at the outset, and appropriately specified in the brief.

5. Where prehistoric sites are suspected, experience elsewhere in the field has shown that it is necessary to apply greater percentages of field evaluation trenching than the 'normal' 2%. Detailed modelling of the results of modern evaluations has indicated that a 6%-10% sample is much more likely to avoid missing significant information (Hey and Lacey 2001, 59), making this a more accurate basis for characterising Bronze Age and Anglo-Saxon sites. For Iron Age sites trenching was the most effective method of finding sites during evaluation, whereas for the Bronze Age sites fieldwalking was nearly as effective as trenching (Hey and Lacey 2001, 31).

6. For data to be comparable between sites there also needs to be an agreed minimum retrieval of data from sites. In the course of excavation, for instance, Haselgrove et al (2001, 10) have advised that a minimum excavation ratio, for instance for enclosure ditches, should be 20%. The material culture deficiencies of the prehistoric period should also be balanced with the higher percentage of features being excavated, including full excavation in specific circumstances, especially in the case of prehistoric remains where remains of any kind are distinctly rare.

7. There is a need to look beyond the more visible sites enclosed with ditches, and to refine other field techniques for the recovery of evidence away from geologies that are most responsive to aerial photography, in order to get a broader picture of the later prehistoric period. For instance greater attention should be given to the recognition of burnt stone in the prospection for sites of prehistoric date, and the tendency of aerial photographers to return to the same areas as in previous years, based on the presence of proven sites, should be resisted (Wigley in prep (b)).

8. There is also a need for more productive environmental work, and this would be more likely to occur if the focus expanded from gravel sites to include sites on other geologies, though some gravel sites are not acidic and bone survival is good (eg Beckford in Worcestershire). Environmental sampling should be carried out routinely for plant macrofossils as an integrated archaeological practice, including, in appropriate circumstances, sampling for pollen etc, as even the negative or poor evidence will be of significance for future reference (Pearson in prep).

9. There is a need to assess the potential of localised natural peat deposits for landscape reconstruction research, based on pollen analysis in particular, as these deposits are not only valuable, but increasingly vulnerable to disturbance. It would be advisable for survey projects to assess the potential

for this sort of localised survival, so that these deposits are appropriately managed for the future through their inclusion in the HER.

10. The production of a final report on major excavations, such as at Beckford, and Wasperton, should remain a regional priority for the future.

11. The detailed survey of uplands should be a priority for the future in areas that have not yet received detailed attention, such as Staffordshire. And publication of previous survey carried out for the National Mapping Programme is to be encouraged.

12. Scientific dating should be undertaken, which will have the likely corollary that bulk environmental sampling should be routinely carried out, as this will be the main way of best guaranteeing the availability of material for radiocarbon dating (especially charred seeds and other small woody materials for AMS dating). Where there are short-lived samples (eg articulated bone) and charcoal from secure contexts (eg hearths) these should also be considered for dating. In addition the dating of residues on pottery is proving invaluable for ceramic dating of earlier prehistoric pottery, and should be extended to other periods. The importance of scientific dating for site chronologies should mean that this should be an essential part of the project brief and design.

13. More effective field strategies, perhaps applying new technology (such as the routine plotting of finds by global positioning system (GPS), and the use of geographical information systems (GIS)), should be developed and evaluated, especially where they offer the opportunity to cover large areas in some detail, as the current sparsity of consistent data over extensive areas severely hampers research.

14. Greater academic engagement in archaeological research from tertiary educational institutions in the region would undoubtedly be beneficial. There are currently projects by the University of Cardiff and University of Worcester, in addition to the long-standing involvement in regional research by the University of Birmingham.

15. There should be adequate funding to realise the full potential of later prehistoric sites, and this should extend to the development of active research programmes. These would be particularly important for the investigation of specific types of sites (eg hillforts) which are highly characteristic of the region, and where developer-funded work is unlikely to ever facilitate any new study.

16. Museum archives and finds from earlier important excavations and other discoveries should also be revisited with a view to fresh study.

17. Archaeology should continue to be a joint endeavour by both amateur and professional, as there are many examples of how this combination brings great advantages both in the scope of research projects and their effectiveness in providing useful data.

18. The metal detectorist working with the Portable Antiquities Scheme (PAS) and other archaeologists has a significant role to play in the detection of new sites, especially if attention is given to pottery finds as well as metalwork, and the PAS data is accessible, including via the HERs. The metal detector may even be the prime equipment for locating Bronze Age and later prehistoric sites where the pottery is not entering the ploughsoil, or where handmade pottery in the ploughsoil has been degraded through intensive arable cultivation over many years.

19. A forum for curatorial and other archaeologists would be useful as a place to discuss issues relating to the recovery and interpretation of data, which is even more important than usual for a region which needs to develop a stronger identity as part of its research framework strategy.

## Acknowledgements

Thanks are owed to the following who delivered papers to the West Midlands Regional Research Framework for Archaeology Assessment session in Worcester in September 2002: Angie Bolton, Hal Dalwood, Annette Hancocks, Mike Hodder, Robin Jackson, Stuart Palmer, Liz Pearson, Chris Wardle, Paul White, Andy Wigley, and Ann Woodward; and to the following who attended the Research Agenda and Strategy meeting at Birmingham in July 2003: Hal Dalwood, Mike Hodder, Robin Jackson, Stuart Palmer, Mike Stokes, Chris Wardle, Phil Watson and Sarah Watt, who, together with Lisa Moffett, Dave Mullin and Simon Woodiwiss, have also commented on an earlier draft of this paper. Angie Bolton (Figs 3.12 and 3.13), Debbie Ford (Fig 3.11), Mike Glyde (Fig 3.5) and Jan Wills (Fig 3.3) kindly made available photographs for inclusion.

Sarah Watt is especially to be thanked for so efficiently keeping an extremely lengthy and involved process of debate on a forward course.

## Bibliography

Allen, D, 1961   A study of the Dobunnic coinage, in Clifford, E M, *Bagendon: a Belgic oppidum: a record of excavations 1954-6*, 75-141, Cambridge

Allen, D F, 1967   Iron currency bars in Britain, *Proc Prehist Soc* 33, 307-35

Applebaum, S, 1975   Some observations on the economy of the Roman villa at Bignor, Sussex, *Britannia* VI, 118-32

Arsdell, R D van, 1994   *The coinage of the Dobunni: money supply and coin circulation in Dobunnic territory* (with a gazetteer of findspots by P de Jersey), Oxford Univ Comm for Archaeol monogr 38

Barfield, L, and Hodder, M, 1989   Burnt mounds in the west midlands: surveys and excavations, in *Midlands prehistory: some recent and current researches into the prehistory of central England* (ed A Gibson), BAR British Series 204, 5-13, Oxford

Bateman, J, 1976-7   A Late Bronze Age cremation cemetery and Iron Age/Romano-British enclosures in the parish of Ryton-on-Dunsmore, Warwickshire, *Trans Birmingham Warwickshire Arch Soc* 88, 1-47

Bolton, A, in prep   The potential of the Portable Antiquities Scheme and treasure finds for understanding the Iron Age in the west midlands, in *Westward on the High-hilled Plains: the later prehistory of the west midlands* (ed J D Hurst a)

Bowden, M, 2005   *The Malvern Hills: an ancient landscape*, Swindon.

Bowker, C M, 1983   Environmental research at Wasperton, 2nd interim report, *West Midlands Archaeology* 26, 29-35

Brown, A G, 1982   Human impact on the former floodplain woodlands of the Severn, in *Archaeological aspects of woodland ecology* (eds M Bell and S Limbrey), BAR International Series 146, 93-104, Oxford

Brück, J, 1995   A place for the dead: the role of human remains in Late Bronze Age Britain, *Proc Prehist Soc* 61, 245-77

Coates, G, 1997   Alrewas: Whitemoor Haye, *West Midlands Archaeology* 40, 66-9

Colledge, S M, 1981   *Report on the charred plant remains from the Midsummer Hill, Herefordshire, excavations*, English Heritage Ancient Monuments Lab rep 3308

Colledge, S M, 1990   (1983-4) *Sampling and human activities: a study of the charred plant remains from the Beckford roundhouse*, Unpub typescript (as revised by L C Moffett)

Colledge, S M,  *Botanical remains from contexts other than the roundhouse*, Unpub typescript

Cunliffe, B, 1984   *Danebury, an Iron Age hillfort in Hampshire: Vol 1, The excavations 1969-1978*, CBA Res Rep 52, York

Cunliffe, B, 1991   (1974) *Iron Age communities in Britain: an account of England, Scotland and Wales from the seventh century BC until the Roman conquest*, 3rd edn, London

Dalwood, H, in prep   'The Bronze Age has lagged behind…' Bronze Age settlement and landscape in the west midlands, in *Westward on the High-hilled Plains: the later prehistory of the west midlands* (ed J D Hurst a)

Earl, G, Morris, E, Poppy, S, Westcott, K, and Champion, T C, 2007   *Later Prehistoric Pottery Gazetteer,* http://ads.ahds.ac.uk/catalogue/archive/lppg_eh_2007

Greig, J, 2004   Prehistoric limewoods of Herefordshire: pollen and seeds from Wellington Quarry, in *Wellington quarry, Herefordshire (1986-96): investigations of a landscape in the lower Lugg valley* (eds R Jackson and D Miller), Unpub internal report 1230, Worcestershire Historic Environment and Archaeology Service

Griffin, S, Dalwood, H, Hurst, D, and Pearson, E, 2002   Excavation at Perdiswell Park and Ride, Droitwich Road, Worcester, *Trans Worcestershire Archaeol Soc 3 ser* 18, 1-24

Griffin, S, Weston, G, Mann, A, and Dalwood, H, 2006   A late Iron Age burial at Old Yew Hill Wood, Church Lench, *Worcestershire Archaeol Soc 3 ser* 20, 1-9

Hancocks, A, in prep   An overview of the ceramic basis within the broader west midlands region, in *Westward on the High-hilled Plains: the later prehistory of the west midlands* (ed J D Hurst a)

Haselgrove, C, Armit, I, Champion, T, Creighton, J, Gwilt, A, Hill, J D, Hunter, F, and Woodward, A, 2001   *Understanding the British Iron Age: an agenda for action,* Salisbury

Hencken, T, 1938   The excavation of the Iron Age camp on Bredon Hill, *Archaeol J* 95, 1-111

Hey, G, and Lacey, M, 2001   *Evaluation of archaeological decision-making processes and sampling strategies*, Oxford

Hingley, R, 1996   Prehistoric Warwickshire: a review of the evidence, *Trans Birmingham Warwickshire Archaeol Soc* 100, 1-24

Hodder, M, 2004   *Birmingham: the hidden history*, Stroud

Hodder, M, in prep   Burnt mounds and beyond: the later prehistory of Birmingham and the Black Country, in *Westward on the High-hilled Plains: the later prehistory of the west midlands* (ed J D Hurst a)

Hunt, A M, Shotliff, A, and Woodhouse, J, 1986   A Bronze Age barrow cemetery and Iron Age enclosure at Holt, *Trans Worcestershire Archaeol Soc 3 ser* 10, 7-46

Hurst, J D, 2000   *The south Worcestershire hoards*, Unpub internal report 812, Worcestershire County Archaeological Service

Hurst, J D, 2001   Dobunnic tribal centres, commodities and trade: the South Worcestershire Hoard, salt and pottery, *West Midlands Archaeology* 44, 84-93

Hurst, J D (ed), in prep a   *Westward on the High-hilled Plains: the later prehistory of the west midlands*

Hurst, J D, in prep b   Middle Bronze Age to Late Iron Age Worcestershire, in *Westward on the High-hilled Plains: the later prehistory of the west midlands* (ed J D Hurst a)

Hurst, J D, and Jackson, R, 2006   *Assessment and updated project design for the Bredon hillfort, Worcestershire, archive: 1935-7 excavations by Thalassa Cruso Hencken,* Unpub internal report 1454, Worcestershire Historic Environment and Archaeology Service

Jackson, R (ed), 2000   *The Roman settlement of Ariconium, near Weston-under-Penyard, Herefordshire: an assessment and synthesis of the evidence*, Unpub internal report 1148, Worcestershire County Archaeological Service

Jackson, R, and Napthan, M, 1998   Interim report on salvage recording of a Neolithic/ Beaker and Bronze Age settlement and landscape at Huntsmans Quarry, Kemerton 1994-6, *Trans Worcestershire Archaeol Soc* 16, 57-68

Kenyon, K, 1953   Excavations at Sutton Walls, Herefordshire, 1948-1951, *Archaeol J* 110, 1-87

Leah, M D, Wells, C E, Stamper, P, Huckerby, E, and Welch, C, 1998   *The wetlands of Shropshire and Staffordshire*, North West Wetlands Survey 5, Lancaster

Macklin, G, Johnstone, E, Brewer, P A, Gnych, P G E, and Jones, A F, 2003   Holocene river development and the archaeological sites in the Arrow valley, in *The Arrow Valley, Herefordshire: archaeology, landscape change and conservation* (ed P White), Herefordshire Studies in Archaeology 2, 52-95

Mann, A C, 2004   *Neolithic and Anglo-Saxon insect assemblages from Wellington Quarry, Herefordshire and the changing landscape of the lower Lugg valley*, Unpub MSc dissertation, Univ Sheffield

Morris, E L, 1982   Iron Age pottery from western Britain: another petrological study, in *Current research in ceramics: thin section studies* (eds I Freestone, C Johns and T Potter), British Museum Occasional Paper 32, 15-25

Morris, E L, 1985   Prehistoric salt distributions: two case studies from western Britain, *Bull Board Celtic Stud* XXXII, 336-79

Morris, E L, 1994   Production and distribution of pottery and salt in Iron Age Britain: a review, *Proc Prehist Soc* 60, 371-93

Mullin, D, 2003   *The Bronze Age landscape of the northern English Midlands*, BAR British Series 351, Oxford

Murphy, P, 2001a   *Review of wood and macroscopic wood charcoal from archaeological sites in the west and east Midlands and the East of England*, Centre for Archaeol rep 23/2001

Murphy, P, 2001b   *Review of molluscs and other non-insect invertebrates from archaeological sites in the west and east Midlands and the East of England*, Centre for Archaeol rep 68/2001

Musson, C R, Britnell, W J, and Smith, A G, 1991   *The Breiddin Hillfort: a later prehistoric settlement in the Welsh Marches*, CBA Res Rep 76, York

Osborne, P, 1994   Insect remains from pit F and their environmental implications, in *Roman Alcester: southern extramural area* (eds S Cracknell and C Mahany), CBA Res Rep 97, 217-20, York

Palmer, S, in prep   Any more old Iron Age?, in *Westward on the High-hilled Plains: the later prehistory of the west midlands* (ed J D Hurst a)

Patrick, C, and Hurst, J D, 2004   *Archaeological survey and excavation along the Cotswold Spring Supply Trunk Main: archive report*, Unpub internal report 1140, Worcestershire Historic Environment and Archaeology Service

Payne, R, and Jordan, D, 2004   Geoarchaeology, in Jackson, R, and Miller, D, *Wellington quarry, Herefordshire (1986-96): investigations of a landscape in the lower Lugg valley*, Unpub internal report 1230, Worcestershire Historic Environment and Archaeology Service

Peacock, D P S, 1965-7  Romano-British pottery production in the Malvern district of Worcestershire, *Trans Worcestershire Archaeol Soc 3*, 15-28

Peacock, D P S, 1968  A petrological study of certain Iron Age pottery from western England, *Proc Prehist Soc 34*, 414-27

Pearson, E, 2004  *Assessment summary of environmental remains from Mill Street, Leominster*, Unpub internal report 1341, Worcestershire Historic Environment and Archaeology Service

Pearson, E, in prep  Cows, beans and the view: landscape and farming of the west midlands in later prehistory, in *Westward on the High-hilled Plains: the later prehistory of the west midlands* (ed J D Hurst a)

Prehistoric Pottery Research Group, 1995  *The study of later prehistoric pottery: general policies and guidelines for analysis and publication*, Occasional Papers 1 and 2

Rippon, S (ed), 2001  *Estuarine archaeology: the Severn and beyond*, Archaeology of the Severn Estuary 11, Annual report of the Severn Estuary Levels Res Comm

Robinson, M, 2003  *English Heritage reviews of environmental archaeology: Midlands region (insects)*, Centre for Archaeol rep 9/2003

Shotton, F W, 1978  Archaeological inferences from the study of alluvium in the lower Severn-Avon valleys, in *The effect of man on the landscape in the lowland zone* (eds S Limbrey and J G Evans), CBA Res Rep 21, 27-32, York

Shotton, F W, Chitty, L F, and Seaby, W A, 1951  A new centre of stone axe dispersal on the Welsh border, *Proc Prehist Soc* XVII, 159-67

Smith, C, 1979  *Fisherwick: the reconstruction of an Iron Age landscape,* BAR British Series 61

Smith, D, 2003  Insect analysis, in *Archaeological evaluation at Morton-on-Lugg, Herefordshire* (ed S Griffin and R Jackson) Unpub internal report 1142, Worcestershire Historic Environment and Archaeology Service, 20

Smith, D, 2004  *An assessment of the insect remains from Mill Street, Leominster*, Unpub typescript

Smith, D N, Roseff, R, and Butler, S, 2001  The sediments, pollen, plant macro-fossils and insects from a Bronze-Age channel fill at Yoxall Bridge, Staffordshire, *Environmental Archaeology* 6, 1-12

Spratling, M G, 1972  *Southern British decorated bronzes of the later pre-Roman Iron Age*, Unpub PhD thesis, Institute of London

Stanford, S C, 1974  *Croft Ambrey*, Hereford, privately printed

Stanford, S C, 1982  Bromfield, Shropshire: Neolithic, Beaker and Bronze Age sites, 1966-79, *Proc Prehist Soc* 48, 279-320

Taylor, M P, and Lewin, J, 1996  River behaviour and Holocene alluviation: the River Severn at Welshpool, Mid-Wales, *UK Earth Surface Processes and Landforms* 21, 77-91

Thomas, N, 2005  *Conderton Camp, Worcestershire: a small middle Iron Age hillfort on Bredon Hill*, CBA Res Rep 143, York

Timby, J, 2004  The pottery, in Patrick, C, and Hurst, J D, 2004 *Archaeological survey and excavation along the Cotswold Spring Supply Trunk Main: archive report*, Unpub internal report 1140, Worcestershire Historic Environment and Archaeology Service, 16-37

Vine, P M, 1982  *The Neolithic and Bronze Age culture of the middle and upper Trent Basin*, BAR British Series 105, Oxford

Wardle, C, in prep   The Late Bronze Age and Iron Age in Staffordshire: the torc of the Midlands?, in *Westward on the High-hilled Plains: the later prehistory of the west midlands* (ed J D Hurst a)

Whimster, R, 1989   *The emerging past: air photography and the buried landscape*, Royal Commission on the Historical Monuments of England

White, P, in prep   Herefordshire: from the Middle Bronze Age to the later Iron Age, in *Westward on the High-hilled Plains: the later prehistory of the west midlands* (ed J D, Hurst a)

Wigley, A, in prep a   Fugitive pieces: towards a new understanding of the later second and first millennia BC in Shropshire, in *Westward on the High-hilled Plains: the later prehistory of the west midlands* (ed J D Hurst a)

Wigley, A, in prep b   Touching the void: Iron Age landscapes and settlement in the west midlands, in *Westward on the High-hilled Plains: the later prehistory of the west midlands* (ed J D Hurst a)

Woodiwiss, S G (ed), 1992   *Iron Age and Roman salt production and the medieval town of Droitwich*, CBA Res Rep 81, York

# 4. The Romano-British period: an assessment

## Simon Esmonde Cleary

a.s.esmonde-cleary@bham.ac.uk

## 4.1. Introduction

Like the Roman god Janus, the west midlands region faces both ways in Roman Britain. It straddles the two archaeological provinces, the south and east with its archaeology of towns, villas, temples, burials, multitudinous artefacts, and the north and west with its forts, *vici* and 'native' settlements, and a low level of artefacts (Fig 4.1). As such, it is in many ways a microcosm of the province of Britannia as a whole. Therefore, how we interpret the Roman west midlands will need to draw on a wide range of approaches to the archaeology of the period, but if some sort of synthesis is achieved it may have wider relevance than just this region.

A 'traditional' resource assessment would in many ways read like a scaled-up excavation report, with sections on settlements and structures, various types of artefacts - coins and pottery first for their dating value, then metal objects ordered by value and aesthetic qualities, then stonework and finally the environmental evidence - reflecting the history of development of the specialisms and all too often their implicit ranking. There would also be discursive sections on relevant topics such as military aspects, towns and urbanism, villas and rural settlement, ritual and religion. Here, rather different approaches will be proposed and a different structure developed in order to try to put in place an assessment that both develops out of the regional database and also responds to current approaches to the archaeology of the Roman period. The need for this became clear from the seminars held as part of the process for producing the frameworks, which showed that the manifestations of the Roman period in the region were much more varied and complex than the 'old' categorisations allow for.

The first important approach is to realise that it is crucial to respond to the nature of the region and its database rather than seek to force it into schemes devised in other areas. The region does have one feature which largely unifies it and sets it apart from many other areas: it is resource-rich, not just in agricultural terms but also in minerals; the implications of this need to be thought through as we try to understand its Roman-period manifestations. Secondly, we are now in a position to understand that the discrepancies in the visibility of the Roman period across the landscape of the west midlands are the results of conscious and unconscious choices made in the past more than of the vagaries of modern recovery. Thus, any new attempt at a resource assessment must embody this variability at its core. Thirdly, the database is increasing not only in quantity but in range, for instance in the results of the Portable Antiquities Scheme for our understanding of artefact distribution across the region (cf Worrell 2005), or in the growing importance of the data from environmental and other specialisms.

Accordingly, it is proposed here that there are four major features of the Roman-period archaeology of the west midlands which can provide the framework for a different sort

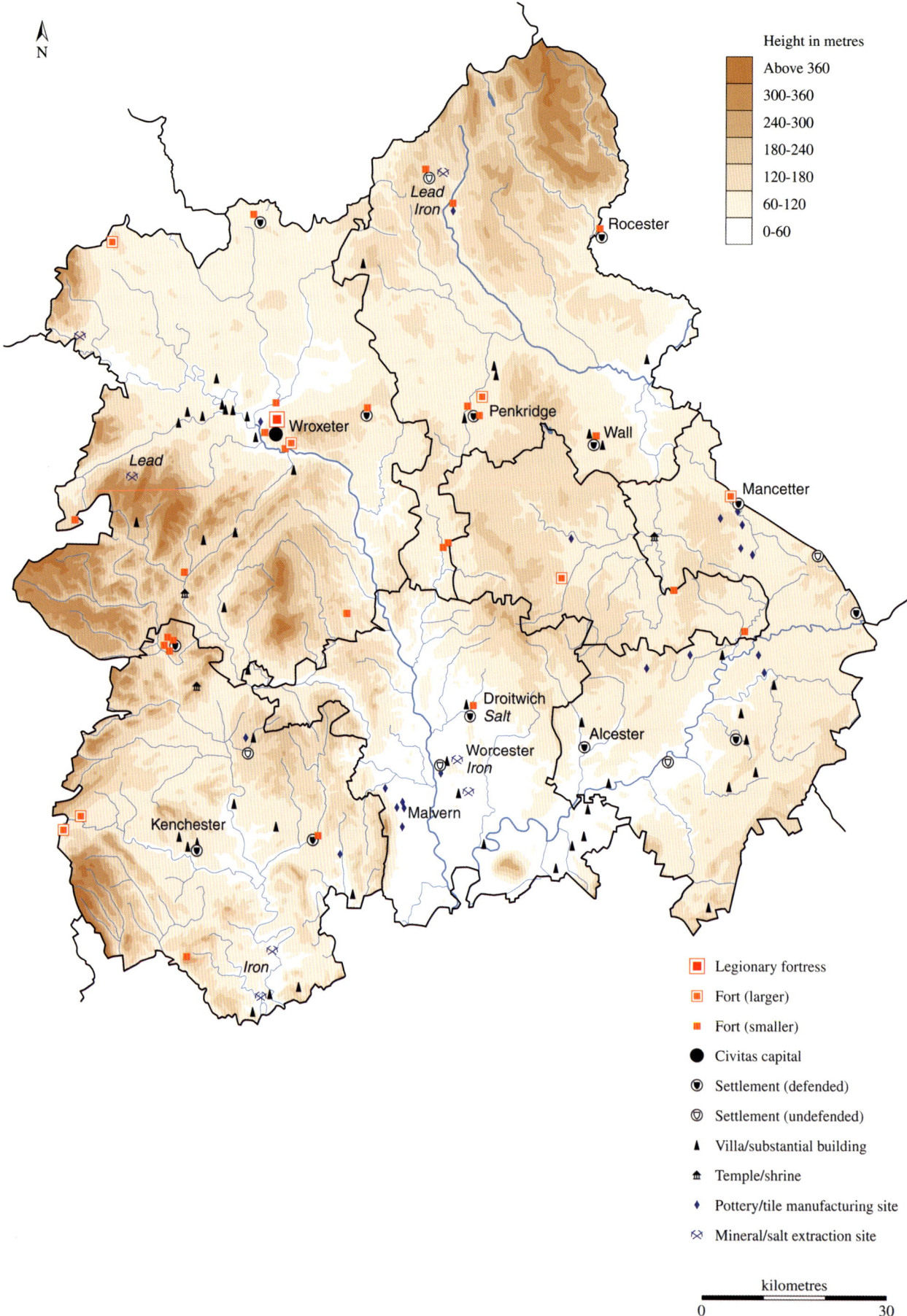

N

### Height in metres

- Above 360
- 300-360
- 240-300
- 180-240
- 120-180
- 60-120
- 0-60

*Lead*
*Iron*

Rocester

*Lead*

Wroxeter

Penkridge

Wall

Mancetter

Droitwich
*Salt*

Alcester

Worcester
*Iron*

Malvern

Kenchester

*Iron*

- ■ Legionary fortress
- ■ Fort (larger)
- ■ Fort (smaller)
- ● Civitas capital
- ◉ Settlement (defended)
- ◎ Settlement (undefended)
- ▲ Villa/substantial building
- ⛪ Temple/shrine
- ◆ Pottery/tile manufacturing site
- ⊠ Mineral/salt extraction site

kilometres

0            30

**Fig 4.1** Site distribution map of the west midlands in the Roman period

of resource assessment, an assessment which will not only seek to elucidate our existing knowledge of the archaeology of the region, but will also help set agendas and provide frameworks for the programming, execution and study of future work on the archaeology of this period. The four over-arching themes of this resource assessment are:

(i)    Resource Mobilisation.

(ii)   Assessing the Evidence.

(iii)  Assessing the Gaps.

(iv)   Tradition and Innovation.

It is to be hoped that the relevance of each of these is clear: the first responds to a defining feature of the region's Roman-period archaeology; the second to the existing and possible future strengths in the database; the third attacks a major problem both in the archaeology of the region for this period and in how we assess the evidence we do have; the fourth seeks to address these major differences while at the same time having more regard to chronological structure. One feature of all four is that they are designed to be essentially integrative, pulling together techniques and analyses from a variety of different materials and approaches not only to benefit from their insights but also to try to counteract any tendency to compartmentalisation. Thus within each of the three major themes are the various minor themes to articulate them. It is hoped that these themes will be of use to curators, contractors and consultants in the field, in order to justify, structure and deliver individual projects, so the themes do need to be ones which they find credible and practicable. This is the more so as most of them are not Romanists by training (still less inclination).

## 4.2. Resource mobilisation

One of the defining features of the archaeology of Roman Britain is the extent to which natural and human resources were exploited, especially compared with the preceding and succeeding periods. A result of this is the vast amount of physical evidence for the Roman period: settlements, buildings, artefacts. But over and above this it can be argued that the west midlands and surrounding areas were a zone where the extraction, processing and movement of natural resources, both mineral and agrarian, were of particular importance.

### 4.2.1. Minerals

The west midlands contain a variety of mineral resources. The most famous and unusual are the brine springs at Droitwich (cf Woodiwiss 1992). These were already a well-established resource by later prehistory, but excavation has shown a very considerable investment in extraction during the Roman period. Some sense of the volume and extent of the distribution of this salt in the earlier Roman period is given by the briquetage, though this still needs to be fully synthesised and published to give an impression of the range and scale of contact. Use of briquetage seems to be essentially a phenomenon of the first half of the Roman period, wooden containers perhaps taking over thereafter. A range of metals were systematically exploited. Argentiferous lead was won around Shelve in western Shropshire (cf Jones and Mattingly 1990, 186-8), though judging by practice elsewhere it was the silver content that yielded most value with the lead as a useful by-product. Iron was clearly a major resource. In the south-west of the region lies *Ariconium*/Weston-under-Penyard, apparently one of the principal centres of the huge iron-mining and -smelting area which extended south into the Forest of Dean. We understand painfully little about the mechanics, organisation and chronology of this industry: in itself it could form an important research objective. Iron-smelting was also a major concern in Worcester where there is evidence for activity on a large scale (Jackson 2004, 100-05). However, there is also the evidence for smaller-scale bloomeries at rural sites in the area; how are the two related? The Worcester iron centre also provokes questions about the source of the ore (whether the iron-fields in areas such as Staffordshire were exploited in the Roman period remains an open question) and about the destination of the product. The siting of Worcester suggests the use of the Severn, so perhaps the end-users of the iron were outside the region.

Mineral resources are an area where the modern administrative boundaries serve us ill. It has already been pointed out that *Ariconium* is only part of a much larger zone extending south out of the region. Just over the northern part of the boundary with Wales lies Llanymynech, probably an important source of copper. North of the region is the area around the legionary fortress at Chester, including sites such as the lead-workings at Pentre Farm, Halkyn and the salt-workings at Middlewich, Nantwich and Northwich. To what extent does the northern part of the west midlands region lie in the resource-procurement zone for Chester? North-east of this region is of course the major lead-mining area of the Peak District. Adding these sites to the west midlands *sensu stricto* gives one of, if not the, largest regions of mineral exploitation in Roman Britain. It is also worth noting the amount of stone quarrying which would have gone on in the region to provide for all the stone-built structures of the period. Much of this would have been small scale and transitory, called into being by the needs of individual projects and then extinguished. However, the requirements of major centres, Wroxeter above all, probably engendered longer-term complexes to exploit the various stones used in the public and private buildings. The south-eastern part of the region, lying near the good freestone of the Cotswolds, would also have been an area of quarrying.

Our evidence for the manufacture of objects in the region is relatively limited. The overwhelming bulk of the evidence is for pottery manufacture (cf Swan 1984), though even for this the evidence is not that great when compared with other regions. The best-investigated industry lies just inside the eastern border of the region at Mancetter-Hartshill, an industry particularly well-known for its widely-distributed mortaria and parchment wares, and operating from the turn of the 1st and 2nd centuries through to the end of the Roman period (cf Tyers 1996, 123-25). The other significant production was of the wares grouped under the appellation 'Severn Valley', originating south of our region and characterised principally by oxidised storage and drinking vessels (Timby 1990 for origins; cf Tyers 1996, 197-99). Unlike the Mancetter-Hartshill industry, this was not a tightly-grouped production centre but rather a series of smaller and larger-scale centres scattered across the region and associated with other productions such as the Malvernian kilns. A few other centres are known, such as the 2nd-century mortaria made at Wroxeter, whose distribution is markedly military and almost entirely outside our region (www.potsherd.uklinux.net/atlas/Ware/WXMO). Otherwise, penetration of the region by wares from other production centres is low, apart from the south-eastern zone in the Cotswold/Avon area. Reasons for the low take-up of pottery production and products over most of the region will be discussed below.

Pottery apart, there are isolated instances of manufacture such as brooches and glass at Wroxeter (Houghton and Ellis 2006) or the two-piece moulds for casting bronze fittings from Rocester (Ferris in Esmonde Cleary and Ferris 1996). Of course, wood-working and textiles would have far outstripped any other manufacture in the region both in terms of labour and of output; unfortunately almost none of the products survive, so we have no means of gauging their overall scale nor their impact on other areas of the economy such as agriculture (woodland management, sheep-rearing, dyestuffs).

The organisation of mining, quarrying and manufacture reflects types and levels of social organisation, so seeking to examine the organisation of these industries in the region is not just of interest in understanding them, it is also of wider interest in understanding the nature of the region's society. Traditionally, the winning of metals, particularly argentiferous lead, in Roman Britain has been seen as one of two systems. One was top-down, essentially created and staffed by the army in direct exploitation. The other sees smaller-scale operations by civilian lessees (franchise-holders) working the ores for the silver and lead on the state's behalf and making their percentage on the deal. A related debate has been in progress over the structure of pottery production, especially the large 'industries'. Were these organised top-down by entrepreneurs who articulated a number of specialists into a form of production line, a model drawn from the evidence for something of this sort in the Gaulish samian production centres? Or were they structured essentially by production site, and the 'industry' is the net aggregate of these individual enterprises?

In turn this relates to the often imprecise terms 'craft' and 'industry'. 'Craft' is seen as something essentially small scale (eg household) and low-tech, whereas 'industry' is centrally organised and profit-driven. However, is there such a neat division in pre-industrial societies? Is the activity long-term and year-round or, as has again been suggested for pottery production, sporadic and/or seasonal? Environmental evidence could be decisive in answering such a question. So it may be that attempting to unravel the structures, systems and cycles of the exploitation of mineral resources in the region could lead onto important insights into the structures of the society which undertook this work.

Another feature of these industries seems to be that across the Roman period there is little in the way of technological or other innovation (unlike, of course, later periods), reflecting one of the major perceived characteristics and weaknesses of the ancient world (cf Greene 1994). Innovation, or the lack of it, is a reflection of complex causalities. However, one regularly identified is the social matrix; are societies 'conservative' or 'traditionalist' and thus inimical to change, or do they allow for the dissent and experimentation that promote change? Can we approach closely enough the social structure and social ideology of the Romano-British west midlands to be able to tackle these big questions?

### 4.2.2. Agriculture

It is not possible to tackle here the whole field of arable and pastoral agriculture in the Roman west midlands. Instead, one can raise two questions which may be worthy of further research from a variety of angles. The first is a resource question. One of the most fundamental resources in the period was timber/wood: for construction, transport, furniture, weapons, tools, fuel; its availability was essential for all other activities. Additionally of course, it is not just a question of any old wood. Different purposes required different types of wood of different scantlings and ages, and these did not just become available without thought. Woodland and wood were a resource that had to be managed and planned for in the long term.

Our general picture of the southern half of Britain in the Roman period is of a land already largely deforested, indeed the north was also undergoing continuing deforestation. The English Heritage Environmental review notes that the south and east in particular may have carried even less woodland than they did in modern times. On the other hand, it also notes that one of the few coleoptera spectrums to indicate the presence of woodland is that from Stourport, and also that some of the wood from late Roman and early medieval water-logged contexts in the region suggest growth starting within the Roman period. This is in no way a basis for firm conclusions, but it does at least suggest an avenue for future research. Was the west midlands an area where timber was a major and managed resource, some of which was distributed outside the region to timber-poor areas? Clearly, a range of environmental evidence and techniques could address this problem as opportunity presented itself. Such a picture would of course accord well with the thesis developed above for the region as a net exporter of other raw materials. Woodland, of course, might help explain away some of the gaps in the settlement distribution maps: there really was no one there. The second feature of a comparison of the west midlands with areas further to the east and south is the apparent low take-up of introduced plant and tree species in this region. The picture overall seems to be one of a mixed agrarian regime, concentrating on the staple crop of spelt wheat and the standard livestock of cattle, sheep and pigs.

One way of reading this might again be in the light of the region as a resource-procurement zone. These are precisely the resources needed by the Roman army, certainly in the first two centuries or so of the province, maybe also later, to feed, clothe and equip its troops. With the forts of Wales to the west and Chester and the garrisons of the north-west, were the requirements of military supply constraining the agriculture of the region? They are the recipients of much of the output of the Wroxeter mortaria production (see above) and, as so often, pottery may be standing as a proxy for the transport of bulk supplies such as grain. Indeed, much of the west midlands might be seen as the southern end of a military-dominated super-region encompassing the north-west all the way up to Hadrian's Wall. The long-distance distribution of Severn valley ware as far as Hadrian's Wall could be, as with other industries such as that at Colchester (Peacock 1982, 102), an archaeologically-visible proxy for long-distance movement of bulk supplies. If substantial value was being removed from the region, this may be part of the explanation as to why the more costly forms of investment in Roman-style buildings and objects was limited. Or, to reprise another theme, are we seeing the effects of a 'conservative' or 'traditionalist' social organisation and ideology, which had little or no place for widespread integration of these novelties into the existing regime?

### 4.2.3. Military involvement

Military archaeology was a major focus of investigation in the region in the 1960s and 1970s under the leadership of Graham Webster. The central concern then was the identification of military sites of the conquest and consolidation (usually through aerial photography cf Frere and St Joseph 1983, Pt.2); these were then trenched to recover dating material in order to assimilate the site to a narrative of the conquest structured by individual governorships (cf Webster 1981). As a result, the region is now a *locus classicus* for the study of the temporary fortification or 'marching camp' (Welfare and Swan 1995). However, the wider enterprise fell into disfavour because of increasing reservations over the idea of using the patchy historical sources to constrain the archaeology, and because of increasing doubts over the possibility of coins and samian being able to yield the sufficiently precise dates required.

Mention of the possibility that the resource mobilisation of and from the region is influenced by military dictates raises the question of whether there is evidence for this. There is a small but significant group of sites and material which may provide a partial answer. The Bays Meadow villa at Droitwich is unique in Britain for its defences. This has long been hypothesised as some sort of official establishment for overseeing the saltworks, in which case these would be some form of imperial monopoly or resource. It has more recently been proposed that the establishment was a *mansio* of the *cursus publicus* (Hurst 2006, 239-41). In a way, this does not affect the argument, since evidence from the wider empire suggests that *mansiones* also acted as sites for resource extraction. So what of other *mansiones* in the region such as *Tripontium* and Wall? Is it significant that the latter were also the sites in the late empire of two of the *burgi* along Watling Street, which have also been proposed as sites for the extraction and/or protection of matériel in transit (cf Gould 1999)? For the same time-frame, there is the large granary or store-building at Coulter's Garage/Gateway Supermarket, Alcester also suggested to be in some way official (Cracknell 1996, 4-41). This was demolished to make way for the town defences; such 'small' town defences may also have been to do with safeguarding installations, personnel or matériel of interest to the late Roman state.

Many towns and other sites in the region have yielded military equipment and fittings of the early or late empire. Traditionally the early ones have been explained away as residual from underlying conquest-period forts. More recently, both early and late material has been accounted for by soldiers in transit. But the surviving documentation from the Roman army (including the Vindolanda tablets) shows clearly that troops were regularly posted to 'civilian' areas in order to secure supplies and commissariat, both under the early empire and with the late empire's increasingly oppressive methods of securing its own existence. In general, a case can be made for the mobilisation of resources being a, perhaps the, defining feature of the archaeology of the Roman period in the west midlands. It may also be that many of the resources were then exported from the region, in particular to supply and service the long-term military garrisons to the west and north of the region.

## 4.3. Assessing the evidence

It was noted above that the traditional site categories (fort, town, villa…) have served us well enough as a means of ordering emerging data; to continue to depend on them risks perpetuating their epistemological weakness, which is that they impose a divisive rather than an integrative approach, more concerned with cataloguing than with articulating the classes of information. Our understanding of the region should benefit from structuring the evidence according to new themes, ones which necessarily involve combining evidence from more than one of the traditional categories. This would also have the advantage that such approaches can be applied to the existing database as well as contributing to the analysis of future work both on-site and off-site. Here it is proposed that the major themes should be Identity and Community and Ritual and Religion, and in each case the relevance of these will be illustrated through reference to examples from the Roman-period archaeology of the west midlands.

### 4.3.1. Identity and community

Identity has become a central concern of archaeologists of the Roman period, subsuming and building on previous concerns with 'Romanisation' (cf Millett 1990). This sought to explain the visible changes in the archaeological record consequent upon assimilation into the Roman empire in terms of the degree of adaptation to Roman ways by indigenous peoples, and was long the implicit agenda in the west midlands. It has been criticised as a linear and teleological view of the past, and it is now preferred to regard 'Roman-ness' as one of a suite of possible ways in which people constructed and expressed their identities, alongside other factors such as age, gender, status, and membership of communities. Identity of course works at various levels: the individual; the family; the kin or 'tribe'; the functional community; the 'people', though all these, of course, overlap and an individual can have multiple identities depending on context – 'situational identity'. All can be expressed through a variety of different types of material evidence. This therefore gives us the opportunity to approach the 'visible' archaeology of the south and east of the region through a new series of themes, each of which allows different types of evidence to be exploited. Here a series of 'levels' will be outlined, ranging from the general of ethnic and cultural identity down to the particular of the construction of the individual's identity.

#### *Ethnicity and cultural identity*

The identification of 'incomer' and 'indigenous' has been one of the central questions of the study of Roman Britain, particularly at its beginning and its end. Likewise, the cultural changes wrought by these incomers and their cultural impact are central to the study of the period. For the earlier part of the Roman period, it is cultural rather than ethnic identity which is the central concern; ethnic identity is usually seen as bound up with the army and its largely Mediterranean-derived legionaries and provincial auxiliaries. Though they would have had a considerable short-term impact on the region, subsequent changes in the archaeological record are investigated through changes in cultural frameworks rather than ethnic identities. At the other end of the Roman period, of course, the emphasis is reversed; the question of ethnicity is central, with identification of 'Germanic' or 'British' ethnicity long seen as the key, with cultural markers an epiphenomenon of those ethnicities.

In the west midlands it is the south-eastern zone which exhibits most clearly the impact of Roman-style cultural markers, through relatively well-known 'small towns' such as Alcester (cf Mahany 1994; Cracknell and Mahany 1994; Cracknell 1996; Booth and Evans 2002), Droitwich (Woodiwiss 1992; Hurst 2006), Kenchester (Wilmott 1980), Rocester (Esmonde Cleary and Ferris 1996), Wall (Gould 1964; Round 1992) or Whitchurch (Jones and Webster 1969). Other such sites are less well understood, such as Blackwardine (Brown 1990) or Chesterton-on-Fosse (cf Booth 1996, 37). Problems of definition between 'urban' and 'rural' are exemplified by sites such as Tiddington (Palmer 1982; Biddulph 2005). It is the same south-eastern zone that has produced many of the villas from the region and it is the zone where coins, pottery and other artefacts are found in relative abundance. In sum, this Cotswold/Avon zone is properly part of the wider culture-province of the south and east of Roman Britain and betokens the uptake by some of the population of the economic and cultural innovations available consequent upon the incorporation of the island into the Roman empire. It is not, though, seen as betokening any major change in ethnic composition of the population. The chronology of these changes is as yet poorly understood, but as elsewhere the turn of the 1st and 2nd centuries seems to mark a major threshold of innovation, developing through the 2nd and into the early 3rd centuries, with the later 3rd and 4th centuries marking something of a change in urban, villa, religious and funerary patterns.

Interestingly, it is the same zone which at and after the collapse of Roman rule in the early 5th century shows further change, in particular with the disuse and disappearance of Roman-style settlements, structure, artefacts and technologies and with the appearance of 'Germanic' material, above all the artefacts and pottery present in certain burial sites (Ford 1996; 2003). Here the dominant interpretation has been in terms of changing ethnicity, the arrival of Anglo-Saxon incomers, rather than of cultural adaptation, though this is beginning to change.

### Burial and identity

When assessing the composition of the archaeology of the region in general and the south-eastern zone in particular, it is worth pointing out that there is one major site-type about which we know little, to our loss: burials and cemeteries. These certainly existed at urban sites such as Alcester (also Wroxeter in the north-western zone) and the rural site at Wasperton, though their presence elsewhere is more open to question, perhaps explaining their poor showing in the literature. The osteological and artefactual analysis of burials for information on age, gender, status, way of life and cause of death is well-established and could make major contributions to studies of individual and group identity. But even more promising are rapidly-developing techniques of mtDNA and stable-isotope analysis, which could have a huge amount to say about the areas of origin of individuals and thus their 'ethnic' identity. This would be particularly important for the identification of incomers in the early Roman period, but also at the end of that period where ethnic identity was crucial both at the time and to modern study of the period.

The potential to distinguish between indigenous and incomer from the 4th century onwards would be critical in assessing the transition from the Roman west midlands to the Anglo-Saxon kingdom of Mercia. To what extent was this a matter of the imposition of an alien culture or of the assimilation of that culture by the indigenous population (as had happened throughout the Roman period)? The cemetery of Wasperton (Crawford 1982; 1983) has already been proposed as a type-site for the indigenous assimilation model on the basis of its artefacts and burial rites, and the cemetery at Stretton-on-Fosse (Warws) (Ford 2003) may be another case in point. Stable-isotope analysis from such sites should be far more definitive.

The above can only be a brief 'taster' of how realigning our categories of interpretation can refocus our perceptions of many aspects of the more visible archaeology of the Romano-British period in the region, but it should be sufficient to show the value of such an exercise both for interrogating the existing database and for devising future fieldwork and research.

### Community

Membership of functional communities can also be visible in the archaeological record. A very obvious one for Roman Britain is the army. Though the direct military occupation of this region was relatively brief, the west midlands were, as has been seen, in all probability affected by the longer-term garrisons in Wales and from Chester northwards. The discussion of the Roman army as a 'community' has recently moved forwards rapidly (cf James 1999; 2001); this was not just the community of the serving soldiers themselves but also all their servants and slaves, their wives and children and the traders and others who earned their living from supplying the army. Such approaches allow a more balanced appreciation of the impact of the early military occupation in general and of particular important sites such as the fortress at Wroxeter, for they do not confine themselves within the defences. The military are, of course, one of the most archaeologically visible and distinctive groups in the landscape of Roman Britain as regards settlement-, building- and artefact-types, thus giving rise to the traditions discussed above of writing a form of military history. However, questions over the relationship of military and civilian and the assumption of an essentially male military world are increasingly being raised, so evidence for the presence of women, children, grooms and slaves inside the forts needs to be assessed. What of the presence of 'feminine' items of apparel or of child-sized items such as shoes within a fortress such as Wroxeter? How does this change our reading of such sites?

The possible longer-term military impact on the region through resource procurement was outlined above. However, as well as grain and quadrupeds such as sheep, pig, goat and horses, what of bipeds? How did the Roman army's need for manpower impact on the region; did men and women leave the region? There is the evidence for a cohort of Cornovii at Newcastle-upon-Tyne in the later Roman period (*Not. Dig. Occ.* XL), or there is the tombstone of a Cornovian woman married to a soldier serving at Ilkley (RIB 639). In return, the men in garrison at Chester or in the Welsh forts may have had a considerable input into the demography of parts of the region. Also, it was argued above that the presence of items of military equipment at towns and other sites in the region might relate to the presence of military personnel in these 'civil' areas in the longer term, perhaps to do with resource procurement, perhaps representing veterans?

### Buildings and the household

At the level of the family, there is another type of evidence which is starting to produce useful discussion: house-plans. Considerable work on the houses of Pompeii has opened up a number of models for discussion which might usefully be applied to the house-plans of Roman Britain (cf Wallace-Hadrill 1994). The Pompeian evidence suggests that the major criterion conditioning the patterning of these houses was access along a public to private axis; how far one was allowed to penetrate was a function of one's status vis-à-vis the head of the household? Curiously, gender and age were much less visible in these houses, with no identifiable women's quarters or nursery areas. Slave and service areas were, though, visible, reinforcing the importance of status as a determinant of layout. Such analyses of the surviving building plans from urban sites such as Alcester, Kenchester and Wroxeter and the villa sites of the region, could be most revealing. On the other hand, Smith (1978; 1997) has proposed an alternative scheme whereby building layout is patterned by kin relationships, his multiple occupancy model. Romano-British houses do not have to conform absolutely to a set pattern, indeed variation may be very revealing of peculiarly British concerns; for instance, it may be that criteria such as age and gender are more visible in Britain than in Italy. These sorts of analysis may of course be extended to the study of settlement layouts, both at the smaller scale such as 'farmsteads', but even up to the 'landscapes' of towns, at all of which functional and other zonings may be discernible.

### Artefacts and the individual

For the individual, the most archaeologically visible statement of identity is dress, which betokens to the viewer age, gender, status, and membership of wider communities (eg the military or a particular ethnic or social grouping). The Roman period is of course rich in dress accoutrements, particularly brooches, belt-fittings and items such as pins, widely distributed on occupation sites in the south-eastern part of the region. Recently, the study of such material has been advancing considerably through theoretically informed questions being put to the rich database (eg Crummy and Eckardt 2003). As yet, this region has not benefited much from such approaches, though the south-eastern zone appears on the edge of some recent distribution maps, showing the potential of this type of study for the area. The evidence for brooch manufacture from Wroxeter does give particular types where the distribution of the finished product could yield important information on the extent of contacts from the town and allow questions to be put over the mechanisms of distribution; trade? group identity?

### Diet and definition

One of the ways in which the Roman military community was distinctive in the earlier Roman period was in its diet (cf Grant 2004). This is of course only part of a wider topic of the ways in which the types, preparation and consumption of food is used to define people's self-definition as part of groups or peoples ('foodways'). There has been some work on the 'Romanisation' of diet through the introduction of new crops, herbs, beverages, butchery practices, and in the preparation and consumption of food and drink, including changes in the related pottery and other vessels. The English Heritage environmental reviews for the region suggest that in fact it was one in which there were few introductions of new foodstuffs, but on the other hand the evidence of pottery and metalware suggests that in the south-eastern zone at least the ways in which food was consumed changed markedly, with the Roman period characterised by vessels for the individual preparation and consumption of food and drink. The osteological evidence for changing preferences in the Roman period away from sheep towards cattle is visible also in the west midlands, though the butchery evidence is so far scarce and remains to be synthesised in detail.

### 4.3.2. Ritual and religion

The west midlands is a region poorly endowed with the sorts of evidence traditionally used to structure consideration of religion in Roman Britain, principally temples (to locate where worship took place) and inscriptions (to show what sorts of deities were being worshipped). A roughly classical temple is known from Wroxeter (Bushe-Fox 1914) and a very probable 'Romano-Celtic' one from aerial survey at Kenchester (Wilmott 1980), and others will have existed at 'small towns' such as Alcester and Droitwich. In the rural areas there is the temple complex at Coleshill (Magilton 2006), a probable temple known from aerial photography near Craven Arms, the very different evidence from Croft Ambrey (Stanford 1974, 131-55) and the carvings from Wall (Henig 2004, 51-3). Apart from the small group of inscriptions from Wroxeter (mainly military tombstones) the region is essentially anepigraphic. However, the recent work at Orton's Pasture, Rocester, has identified what is most probably a ritual or religious site (Ferris et al 2000), albeit one lacking the traditional appurtenances of temple structure or inscription. This identification was made possible by the recent development of alternative ways of identifying ritual or religious behaviour and the continuing development of new ways of thinking about religion.

This has again been much influenced by developments in prehistory, particularly the realisation that much deposit formation and associated presence of artefacts at Iron Age sites was not solely functional or random rubbish, but the product of processes of 'structured deposition'. Particular types of 'special' deposits have long been recognised in Romano-British archaeology, most obviously burial, but also deposition of objects at temples or in temple precincts, and also the burial of hoards of coin and plate (though these have tended to be analysed more for their contents than their contexts). However, what is becoming clear is that there is a variety of Roman-period contexts where the deposition of material is clearly not random or rubbish. Contexts such as pits and wells, where the backfills have clearly taken place over time, and with the inclusion of objects and of animal and human remains in significant associations, are a good example of this. For instance, the presence of altars and other material in the backfill of wells in the extra-mural areas of Alcester strongly suggests this sort of practice (Mahany 1994, 113, 144). Roman period pits at Wasperton contained unusual deposits, including in one instance a stone inscribed FELICITER associated with two sets of antlers (Crawford 1981, 124). Ditches also, particularly boundary ditches, are now recognised as places for unusual deposits such as human burials, for instance at Tiddington (Palmer 1982) or the household deity from Berwick Alkmund Park (White and Gaffney 2003). The list could be multiplied, but what is important is that such locations are now recognised. It is also becoming important to be more attentive to the artefactual and other material from such locations, for instance finds of human bone, traditionally either ignored or assumed to be from disturbed formal burials, but now increasingly realised to be purposive (cf Esmonde Cleary 2000).

If the phenomenon of the structured deposition of selected artefactual and other material is now more widely recognised, how is it to be interpreted? The approach to these deposits has often been spatial, looking at them in relationship both to the features in which they are contained and these features in relationship to the site as a whole or in part. Spatial analysis tends to lead to cosmological interpretations, trying to use these features as a guide to how their creators divided up and assembled the world around them. It can also reveal structures of binary opposition by place (inside/outside), but also by criteria such as gender and possibly age, suggesting that it may be possible to approach other religious themes such as rites of passage. Furthermore, the artefacts and other material represented in these deposits are often also present in formal human burials and cemeteries, arguing that we are looking at a suite of ritual activities across a wide range of religious contexts.

It should be clear that all major types of evidence – settlement, structural, ritual, funerary, artefactual and environmental – have their contribution to make to these over-arching themes (as well as to others such as Resource Mobilisation and Tradition and Innovation). Furthermore, the themes entail the use of suites of evidence from across the major types in new ways and combinations, thereby increasing the range and sophistication of the analyses and militating against continuing to run in the same well-established ruts.

## 4.4. Assessing the gaps

Our knowledge of the archaeology of much of the west midlands region remains patchy and, consequently, our understanding even more so. The characteristic definition of this zone is in negative terms; it lacks the sorts of archaeological evidence which characterises the civil archaeology of the south and east of Britain. Wroxeter is the only major town, and has of course been the focus of large-scale excavations over the last century (cf White and Barker 1998, ch 1), with more recent geophysical surveys filling out remarkably our picture of activity within the defences (Gaffney and Gaffney 2000). Kenchester is the only 'small town' which conforms with those seen further south and east, indeed it is a classic example of the type (Wilmott 1980). Otherwise, putative 'small towns' such as Blackwardine and Leintwardine remain poorly characterised. Wroxeter (in particular) and Kenchester each have a group of satellite villas, with Acton Scott, Whitley Grange and Yarchester among the better-known near Wroxeter and Magna Farm and New Weir near Kenchester, but these apart, this type of rural settlement is generally absent. So also is any settlement that looks like the 'villages' to be found in parts of the south and east (cf Hingley 1989, ch 6). Largely absent too are temples and shrines of 'Romano-Celtic' type (apart from a probable 'Romano-Celtic' temple near Craven Arms), as too, by and large, are burials (cf Philpott 1991, *passim*). Artefacts too are thin on the ground, be it from settlement sites or more generally in the landscape with, for instance, very few coin hoards from the area. The Portable Antiquities Scheme is beginning to add some dots to the distribution maps for counties such as Herefordshire and Shropshire (eg Worrell 2005), but these remain few relative to other areas of Roman Britain. It is important not to over-schematise the differences; there is a penetration of Roman-style markers into this zone, but only patchily as regards both the type of evidence and its geographical distribution, so the type and distribution of this material need further definition and explanation.

Interpretatively, such a region was all too often either largely ignored in favour of the more archaeologically visible regions of the south and east and the military north; or else it was written off as a 'failure' because it did not evince the assimilation to Roman-style

**Fig 4.2** Statements through the extent and complexity of settlement earthworks: Chirbury (Salop)

practice implicitly assumed to be the goal of any self-respecting provincial (the élite, at least), remaining at a 'peasant' or 'prehistoric' cultural level. Another approach, which may still have some validity, was to interpret the difference in terms of what little is known of the political geography of Roman Britain, with the south-eastern zone belonging to the civitas of the Dobunni and the north-western to that of the Cornovii. The 'fit' is, of course, not exact, with Kenchester belonging to the Dobunni despite the low level of Roman-style archaeology in this area.

However, as will be seen below in the Tradition and Innovation discussion, there is much more to it than that. This essentially negative characterisation restricts our understanding, so the zone needs to be characterised in more positive terms which reflect what is there, rather than what is not.

What we are left with is essentially a series of landscape areas archaeologically characterised either by enclosed (Fig 4.2) or unenclosed settlements and by field-systems, or by a lack of anthropogenic features. As a result of survey projects such as that by the RCHM(E) (Whimster 1989), the Wroxeter Hinterland survey (Gaffney and White 2007) or the Marches Upland Survey all depending heavily on aerial photographic data, there is now a considerable body of systematised data to be drawn on. These can be supplemented by the county period assessments drawn up as part of the present Research Framework exercise (White in prep). One avenue of approach might be to define a number of areas within the broader zone on the basis of physiographical characteristics – elevation, drainage, solid geology, drift geology – creating essentially a number of areas of differing agricultural potential (arable, pastoral, forestry). This would define relatively small-scale landscape blocs (what the French might call *pays*) susceptible to individual analysis in terms of their natural resources, and onto this the map of human activity could be overlaid. Some of these landscape blocs would also be susceptible to current techniques of landscape analysis through GIS, as has been tested in the Wroxeter Hinterlands Project, or to phenomenological approaches for highly distinctive blocs such as the Stiperstones.

Essentially, discussions have had to be based on morphological characteristics of the settlements located by aerial photography (size, shape). These have shown that there is a small number of general correlations that can be made: rectilinear enclosures are more common in the eastern part of the zone than the western; larger and more elaborate enclosures (eg multivallate) tend to be more common in the river valleys than on the surrounding uplands; so also do unenclosed settlements, rare outside the valleys. There would therefore seem to be a broad distinction between the major river valleys such as the Severn and the Lugg and their adjacent uplands. It must be emphasised that these are trends, not hard-and-fast divisions. Unfortunately, due to the paucity of excavation at these sites, it is at present not possible to understand the variations and explain the reasons for them, or instance whether they are related to factors such as date, status, agricultural regime or social structure (cf Wickham 2005, for an illuminating discussion of a predominantly pastoral society in early medieval Ireland, its social formations and its archaeological manifestations). Nevertheless, it is clear that the broad zone of the north and west of the region is susceptible to being broken down into these smaller areas or blocs.

In broad terms also, it would seem to be the case that the relatively thin and poor soils of much of the upland meant that these areas were much more suited to pastoralism than to arable agriculture. The latter, of course, could be carried out profitably on the richer soils of the river basins, perhaps accounting in part for the observable differences in settlement morphology and for the presence in these areas of evidence for field-systems and other patterns of enclosure. Indeed the two might have been intimately linked in patterns of seasonal short-range transhumance, so even parts of the lowland landscape might have pastoral elements alongside arable. It has been argued for instance (White and Gaffney 2003, 223) that the pattern of enclosures visible in the immediate vicinity of Wroxeter is better linked with cattle rearing than with crop cultivation. The landscape of the north and west of the region may therefore have been one dominated by pastoralism. Given the demands of the long-term garrisons of the Roman army just outside the region for leather, wool, meat and bone, pastoralism might well have been the 'rational' response to the landscape. It may also be that some of the areas currently devoid of settlement or field-systems really are 'blanks', having been areas of managed woodland, responding to the military and other demands discussed above.

The north and west of the region is a zone likely to remain difficult to understand until such time as a great deal more fieldwork, particularly extensive excavation with particular emphasis on the recovery of environmental data, has been undertaken. This is particularly evident in the difficulty of tracking change through time at the level above the individual site; this may relate to the suggestion made below of a traditionalist society where change happened over the longer rather than the shorter term. Nevertheless, even at present it is possible to see the overall outlines of a system by which this much more problematic database can be interrogated. It is also worth remembering that even in the south and east of the region there are extensive areas where the archaeology is of 'farmsteads', field- and enclosure-systems and apparent 'blanks', reminiscent of the north and west, so even there we must not allow our vision of the archaeology to be dominated solely by the highly visible towns and villas.

## 4.5. Tradition and innovation

The division of the archaeology of the west midlands into the two broad zones of the south and the east and the north and the west is one which of course is an expression of deeper social and ideological structures. In order to approach these and thus to try to explain, at least in part, the divergences in the archaeology, this section of the discussion will address explicitly a theme already touched upon: tradition and innovation. In broad terms it could be said the south and the east exhibit more innovation in their archaeology because of the adoption of a range of settlement and artefact types derived from provincial Roman practice, whereas the north and the west are more traditional in eschewing such developments. However, tradition and innovation should not be taken as proxies for inertia and for progress, this would be too simple. Each is the result of a series of positive choices rooted in the social and ideological structures and it must be our task here to try to unravel and understand these structures. Therefore, this section will also be the most explicitly chronological. The discussions above have tended to be a-historical in the sense of presenting the evidence undifferentiated by date; here the time-line will be much more important. This also means that it is this section which will allow us more easily to address the questions of how the Romano-British archaeology relates to what immediately preceded and succeeded it – late prehistory and the early Middle Ages. It is proposed here to start by considering the 'traditional' areas of the north and the west of the region. In part this is to get away from the assumption that it is change ('Romanisation') that is the more interesting; in part it is because it might well be easier to describe and understand innovation if we have an understanding of the base-situation out of which it develops and with which it is to be contrasted.

The extreme shortage of 'Roman' settlement-, structure- and artefact-types, as well as of evidence for religious practice and burial in this zone is striking. Comparison with the medieval period reveals the potential wealth of the zone, so the explanation is not determined by environmental or other natural factors; it must be anthropogenic, the results of explicit or implicit human choices. The reasons for the lack of uptake of Roman-style material culture have been the subject of considerable debate in the last decade or so (eg Metzler et al 1995; Webster and Cooper 1996; Mattingly 1997; Mattingly 2004), provocatively summarised by Whittaker (1997, 145) as 'If received enthusiastically, the process is called 'Romanization'; if less so, 'resistance''. 'Resistance' has enjoyed a certain vogue as a supposed explanation, but it is, of course, a term currently implying a strong political agenda; it is also problematic in that it is essentially negative in its construction of motivation. 'Resistance' is in fact not only a reaction against something, more importantly perhaps it is a statement in favour of something else, most often the status quo ante. If we can characterise the grounds for the people of much of the Romano-British west midlands to prefer to retain the established order of things, then not only may this explain (away) 'resistance', more helpfully it may aid in establishing further ways of understanding and interrogating the existing archaeological record and thus of formulating future fieldwork and research.

A useful comparison and point of entry for a different understanding of what was (not) taking place in the region in this period is afforded by arguments arising out of the situation in the Netherlands, encompassing essentially the Roman province of Germania Inferior. There in the Roman period there was a similar situation to that found in Roman Britain – a heavily militarised frontier zone full of military installations and personnel co-existing with an immediate hinterland with few visible signs of 'Romanisation', then further to the south in the province of Gallia Belgica a 'Romanised' landscape of towns, villas, temples etc. Rather than polar oppositions of 'Romanisation' and 'resistance', Dutch workers have proposed an explanation more grounded in the nature of the archaeology of the pre-Roman and Roman periods. It is argued (for a clear and convenient summary see Roymans 1996) that in the Late Iron Age economic and social worth (particularly for adult males) was grounded in cattle and warfare, because of the particular environmental conditions of the lower Rhine and the delta. This created a very particular ideology of society and of male values. Religious and ritual practice were also heavily conditioned by these factors, further reinforcing the ideological structures of the society. These were all reflected in the archaeology of settlements, building and deposition.

After the Roman conquest, the martial ideals could be perpetuated through service in the Roman army, and indeed the province yielded an exceptional number of auxiliary units for such a small area, particularly the multiple cohorts of Batavians. But on the other hand, the economic, social and ideological/religious formations promoted by the centrality of cattle and pastoralism meshed poorly with 'Roman' social and ideological/religious practice, not necessarily through antipathy or resistance, but simply because these made little or no sense in the existing structures. Thus, the hinterland of the Germania Inferior remained notably un-Romanised. Interestingly, even all the men who had served in the Roman army and had adopted Roman military identities become largely invisible when they retire and return home, resuming their 'indigenous' identities. It is only further south, in the grainlands of Gallia Belgica, that Roman-style practices took root.

The moral of this for the west midlands is clear and instructive. If the north and west of the region (the lands of the Cornovii?) is one where pastoralism was an important (the dominant?) agrarian mode, then we may be looking at a similar situation. The late prehistoric archaeology of the zone is even more fugitive than the Roman-period, but it may be that the importance of pastoralism was pronounced, and the presence of all those hillforts suggests that warfare (however ritualised) may have been a significant activity. If so, then we may hypothesise along the lines proposed for Germania Inferior. The theatre of warfare may have been transferred to the Roman army, not so much in the short term of the conquest, but in the longer term as the units in garrison in Britain increasingly turned to local recruitment. Thus, we may have an aristocracy for the north and west of our region (peoples such as the Cornovii), it is just that we have been looking for it in the wrong place. Instead of looking for it only within the region at sites such as Wroxeter, we should perhaps be looking to Chester, to Wales and to the military north and for its expression in the form of the Roman army. If these men retired back to their homeland, then it may be that like the Batavians in Germania Inferior, they resumed their indigenous identity rather than perpetuating their Roman military identity; the presence of a military discharge certificate ('diploma') at Wroxeter is interesting in this regard. So here we may have another aspect of the west midlands as a resource-procurement zone, as a recruiting-ground for the Roman army. However, this may have had further demographic and social impacts on the region by removing from it many of its most innovative young men, thus helping perpetuate the status quo. It may also explain why at least one Cornovian woman, commemorated at Ilkley, left her homeland for a husband.

But for those who stayed at home, the Dutch analysis may also offer a model to help explain the archaeological evidence of this north-western zone. The population of the zone remained attached not only to the largely pastoralist economic basis of their life as developed in later prehistory, but also to the social and ideological structures founded upon that basis. So, when they came in contact with Roman concepts and material, these were essentially alien to them and had little meaning or value within their frame of reference; as a result they by-and-large did not adopt them, or adopted only specific elements which they found useful/meaningful. A specific instance of this may be the site at Whitley Grange where the architecture and values of the 'villa' and of Roman-style bathing and dining were adopted (all markers of aristocratic status in the wider Roman world), but pottery by contrast was not significant (only 325 sherds). Such a model allows us to forge a possible understanding of the rationales which lay behind the near-total absence of Roman-style material culture over much of the region. Moreover, it allows us to do this through an appreciation of the particular nature and consequences of the zone's archaeology rather than through the imposition onto it of teleological categories such as 'Romanisation' or 'resistance'. What is more, 'tradition' is not a default position arrived at through inertia, it is rather a positive choice and one which, moreover, has continuously to be redefined and restated. This may mean that there is observable change over time, not stagnation, as successive generations redefine 'tradition'.

If the argument proposed above has merit for the zone of the region which we have characterised as 'traditional', what contribution can this make to an understanding of the motives for and expressions of the 'innovative'? Again, the nature of the Late Iron Age evidence of the south and east of the region will be crucial for an understanding of what follows. Are there observable differences in the environmental evidence for economic basis (e.g. arable rather than pastoral) or for the social structures of the zone and consequently in the patterns of settlement and of artefact use and deposition? If so, then this may have been a zone more open to the adoption of innovative practice consequent upon the arrival of Roman-style practices. Clearly, in gross terms this was a zone which in the Roman period did refashion its ideologies, allowing features such as towns, villas and objects to become widely diffused as meaningful signifiers of identity. There is one medium which may allow us to detect and calibrate such changes (or lack of them) not only in the south-eastern zone, but across the whole region more widely. This is the most prolific of all Romano-British goods and one which has so far been (curiously) absent from this discussion: pottery.

### Pottery and cultural change

In the west midlands, as elsewhere in Roman Britain, the principal use of pottery has for a long time been for dating, and this use will undoubtedly and rightly continue.

**Fig 4.3** The impact of Rome: the Roman road from Wroxeter to Leintwardine framed in upland and lowland landscapes.

Nonetheless, it is two other features of pottery that must concern us here: overall distribution and trade. The huge variability over the region in the incidence of pottery in general and of fabrics and of functional types in particular, is of course one of the most noticeable and characteristic features of Roman-period archaeology. For example, two comparable projects, the Arrow valley pipeline in Warwickshire (Palmer 2000) and the M6 Toll motorway in Staffordshire, both produced linear transects across the landscape and a range of settlements and other indications of human activity. However, the disparity in the quantity and range of pottery between the two projects was remarkable, and when the latter is published it should be possible to make precise comparisons. Additionally, clearly it should be possible on present data to produce distributions which can be manipulated (eg by trend surface analysis) to show the extent of the south-eastern zone with strong presences of ceramics and equally importantly the fall-off line between that zone and the north-western one. Beyond this there would of course be islands of pottery use such as early military bases at Mancetter and Wroxeter or later towns at Kenchester and Wroxeter, but this would again emphasise the exceptional nature of such ceramic islands in a sea of general indifference.

As well as gross presence/absence patterns, the distributions of wares from particular production centres should also be revealing. It was noted for Rocester, for instance (Esmonde Cleary and Ferris 1996), that its ceramic relations lay to the east and south (Derbyshire, Mancetter products) rather than the west (Severn Valley wares), suggesting different zones of economic and/or social interaction characterised by the variations in the ceramic assemblage. However, pottery as a commodity transported over longer or shorter distances can stand as a proxy for the distribution of other things. The presence of Severn Valley wares on Hadrian's Wall is probably a proxy for the long distance transport of grain or other matériel from the west midlands to the military north, and we have also noted the distribution of 2nd-century Wroxeter mortaria largely to military sites. It could also be argued that the movement of pottery stands as a proxy for the movement of ideas and information. The very long distance movement of samian, the regional distributions of major fine wares, and the more local distributions of coarse wares could indicate the penetration not only of goods but also of ideas, and their distribution within the west midlands shows the areas more open to such interaction and those to which it was not a matter of importance (cf. Peacock 1982). The tradition of study of Romano-British pottery for chronology would mean that variations in these patterns would be at once apparent. Another approach is through the spatial distribution of functional types. In particular, which vessel types do manage to penetrate into the north and west of the region and when? Do these types tell us about aspects of Roman-style practices making some headway in the region, in domains such as the storage, preparation, and consumption of foodstuffs and beverages?

## 4.6. The Roman period and the longer term

To conclude this essay the relatively short Roman period will be set in the longer *durée* of its adjacent periods to see to what extent the Roman interlude conformed to longer term rhythms of the region's archaeology or stood outside them (Fig 4.3).

At some levels, the archaeology of the Romano-British period does show distinctive features. Perhaps most important is the great upsurge in resource exploitation and transformation which characterises the period. The archaeology of the later prehistoric and early medieval periods show nothing like this; individual resources, notably the Droitwich brine-springs, were exploited, but there is no evidence for the sort of systematic and intensive exploitation of a whole range of mineral and agrarian resources that it has been argued here is a determining feature of the Roman period. If one is to look for parallels to such behaviour, then it comes a millennium and more later with the later medieval period, leading of course to the early modern and Industrial Revolution periods when the winning and transformation of the natural resources of the west midlands again come to mark and define the archaeology of the region.

Equally, other features of the Roman period mark a break with what came before and after; this is particularly true of elements such as the creation of an urban hierarchy, masonry construction, and the relatively widespread use of artefacts in the 'Roman' style. This was very much the case for the south-eastern zone of the region and of course marks its assimilation into the wider context of the south and east of Roman Britain. These are features which recur in the archaeology of the region, starting in the 7th century AD but not developing fully until the end of the first millennium AD or after. Overall, the Roman period sees the west midlands far more integrated into the wider economic and social order of the province of Britannia and beyond it the wider imperial military, economic and cultural framework. This is, of course, the archaeology which suffers a catastrophic collapse in the first half of the 5th century, the archaeology linked to the Roman economic and cultural system. It is now widely accepted that the reasons for this collapse lie ultimately in the wider provincial and imperial frameworks, that the parts of society which maintained the towns, villas, coins, pottery, etc., were precisely the parts which suffered the deepest, irreversible crisis with the cessation of Roman rule in Britain (Esmonde Cleary 1989; cf Wickham 2005, 306-10). Interestingly, it is the south-eastern zone of the region that also seems most receptive earliest on to 'Germanic' material culture, particularly evinced by grave-goods in what is now southern Warwickshire and shading into eastern Worcestershire: are we again seeing an expression of the social and ideological divide in the modern region? What of the differences between the archaeology of the *Arosaetna* as opposed to the *Magonsaetan* or the *Wreoconsaetan*?

On the other hand, the archaeology of much of the west midlands through the Roman period seems to fit better with that of much of the first millennium BC and the later first millennium AD. This is the poorly visible archaeology of a rural landscape operating apparently at local levels with little evidence for economic or social complexity or innovation. The archaeology of the north and west of the region in the Roman period looks little different from that for centuries before and after; the longer-term formations of the agrarian economy and society were what characterised so much of the region for over a millennium, if not deeper into prehistory. In this case, then, the contrasting face of the archaeology of the region may help us to another view of the ending of Roman Britain and of the relationship of the Roman to the early medieval. It can be argued that over much of the region and for most of the population, the terminal crisis of the wider Roman system in Britain at the beginning of the 5th century was not central to their lives. The longer-term rhythms of the agrarian landscape continued as probably did the social and ideological frameworks based on them, even if economic formations such as taxation and other resource extraction ceased. Paradoxically, therefore, the late survival of sites such as Wroxeter (Barker et al. 1997) and Whitley Grange may be an expression of the persistence of the 'un-Romanised' society in which they were embedded rather than of the survival of 'Roman' practices and values. In this case, it is not surprising that the archaeology of the early medieval period in the west midlands is so fugitive; it is continuing a long-established tradition.

It is not until the 7th century that this part of the region sees the appearance of 'Germanic' material culture. Historians (cf Gelling 1992; Bassett 2000) are now pretty much agreed that the Anglo-Saxons arrive into a landscape peopled by Britons, who are almost as fugitive in the surviving documentary sources as they are in the archaeology. The heartlands of Mercia noticeably lay in the eastern part of the region, the western part remains much more shadowy to us. Again, it is not until late into the first millennium or later that many of the characteristic features of medieval archaeology become established in the region (for instance, widespread pottery use is a late development, cf Vince 1988), quite probably under the influence of the southern kingdom of Wessex, with the last elements to be put in place perhaps being associated with another set of intruders from overseas, the Normans.

## Bibliography

Barker, P, White R, Pretty K, Bird H, and Corbishley, M, 1997  *The Baths Basilica Wroxeter: Excavations 1966-90*, English Heritage Arch Rep 8, London

Bassett, S R, 2000  How the west was won: the Anglo-Saxon takeover of the west midlands, *Anglo-Saxon Studies in Archaeology and History* 11, 107-18

Biddulph, E, 2005   Excavations of a Roman settlement at 121 Tiddington Road, Stratford-upon-Avon, *Trans Birmingham Warwickshire Archaeol Soc* 109, 27-37

Booth, P M, 1996   Warwickshire in the Roman period: a review of recent work, *Trans Birmingham Warwickshire Archaeol Soc* 100, 25-57

Booth, P M, and Evans, J, 2002   *Roman Alcester Volume 3: Northern Extra-Mural Area*, CBA Res Rep 127, York

Brown, D, 1990   The Romano-British settlement at Blackwardine (HWCM 737), *Trans Woolhope Natur Field Club* 46, 390-406

Bushe-Fox, J P, 1914   *Second Report on the Excavations on the Site of the Roman Town at Wroxeter Shropshire, 1913*, Reports of the Research Committee of the Society of Antiquaries of London II, Oxford

Cracknell, S (ed), 1996   *Roman Alcester: Defences and Defended Area: Gateway Supermarket and Gas House Lane*, CBA Res Rep 106, York

Cracknell, S, and Mahany, C (eds), 1994   *Roman Alcester: Southern Extramural Area: 1964-1966 Excavations, Part 2: Finds and Discussion*, CBA Res Rep 97, York

Crawford, G, 1981   Wasperton, Warwickshire, *West Midlands Archaeology* 24, 121-29

Crawford, G, 1982   Excavations at Wasperton: second interim report, *West Midlands Archaeology* 25, 31-44

Crawford, G, 1983   Excavations at Wasperton: third interim report, *West Midlands Archaeology* 26, 15-28

Crummy, N, and Eckardt, H, 2003   Regional Identities and Technologies of Self: Nail-Cleaners in Roman Britain, *Archaeol J* 160, 44-69

Esmonde Cleary, A S, 1989   *The Ending of Roman Britain*, London

Esmonde Cleary, A S, 2000   Putting the dead in their place: burial location in Roman Britain, in *Burial, Society and Context in the Roman World* (eds J Pearce, M Millett and M Struck), Oxford, 127-42

Esmonde Cleary, A S, and Ferris, I M, 1996   Excavations at the New Cemetery, Rocester, Staffordshire 1985-87, *Trans South Staffordshire Archaeol Hist Soc* 35, Stafford

Ferris, I M, Bevan, L, and Cuttler, R, 2000   *Excavation of a Romano-British Shrine at Orton's Pasture, Rocester, Staffordshire*. BAR British Series 314, Oxford

Ford, W, 1996   Anglo-Saxon cemeteries along the Avon valley, *Trans Birmingham Warwickshire Archaeol Soc* 100, 59-98

Ford, W, 2003   The Romano-British and Anglo-Saxon settlement and cemeteries at Stretton-on-Fosse, Warwickshire, *Trans Birmingham Warwickshire Archaeol Soc* 106, 1-116

Frere, S S, and St Joseph, J K, 1983   *Roman Britain from the Air*, Cambridge

Gaffney, C, and Gaffney, V (eds), 2000   *Archaeological Prospection* 7, 2

Gaffney, V, and White, R, 2007   Wroxeter, the Cornovii and the Urban Process: Final Report on the Wroxeter Hinterland Project, 1994-1997. Vol 1, *Journal of Roman Archaeology Supplementary Series No 68, Portsmouth*

Gelling, M, 1992   *The West Midlands in the Early Middle Ages*, Leicester

Gould, J, 1964   Excavations at Wall, 1961-63, *Trans South Staffordshire Archaeol Hist Soc* 5, 1-50

Gould, J, 1999   The Watling Street Burgi, *Britannia* 30, 185-97

Grant, A, 2004  Domestic Animals and their Uses, in *A Companion to Roman Britain* (ed M Todd), Oxford, 371-92

Greene, K, 1994  Technology and innovation in context: the Roman background to medieval and later developments, *Journal of Roman Archaeology* 7, 22-33

Henig, M, 2004  *Roman Sculpture from the North-West Midlands*, Corpus Signorum Imperii Romani/Corpus of Sculpture of the Roman World: Great Britain, Volume I, Fascicule 9, Oxford

Hingley, R, 1989  *Rural Settlement in Roman Britain*, London

Houghton, J, and Ellis, P, 2006  The excavation between *insulae* XXVII and XXVIII, and evidence for glass-working, in *Wroxeter Archaeology: excavation and research on the defences and in the town, 1968-1992* (P Ellis and R White), Trans Shropshire Archaeol Hist Soc 78, 125-38

Hurst, D, 2006  *Roman Droitwich: Dodderhill Fort, Bays Meadow Villa, and Roadside Settlement*, CBA Res Rep146, York

Jackson, R, 2004  Production: Roman ironworking, in Dalwood, H, and Edwards, R (eds), *Excavations at Deansway, Worcester 1988-89: Romano-British small town to late medieval city*, CBA Res Rep 139

James, S T, 1999  The community of the soldiers: a major identity and centre of power in the Roman world, in *TRAC 98: Proceedings of the eight annual Theoretical Roman Archaeology Conference, Leicester 1988* (eds P Baker, C Forcey, S Jundi and R Witcher), Oxford, 14-25

James, S T, 2001  Soldiers and civilians: identity and interaction in Roman Britain, in *Britons and Romans: advancing an archaeological agenda* (eds S T James and M Millett), CBA Res Rep 125, 77-89

Jones, G D B, and Mattingly, D, 1990  *An Atlas of Roman Britain*, Oxford

Jones, G D B, and Webster, P V, 1969  Mediolanum: Excavations at Whitchurch 1965-6, *Archaeol J* 125, 193-254

Magilton, J, 2006  A Romano-Celtic Temple and Settlement at Grimstock Hill, Coleshill, Warwickshire, *Trans Birmingham Warwickshire Archaeol Soc* 110, 1-231

Mahany, C (ed), 1994  *Roman Alcester: Southern Extramural Area 1964-1966 Excavations, Part 1 Stratigraphy and Structures*, CBA Res Rep 96

Mattingly, D, 2004  Being Roman: expressing identity in a provincial setting, *Journal of Roman Archaeology* 17, 5-25

Mattingly, D (ed), 1997  Dialogues in Roman Imperialism: Power, discourse and discrepant experience in the Roman Empire, *Journal of Roman Archaeology* Supplement 23, Portsmouth RI

Metzler, J, Millett, M, Roymans, N, Slofstra, J (eds), 1995  *Integration in the Early Roman west: The Rôle of Culture and Ideology*, Dossiers du Musée National d'Histoire et d'Art IV, Luxembourg

Millett, M, 1990  *The Romanization of Britain*, Cambridge

Palmer, N, 1982  *Roman Stratford: Excavations at Tiddington 1980-81*, Warwick

Palmer, S, 2000  Archaeological Excavations in the Arrow Valley, Warwickshire, *Trans Birmingham Warwickshire Archaeol Soc* 103

Peacock, D, 1982  *Pottery and the Roman Economy*, London

Philpott, R, 1991  *Burial Practices in Roman Britain: A survey of grave treatment and furnishings A.D.43-410*, BAR British Series 219, Oxford

Round, B, 1992  Excavations on the *mansio* site at Wall, *Trans South Staffordshire Archaeol Hist Soc* 32, 1-78

Roymans, N, 1996  The sword or the plough: Regional dynamics in the Romanisation of Belgic Gaul and the Rhineland area, in *From the Sword to the Plough: three studies on the earliest romanisation of northern Gaul* (ed N Roymans), Amsterdam, 9-126

Smith, J T, 1978  Villas as a key to social structure, in Todd, M (ed), *Studies in the Romano-British Villa*, Leicester, 149-85

Smith, J T, 1997  *Roman Villas: a study in social structure*, London

Stanford, S C, 1974  *Croft Ambrey*, Hereford

Swan, V G, 1984  *The Pottery Kilns of Roman Britain*, London

Timby, J, 1990  Severn Valley Wares: A Reassessment, *Britannia* 30, 243-51

Tyers, P, 1996  *Roman Pottery in Britain*, London

Vince, A, 1988  Did they use pottery in the Welsh Marches and the West Midlands between the 5th and 12th centuries AD?, in Burl, A (ed), *From Roman Town to Norman Castle: essays in honour of Philip Barker*, Birmingham, 40-55

Wallace-Hadrill, A, 1994  *Houses and Society in Pompeii and Herculaneum*, Princeton

Webster, G, 1981  *Rome against Caratacus*, London

Webster, J, and Cooper, N (eds), 1996  *Roman Imperialism: Post-Colonial Perspectives*, Leicester Archaeol Monogr 3, Leicester

Welfare, H, and Swan, V, 1995  *Roman Camps in England: The Field Archaeology*, London

Whimster, R, 1989  *The Emerging Past: Air Photography and the Buried Landscape*, London

White, R (ed), in prep  *The Making of the West Midlands, Vol. 3: The Roman Period in the West Midlands*, Oxford

White, R, and Barker, P, 1998  *Wroxeter: Life and Death of a Roman City*, Stroud

White, R, and Gaffney, V, 2003  Resolving the paradox: the work of the Wroxeter Hinterland Project, in Wilson, P (ed), *The Archaeology of Roman Towns: studies in honour of John S. Wacher*, Oxford, 221-32

Whittaker, C R, 1997  *Roman Frontiers: a social and economic survey*, Baltimore and London

Wickham, C J, 2005  *Framing the Early Middle Ages: Europe and the Mediterranean, 4000-8000*, Oxford

Wilmott, A, 1980  Kenchester (Magnis): a reconsideration, *Trans Woolhope Natur Field Club* 43, 117-33

Woodiwiss, S, 1992  *Iron Age and Roman Salt production and the medieval town of Droitwich: excavations at the Old Bowling Green and Friar Street*, CBA Res Rep 81, York

Worrell, S, 2005  Roman Britain in 2004: II. Finds Reported under the Portable Antiquities Scheme, *Britannia* 36, 447-72

# 5. The post-Roman and the early medieval periods in the west midlands: a potential archaeological agenda[1]

## Della Hooke

d.hooke.1@bham.ac.uk

## 5.1. Introduction

The early medieval period is probably one of the periods least visible archaeologically. Yet documentary and place-name evidence, together with historical narrative, reveals a period of intense activity in a closely settled and developed landscape in the west midlands, as elsewhere in the country. This was undoubtedly also a period in which changes occurred that underpinned much subsequent development: new settlements were established and new settlement patterns emerged; most of our churches and many of our towns were established; field systems in many areas underwent change with the introduction of open-field agriculture (especially in the south-east of the region) while older patterns remained in others or different ones evolved. Kingdoms coalesced, with all this region becoming part of Greater Mercia, a kingdom that expanded from a heartland in the valley of the Trent to subsume the territories of the Hwicce, Magonsæte and Wreocensæte that lay to the south and west (Hooke 2001, 160, map 4). At a smaller scale, estate fragmentation enhanced the role of the 'township' community and gave way to the proto-manor that became the kingpin of much medieval organisation and the components of the ecclesiastical parishes. Although Domesday Book was compiled after the Norman Conquest it mostly reveals a situation that had developed by late Anglo-Saxon times, a situation that has been called the 'Anglo-Saxon achievement' (Hodges 1989). Indeed, the administrative framework that was established has lasted ever since with remarkably little change. However, history is beset with such terms as 'perhaps' and 'maybe' and, to date, archaeology has played only a very minor role in resolving the problems raised. We are not even able to guess at population numbers: there can be little doubt that the people of this period are going to be most difficult to find.

## 5.2. Ethnicity, burial, territory and belief

### 5.2.1. Ethnicity and burial evidence

The question of ethnicity remains one of the fundamental questions of the age. Opinions still veer between an 'invasionist' theory (now increasingly tempered to be interpreted as more an 'immigrationist' one), with Anglo-Saxons entering the country in some numbers, and 'population continuity', a situation in which the 'Britons' remained the main section of the population but slowly absorbed or aspired to assume Anglo-Saxon cultural traits (including language; discussed by Hooke and Ray: WMRRFA 4; Esmonde Cleary 1989, 200-1). The latter view seems to be gaining ground at the present (see Pryor 2004) and Bassett (2000) has argued that the population of the western and southern parts of the west midlands region chose deliberately to put themselves under Mercian protection by the late 7th century, opting 'for an Anglo-Saxon future' (Gelling 1992, 76-7). Ray (WMRRFA 4) raises the possibility of a third 'isolationist' scenario that he finds suggested by *walh* place-names in which British populations in some enclaves of the

Borderland actively shunned Anglo-Saxon influence, strengthened by their Christian faith (a different interpretation is suggested by Hooke 2003b, 68[2]). These communities were to 'evaporate by one means or another' as Mercia became politically dominant in the middle Anglo-Saxon period and they may have given way in the west of the region only through 'violent onslaught' (Ray WMRRFA 4), with Anglo-Saxon settlement spreading up the major river valleys as far as central Powys.

New archaeological techniques of genetic testing will need to become more refined if they are to provide answers and examine the evidence across the country. An initial suggestion that DNA tests showed massive dominance by those of Germanic or Scandinavian blood, which could only have resulted from population movement in this period (Weale et al 2002), has subsequently been questioned. This study, in any case, failed to address evidence from the west midlands region where greater native survival is likely to have occurred. Further studies of the Y chromosome evidence (Capelli et al 2003) suggested that differences were caused mostly by the presence of Danes in eastern England (including a strong presence in eastern Staffordshire) and that there was probably greater population stability beyond this zone. However, a recent study by Stephen Oppenheimer argues that the genetic make-up of the British population has changed only slightly since the Neolithic period, although he identifies a clear west–east divide. Moreover, he argues that the Anglo-Saxon incursions of the 5th and 6th centuries were made easier by the fact that, in some parts of the country, the population already had strong genetic links to continental peoples and that at least some were already speaking a Germanic language. He concludes:

> Overall, 4% of Anglo-Saxon male intrusion into the British Isles (maximum 9–15% in those areas of eastern England which from the archaeology would have been expected to bear the brunt) seems more reasonable than the wipeout theory (Oppenheimer 2006, 381).

The analysis of strontium isotope ratios might also help to distinguish newcomers from natives in early cemeteries but also has its limitations (J Hunter, pers comm).

Certainly, known pagan Anglo-Saxon burials are concentrated across the south-eastern parts of the region in south Worcestershire and south-east Warwickshire, with further groups in the Trent valley area of south-eastern Staffordshire and in the Staffordshire Peak District to the north (Fig 5.1). Although it is now accepted that the fashion of grave goods is no reliable indicator of race, the early burials, in particular, do seem to indicate the presence of Anglo-Saxons and suggest that many individuals buried in the cemeteries had played a role among a warrior or social elite. At Wasperton in Warwickshire, a cemetery appears to have continued in use from late Roman into Anglo-Saxon times (Esmonde Cleary 1989, 201; Crawford 1982), perhaps implying the acquisition by an existing native community of cultural traits that were 'Anglo-Saxon' in origin. Others seem, however, to represent the burials of a predominantly youthful population that may have been made up of incomers. At Alveston, Warks, there are hints that the community was suffering from stress and starvation (Ford in prep), and the early cemetery at Beckford, Worcs, is also characterised by the apparent poverty of its grave goods (Evison 1996). (But a settlement of both sunken-floored and post-built structures has now been identified nearby at Ryall Quarry that may cast doubt upon this assumption: Barber and Watts 2003.) Burial of a leading elite, on the other hand, is suggested for the pagan barrow burials that spill over into the north-east Staffordshire Peak District from Derbyshire. Here leaders may have grown rich from the lead resources of the area and for the most part these are late (mid 7th-century) secondary burials that have been attributed to the *Pecsætan* tribe. Burial here took place at a time when paganism was facing the threat of being overwhelmed by Christianity and the barrows were perhaps a deliberate statement of pre-Christian belief. Final phase burials with rich grave goods that again suggest the emergence of a 7th-century elite also seem to be suggested in some Warwickshire cemeteries (Crawford WMRRFA 4). Although the context of individual finds can be difficult to understand, the discovery of a fine dagger pommel at Dinham in Ludlow seems to show the presence of high-status people in that region in the 7th century.

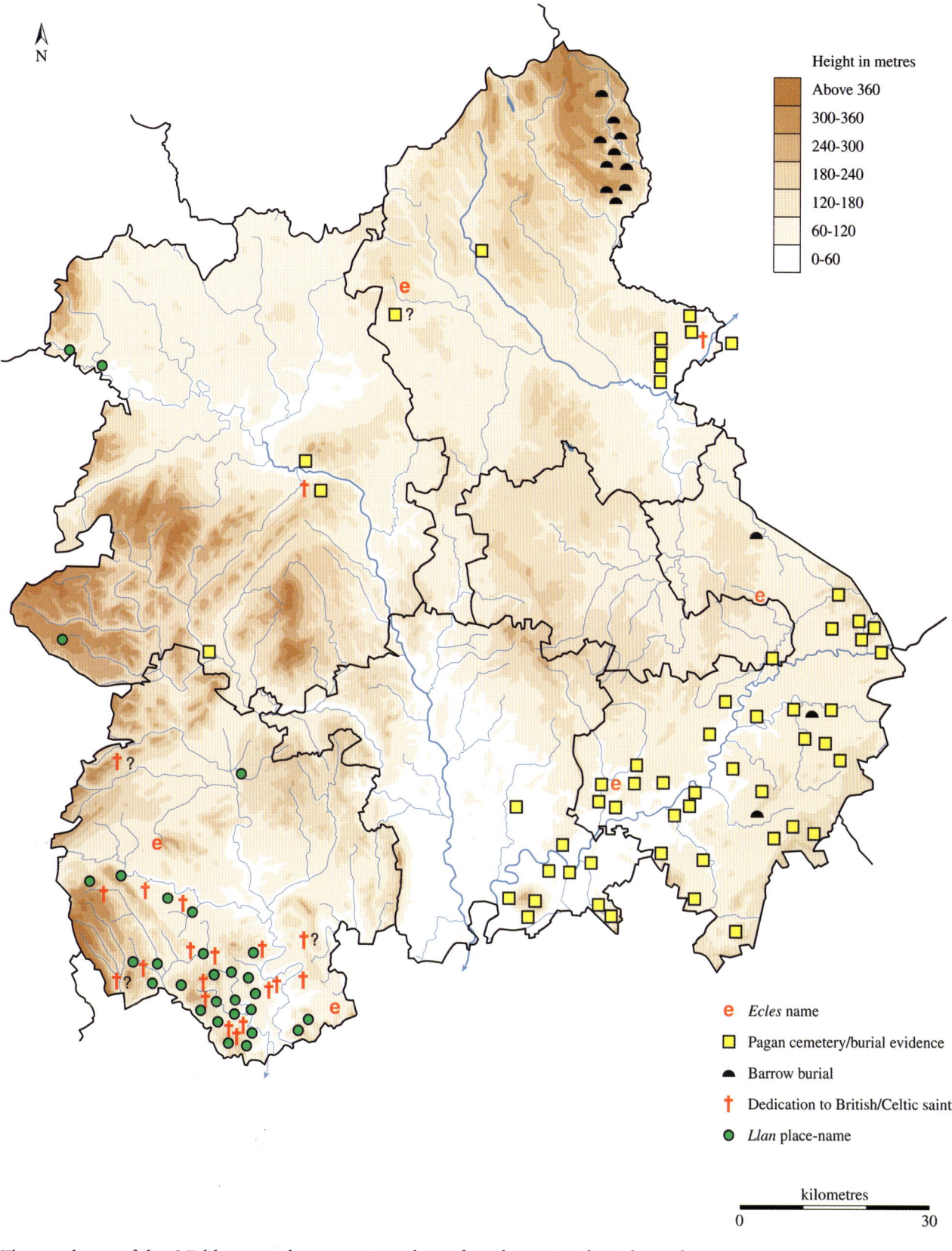

**Height in metres**

Above 360

300-360

240-300

180-240

120-180

60-120

0-60

*e*    *Ecles* name

☐    Pagan cemetery/burial evidence

⬤    Barrow burial

†    Dedication to British/Celtic saint

●    *Llan* place-name

kilometres

0                       30

The incidence of the OE *hlaw* term has sometimes been found to coincide with Anglo-Saxon burial (Hooke 1981b) and this term also occurs in the west of the region. However, mounds may have been constructed to mark meeting places etc, perhaps following a tradition of barrow burial in which the barrow marker established a claim to land proved by ancestral ownership, and actual interment need not have been present in later periods. (The extent to which pagan 'superstitions' continued among the general populace after conversion is difficult to determine but the early Church had continually to fight

**Fig 5.1** Pagan Anglo-Saxon cemeteries and British Christianity

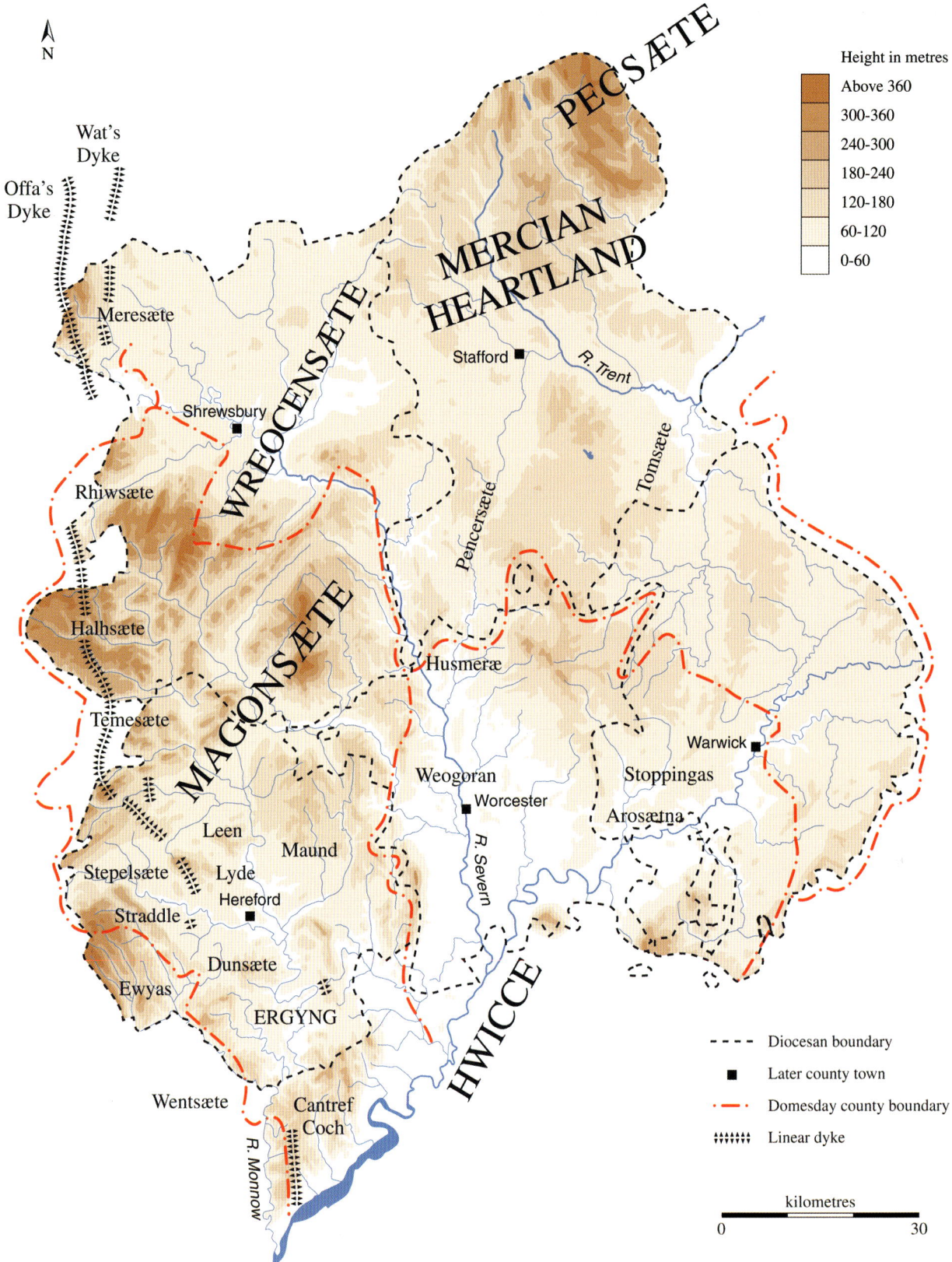

N

Height in metres

Above 360

300-360

240-300

180-240

120-180

60-120

0-60

Wat's Dyke

Offa's Dyke

PECSÆTE

MERCIAN HEARTLAND

Meresæte

WREOCENSÆTE

Stafford

R. Trent

Shrewsbury

Rhiwsæte

Pencersæte

Tomsæte

Halhsæte

MAGONSÆTE

Husmeræ

Temesæte

Warwick

Leen

Maund

Weogoran

Stoppingas

Lyde

Worcester

Arosætna

Stepelsæte

Hereford

R. Severn

Straddle

Dunsæte

Ewyas

ERGYNG

HWICCE

Wentsæte

Cantref Coch

R. Monnow

– – –  Diocesan boundary

■  Later county town

–·–·–  Domesday county boundary

✝✝✝✝  Linear dyke

kilometres

0                    30

**Fig 5.2** The Anglo-Saxon kingdoms

remnants of such belief.) If a language change occurred over the first few centuries of Anglo-Saxon cultural domination this still awaits a full explanation and there is little indication of how strongly the British (Primitive Welsh) tongue had been current in the west midlands area or had continued in everyday use. Oppenheimer (2006, 415-16) has argued for the presence of a strain of the Germanic language (closer to Norse) being present in parts of England from pre-Roman times. In this area the survival of British place-names suggests that neither this, nor population change, were major factors here (Hooke 1997). Even among British-speaking communities, it is likely that, as on other numerous similar occasions, one language slipped down the social scale as another became the accepted speech among landowners, scribes etc (cf Gaelic in Lowland Scotland) (Hooke 1997).

### 5.2.2. Territory

Metalwork located as stray finds cannot always be tied in with a known burial place but can sometimes add to our understanding of the identity of Anglo-Saxon tribal groupings already suggested by grave goods. In particular, Ford (1996, 92-6) has noted how the latter suggest a territorial divide through Warwickshire in the Anglo-Saxon period, with the Avon region of central Warwickshire being first subject to cultural and trading influence from Anglian regions to the east (indicated largely by cruciform, small-long, annular, cut-away disc, some great square-headed and possibly pennanular brooches) but with, at some time in the first half of the 6th century, the introduction of disc, followed by saucer, brooches indicating a more dominant commercial link to the south for the lower part of the Avon valley. He argues that the division between what was to become the kingdom of the Hwicce and that of Greater Mercia can be discerned, therefore, by the end of the 6th century. Indeed, some political boundaries may have perpetuated much older territorial groupings, for the Hwiccan kingdom seems to have been established over part of the former late Iron Age Dobunnic territory (which seems to be perpetuated in the distribution of Romano-British coarsewares) (Hooke 1985b, 17-18). Until the Anglo-Saxon period the midland region had no cultural uniformity, looking outwards to core regions beyond. Although the eastern parts of the region continued to look eastwards in pagan Anglo-Saxon times the dominance of Mercia by the 8th century brought a measure of cohesion as this kingdom, spreading from a core region in the valley of the Trent, extended its boundaries as far as the estuary of the Dee and subsumed the kingdoms of the Hwicce and Magonsæte to the south and south-west.

Documentary and place-name evidence has helped to identify folk regions within the 7th-century Anglo-Saxon kingdoms (Hooke WMRRFA 4; Fig 5.2). Because of their location in the Borderland region, some have suggested that the tribal groups that carried a -sæte name may have been of British origin, unlike the *ingas-*, *inga-* groups common in eastern England (Higham 1993, 85, 89, fig 3.6) (although the appearance of such names may itself denote assimilation and Anglicisation: J Hines, pers comm). There is one *ingas* name in the region that applies to a recognisable territory – the *Stoppingas* of Wootton Wawen. This type of name seems to indicate land given to an Anglo-Saxon leader and his followers relatively early on in the period of post 5th-century Anglo-Saxon colonisation, here apparently granted a block of land with an assessment of about 50 hides across the headwaters of the River Alne in Warwickshire. But *who* gave this land unit and why did the bulk of the population – if, indeed, large numbers of 'British' survived – eventually aspire to identify itself with an immigrant culture? It is important to note that in the midlands we have as much (if not more) evidence for the territorial and political geography of early medieval England as anywhere else in the country.

### 5.2.3. Pre-Christian belief and the Christian Church

Little is yet known about pre-Christian ritual, rather than funerary, sites in the region in this period. But Christianity probably helped to eradicate many such sites beyond the main areas of Anglo-Saxon influence. Springs may have played a part as pre-Christian cult centres but, as sources of purifying water, were readily taken over by the Christian Church. Particular trees too lost their significance although the yew, probably already accepted by Roman Christianity, became a feature in many churchyards (where it has been claimed that a few may pre-date the standing church near by). In spite of numerous edicts issued by the early Church banning worship at pagan sites, trees, springs and stones continued to be associated with healing powers. Place-names and landmarks along estate boundaries may indicate other Anglo-Saxon pagan sites, with a number clustered around the area of the Birmingham Plateau. This perhaps indicates a region, close to the border of the Hwiccan kingdom and Greater Mercia, in which paganism lingered (Gelling 1961; 1973; 1978, 158-60, fig 11): the names Wednesbury and Wednesfield are associated with Woden and may owe their existence to Penda, the last pagan Mercian ruler. Close to the northern boundary of the Hwiccan kingdom was *Tyes mere*, 'the mere of Tíw', a Germanic war-god, while Tysoe, 'the hill spur of Tíw', lay on the side of Edge Hill, close to its southern boundary, where traditionally a horse figure had been carved on the hillside. (The horse appears, too, in the Godiva legends attached to Coventry, and may even be derived from the Gaulish horse-goddess, Epona, riding out to confer benefits upon her people.) Legend and tradition are other sources that archaeologists can consider. Archaeologically known 'heathen' shrines are few: at Blacklow Hill in north Warwickshire two large enclosures full of pits were associated with two, possibly 7th-century, Anglo-Saxon graves, a type of monument which may have drawn upon older roots in its concept but was apparently constructed at a time when Christianity was becoming popular even among the Anglo-Saxons (Blair 1995, 18, 22).

Evidence from the west of the region seems to show Christianity firmly established before the conversion period, although it is not yet clear how much this derived from late Roman Christianity. There are hints of religious continuity at Acton Trussell, Staffs, where the medieval (possibly 11th-century) church stands on a high-status Roman (villa?) site (C Wardle, pers comm). Religious continuity may also be suggested by the *ecles* place-names which have been taken to indicate surviving British Christian communities in the vicinity. Many scholars have argued that the religion was reintroduced from Gaul in the 5th and 6th centuries, gaining ground amongst British populations, but others see this as the reinforcement of an already established faith. Early 'British' Christian inscribed stones are known from Wroxeter in Shropshire and Lanveynoe in Herefordshire.[3] The influence of late Roman organisation in the Church has been effectively argued by Bassett (1989).

Burials and cemeteries from the 5th century onwards have been located in small numbers across the Borderland (some others are of uncertain age) and many have interpreted some features as illustrative of British Christian belief, although the presence of a small Anglo-Saxon element is not denied: suggested, for instance, by a (possibly mid 7th-century) potsherd in a ring ditch at Sutton St Michael in Marden, Heref (K Ray, pers comm), or two scramasax-type iron knives and fragments of iron buckle found in a post 7th-century cemetery at Bromfield, Shrops. Other burials, however, were orientated and lacked grave goods (eg three north-east/south-west orientated graves, one certainly in a coffin, from Much Wenlock), perhaps indicative of Christian burial. The recently found 7th- or 8th-century cemetery at Dewsall Court, Heref, is another significant example of a likely Christian cemetery, coinciding here with a dedication to a Celtic saint, St Dewi, and overlying late Roman deposits but lying in a different location to the medieval church (Cotton WMRRFA 4). Ewyas and Archenfield, in south-western and southern Herefordshire respectively, remained Welsh districts until the time of Domesday Book, with British bishops controlling the Church until at least the 10th century. The possibility of re-examining church enclosures (Br. *llan*) offers another line of enquiry.

## 5.3. Settlements and settlement hierarchy

Early medieval rural settlement sites have also rarely been identified archaeologically. Even when excavation has located continuous occupation from prehistoric into Roman times, with additional evidence from the medieval period (as at Throckmorton, Worcs), the intermediate occupation layers remain elusive. Roman pottery has, indeed, been located on many deserted medieval sites in Warwickshire but any early medieval phase of settlement on most of these sites remains undiscovered or unidentified. Early sunken-featured buildings (SFBs) have been found in this county at Baginton, Brandon, Stretton-on-Fosse, Hatton Rock, Wootton Wawen and Broom (three dating to the 6th century?). Building features such as postholes have been identified at a number of locations which include a site close to a pagan cemetery at Alveston, Broom (two possible post-built structures, one a hall-house), Bidford-on-Avon, and possibly Wootton Wawen (Palmer 2000). Buildings of the 10th/11th century have been identified at Coton in Churchover parish, and in Worcestershire similar features have been noted at Fladbury (substantial mid 10th-century buildings) and Ipsley (a possible cattle pen) with sunken-featured buildings at Kemerton (Dinn and Evans 1992), and no fewer than seven SFBs at the Ryall

Quarry site in Ripple. For Herefordshire, however, Cotton is forced to conclude that 'there are no rural non-ecclesiastic settlements of this period … whose presence can be clearly verified by reliably contexted ground evidence' and for Staffordshire Kinsley adds that 'Apart from Catholme (in Barton-under-Needwood), no finds of the Anglo-Saxon period have been made in rural settlement contexts' (WMRRFA 4) (although Roman pottery has been found on a small number of medieval village sites, possibly indicating continuous occupation since the late 4th century: Smith 1980, 11, and possibly at Barton-under-Needwood itself). The reason usually given for this is that domestic settlements in the early part of the period were small scale, non-intrusive and probably subject to shift, some perhaps hidden beneath later settlements.

The only substantial post-Roman hamlet to have been located and excavated in the region is that of Catholme in the Trent valley of Staffordshire (Losco-Bradley and Kinsley 2002). Some 65 buildings of various sizes and structures that included wall-post buildings and *grubenhäuser* were identified on this site, representing several phases of building within clearly defined settlement zones. Occupation on the gravel river terrace may have begun in the Roman period, when the area was at least farmland, with an early Anglo-Saxon settlement and a related cemetery (at Wychnor) continuing in the northern part of the original site. Settlement gradually drifted north-eastwards along the gravel terrace to the area that was excavated after 1973 when quarrying threatened its survival. The excavated settlement apparently consisted of a number of individual farmhouses, with their ancillary buildings, that were established in the mid to late Anglo-Saxon period but went out of use at a date any time between the late 9th and 13th centuries (ibid, 123). Even with extensive excavation, the problem of ethnicity remains unresolved but no major disruption of the agricultural regime was evident at the end of the Roman period. The presence of a north-west European burial rite at Wychnor, 'Anglo-Saxon' grave goods and the presence of some 14 *grubenhäuser* may indicate at least a degree of Anglo-Saxon involvement but, as at Wasperton, arguments have been advanced that the earliest inhabitants of the settlement were Britons:

> If indeed the earliest buildings and enclosures pre-date c. AD 600, it seems likely that it was originally peopled largely or entirely, by Britons. Whatever its origins, however, the community swiftly adopted 'Anglo-Saxon' architectural forms and buried at least some of its dead with distinctively Germanic artefacts. The buildings and burials could be manifestations of a local British population which had never gone away, but which merely emerged from archaeological invisibility in the later sixth and seventh centuries by adopting the trappings of the 'Anglicised' society to the east (Losco-Bradley and Kinsley 2002, 128-9).

Andrew Reynolds' (2003) recent discussion of rural domestic settlements in early medieval England notes no others in the midland region and a gazetteer updating that produced by Rahtz in 1976 would make a welcome addition to the literature. Our knowledge of settlements is still dominated by the evidence from eastern England and the east midlands where pottery was in greater use. There, Romano-British farmsteads seem to have gone out of use, as pottery scatter also suggests in the west midland region, but a pattern of equally dispersed farms and hamlets took their place (however, it should be noted how frequently Romano-British pottery turns up on later village sites, suggesting a degree of continued preferred site selection, if nothing else). By the mid Saxon period an element of nucleation was taking place in the east midlands, even involving a degree of regularly planned layouts (Brown and Foard 1998, 77). Whether this represents the failure of outlying farmsteads or a deliberate change in social organisation is uncertain and is discussed further below.

The importance of pottery and other artefacts for dating settlements and placing them within the estate network is shown by the evidence from eastern England, but in much of the midlands domestic pottery seems to have gone out of use in the immediate post-Roman period apart from its use for funerary urns. However, this absence may be more illusory than real, as the detailed excavations carried out in the Trent valley site of Catholme show, for over 2000 sherds of handmade pottery, mostly coil-built and probably locally made, were found scattered widely across the site, possibly beginning as early as the 6th century (Vince 2002, 102-10; Losco-Bradley and Kinsley 2002, 123). There were 757 sherds of sub-Roman/Anglo-Saxon pottery from the excavation of well-stratified deposits of c 5th- to 7th-century date at the Upwich salt-making site in Droitwich (Lentowicz 1997), where the dating of the deposits did not solely rely on the ceramics but was rather based on extensive radiocarbon dating. This included 'grass'-tempered pottery and a range of other well-defined fabrics, some of the pottery being non-locally produced (Hurst & Hemingway 1997, 23). More recently 'grass'-tempered pottery has been discovered during fieldwalking at Bretforton in south Worcestershire (D Hurst, pers comm), suggesting that it may after all be possible to trace settlement occupation by this means. Some 736 sherds were also found at Broom in the Arrow valley of Warwickshire during excavations carried out in advance of the construction of a new bypass between Evesham and Alcester (Palmer 2000), some of it apparently datable again to the 6th century, and organic-tempered pottery was also obtained from the 6th- to 8th-century settlement site at Ryall Quarry in Ripple, Worcs (Barber and Watts 2003).

Over most of the region, however, it is not until the mid Anglo-Saxon period that pottery begins to appear in the known archaeological record, and then mainly on urban sites, the exception being a number of isolated royal palace sites (see below). Interestingly, pottery found on a small number of Warwickshire rural sites is late Saxon in date, consisting of imported Neots ware and Cotswolds oolitic tempered ware, possibly carried in along the Roman road network — the Fosse Way and Watling Street (S Ratkai, pers comm): does this indicate the late emergence of these sites? At Coton in Churchover, occupation appears to have begun in the 10th/11th century and enclosures and buildings of the period have been found (Palmer WMRRFA 5), and a number of other Warwickshire rural sites have produced 10th- and 11th-century material, among them Pillerton Priors, Goldicote, Loxley, Flecknoe and Ettington, all in the Warwickshire Feldon. The picture is similar in Worcestershire where Cotswold oolitic pottery has been encountered on some rural sites (D Hurst, pers comm). Yet there is no indication, even here, of the *frequent* usage of pottery found in regions to the south by the late 10th century. Only after the mid 11th century do locally-made wares come into general usage for such items as cooking pots and jugs and pitchers (although a 'potter's wood or clearing' is recorded on the northern margin of Needwood, Staffs, in the mid 10th century: Hooke 1983, 103-7; Sawyer 1968, S 557). Clearly, the list of known sites yielding pottery is likely to grow with excavation.

Nucleation was clearly a gradual process in many areas, often associated with later re-planning, but charter evidence shows conclusively that small farms and hamlets still existed close to estate boundaries in the later part of the early medieval period (Hooke 1985a), in north-east and south-east Worcestershire at least. None of these sites has been investigated archaeologically and habitative field-names elsewhere may suggest other 'lost' sites. Another priority must be to try to establish the date of origin of many of the minor farmsteads that first find their way into the documentary record in the medieval period (again, Roman pottery has been found close to some medieval farm sites: Hodder WMRRFA 3). Even less can be said about the region's villages. It has been argued (Brown and Foard 1998) that nucleation began even before the fragmentation of multiple estates, perhaps under royal or ecclesiastical influence, and at Goltho in Northamptonshire nucleation appears to have preceded the building of a manorial complex (Reynolds 2003, 123-5, 131; Beresford 1987), a point also recently made about settlement nucleation by Tom Williamson (2003). Dating in East Anglia and the east midlands has depended very much upon the ceramics found during intensive fieldwalking projects like those carried out by David Hall in the East Anglian Fenland and the east midlands or by Williamson in Essex (eg Hall 1981; Hall and Coles 1994; Williamson 1986), but there is limited evidence so far from the west midland region to cast light upon the matter (see discussion of the ceramic evidence above). As Crawford (WMRRFA 4) concludes,

> the desperate lack of excavated settlement evidence for this area should put the need to conduct a more careful excavation of a settlement, should the ghost of an opportunity arise, at the top of the research agenda.

The greatest hope of locating 'lost' settlement sites may lie with less intrusive forms of archaeological investigation such as the use of geophysical prospecting, at least in preliminary investigations, and deliberately aimed small-scale excavations not led by the location of building development.

The reoccupation of prehistoric hillforts in the immediate post-Roman period by a lordly elite has been suggested, with The Berth at Baschurch being put forward as a likely candidate (White WMRRFA 3) and perhaps, too, the hillforts of Sutton Walls, Old Oswestry and the Wrekin, but corroboratory evidence is so far lacking. Air photography has, however, produced evidence of another kind of high-status site, for ranges of timbered buildings, interpreted as 'palaces', have been identified at Hatton Rock and Long Itchington in Warwickshire and at Atcham in Shropshire. The site at Hatton was, however, in the hands of the Church of Worcester after AD 781 (Sawyer 1968, S 1257) and this may have been an ecclesiastical 'palace' building, perhaps with a church — again, this depends upon the dating of the pottery, judged by Hirst and Rahtz (1972–3) to be of 8th- or 9th-century date. A type of black pottery found by fieldwalking on the first of these sites was also found beside the River Dene at Wellesbourne in Warwickshire after bridgeworks upstream — suggesting the presence of another, so far undiscovered, high-status site in a location in which royal assemblies are known to have been held (Hooke 1985b, 204). There are other known royal centres, like Sutton in Marden in central Herefordshire, which may eventually produce further evidence for a focal building or royal residence.

### 5.3.1. Urban development

The evolution of the region's towns is better understood. The 'dark earth' deposits found in many sub-Roman centres suggest that in the immediate post-Roman period, or even earlier than this, towns were losing their focal role, although in some places such deposits may represent the wattle and daub of fallen buildings, the role of earth-based buildings having perhaps been underplayed on British, as opposed to continental, sites (R Macphail, pers comm). Places that had been urban have produced evidence, from late Roman times, of silty soil brought in on the feet of livestock mixed with other refuse. At Worcester these soils supported grassland from the 4th to the 10th century, suggesting that parts of the former settlement were being farmed as pasture fields, and there is direct archaeological evidence here, probably within the Roman period defensive circuit, for continuity of occupation through the 5th and 6th centuries, together with continuity in the management of fields around the town (Dalwood 2004; Macphail 2004). Similarly, there seems to have been continuity of occupation at Wroxeter into the 5th and 6th centuries. A tombstone commemorating one Cunorix (c 475) may imply the use of Irish mercenaries to defend the town (White WMRRFA 3). A mid 6th-century resurgence led to the construction of some buildings of considerable size and status (White and Barker 1998, 2002). After that, urban settlement at Wroxeter apparently diminishes. Settlement is also likely to have continued at Droitwich, where salt production continued (Hurst 1997), and 5th-century occupation has been inferred at Kenchester and Leintwardine in Herefordshire, although a break seems to be evident in the east of the region at Alcester and Wall (Ray WMRRFA 4). (But a sword mount found at Alcester on the edge of a Romano-British burial site, and a later crozier head of ivory, may be indicative that more remains to be found here on the outskirts of the Roman town: S Ratkai, pers comm).

If the towns lost their role in the early part of the Anglo-Saxon period, their re-growth seems to have been brought about by further threats. Burh defences are some of the most noteworthy features of the period and many of the early towns of the west midland region developed as defended urban centres during the Danish invasions. However, the deliberate fostering of trade and markets is a feature sometimes overlooked. Tamworth was already an important Mercian royal vill in the 8th century; it may have earlier borne the name *Tomtun*. Offa had a palace there and it was already defended before it became a centre for the reconquest of the Danelaw under Æthelflæd. Hereford may have originated as an ecclesiastical centre in the later 7th century but its defences appear to have been built in the mid 9th century before those of any other midland burh (Boucher 2002, 4; Baker WMRRFA 4), presumably constructed against Welsh attack. Worcester, already described as *(ad) metropolim Huicciorum* '(at) the metropolis or capital of the Hwicce' in the mid 8th century (Sawyer 1968, S 1254; Birch 1885–99, B 166) and another episcopal city, was defended by Æthelflæd and her husband Æthelred, ealdorman of Mercia, in the late 9th century, when it was ordered that the burh should be built 'for the protection of all the people' (Sawyer 1968, S 223), and they shared market dues there with the Church of Worcester. The defences were located during the Deansway excavations in 1989 and suggest a defended annexe added to the north side of an earlier enclosure around the cathedral with later suburban development at Sidbury. Later Æthelred and Æthelflæd established a burh at Shrewsbury and refortified Hereford and Worcester (AD 910). After her husband's death, Æthelflæd went on to build fortresses at Bridgnorth on the Severn (AD 912), Stafford (AD 913), and Warwick (AD 914). Both Stafford and Shrewsbury made use of the defence offered by marshland and a river meander, Shrewsbury on the Severn and Stafford on the Sow.

The burhs, whether defended against the Welsh or the Danes, are likely to have made a considerable impression on the landscape of early and later medieval England and were well populated by the mid 11th century: Baker (WMRRFA 4) estimates populations at that time of around 2000 for Worcester, 1200 for Shrewsbury, about 1500 for Warwick, and 1300 for Stafford. But the defended towns were also meant to develop as economic centres, with good roads serving a market for the surrounding countryside (Hooke 1980). The burhs were not alone, for the salt-producing centre of Droitwich, a *wic* or 'place of trade', may have had 800 inhabitants by that date. Neither were the burhs set at new locations, for several coincided with ecclesiastical minster foci, among these Hereford and Worcester.

Other aspects of commercial activity before the development of urban markets urgently demand enquiry: although it has been suggested that the production of pottery at Stafford pre-dated the establishment of the burh, others prefer to accept a later industry developing there once the burh had begun to develop (S Bassett and S Ratkai, pers comm), as at Derby and Northampton. Neither is a great deal known about the region's place within the commercial activity of the country as a role. When Mercia spread its authority as far as the Thames in the 8th century, the Church of Worcester maintained a trading post on the river which presumably brought profits back into the region but apart from salt, originally a commodity over which the kings of the Hwicce had claimed control, little is known about the goods being traded — such as agricultural produce or wool — and whether wealth was actually coming into the region or being exploited elsewhere. On urban sites, however, pottery, perhaps associated with high-status sites, is not uncommon. Much of the pottery found within towns was imported from outside the region (eg Stamford and St Neot's wares) although Stafford ware, produced between the late 9th century — or later — and the 11th century, was widely distributed across the west midland region (and along the north Welsh coast, even reaching as far afield as Dublin: Ford 1998–9, 33, fig 18). An urgent review of other midland pottery collections is necessary.

Baker (2003) has raised many questions regarding urban growth in the early medieval period which could be archaeologically addressed: what authority supplied the impetus for growth and how did the Church and political leaders interact, given the factors of military necessity and commerce? How fast did towns develop as urban centres in the pre-Scandinavian period? What elements of planning can be detected (*haga* enclosures within towns are noted in the charters of pre-Conquest England, sometimes with their dimensions) and when did burgage plots come into being? Crafts were well established in the later Anglo-Saxon towns but how much evidence is there of zoning within the towns? This seems to be evident, for instance, in the location of pottery manufacture at Stafford. Furthermore, how did towns react with the countryside? Again, links between town and country are attested in Domesday Book that may have had their origins in the burh's role as a centre of refuge but which continued to play an economic and marketing role. Archaeological excavation can reveal much about the status and quality of life of those occupying urban locations — about the crafts practiced and where they were located, or about building types and roads. Pottery found in urban settings is one form of evidence for the development of towns and the extent of trade: Hereford may have had a local pottery industry by the end of the 10th century (Vince WMRRFA 4; but the kilns at Stafford were earlier). Some towns acquired a new function when they became the foci of the new counties established at the end of the early medieval period. Warwick had been a border town and probable place of exchange on the boundary between the Hwiccan and Greater Mercian kingdoms (Fig 5.2); Hereford and Worcester had been important ecclesiastical centres and, together with Stafford and Shrewsbury, had been defended burhs before they took on the new administrative role. But many other small medieval towns have seen little archaeological investigation and the beginnings of their urban character remain little known.

### 5.3.2. Rural marketing

The system of marketing before the growth of towns also needs investigation. What have been termed 'productive sites' have been identified in a number of non-urban sites such as the area to the east of Bidford-on-Avon, Warks, where metal detecting has produced items such as silver coinage (15 coins) and bronze metalwork (12 pieces: brooches, strap-ends and ornamental fragments) of middle Saxon (8th/9th- century) date, together with an Anglo-Saxon gold mount decorated with a calf's head in beaded wire filigree, probably of 8th-century date and perhaps part of a hanging bowl or an ecclesiastical object (representing the symbol of St Luke). This represents a concentration of objects that are unlikely to have been casual losses and may have accumulated at a market site, perhaps one at which 'cattle, sheep, horses and other commodities were bought and sold' and goods perhaps exchanged (Wise and Seaby 1995). Beyond the great emporia, mostly lying outside our region, were other smaller places involved in the distribution and collection of low-value goods, sometimes with organised production workshops. How far can such sites be identified in the west midlands?

### *Defensive features*

The burhs were defended centres, often with inner enclosures known as *hagæ*, a term that suggests protection and defence (Hooke 1981a, 247-8), but the most impressive linear defence system is the earlier Offa's Dyke that runs north–south through the Borderland close to the Welsh border (Fig 5.2). Opinions may differ about the reasons for its construction: Hill and Worthington (2003, 110-12) envisage it as a border earthwork constructed when the Welsh of Powys were attacking sites in Mercia. (Brooks 1989, 168-9, suggests another reason for early Welsh raids on the midlands.) The dyke is likely to have been constructed on the instigation of Offa, a powerful leader who was not averse to using the trappings of Imperial Roman power to promote his own image: the dyke in many ways emulates Hadrian's Wall in its symbolism and scale. (Indeed, it has been claimed that the dyke follows an earlier earthen rampart built by the Roman emperor Severus at the beginning of the 3rd century AD.) Shorter stretches of linear boundaries in the same region seem to have been earlier than Offa's Dyke: Wat's Dyke may have been of mid or later 6th-century construction, protecting the area around Chester (White WMRRFA 3 but dating N Baker, pers comm), while excavations at points on the Rowe Ditch, which cuts across prehistoric field systems in the Arrow valley in Pembridge, suggest a date for its construction *c* AD 650, ie in a post-Roman context in a period that suffered major cultural dislocation, perhaps in the face of some other rapid and major incursions by the Anglo-Saxons into British territory (Ray WMRRFA 4). Other stretches of linear earthwork or cross-valley dykes, like the Birtley dyke near Lingen and another near Wigmore, both in north Herefordshire, have yet to be placed into context but may mark out other British enclaves (see Ray WMRRFA 4). While most castles in the region date from after the Norman Conquest, Norman intervention began in Herefordshire at an earlier date when Edward the Confessor granted lands to his Norman associates: mottes at Richard's Castle, Ewyas Harold and Hereford itself date from the pre-Conquest period, reflecting the troubled political background of the Border region and the presence of new Norman landholders.

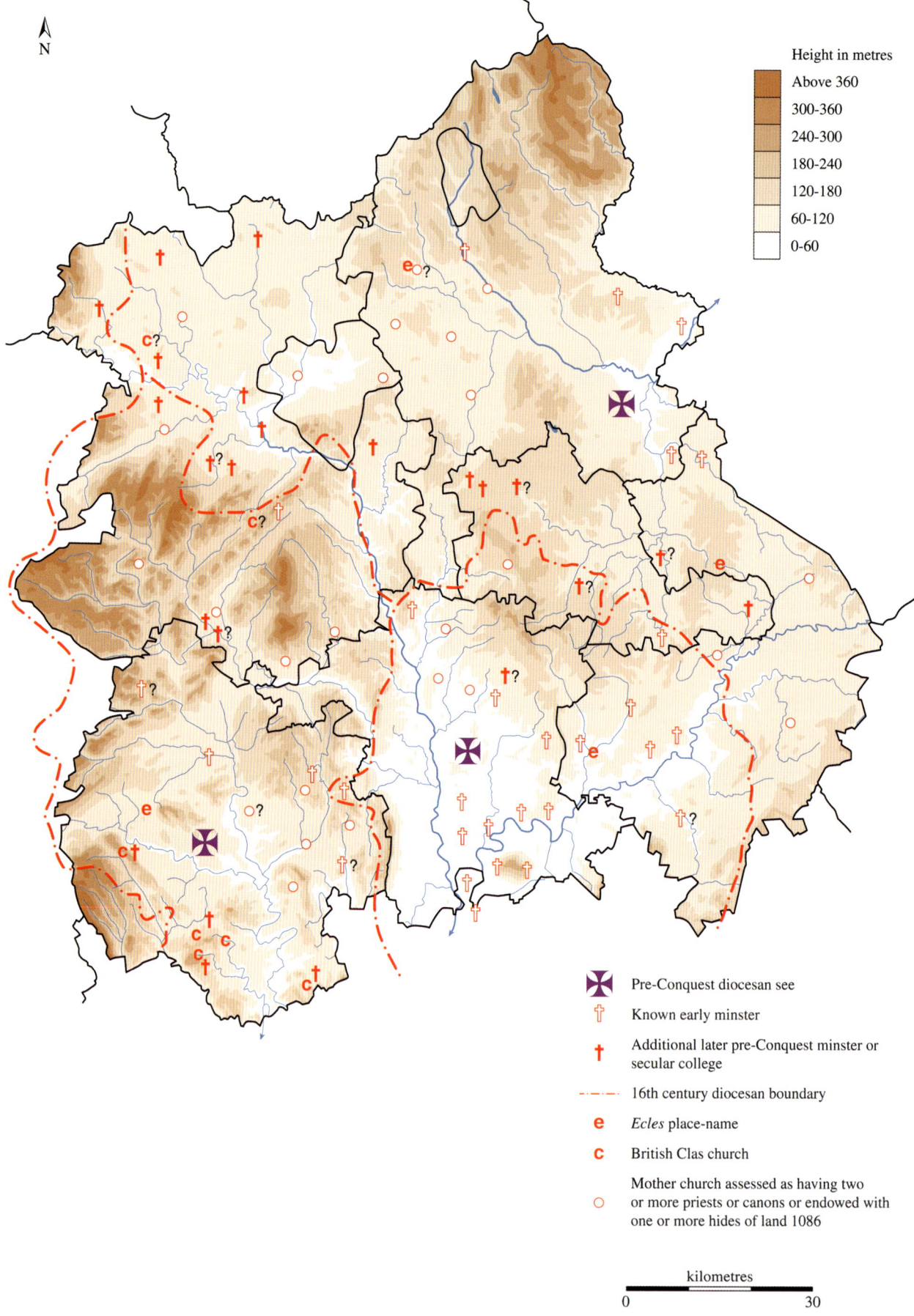

Height in metres

Above 360

300-360

240-300

180-240

120-180

60-120

0-60

✠  Pre-Conquest diocesan see

✝  Known early minster

✝  Additional later pre-Conquest minster or
    secular college

–·–·–  16th century diocesan boundary

e  *Ecles* place-name

c  British Clas church

○  Mother church assessed as having two
   or more priests or canons or endowed with
   one or more hides of land 1086

kilometres

0                                    30

**Fig 5.3** Known early and later pre-Conquest minsters in the region

### Minster foundations

Apart from the burhs, it has been claimed (Blair 1988) that minster foundations were the nearest thing to urban sites in early Anglo-Saxon England; many, indeed, became towns in their own right (above), gaining revenue from the control of marketing and acting as consumers of goods and services. Lichfield, never a burh but a short-lived diocesan centre by the 8th century, is a candidate for early medieval urban status (Wardle, notes submitted to WMRRFA). Again, archaeology has begun to supply information about many of these centres: at Evesham, for instance, the reformed Benedictine community appears to have developed the town in the later 11th century, with a degree of urban planning, and similar initiatives probably took place at Pershore and Coventry. But what of the other early minsters (Fig 5.3)? Hanbury stood within the ramparts of an Iron Age hillfort, a location which perhaps provided an expression of power over the surrounding landscape. Although Alcester was probably the 'celebrated place called Alne' where an ecclesiastical council was held in AD 709, and remained a royal estate, no evidence of its probable early minster has been found. This was perhaps because its ecclesiastical role was taken over by Evesham Abbey, which by the time of the Norman Conquest had managed to gain control of most of the area in the Arrow valley that seems to have been earlier dependent upon Alcester. A territory initially dependent upon Alcester, assessed at very close to 100 hides, can be reconstructed (Hooke 2003a, 73-4, also fig 3). The location of early minsters is better known within the Hwiccan kingdom due to the full records maintained by the Church of Worcester but even here many have yet to be identified on the ground (Inkberrow, Ismere, Bredon etc). In Herefordshire and Shropshire, estate groupings and sculpture may suggest the location of pre-Conquest minsters (Croom 1988; Cotton WMRRFA 4). Sculpture fragments can be indicative of early church foundations and the role of the Church in acting as a focus for local territories also offers important evidence when the extent of their medieval *parochiae* can be reconstructed (eg for Hanbury see Dyer 1991, 18; for Wootton Wawen see Bassett 1983, 70; Hooke 1985b, 136, fig 33). By the end of the period, the great minsters stood out as virtually the only stone buildings (eg the churches at Wootton Wawen and Tredington) in a landscape where other buildings were small and constructed out of timber and thatch. The minster buildings not only expressed the power of God on earth but, perhaps inadvertently at this stage, the role and status of the Church itself.

### Communications

Most of the major Roman roads appear to have remained in use (Hooke 1981a, 300-14), facilitating communications across the region, although some towns like Tamworth and Burton developed on sites a little distance away from the main network lines. A network of saltways, some using stretches of the Roman network, was also used for one of the region's main commodities of trade (Fig 5.4). River transport also gave access to the region and Worcester developed its river trade by the 10th century (Dalwood WMRRFA 4) but the dates at which bridges were constructed across the region's rivers remain largely unknown (the bridge at Worcester was repaired in 1088); fords and ferries were earlier means of effecting crossings.

### 5.3.3. The rural landscape: settlement and land use

An understanding of the rural landscape offers more of a challenge. Opportunities in advance of redevelopment are less concentrated than in towns and rarely coincide with research questions. Neither does archaeological excavation necessarily reveal a great deal about field systems etc, although the techniques of environmental archaeology can be invaluable in suggesting land use over a limited area. In the early medieval period, a change seems to have taken place in the organisation of large estates. The collection of taxes under Roman rule seems to have given way, in many areas, to the more traditional form of taking tribute in kind, perhaps linked to other changes taking place in the rural economy (Faith 1997, 4-5, 102). The need to provide urban centres and the army with grain was removed, and traditional pastoral farming may have increased in importance, also perhaps a response to a deteriorating climate, although excavations at Salford Priors and Broom indicate continued exploitation of the cleared and cultivated river terraces along the Arrow, perhaps accompanied by settlement 'drift'. New 'multiple' estates were

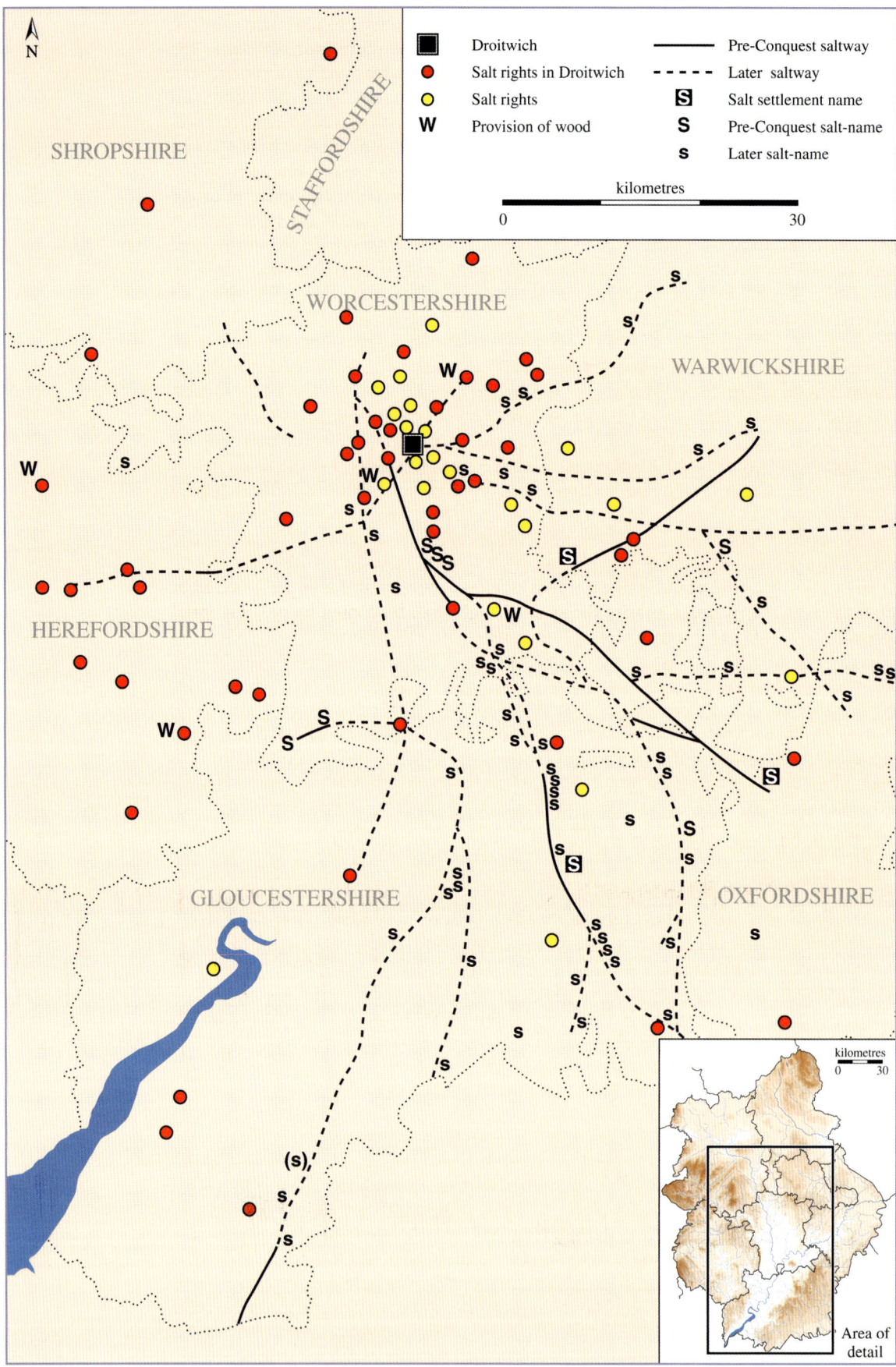

**Fig 5.4** Pre-Conquest saltways in the midland region (after Hooke 1998, 8, fig 4)

to emerge, and some of their central places may have continued to occupy sites that were previously important. It is within such estates that the settlement patterns characteristic of the period may have emerged. Brown and Ford (1998, 81) have conjectured whether 'the process of nucleation was associated with a fundamental reorganisation of the decayed late Roman landscape' as 'the middle Saxon economy was dominated by pastoralism', but the change seems generally to have occurred later, in the mid to late Anglo-Saxon period, when the amount of land used for cultivation was again being extended, as attested by alluviation in river valleys arising from soil erosion on newly cleared land. The end of a major period of relatively well-dated alluviation has been radiocarbon dated to the 8th century at Droitwich, perhaps signifying such a change in land use, with the onset of the alluviation occurring in the 7th or 8th centuries (Hurst and Hemingway 1997), although in the vicinity of Droitwich such evidence may, alternatively, reflect the fresh removal of tree cover upstream in association with fuel provision for salt making (D Hurst, pers comm).

It has also been commonly suggested that intensified land use coincided with the fragmentation of estates into 'township' communities and the rise of the 'proto-manor' (Fox 1981; Hooke 1998, 114-21) as lords were under pressure to augment the economies of their individual estates, and that it was also associated with the introduction of open-field farming as a means of achieving increased revenue. But fresh thinking has suggested that these changes, involving the development of open-field agriculture, occurred *before* estate fragmentation, taking place upon the *inland* of the great estates (Williamson 2003, 18). As noted earlier, this places the move towards settlement nucleation and open-field agriculture within large ('multiple'?) estates rather than within splintering local lordships, attributing nucleation to the improvement of efficiency within the larger unit rather than the smaller. In this scenario, the system might well be copied by new manorial lords. But estate fission is again almost impossible to date. Williamson (ibid, 155-9) has gone further in examining the influence of soils and geology, for he has pointed to the narrow window of opportunity for ploughing on pelo-stagnogley soils that may have encouraged farmers to live in a nucleated settlement, adopting the centralised open-field system of agriculture. He also argues that the presence of meadowland encouraged settlement nucleation and that an abundance of hay enabled growing populations to expand the arable at the expense of woodland and pasture. However, ceramic evidence (Warwickshire, above) may point to the relatively late establishment of nucleated village centres in the 'champion' regions of the west midlands.

### Farming and field systems

Can archaeology help to identify the nature of early field systems? Methods of retrogressive analysis have shown some promise but have again thrown up as many questions as they have answered. In north-west Herefordshire a pattern of coaxial fields near Pembridge was apparently established in the prehistoric period for it was cut by the post-Roman Rowe Ditch in the Arrow valley to the west of Kington (White 2003, 74-5). Bassett (1986) attempted to show other coaxial systems in west Warwickshire but, if genuine, these would need to have survived through later patterns of open-field farming. Neither can the extent of the early open fields yet be verified. Charter boundaries seem to suggest that there were often enclosed fields beyond the open-field nucleus in the later part of the early medieval period although these were subsequently taken into the medieval open fields. This seems to have been the case near the western boundary of Tredington in Warwickshire and in Bishopton near Stratford in the same county (Hooke 1999, 85-6, 123), some of these perhaps associated with boundary settlements lying some distance from the manorial nucleus. The areas under open field were often those that had already been most intensively developed in the Roman period, extending, especially, across the Feldon of Warwickshire and the Vale of Evesham in Worcestershire. It was these regions that became the classic 'champion' lands of medieval times, with extensive and regular open-field systems.

Far less is understood about farming outside these regions. Most have been classified as regions of 'irregular' field systems with more limited areas of open field often associated with smaller but more numerous settlement clusters. Only where populations were denser in medieval times, as in the more fertile plain areas of Shropshire, the Wye valley of Herefordshire and central and south-east Staffordshire, did extensive and regular open-field systems develop. An argument for the intensity of arable farming and settlement nucleation over much of Herefordshire has, however, been advanced by the county's chief archaeologist, Keith Ray, who bases his arguments upon the number of deserted medieval settlements now known and the amount of ridge and furrow recorded, which he links with the surprisingly large number of plough teams recorded in Domesday Book (Darby 1977). Landscape archaeology can thus suggest possible land use but cannot always offer proof or period of settlements: the number of ploughs recorded in 1086 may still indicate a landscape of scattered manorial nuclei, often small, surrounded by scattered farms with plough teams that had still not been drawn into a central estate focus and thus reduced in number. Archaeology has yet to take up this challenge as well as so many others. However, it is clear that a multidisciplinary approach is needed to establish the framework of estates and territories within which settlements developed and field patterns emerged. Neither should geology and soils be ignored, as Willliamson's (2003, 155-9) theories indicate (above).

### Changing estate and settlement patterns

There is a need to understand the region not only in a wider English setting but in the light of changes that were occurring in the early medieval period across Europe. A major reorganisation and stabilisation of settlement was taking place in many parts of north-west Europe during the later 7th and the 8th centuries, although the trend could continue later, as in Denmark (Hamerow 2002). It seems to reflect an intensification of production, new systems of distribution and the changed socio-economic structure of rural communities within larger territories. New administrative structures replaced old tribal loyalties and distant centres became important foci of activity. Hamerow (ibid, 123) rejects the break-up of multiple estates as a prime factor in settlement shift but agrees with those who see the shift to heavier soils as a means of meeting 'the demands of new secular and ecclesiastical landlords for surplus, and to provision the populations of the newly established emporia'. She envisages a process that began here in the 8th century but lasted at least a century, proceeding at different rates in different regions. Crucially, crop and animal husbandry was also changing: agricultural production was intensifying in the 8th and 9th centuries after a period dominated by a strong pastoral element: monasteries and towns were growing 'consumer' communities and the demesne system was asked to produce a substantial agricultural surplus, perhaps most readily effected in open fields, by crop rotation and greater use of the mouldboard plough. A bigger labour force was required and labour was pooled, and plough oxen shared, with a collective right over such resources as pasture and pannage.

### Water resources

Another feature of economic development is the watermill, the best known that found on the royal vill of Tamworth, Staffs, and thought to date from the 8th century. Two others have recently been found close to the royal centre of Marden in Herefordshire. On rural manors, mills were being built in Warwickshire in the 10th century, recorded in charters and place-names. Most sites recorded lay in the central Avon valley: at Milcote, Alveston, Clopton and Ruin Clifford in Old Stratford and in the Stour valley at Blackwell in Tredington, although a mill at *Bluntesige* may have been at Blunt's Green in Tanworth (Hooke 1996). In Worcestershire there was a mill on the Church of Worcester's manor of *Caldinccotan* in Bredon, recorded in the later 10th century (Hooke 1981a, 267-9, fig 3.28) and mills also on estates of Pershore Abbey. It is not perhaps fortuitous that these were all church estates, for innovation was probably first effected on important royal and ecclesiastical estates. Mill pools were often associated with the capture of eels in Domesday Book but river and estuarine fisheries were already operating at an earlier date (ibid, 268-72).

### Marginal land use

Some of the most intriguing questions are concerned with the regions of more marginal land use. Abandoned field systems at the Burrels in Sutton Coldfield (M Hodder, pers comm) and recent studies of palaeobotanical data of the area around Metchley Roman fort on the Birmingham Plateau suggest that wood pasture was re-emerging as the dominant land use of the area in the post-Roman period although there was some subsequent cultivation of rye (Greig 2005). This would tie in with the place-name evidence for much of north Worcestershire, north Warwickshire and elsewhere in the region (similar results have been obtained at King's Pool in Stafford: J Hunt, pers comm). Pre-Conquest charters reveal a pattern of resource management in which links were maintained between estates in regions of intensive agricultural development and those in more marginal areas. Ford (1976) has argued that such links may go back into at least the late Iron Age when, in a similar economy, herds and flocks were driven to seasonal pastures many kilometres distant. Some of these links may have survived or been initiated anew in the Anglo-Saxon period. Whether actual movement of stock always occurred is not known but a pattern of north-west/south-east route ways across Warwickshire linking the Arden and Feldon may have begun as drove ways linking the two regions (Hooke 1998, 161, fig 55; 2003a, 71, fig 2). By the early medieval period, estate links seem to have continued as a means of utilising contributory resources, wooded regions in particular providing pasture for herds of swine as well as timber resources.

Another use of marginal regions that emerged in the early medieval period was that of hunting. Again, place-name terms cannot be accurately interpreted but a boundary feature referred to in charters as a *haga* apparently bounded areas of ground in wooded countryside and seems to have been the forerunner of the game reserve or park, often found on the boundaries of royal estates. By the time of Domesday Book, *haia* features represented the same enclosures and were stated in that source to be enclosures for the capture of deer (Hooke 1989). They were particularly frequent in the Welsh Borderland where much land had been laid waste by Welsh attacks and were also frequent in areas due to be designated as Royal Forest by the Normans. Landscape archaeology in the midland region has so far failed to identify these features on the ground but detailed studies of hedges, hedgebanks and woodbanks might yet provide more information.

### The recognition of regional pays

The recognition of regional variation, expressed as landscape *pays*, must be a major aim if causal factors are to be fully understood. Historic Landscape Characterisation projects are underway or nearing completion across the region and have helped to identify landscape regions across the west midlands. One of the first studies of this kind was carried out in Warwickshire in the early 1990s under the auspices of the Countryside Commission and Warwickshire County Council. It included an analysis of the historical landscape regions of the county, primarily as a guide to future countryside planning and management, and involved the production of detailed maps and reports covering the whole of Warwickshire and adjacent parts of surrounding counties (Warwickshire City Council, 1991, 1993; Hooke 1993). Since then, English Heritage has fostered similar projects more closely geared towards archaeology and the historical landscape, developing models for the analysis, management, protection and enhancement of the historic environment. Such studies have enabled archaeological and historical monuments to be seen within the wider landscape setting that is unique for each character area recognised. Evolutionary trends can also be examined and perhaps better understood, together with the factors that have led some regions to include areas where ancient features have apparently had a better chance of survival whereas, in others, rural landscapes have been irrevocably changed, largely by enclosure or urbanisation.

The recent development of Historic Environment Records, replacing Sites and Monuments Records, must also be a step forward but at present the evidence for the early medieval period is seriously incomplete. Gaps in the settlement record, in particular, cannot necessarily be taken to indicate an absence of population. For the first time in history, the documentary record for parts of the region offers a substantial body of information about the nature and development of the rural landscape. Pre-Conquest charters provide detail about land use features in some regions, as such much of Worcestershire, which is difficult to match from any other source, although place names are a more ubiquitous source of information (Hooke WMRRF 2004; 1981a, 1985b, 1990, 1999; volumes of the English Place-Name Society where completed; for Herefordshire see Coplestone-Crow 1989). Charters are few in number for the Borderland, however, and the charters of the *Book of Llan Dâv* that describe estates in southern Herefordshire may offer details about local topography but do not disclose a great deal about land use other than indicating the presence of woodland in some areas now relatively open (Davies 1978; *Book of Llan Dâv* 1979; Hooke WMRRFA 4). Most regional classifications have been based upon medieval and later landscapes (eg designations such as Rackham's (1986, 4-5) 'Ancient' and 'Planned Countryside'; this and others are discussed more fully in Hooke 2006, 9-22). It is clear, however, that later regional characteristics were already clearly evident in the early medieval period and a priority is to establish how early they became apparent. Here research must clearly look beyond the beginning of the period back into prehistoric and Roman times. One of the clearest distinctions evident is that between the Warwickshire Arden and Feldon but that reality was rather more complicated is shown by detailed study (eg Hooke 1981a, 1985b; Fox 1989).

Archaeobotanical evidence is urgently needed to provide more information about the nature of early medieval woodland. Well-wooded regions are clearly indicated by place-name evidence but the exact interpretation of the terms used needs clarification. Unprotected areas of woodland, such as the extensive areas used as wood pasture where stock foraged and often destroyed tree seedlings, are not likely to have consisted of dense woodland and the ubiquitous *leah* term in such regions has been interpreted by Wager (1998) as 'secondary woodland'; the term may, however, have implied the specific economic usage of 'open woodland used as wood pasture' (as at Metchley) (Hooke 1989 and 2008). The distribution of marginal areas is also closely related to frontier regions and, hence, territorial organisation (Hooke 1986). Waterlogged deposits, in particular, offer considerable potential for archaeological investigation, as attested by the discovery of the two water mills near Wellington associated with the royal centre of Marden.

Concentrated activity such as that currently being directed towards an understanding of the manors of Marden, with specific enquiries in mind, may offer the best way forward rather than leaving archaeology to the vagaries of 'rescue' archaeology. The Arrow Valley Project in Herefordshire that was funded by English Heritage and Herefordshire Council is an example of what a systematic study of a clearly defined area can hope to produce, providing as it does a framework for subsequent archaeological investigation. There have been similar earlier studies, usually carried out on a much smaller scale, such as my own work in the Arrow Valley of Warwickshire in the late 1970s/early '80s or Bassett's (1983) in Wootton Wawen, or studies of single parishes like Dyer's (1991; 1994, 51-76) work at Hanbury and Pendock, but these lacked the funding and organisation allotted to the Herefordshire project, which also involved 'key-hole' excavation on a Roman settlement site and at points along the Rowe Ditch. Here, field survey and aerial photography revealed earthworks of medieval settlements and even a new medieval town at Lyonshall, showing that there was a large population living in the area during the medieval period with hints of greater settlement nucleation than hitherto expected. It is a sobering thought, however, that the marshalling of known information, studies of aerial photographs, fieldwalking, and even some selective trenching, failed to produce evidence of early medieval settlements.

## 5.4. Re-examination of existing data

Discussion during the Framework meetings also noted the importance of re-examining existing collections, perhaps subjecting some to modern analytical techniques, and the need to complete the examination and publication of some early work. Other problems have arisen because of the constraints of present planning policies, for developers cannot be expected to fund primary research, and the costly examination of such features as palaeochannels is hard to guarantee: the need for detailed pollen studies of a general area such as the Avon valley of Warwickshire has to be a deliberately funded project. The maintenance of a midland database might be a particularly useful tool. In investigating the evidence for the early medieval period in the west midlands, the inconsistency of the region's Sites and Monuments Record (now Historic Environment Record) has been especially highlighted. This is especially obvious for this period, when almost every medieval village in Staffordshire is classified under the date AD 410+ as the category runs from this date to 1066, with only a handful of villages classified under this date in Shropshire and Warwickshire (the latter reflecting actual archaeological evidence). Above all, the necessity to adopt a multidisciplinary approach to problems is clearly evident if archaeology is to answer specific questions. A selected estate entity might provide a suitable framework for investigation but the need for archaeological intervention is shown by the failure of historical/documentary studies to answer unresolved problems.

## 5.5. Suggested research priorities

- Population make-up: use of strontium isotope ratios and continued DNA testing to explore racial affinities.

- Re-examination of burial evidence: bones, metalwork and pottery, in existing collections.

- Urgent publication of unpublished or partially published archaeological investigations.

- Evaluation of pre-Christian ritual sites.

- Evaluation of the possible reuse of Iron Age hillforts in the post-Roman period.

- Continued search for evidence of all forms of early medieval rural settlements with particular attention to sites where Roman and medieval settlements are juxtaposed.

- Identification of early minster sites, especially within Greater Mercia, using all available documentary evidence (including the extent of medieval parochiae) together with church sculpture and church fabric etc.

- Continued work on urban sites with detailed studies of ceramic evidence. Need to understand the role of commerce and markets.

- Prominence needs to be given to environmental archaeology and results need to be easily accessible within the region. Definition needed of areas where environmental evidence of previous land use is likely to be well preserved (eg alluviated river valleys). An allotted programme in a selected area would be beneficial. Recognition of the potential of soil micromorphology to determine 5th- to 9th-century occupation or land use.

- Need to adopt a multidisciplinary approach embodying archaeology: selected area studies likely to be most productive. However, no area can be examined in isolation.

- Need to record areas of specific land use such as early field systems, etc. The difficulty of dating such features should not mean that they are ignored.

## Notes

1. Many of the themes highlighted in this paper are addressed further in my contribution to the WMRRFA Seminar 4 (http://www.iaa.bham. ac.uk/research/projects/wmrrfa/index.shtml).

167

2.  Some peasants on royal or similar estates, such as the British *maerdrefi*, were responsible for the upkeep of the vill. Alongside these responsibilities, they held a servile position that would have been inherited by their offspring; this may have discouraged marriage into this community, thus perpetuating the *walh* segment of the population well into the 8th century when this term becomes recorded in place-names (such as Walton, Walcot etc) for communities linked to estate centres.

3.  http://www.ucl.ac.uk/archaeology/cisp/database.

## Abbreviations

WMRRFA 2004: West Midlands Regional Research Framework for Archaeology, series of seminars 2003–4. It must be noted that some of the papers presented at this seminar were never submitted to the Management Committee and could not, therefore, be used to produce this report.

## Bibliography

Baker, N, 2003   *The Archaeology of the Larger Medieval Towns, West Midlands Research Framework* (Seminars)

Barber, A, and Watts, M, 2003   Excavations at Saxon's Lode Farm, Ryall Quarry, Ripple, *Worcestershire Recorder* 67, 11-13

Bassett, S, 1983   The Wootton Wawen project, *West Midlands Archaeol* 26, 66-71

Bassett, S, 1986   *The Wootton Wawen Project*, Unpub interim rep 4, Univ Birmingham School Hist

Bassett, S, 1989   Churches in Worcester before and after the conversion of the Anglo-Saxons, *Antiq J* 69, 225-56

Bassett, S, 2000   How the west was won: the Anglo-Saxon takeover of the west midlands, *Anglo-Saxon Studies in Archaeol & Hist* 11, 107-18

Beresford, G, 1987   *Goltho. The development of an early medieval manor c. 850–1150*, English Heritage Arch Rep 4, London

Birch, W de Gray, 1885–99   *Cartularium Saxonicum*, London

Blair, J, 1988   Minster churches in the landscape, in Hooke, D (ed), *Anglo-Saxon Settlements*, Oxford, 35-58

Blair, J, 1995   Anglo-Saxon pagan shrines and their prototypes, Griffiths, D (ed), *Anglo-Saxon Studies in Archaeol & Hist* 8, Oxford, 1-28

*Book of Llan Dâv, the Text of,*   reproduced from the Gwysaney manuscript by J, Gwenogvryn Evans, facsimile edn, 1979, Aberystwyth

Boucher, A, 2002   Understanding Hereford's Past, in Thomas, A, and Boucher, A (eds), *Hereford City Excavations. Vol. 4: 1976–1990*, Almeley, 1-11

Brooks, N, 1989   The formation of the Mercian kingdom, in Bassett, S (ed), *The Origins of Anglo-Saxon Kingdoms*, London, 159-70

Brown, T, and Foard, G, 1998   The Saxon landscape: a regional perspective, in Everson, P, and Williamson, T (eds), *The Archaeology of Landscape*, Manchester, 67-94

Capelli, C, Redhead, N, Abernethy, J K, Gratrix, F, Wilson, J F, Moen, T, Hervig, T, Richards, M, Stumpf, M P H, Underhill, P A, Bradshaw, P, Shaha, A, Thomas, M G, Bradman, N, and Goldstein, D B, 2003   A Y chromosome census of the British Isles, *Current Biology* 13, 979-84

Coplestone-Crow, B, 1989 *Herefordshire Place-Names*, BAR British Series 214, Oxford

Crawford, G, 1982 Excavations at Wasperton: 2nd interim report, *West Midlands Archaeol* 25, 30-44

Croom, J, 1988 Fragmentation of the minster parochiae of south-east Shropshire, in Blair, J (ed), *Minsters and Parish Churches. The local church in transition 950–1200*, Oxford Univ Comm Archaeol Monogr 17, Oxford, 67-81

Dalwood, H, 2004 Chronological synthesis, in *Excavations at Deansway, Worcester* (ed H, Dalwood and R, Edwards), 36-76

Dalwood, H, and Edwards, R, 2004 *Excavations at Deansway, Worcester, 1988–89: Romano-British small town to late medieval city*, CBA Res Rep 139, York

Darby, H C, 1977 *Domesday England*, Cambridge

Davies, W, 1978 *An Early Welsh Microcosm: studies in the Llandaff charters*, London

Dinn, J, and Evans, J, 1992 Aston Mill Farm, Kemerton: excavation of a ring-ditch, middle Iron Age enclosures, and a grubenhaus, *Trans Worcestershire Archaeol Soc*, 3rd ser 12, 5-66

Dyer, C, 1991 *Hanbury: settlement and society in a woodland landscape*, Univ Leicester Depart Engl Local Hist Occas Pap, 4th ser 4, Leicester

Dyer, C, 1994 *Everyday Life in Medieval England*, London

Esmonde-Cleary, A S, 1989 *The Ending of Roman Britain*, London

Evison, V I, 1996 *Two Anglo-Saxon Cemeteries at Beckford, Hereford and Worcester*, CBA Res Rep 103, York

Faith, R, 1997 *The English Peasantry and the Growth of Lordship*, London

Ford, D, 1998–9 A late Saxon pottery industry in Staffordshire: a review, *Medieval Ceramics* 22–3, 11-36

Ford, W J, 1976 Settlement patterns in the central region of the Warwickshire Avon, in Sawyer, P H (ed), *Medieval Settlement, Continuity and Change*, London, 274-94

Ford, W J, 1996 Anglo-Saxon cemeteries along the Avon valley, *Trans Birmingham and Warwickshire Archaeol Soc* 100, 59-98

Ford, W J, in prep The Anglo-Saxon cemetery and settlement at the Alveston Manor Hotel, Tiddington, Alveston, Stratford upon Avon, Warwickshire, *Trans Birmingham Warwickshire Archaeol Soc*

Fox, H S A, 1981 Approaches to the adoption of the Midland system, in Rowley, T (ed), *The Origins of Open-Field Agriculture*, London, 64-111

Fox, H S A, 1989 The people of the wolds in English settlement history, in Aston, M, Austin, D, and Dyer, C (ed), *The Rural Settlements of Medieval England*, Oxford, 77-101

Gelling, M, 1961 Place-names and Anglo-Saxon paganism, *Univ Birmingham Hist J* 8, 7-25

Gelling, M, 1973 Further thoughts on pagan place-names, *Otium et Negotium: studies in onomatology and library science presented to Olof von Feilitzen*, Stockholm, 109-28

Gelling, M, 1978 *Signposts to the Past. Place-names and the history of England*, London

Gelling, M, 1992 *The West Midlands in the early Middle Ages*, Leicester

Greig, J, 2005  Pollen and waterlogged seeds, in Jones, A, Metchley II, *Trans Birmingham Warwickshire Archaeol Soc* 108

Hall, D, 1981  The changing landscape of the Cambridgeshire silt fens, *Landscape History* 3, 37-50

Hall, D, and Coles, J, 1994  *Fenland Survey. An essay in landscape and persistence*, English Heritage Arch Rep 1, London

Hamerow, H, 2002  *Early Medieval Settlements. The archaeology of rural communities in north-west Europe 400–900*, Oxford

Higham, N, 1993  *The Origins of Cheshire*, Manchester

Hill, D, and Worthington, M, 2003  *Offa's Dyke. History and guide*, Stroud

Hirst, S, and Rahtz, P A, 1972–3  Hatton Rock 1970, *Trans Birmingham Warwickshire Archaeol Soc* 85, 160-77

Hodges, R, 1989  *The Anglo-Saxon Achievement*, London

Hooke, D, 1980  The hinterland and routeways of Anglo-Saxon Worcester: the charter evidence, in Carver, M O H (ed), *Medieval Worcester. An archaeological framework*, Trans Worcestershire Archaeol Soc, 3rd ser 7, 39-49

Hooke, D, 1981a  *Anglo-Saxon Landscapes of the West Midlands: the charter evidence*, BAR British Series 95, Oxford

Hooke, D, 1981b  Burial features in West Midland charters, *J Engl Place-Name Soc* 13, 1-40

Hooke, D, 1983  *The Landscape of Anglo-Saxon Staffordshire: the charter evidence*, Keele

Hooke, D, 1985a  Village development in the West Midlands, in Hooke, D (ed), *Medieval Villages, a review of current work*, Oxford Univ Comm Archaeol Monogr 5, Oxford, 125-54

Hooke, D, 1985b  *The Anglo-Saxon Landscape: the kingdom of the Hwicce*, Manchester

Hooke, D, 1986  *Anglo-Saxon Territorial Organization: the western margins of Mercia*, Univ Birmingham Dep Geogr Occ Pap 22, Birmingham

Hooke, D, 1989  Pre-conquest woodland: its distribution and usage, *Agric Hist Rev* 37, 113-29

Hooke, D, 1990  *Worcestershire Anglo-Saxon Charter-Bounds*, Woodbridge

Hooke, D, 1993  *Warwickshire's Historical Landscape - the Arden*, Univ Birmingham School of Geogr, Birmingham

Hooke, D, 1996  Reconstructing Anglo-Saxon landscapes in Warwickshire, *Trans Birmingham Warwickshire Archaeol Soc* 100, 99-116

Hooke, D, 1997  The Anglo-Saxons in England in the seventh and eighth centuries: aspects of location in space, in Hines, J (ed), *The Anglo-Saxons from the Migration Period to the Eighth Century*, Woodbridge, 65-85

Hooke, D, 1998  *The Landscape of Anglo-Saxon England*, London

Hooke, D, 1999  *Warwickshire Anglo-Saxon Charter-Bounds*, Woodbridge

Hooke, D, 2001  Mercia: landscape and environment, in Brown, M P, and Farr, C A (eds), *Mercia, an Anglo-Saxon Kingdom in Europe*, London, 160-72

Hooke, D, 2003a   Names and settlement in the Warwickshire Arden, in Hooke, D, and Postles, D (eds), *Names, Time and Place. Essays in memory of Richard McKinley*, Oxford, 66-99

Hooke, D, 2003b   Landscape studies, in Ecclestone, M, Gardner, K S, Holbrook, N, and Smith, A (eds), *The Land of the Dobunni, Sons of Woden – Soldiers of Christ?*, Comm for Archaeol in Gloucestershire and CBA – South West, 68-76

Hooke, D, 2006   *England's Landscape. The West Midlands,* London

Hooke, D, 2008   Early medieval woodland and the place-name term *léah*, in Padel, O J, and Parsons, D N (eds), *A Commodity of Good Names: essays in honour of Margaret Gelling*, Donington, Lincs, 365-76

Hurst, J D (ed), 1997   *Multi-Period Salt Production Site at Droitwich: excavations at Upwich*, CBA Res Rep 107, York

Hurst, J D, and Hemingway, J, 1997   The Excavation, in Hurst, D (ed), *A Multi-Period Salt Production Site at Droitwich*, 9-67

Lentowicz, I J, 1997   Pottery, in *A Multi-Period Salt Production Site at Droitwich* (ed D, Hurst), 68-89

Losco-Bradley, S, and Kinsley, G, 2002   *Catholme. An Anglo-Saxon settlement on the Trent gravels in Staffordshire*, Nottingham Studies in Archaeol 3, Nottingham

Macphail, R I, 2004   Soils and land-use history: results and potential of soil micro-morphology, in *Excavations at Deansway, Worcester, 1988–89: Romano-British small town to late medieval city* (eds H Dalwood and R Edwards), CBA Res Rep 139, York

Oppenheimer, S, 2006   *The Origins of the British. A genetic detective story*, London

Palmer, S C, 2000   Archaeological excavations in the Arrow Valley, Warwickshire, *Trans Birmingham Warwickshire Archaeol Soc* 103

Pryor, F, 2004   *Britain AD, A Quest for Arthur, England and the Anglo-Saxons*, London

Rackham, O, 1986   *The History of the Countryside*, London

Rahtz, P, 1976   Gazetteer of Anglo-Saxon domestic settlement sites, in Wilson, D M (ed), *The Archaeology of Anglo-Saxon England*, Cambridge, 405-52

Reynolds, A, 2003   Boundaries and settlements in later sixth to eleventh-century England, in Griffiths, D, Reynolds, A, and Semple, S (eds), *Boundaries in Early Medieval Britain*, Anglo-Saxon Studies in Archaeol & Hist 12, Oxford, 97-136

Sawyer, P H, 1968   *Anglo-Saxon Charters. An annotated list and bibliography*, London

Smith, C, 1980   The historical development of the landscape in the parishes of Alrewas, Fisherwick and Whittington: a retrogressive analysis, *Trans South Staffordshire Archaeol Hist Soc* 20, 1-14

Vince, A, 2002   The Anglo-Saxon pottery, in Losco-Bradley, S, and Kinsley, G, 2002 *Catholme. An Anglo-Saxon settlement on the Trent gravels in Staffordshire*, Nottingham Studies in Archaeol 3, Nottingham

Wager, S J, 1998   *Woods, Wolds and Groves, the woodland of early medieval Warwickshire*, BAR British Series 269, Oxford

Warwickshire City Council 1991, repr 1993   *Warwickshire Landscapes Guidelines*, 3 vols, Warwick

Weale, M E, Weiss, D A, Jager, R F, Bradman, N, and Thomas, M G, 2002   Y chromosome evidence for Anglo-Saxon mass migration, *Molecular Biology and Evolution* 19, 1008-21

White, P, 2003   *The Arrow Valley, Herefordshire: archaeology, landscape change and conservation*, Herefordshire Stud Archaeol 2, Hereford

White, R, and Barker, P, 1998 revised edn 2002   *Wroxeter: the life and death of a Roman city*, Stroud

Williamson, T, 1986   The development of settlement in north west Essex: the results of a recent field survey, *Essex Archaeol and Hist* 17, 120-32

Williamson, T, 2003   *Shaping Medieval Landscapes: settlement, society, environment*, Macclesfield

Wise, P, and Seaby, W A, 1995   Finds from a new 'productive site' at Bidford-on-Avon, Warwickshire, *Trans Birmingham Warwickshire Archaeol Soc* 99, 57-64

# 6. The medieval period

## John Hunt

### 6.1. Introduction

As Professor Hilton observed (Hilton 1983, 8), the medieval west midlands is a region with extremely vague frontiers, particularly if attempting to define it in terms of economic and social structure. In his study, Hilton defined the region by the boundaries of the diocese of Worcester, which in turn referred back to those of the former Hwiccian kingdom. However, for the purposes of this review, the west midland region is more widely defined, encompassing Staffordshire, Shropshire, Worcestershire, Warwickshire and Herefordshire, but, contrary to Hilton, excludes Gloucestershire. This includes shires that looked towards the Welsh March, Cheshire, Derbyshire and Leicestershire, all areas interlocking with their neighbours in some way. While a county like Staffordshire might look towards Derbyshire and the Trent valley, it also had aspects in its socio-economic and socio-political 'make-up' that served to link it with Shropshire, Worcestershire and Warwickshire. It clearly is possible to look upon the medieval west midland region on a broader basis than that selected by Hilton in his seminal study, and inevitably, with a larger area, there also comes greater diversity.

The centuries between the Norman Conquest and *c* 1500 saw, among other things, the introduction and development of a new political and social order, and new frameworks within which it operated. Society expanded. Considerable demographic growth (and decline), the emergence of the gentry, the expansion of settlement, the growing commercialisation of society, changing relationships between landlords and their tenants, and expansion and developments within the church were all aspects of these years, and many had a significant impact on the medieval landscape. These have left an archaeological imprint, as well as a documentary one.

This review of our current state of knowledge and priorities for future research has fallen at an opportune moment. New approaches to the protection and management of the historic environment are under development, together with moves to enhance the role of Historic Environment Records (HERs). Furthermore, this has been the first broadly based review that has taken account of the important and positive impact that the introduction of PPG16 in 1990 has had on the archaeology of the region. The message is a consistent one. Development-led archaeology has brought about a significant increase in the number of archaeological interventions that are undertaken. The majority of these are on a small scale, and are often relatively uninformative when viewed alone. However, they all represent accumulating data and, if this is viewed together, there are contexts where a number of small-scale interventions can make significant contributions to our wider understanding. Such is the case, for instance, in the archaeology of medieval towns and, although not arising from PPG16 work, similar observations might be made on the small-scale intervention approach of the Whittlewood Project in investigating rural settlement (Dyer et al 2002, 42; Jones and Page 2003a, 37-45; Jones and Page 2003b,

53-83). However, we have not yet been able to gain the full benefit of this accumulating data. This arises partly from the speed with which it is produced, posing HERs with problems of properly assimilating this information, but more so from the fact that there is at present a lack of, and an urgent need for, works of synthesis and analysis that can bring this material together and set a 'baseline' for the next generation of work. This aspiration lies well beyond the scope of this present chapter, but it does serve to highlight the need for it.

## 6.2. Town and country

### 6.2.1. Rural settlement

The study of rural settlement can claim a long pedigree in the west midlands, particularly in Warwickshire. In the late 15th century John Rous was recording the desertion of villages, and in 1656 William Dugdale produced the first county distribution map of deserted medieval villages. The region has made some significant contributions to the study of this topic, and with it the emergence of medieval archaeology and landscape history as distinct and recognisable disciplines. Key studies include Roberts' (1965; 1968) discussions of the Arden, Thorpe's (1965) important study of Wormleighton in the Warwickshire Feldon and Dyer's (1990; 1991) examination of dispersed settlement patterns in the Worcestershire woodland parishes of Pendock and Hanbury. Despite some singular contributions and case studies, across the region as a whole some fundamental questions remain unanswered, and areas like Shropshire and Staffordshire have not attracted the same intensity of study.

It is widely recognised that the landscape and environmental context provides the most obvious framework within which to approach the study of rural settlement, a point eloquently reiterated recently by Williamson (2003). However, the local and regional environmental circumstances will also mediate a range of other factors that might have a part to play. Technological and demographic developments were clearly important, and social, economic and tenurial factors might also prove influential. For instance, the growth of lordship and its implications have been vigorously debated. The proliferation of local lordships, whether pre-Conquest fragmentation of multiple estates, or post-Conquest subinfeudation and estate subdivision, brought new settlement foci and increasing tenurial complexity. This was accompanied by seigneurial concerns to provide for the needs of their demesnes which, in turn, had to be responsive to changing social and economic circumstances. For example, the 12th and 13th centuries saw aristocratic responses to their incomes under pressure and changing relationships between lords, peasants and land. While the trends were general, the precise nature of the local implications varied. Hence the often contentious question of the extent to which lordship played a direct role in the ordering of medieval settlements and their fields. In the honor of Dudley, for instance, it was noted that the interests and actions of lordship had the capacity to influence the local settlement pattern, but that this was generally incidental to other factors, such as the formation of parkland, rather than any deliberate or planned scheme. Here, the environment remained the overriding factor (Hunt 1997, 130-140). Other studies, like that of Thorpe (1965) on Wormleighton, have emphasised a more assertive and direct impact by lordship. It is the case that the exercise of lordship in woodland areas is frequently perceived as having a 'lighter touch' than in the 'planned' or 'champion' countryside, but whatever landscape lordship was exercised in, it should not be overlooked that its effectiveness and expectations could vary greatly from manor to manor.

Tradition and custom were also of vital importance. For Williamson (2003, 192), 'custom was the single most important articulating force in the organisation of early medieval peasant communities', impacting on the management and structure of the landscape. In this vein, in Herefordshire, arguments have been put forward for the influence of the cultural inheritance from the late Anglo-Saxon period upon the settlement pattern, together with the social and political upheavals of the 11th and 12th centuries (K Ray, pers comm).

Whatever the critical factors might be, it is the case that across the west midlands it is possible to recognise patterns of nucleated and dispersed settlement, in which the former tends to be associated with intensively settled, open landscapes, often established at an early date (Rackham's 'planned', or champion countryside) (Roberts and Wrathmell 2000, 27; Roberts and Wrathmell 2002, 80, 169). The latter, on the other hand, tends to be associated with woodland landscapes and economies (Rackham's 'ancient' countryside). The classic illustration of this contrast is the distinction within Warwickshire between the Arden and Feldon regions of the county. While there is a tendency for dispersed patterns of settlement to be prevalent in the more westerly parts of the region, there is in fact a good deal of sub-regional diversity such that nucleated and dispersed settlement forms may be found throughout the region. Indeed, the reality is that sharp boundaries are generally difficult to draw and each countryside or 'pays' embraced a range of different landscapes. As our consciousness of this issue has been increasingly raised over recent years, Roberts and Wrathmell (2002, 173) felt able to propose that the opposition of dispersed and nucleated settlement was now a construct that should be discarded as having served its purpose. All would accept that this is an oversimplification. Both 'pays' could support a range of variation, but within which it is possible to detect local or regional emphases.

In terms of these broad trends, the Arden/Feldon contrast in Warwickshire has already been noted. In Worcestershire, the emphasis on nucleated settlement occurs in the Cotswold scarp, with an increasing tendency towards dispersion to the west, most emphatically in the Wye–Teme area. In Staffordshire, nucleated settlement is most evident in the river valleys of the Trent–Tame, and to a lesser extent in the Penk and Smestow valleys and parts of central Staffordshire, a number of which subsequently emerged as rural boroughs. Dispersed forms of settlement, however, are found throughout the county.

Recent work in Herefordshire has identified evidence for former villages centred on parish churches and tightly clustered hamlets, together with open-field systems, but is suggesting that the actual form and density of settlement is not always obvious, as the 'visibility' of former settlements is not as clear as might have been assumed, especially in those areas long under arable. Quite simply, sites have been missed and the resulting deficit in recording such sites has led to a false picture of the character and intensity of settlement. This is consistent with the broader picture, and may receive some indirect support from calculations offered by Roberts and Wrathmell (2002). Based on ploughteams recorded in Domesday Book, they suggest that in Herefordshire in 1086 tilled land accounted for some 44.7% of the whole (Roberts and Wrathmell 2002, 187). They note that this is unusual, since they suggest that the average is around 35%-36%. Such levels of agricultural activity would surely be consistent with the greater intensity of settlement that is being suggested. However, while it might indicate intensity of settlement, it does not necessarily indicate the form and nature of that settlement. The remainder of the land, that is, the uncultivated land, comprised mixtures of woodland, scrub and heath lands, and grass pastures, which they collectively term as 'temperate savanna'.

Interesting also in the methodology suggested by Roberts and Wrathmell (2002) is the profile that it offers of the west midlands region. Warwickshire, with 32.5% tilled land, broadly conforms to their proposed national average of 35.5%. Herefordshire, however, was not alone in its high proportion of tilled land in 1086. Application of their methodology produces a figure of 44.5% for Worcestershire. In Shropshire, where settlement sites remain poorly defined and, as at Abdon, medieval settlement sites may occur in areas largely without modern dwellings, they give a figure of 20.3%. Perhaps most startling of all is the calculation that can be made for Staffordshire, suggesting that only 13.9% of the land was tilled in 1086, which clearly has bearing on the intensity of settlement and its economic base. However, this statistic has to be set alongside the record in Domesday Book of some 63 mills in Staffordshire in 1086. If confidence can be placed in the methodology, the outcomes emphasise both the diversity of the west midlands and some of the aspects requiring further research.

There is no area that would not benefit from further work on rural settlement, as in even relatively well studied counties like Warwickshire there are issues to resolve. Here, knowledge of the Feldon is much more comprehensive than for the Arden, such that the latter is regarded as a local priority. In Worcestershire, despite some significant, essentially documentary, case studies, rural settlement has not been sufficiently prioritised. However, it is Staffordshire and Shropshire that are perhaps the most neglected in studies of rural settlement. This is certainly not a reflection of any lack of potential. For instance, even in the conurbation that now dominates what was once the southern part of Staffordshire, fieldwork might reveal previously unrecorded settlement sites, like that known as Cooper's Bank, near Dudley, recorded in 1990 by Peter Boland (Hunt 1997, 134-6). Such instances highlight the need for more coherent studies of settlement in Staffordshire, and the same is certainly true of Shropshire. What is required of this work, as the researches in Herefordshire remind us, is the need to confirm and map settlement density in the medieval period, and to examine more closely the form that it took. This latter point is given greater weight in light of recent developments. Firstly, there is the increasing sophistication that is being urged in the interpretation of medieval landscapes and their settlement patterns – simple 'nucleated' or 'dispersed' tags are no longer sufficient. This requires a review and possible re-evaluation, even of those areas considered as having been fully examined, while for other areas the process is considerably enriched by the work done around the country over the last 20 years or so. Secondly, the work of Roberts and Wrathmell that culminated in the publication of their *Atlas of Rural Settlement in England* (2000) and then of an interpretative essay (2002) has offered ready access to a model that might be applied and its veracity interrogated. Indeed, as the authors recognise, if their work is to be widely applied, and if it were to be adopted as one context in which the vulnerability of the archaeological resource might be assessed, then there is a need to rigorously test it at the level of region and locality (ibid, 192). As Dyer (2001, 117-118) commented, there is value in their 'top-down' approach, but there is now a need for 'bottom-up' case studies to test it.

The archaeological information that we have for medieval rural settlement naturally falls into two basic categories. Firstly, there is that which informs on layout and distribution arising from survey work, ranging from parish surveys, like Pendock and Hanbury, to individual sites like Baginton in Warwickshire, or Chartley (George 1997) and Wychnor in Staffordshire. These reflect ongoing programmes of work of a kind found across the region that are certainly needed, but it is problematic that more often than not the results of the work may not be fully assimilated, beyond being recorded in the SMR. In some cases this is because, as at Wychnor, the work was done partly under the guise of PPG15 (or elsewhere, PPG16), and partly as a project undertaken by Continuing Studies students (Meeson 2003, 4). Non-excavation fieldwork of this kind lends itself to the attentions of local societies and community groups, and important contributions may be made (eg Barston, Warwickshire).

In the region as a whole, there is clearly a lack of excavated sites, again a concern that is particularly acute in some areas like Shropshire and Staffordshire. On the whole, the trial trenching often undertaken as PPG16 related work, but which does not progress further, fails to adequately address this lacuna, all the more so when it is noted that what has been recorded remains largely unassimilated. Generally speaking, at best this process will confirm the presence of medieval activity, but may well fail to demonstrate its nature.

While the current trend has been to move away from large-scale excavations, there can be no doubting the contribution that such work has made to our knowledge of medieval settlement in the region. Warwickshire has an enviable record in this regard, even though this is work that has largely come about in the last 25 years or so. At Burton Dassett Southend (1986-1991; Fig. 6.1) excavation revealed the plans of 20 houses, largely stone built, and with evidence of occupation from the mid 13th to the late 15th century. Outbuildings and a smithy were also excavated (cf Dyer 1996, 126-8; Palmer and Dyer 1988, 216-19). At Coton on the Wolds excavation has revealed a site with over 20 post-built structures, and demonstrated occupation that began in the 10th/11th century and lasted to the late 13th/14th century. Among smaller excavations in Warwickshire, most of which produce only partial plans, mention should be made of Botelers Castle, Oversley (1993) (Jones et al 1997). Here, medieval occupation within an enclosure has been interpreted as a settlement site of 12th-/early 13th-century date associated with, and dependent upon, the motte and bailey castle. This pattern of excavation on settlement sites is difficult to match elsewhere in the region, but even in Warwickshire there remain lacunae in our knowledge, most obviously in the Arden.

The lack of excavation has other implications. Firstly, we are relatively poorly informed about building types in rural settlements. A consequence of this is that frameworks of reference are set by returning to sites now excavated some time ago, generally outside our own region, such as the Upton longhouse (Hilton and Rahtz 1966), Barton Blount (Beresford 1975) and Wharram Percy (Hurst et al 1979). The documentary studies of historians such as Field (1965) and Dyer (1986) have 'offset' this gap in our information, but they cannot obviate the need for archaeological work as well, particularly when considering questions of possible regional characteristics.

Undoubtedly of growing importance is the contribution made by standing buildings. For example, 14th-century buildings have been identified in Staffordshire. In Yoxall, Reeve End Cottage has been identified as an early 14th-century timber-framed building that was once an open aisled hall (Hislop 1985-6), and another 14th-century building has recently been discovered here. At Longdon, in 1995 following fire damage, a medieval aisled hall and cross-wing of possible 14th-century construction was surveyed, and identified as a probable house-byre (Meeson 2001). Staffordshire is hardly unique in this respect. In Shropshire, a programme of dendro-dating has greatly enlarged the number of known medieval buildings in the county, the results of which have recently been summarised by the late Eric Mercer (Mercer 2003). Over 250 cruck houses have been identified, ranging in date from the late 13th to the mid 16th century, although most are of mid to late 15th-century date (ibid, 125). Mercer (2003, 123) concluded that many had been the dwellings of peasants, albeit relatively affluent members of their class. There are also instances of box-framed halls from around 1300, perhaps to be associated with the minor gentry.

Dendro-dating across the region has demonstrated the presence of structures surviving from the 13th century – the West Bromwich manor house is another good illustration – and furthermore, the relative frequency of 15th-century examples. In Birmingham, buildings such as the 'Saracen's Head', and the 'Old Grammar School' (Kings Norton) may be added to their number (Fig. 6.2). At the same time, some studies have suggested a 14th-century 'gap' in the record (Esling et al 1989, 22-9), the significance of which requires fuller exploration. The importance and number of surviving medieval buildings will surely grow in future years, posing further challenges to those engaged in heritage management and development control, and will inevitably have implications for the approaches adopted by archaeologists.

However, there are some questions on rural buildings that only excavation is likely to answer. For example, were there sub-regional differences in rural buildings, and did differences occur between the buildings that one might expect within a nucleated settlement, as opposed to one of a more dispersed character? Similarly, it is excavation

**Fig 6.1** Excavations at Burton Dassett, Warwickshire, in 1987 (copyright John Hunt)

**Fig 6.2** 'The Saracen's Head', Birmingham; the north and northwest ranges (copyright Mike Hodder)

that has the potential to provide our most satisfying evidence for the material culture on medieval rural settlement sites, but at present our knowledge in the west midlands is 'broad brush' in nature, often informed from outside the region, and we still know least about the dwellings and material culture of the poorest in society.

When the current position is reviewed, what is striking is the relative ease with which research priorities can be identified, and the extent to which these are actually quite fundamental questions that one might have expected to have already been tackled. The discipline of 'medieval archaeology' only emerged as a taught academic discipline in the 1960s and 1970s, and there is now a need for the data collected in the second half of the 20th century to be assimilated and analysed, in addition to which, of course, there is the constant torrent of data arising from PPG16 and PPG15.

What questions and issues emerge from this review?

- The question of village origins remains as critical as ever it was, particularly in light of the regional imbalances in the distribution of work relevant to this issue. Clearly there is a need to work on settlements with pre-Conquest phases, and which might be related to the major socio-economic shifts occurring in English society, such as the development of open fields, the growth of dependent tenure and the onset of manorialism. The precise distribution of nucleated settlement, the point at which it appears in the landscape, and the factors that gave rise to it are critical. On this, the recent contribution of Williamson (2003, 23-7, 180) identifies one approach that should be tested, that is, the influence of soils, topography and the environmental context. Over the last decade, Warwickshire has started to produce sites of 10th- and 11th-century date, such as Pillerton Priors, Goldicite, Loxley, Flecknoe and Ettington. Coton on the Wolds also seems to have originated at this time, having produced evidence of enclosures and buildings of this period. While it seems reasonable to suppose that such settlements were emerging in the 9th and 10th centuries across the region it has not elsewhere been evidenced so directly by archaeology. Dyer's (1996, 118) observation, made in the context of Warwickshire, that sites with 10th- and 11th-century activity are relatively few, remains broadly true.

- The fluidity of settlement has long been recognised, but the nature and context for it remain valid questions to address. Re-planning is clearly a phenomenon that affected many settlements, as at Coton on the Wolds where there was a phase of such activity in the 12th century. How widespread was this phenomenon, at this and other dates, and what was the socio-economic context to which it related? Was this a feature of all settlement types, or does it only manifest itself on nucleated sites?

- The desertion and/or shrinkage of rural settlements is another long recognised and studied phenomenon, but again there remains much scope to explore this in detail. This has to be done within the wider context of settlement 'life cycles', of how and why settlements of various types grow, and against trends that might be observed within urban settlement. Indeed, settlement development must be studied in the context of the wider landscape within which it was set. In Warwickshire, Coton was abandoned in the late 13th/early 14th century, Oversley in the early 13th century, and Spennall and Loxley both experienced shrinkage in the mid/late 14th century. All these contrast with the late 15th-century desertion of Burton Dassett and elsewhere which, in the past, has been regarded as the norm. In Worcestershire, desertion is no longer associated only with nucleated settlement in the south-east of the county, and nor is it seen as simply a late medieval phenomenon; it is now known to have affected all parts of the county, including the hamlets in the north. However, the study of such issues in Worcestershire is again hampered by a lack of archaeological data and excavated sites, and has hardly been addressed in other parts of the region, such as Staffordshire.

The scope for further work is immense, but is unlikely to be addressed through the opportunities afforded by developer-led work. The future prospects are not necessarily all negative. While opportunities for large-scale excavation must be seized wherever they arise, it is difficult to envisage the likelihood of such extensive and structured research opportunities. However, the Whittlewood project is demonstrating the potential value of small-scale interventions, within the context of an integrated research methodology, and there remain the constant contributions of field survey work (Dyer et al 2002). There are areas where the mapping of data is still a basic requirement, and there is no shortage of models to be tested. This is one way of capitalising on specialised academic studies, which in turn might be related to developing and enhancing the role of HERs as research tools. However, there is an urgent fundamental need for publication, which touches on all aspects of medieval archaeology in the west midlands region.

### 6.2.2. Urban settlement

Towns have been a theme of particular interest in the west midlands and, like rural settlement, they have attracted the interest of historians and geographers as well as archaeologists. It is this multidisciplinary dimension, with its various methodological approaches, that has provided the foundations upon which we need to build. Rescue archaeology, the foundation of which was one of the defining points in the development of British archaeology, had urban origins and a west midlands profile.

Although often blurred, it has become customary and useful to make a distinction between large towns and small towns, even though the key issues facing both are essentially the same. Not surprisingly, it is the study of the larger towns that is the longer established, reflected in the large-scale excavations and synthetic publications of the 1960s, 70s

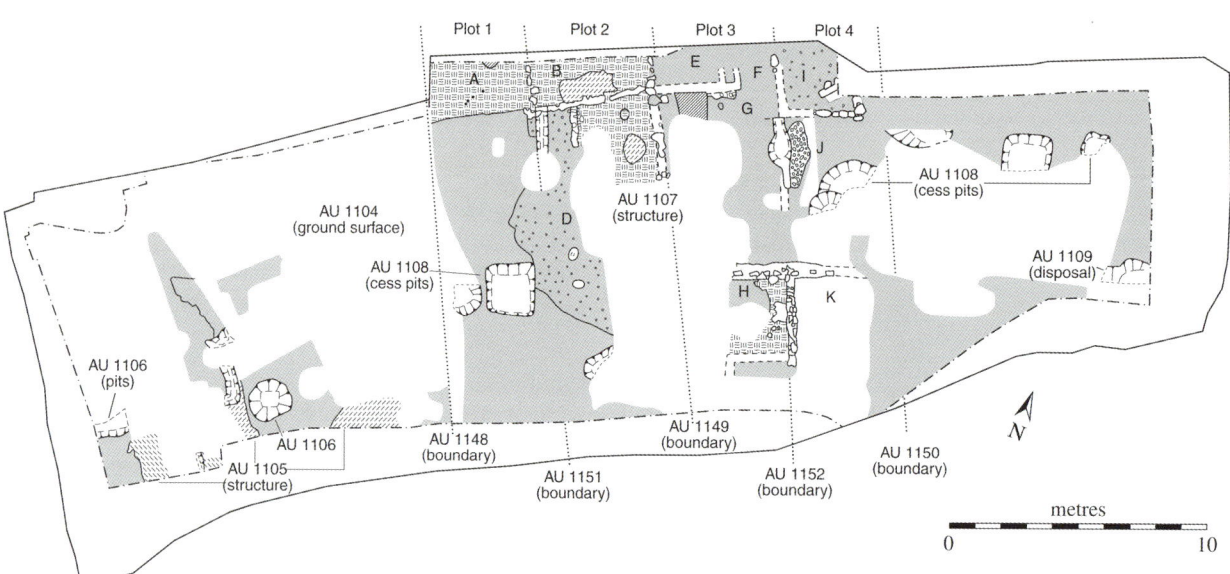

**Fig 6.3** Deansway, Worcester; aerial photograph of site, combined with plan of medieval urban cottages (copyright Worcestershire Historic Environment and Archaeology Service and Council for British Archaeology)

and 80s, and which still largely form the basis of our current understanding of larger towns in the region. During this period there were major excavations, some of national importance, in Worcester, Hereford, Shrewsbury and Stafford. Some of the later work in this sequence is still in the process of publication and assimilation. In the case of small towns, it has only been over the last ten years or so that there has been any appreciable advance in our knowledge of their archaeology. A perception that such towns offered low archaeological potential seems to be the principal reason for this 'late start', but this has now been reversed. The demonstrable increase in our archaeological understanding of small towns since the 1990s is related to both the provoking contributions of other disciplines, and the stimulus that PPG16 has provided for archaeology. Often dealing with relatively shallow stratigraphies in small towns, even small-scale interventions in such places can be informative, as at Pershore, Evesham and Leominster. For both large and small towns, the 1990s also saw the development of urban surveys supported by English Heritage, another factor in the rapid development of archaeological evidence for towns. An urban database has been completed for Shrewsbury and is in progress for Worcester, while in 1992 an 'extensive urban survey' was launched across the smaller towns of Worcestershire, Herefordshire and Shropshire, producing a detailed study of over 50 urban settlements.

While it is the case that the extent of survey and archaeological fieldwork varies across the west midlands, and that there are outstanding issues to address, it is also clear that work on towns is broadly based. Worcestershire has been fairly fortunate in this regard, including important early work on the small town of Droitwich. This town has been the focus of sustained and concentrated archaeological attention from the mid 1970s, leading to a detailed understanding of medieval salt production (Hurst 1997). Such work on a small town was unusual in its day, but Droitwich was always something of a special case because of its regional role in the salt trade. Excavations in Pershore and Evesham have revealed tenement plots that had become gardens by the late 14th century (Dalwood 2000). Similarly, excavations in Worcester have provided some fresh insights into the character of the medieval built environment (Dalwood and Edwards 2004). The important Deansway excavation has demonstrated the intensive occupation of this part of Worcester from the late 11th century to the mid 14th century (Fig. 6.3). In the mid 14th century an area of small plots with one- and two-roomed buildings was abandoned and became a garden plot until a bronze foundry was established on it in the late 14th century. This distinct hiatus in the intensity of occupation, albeit short-lived, perhaps reflects the impact of the Black Death. Such work has demonstrated the opportunities for examining fluctuations in town development and for comparative work, also highlighting the need to pay attention to the suburbs of towns, which might be expected to be particularly sensitive to fluctuations in population and serve as one indicator of prosperity or decline.

Among the larger towns of the region a significant contribution has been made by the archaeology of Coventry (Fig. 6.4). Excavations here have embraced major church sites (Whitefriars, Charterhouse and the Cathedral Priory), town defences, the problems of an urban castle site, and various sites within the medieval city. These have included a small but well-known corpus of buildings from Much Park Street, producing some of the best excavated sequences of structural remains from the region (Wright 1982). The below-ground archaeological resource of Coventry remains considerable.

Large-scale projects within the major towns of the region now seem largely to be a thing of the past. Warwick, for instance, has not hosted an area excavation within its defences since the early 1970s, and still lacks building plans or work on frontages in the town, but work has continued. Among the more significant recent works have been excavations on the Market Place, where 11th-century occupation was revealed at the rear of the 'Woolpack'. Medieval stratigraphy has been seen in Castle Park and High Street, and much small-scale work has also been carried out on Warwick's suburbs, although with limited results. In Shrewsbury there has been a major study of urban monasticism (Baker 2002), and Baker has also undertaken an intensive survey of the town's archaeological resource, providing a better understanding of the town's origins and growth. Stafford

**Fig 6.4** Excavation of a late medieval cellar in Bayley Lane, Coventry, in 1988 (copyright Coventry Museum)

has also seen continued activity, although not on the scale of Carver's work in the late 1970s (Carver 1981). More recent excavations have produced another possible Stafford ware kiln (Darlington 1997, 5-6), a substantial garderobe, a water mill with a sequence commencing in the late 12th century, and a series of ditches. It is suggested that the latter represents the first archaeological evidence for the site of the 11th–century royal castle within the town of Stafford and a possible pre-conquest enclosure (Cuttler, Hunt and Rátkai, 2009).

However, the main area of growth in urban archaeology since the 1990s has been in its focus on smaller towns. Perhaps the most significant in the region has been the recent series of excavations attendant upon the extensive redevelopment at the centre of Birmingham, which in the medieval period was a small town within the honor of Dudley. Substantial archaeological deposits from the city centre, from excavations initiated as a result of the PPG16 process, have informed on Birmingham's medieval development and transformed our knowledge of it, with evidence recovered for medieval tenements, boundaries, and industrial activity, together with environmental data (Buteux 2003; Hodder 2004). The 'Birmingham experience' also serves to highlight a warning. The excavations have established the city's 'medieval credentials' beyond doubt, but lacking an extant medieval profile in its surviving urban fabric, it is unlikely that Birmingham would ever have attracted the resources of an English Heritage urban survey.

The survival of archaeological deposits has also been demonstrated at the historic core of Dudley, and in Staffordshire there has been the opportunity for a significant series of excavations on several sites in Lichfield (eg Nichol and Ratkái 2004), while medieval occupation layers have also been examined in Newcastle-under-Lyme (Hunt 2007, 38-58). In Warwickshire several small towns have attracted work, although the results have been mixed. Evaluations on frontages in High Street in Henley-in-Arden generally produced only isolated pits, but did reveal a 14th-century standing structure. In Atherstone, excavations in the market place produced 14th- and 15th-century surfaces and timber settings and further pits and a possible tanning site have been found at Stratford-on-Avon (Fig. 6.5). Back plot survival has also been demonstrated in Sutton Coldfield (Hodder 2004, 96). In Shropshire, back garden trenching in Much Wenlock again revealed that

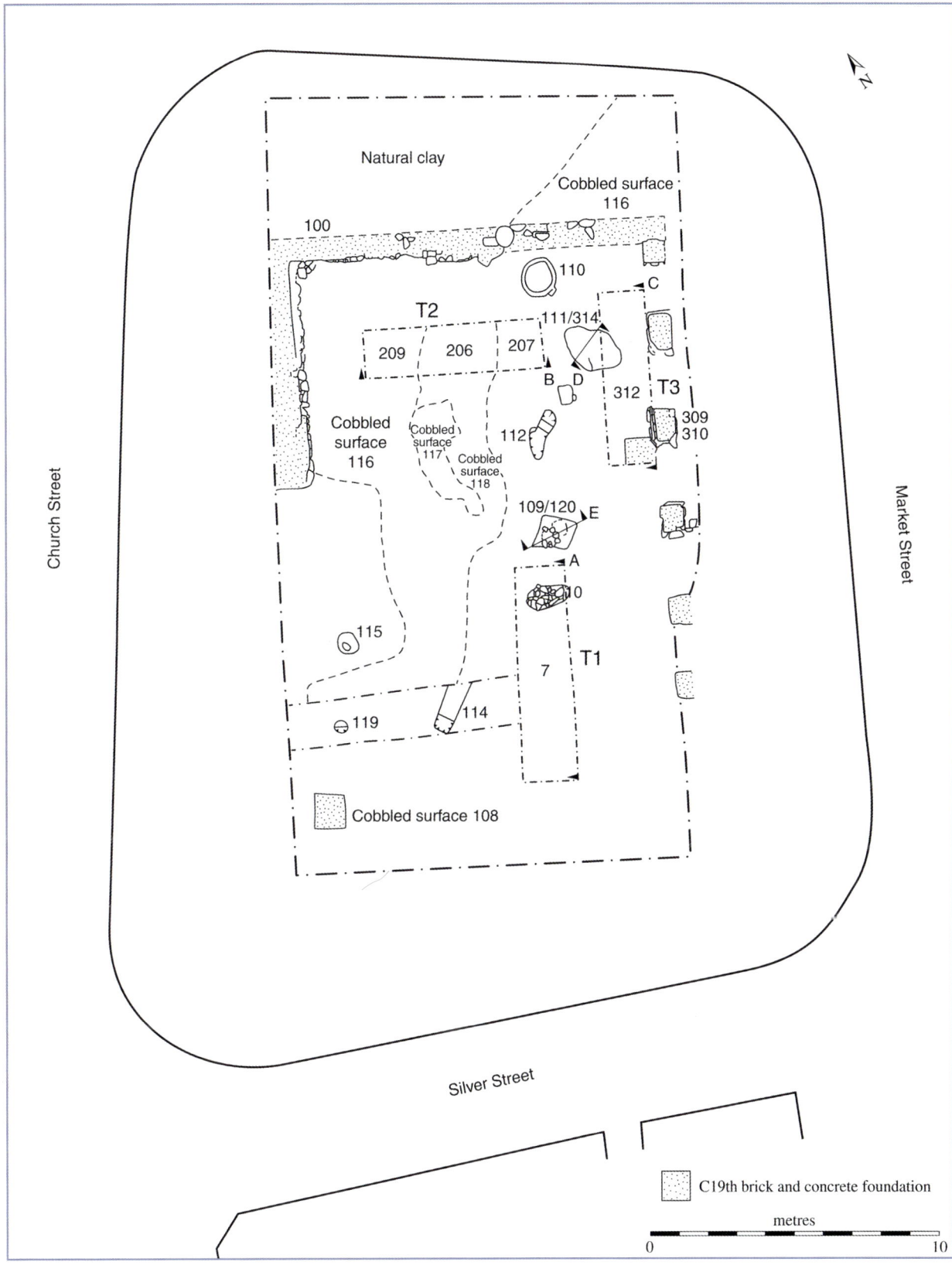

Natural clay

Cobbled surface
116

100

110

T2

111/314

209  206  207

B  D

Cobbled
surface
116

Cobbled
surface
117

Cobbled
surface
118

112

C

312  T3

309
310

109/120  E

A

Church Street

Market Street

0

115

7  T1

119  114

Cobbled surface 108

Silver Street

C19th brick and concrete foundation

metres

0                    10

medieval and earlier archaeology can be well preserved, enabling an investigation by 'Time Team' of the rear boundary of a burgage plot in Sheinton Street, confirming its origin in the early post-Conquest period. Shropshire, however, also illustrates some outstanding issues. Places like Ludlow and Bridgnorth represent complex multi-phase planned centres alongside castles, and are of outstanding potential, deserving of, but still awaiting, the same kind of study that Baker (2002) conducted in Shrewsbury.

**Fig 6.5** Excavations in Atherstone Market Place (copyright Warwickshire Museum)

While there is some common ground in the emerging issues for urban archaeology, it serves clarity to observe the distinction between large and small towns, and address them separately. What does hold for both, however, is the general scarcity of frontage excavations, particularly on major commercial streets. The continuous redevelopment of these main thoroughfares inevitably leads to the situation where the archaeological record is dominated by evidence from backyards and rear wings. There is a need to identify potential for frontage excavations in both large and small towns, as in Shrewsbury where Baker (2002) has identified such a site at 58-59 Mardol. Recent city centre development in Worcester has resulted in the loss of medieval burgage frontages. In many cases there is no substitute for excavation, and opportunities for research excavations are clearly needed. A further common feature, widely shared, is the lack of works of synthesis, which are needed to facilitate the comprehension of the work to date, and enable the contextualisation of future work.

With regard to the large towns, the key issues might be identified as follows –

- *Cycles of urban growth and decline, and the accompanying trends in urban populations.* The immense contribution made by the Deansway excavation is an encouraging marker, but rarely will the results of a single project be sufficient to define the development of a whole neighbourhood. Another significant recent contribution with wider potential has been a mass programme of dendro-chronological dating of town buildings in Shrewsbury. This has shown that the chronology of construction parallels the documented evidence for the changing fortunes of the town between the 15th and 17th centuries. Finally, as already noted above, the study of suburbs is central and essential to questions on urban growth and decline. However, this presents challenges for those charged with protecting and managing the archaeological resource, as it requires that planners recognise that there are issues within the historic environment beyond historic urban cores.

- *Industry and production.* Not all industrial activities are well represented archaeologically, and it is generally difficult to assess the scale and intensity of production. The study of production sites is clearly a priority.

- *Housing and buildings.* Although our knowledge of medieval housing varies from town to town, it is generally poor, all the more so before the 14th century.

- *Defences and urban castles.* The demand for ring roads since the 1960s has ensured that public urban defences are among the more closely studied aspects of the archaeology of towns. While individual studies have emerged, there is an urgent need for a regional review addressing fundamental questions such as chronology, building practice and impact. Our knowledge of 'urban castles' is more limited, particularly in the phases following immediately after the Conquest. Shrewsbury has potential in this regard, but those at Worcester, Coventry and Stafford pose particular challenges, even in terms of establishing locations or extent.

- *The church.* Important work has been done on major churches, including Hereford Cathedral and Worcester Cathedral, and a number of monastic sites, but there remains a crucial gap in our knowledge at the level of the parish.

In the case of small towns, the key priorities that emerge are –

- *Towns and their role within their wider landscapes.* Small towns were not as varied or complex as large towns, but they none the less functioned as focal points in the local area. It is of fundamental importance that a closer understanding is developed, from an archaeological perspective, on how small towns worked within their hinterlands and the wider region. Multidisciplinary studies that engage with these aspects are urgently required.

- *Town planning and urban landscapes.* Building further on the work to a large extent developed in the west midlands by Terry Slater (Baker 2003). While this is work that has been progressing since the 1970s, it would be advantageous for all small towns to be included, not least because of its value in identifying areas of archaeological sensitivity.

- *Buildings.* Some small towns in the region contain buildings of national significance, as in Weobley (Herefordshire), but there is no coherent regional approach to researching medieval urban buildings. This must be developed, combining the study of standing buildings with archaeological investigations, providing an approach to the study of building types in small towns. Account must also be taken of fragmentary survivals, of the kind exemplified in a largely 19th-century town house in Sutton Coldfield which has a medieval smoke hood.

- *Crafts and trades.* It is the presence of non-agricultural occupations that plays a crucial role in defining a place as a town, but the range of such occupations was not as great as in the case of large towns, and tended to be more closely related to the needs of the local rural population. The range and nature of these occupations needs to be established, and their role in contributing to the material culture of a place.

- *Development patterns.* There are several issues to explore here. Small towns are generally considered to have developed in broadly similar ways, and to have similar economic structures. However, there is a need to investigate the diversity of small towns, particularly within the context of a region. The origins of small towns, their rates of growth, patterns of expansion and decline, and the factors that impacted on each of these are in need of closer study. The study of 'failed' towns, like that at Oversley (Warwickshire) also has a critical role to play in this theme.

The overall impression for urban archaeology in the region is a positive one, but there remain key and fundamental issues to address. While large and small towns have specific aspects on which to focus it is clear that they share a number of similar issues, and would benefit from the same initiatives. For many of the fundamental questions, it is likely that only significant opportunities for area or frontage excavations will bring satisfactory answers. This is largely beyond the control of archaeologists, who are dependent upon the opportunities that the developers' plans might create. However, there are aspects that the archaeological community can engage with. PPG16 work will continue apace, and represents a valuable asset, but if best use is to be made of it, there is an urgent need for works of synthesis that properly analyse the material that has already been recovered, to inform both curators and contractors. Similarly, there is an urgent need for a successor to the urban survey projects that now appear to have stalled. The value of these projects in identifying the archaeological resource in towns, and in providing a clear intellectual context for subsequent archaeological work, is manifest. It is a clear regional priority that this kind of stimulus is again established.

## 6.3. Hinterlands

The study of hinterlands is central to understanding more fully the relationship between town and country, not only in terms of patterns of trade and exchange, but also with regard to social and economic structures and change within medieval society (cf Perring 2002, 2-4). Hinterland studies also provide an appropriate framework for the discussion of settlement hierarchies, for examining the impact of urban settlement on the landscape, and for the key issues already identified by Perring (2002, 3).

While recognising the immense potential inherent in the study of hinterlands, there is an issue of how they should be recognised and defined. The historian might use the evidence of debts, landholding, migration, trade links and membership fraternities to identify a hinterland, as has Dyer (2000, 34-9) for Bromsgrove between 1275 and 1520. However, Ratkái (2003) points out that hinterlands so defined are much smaller than the areas suggested by the pattern of pottery distribution. There are also the inevitable differences of scale between the likes of Bromsgrove and a major urban and trading centre such as Coventry.

What are the most appropriate ways of defining hinterlands? This question is a key issue that must be explored within the west midlands region to develop a consistent approach and framework for comparative studies. However, as noted by Perring (2002, 11), this is a complex theme to address. Archaeology might turn to use the spatial distribution of certain items, such as pottery, but in the medieval period the movement of such items was not constrained by modern notions such as transport costs. Invisible controls such as networks of patronage, obligation, tradition, or estate and seigneurial links, are also influential. However, these are also factors that might leave archaeological traces, and enable more sophisticated models to be developed. As has been recognised, we are dealing with complex, overlapping zones of influence acting diversely across the landscape (Perring 2002, 11). They were not homogeneous or uncontested regions. The application of 'urban fields' theory offers the most coherent and broadly-based approach. Having developed a consistent approach relevant to the region, it will be possible to undertake comparative studies, not only between towns of similar standing, but also between urban places of different size and status. Such studies of smaller towns have particular potential to investigate the socio-economic fabric of medieval life.

## 6.4. Life and death in the medieval west midlands

### 6.4.1. Life in town and countryside

An important area to prioritise and maximise is the contribution made by environmental archaeology to our knowledge of medieval life in town and country. A number of sites across the region have produced information, although these samples derive predominantly from urban sites, and many are small-scale. Human activity obviously does much to preserve environmental data from the period, as a result of pit and ditch digging, wells, cesspits and refuse dumping.

The value of this work may be illustrated in a simple case study. Stafford has been the subject of environmental sampling on several occasions, including an area known as King's Pool, a post-glacial hollow infilled by a sequence of deposits, offering 21m of organic sediments (Bartley and Morgan 1990; Pearson et al 1999). Work here has demonstrated the value of so-called 'off-site' studies, sampling deposits in landscape features as well as those in more conventionally defined archaeological sites. Analyses of pollen, sediments and plant microfossils, undertaken in the context of watching briefs, have illustrated an environmental history running from the Mesolithic to the medieval period. Investigations here have been supplemented by several other sites in the town, which has demonstrated the need for a corpus of material rather than single samples.

Work in 1990 suggested continuous occupation and no evidence for woodland regeneration in the post-Roman period, whereas later work in Stafford has challenged this, indicating an abrupt break in the cereal pollen record and some signs of woodland regeneration in this period (Bartley and Morgan 1990; Pearson et al 1999). This phase was followed by a renewal of agricultural activity in the Anglo-Saxon period, with sharp increases of rye in particular, apparently processed in the town. The evidence for farming became increasingly significant from the 10th century, with suggestions of a three-fold increase in cereal production, reflecting the growth of Stafford itself. Samples of charred plant microfossils taken in Gaolgate Street (Dodd et al 2004) from 13th- and 14th-century contexts were dominated by cereal grains, particularly oats suited to less favourable soils, and weeds of cultivated and disturbed ground. Arable fields are indicated (bread-type and rivet-type wheats are present), together with material brought in from upland heathland environments, presumably for use as bedding, flooring, fodder, thatch, and perhaps fuel.

Insect assemblages (Robinson 2003) have been produced from sites in Hereford, Birmingham, Stone, Worcester and elsewhere. Cesspits, particularly common in urban medieval sites, suit some insects and it is on such sites that the insect evidence has proven most informative. However, small organic deposits may also be preserved by very local conditions (eg Fishgate Street, Worcester). Medieval town life brought together large quantities of organic material, of which the insect fauna took advantage. Urban conditions included decaying organic material, foul stable cleanings, cesspits with maggots and timber buildings with woodworm and deathwatch beetle, but the presence of clean areas demonstrates that caricatures of medieval life should be avoided.

Mollusc assemblages (Murphy 2001b) have the potential to inform on landscape change and the nature of the immediate environment, although they are often poorly preserved in the soils of the region. The potential of mollusc assemblages is well illustrated by their aid in the interpretation of two moated sites in Stansted (Molehill Green and Round Wood; Murphy 2001b, 20) where they were used to identify a hay meadow and an assart, but such approaches have not yet emerged in the west midlands. However, mollusc assemblages have been used to effect in Friars Road, Coventry, where ten species showed the wet marshy medieval town ditch fills lingering as late as *c*.1800 (Soden 1990). While there is a need to expand our environmental database in the region, this is particularly acute in rural contexts.

### 6.4.2. Population studies

In the west midlands, in so far as medieval demography has been studied, it has primarily been the preserve of historians (eg Razi 1980). This was inevitable. Apart from the fact that until recently the study of human bones was not a high priority in British archaeology (Mays 1998, 195), it is also the case that there have been relatively few opportunities presented archaeologically to undertake such studies. While small-scale finds of human remains are not unusual, such as those found in Bird Street, Lichfield (Stone 1999), the problem is one of finding sufficiently large numbers in a satisfactory condition to permit meaningful study. This Lichfield sample of at least 14 individuals was studied, but the bone was found to be in a poor condition, friable and abraded. Similarly, at Haughmond Abbey, 55 cloister burials were excavated, clearly of benefactors, but the bones were not in a good enough condition to do much with (Pearson 2003). There have been more successful opportunities, such as the assemblage of 91 human skeletons from the Greyfriars cemetery in Stafford (Booth 1998), the burials excavated at Sandwell Priory (Hodder 1991), and about 130 burials from various sites in Coventry (Soden 1995; Rylatt and Mason 2003). Excavations at Hereford Cathedral in 1993 produced a total of 1129 recognisable inhumations, with the likelihood that overall there were perhaps some 5000 individuals represented. The condition of the bone was variable, and although the majority were described as 'fair', the nature of the deposit did mean that only 13% of the skeletons were complete and undisturbed (Stone and Appleton-Fox 1996, 58-61).

It therefore remains a regional research priority to find reasonable sized skeletal groups for study, and which need to be closely dated and in good condition. It would be particularly beneficial if it were possible to study such an assemblage within the context of the community that it represented, as has been possible at Wharram Percy (Yorkshire). Such assemblages offer the opportunity for the study of burial practices, demographic trends and a range of palaeopathological studies. Such studies would be further enhanced if the opportunity arose to examine both rural and urban assemblages, particularly within the context of a hinterland. Such opportunities would not only inform on the west midlands region, but provide important comparative data to set alongside other parts of the country, such as York. The value of comparative studies within the region is also obvious. The region is unlikely to produce several major assemblages for comparison, but the examination of one major assemblage will at least provide a potential reference point for the occasional burials discovered within the context of PPG16 work.

The current trends being advocated in the study of human bones (Mays 1998), that is, employing the material to address archaeological problems relevant to the interpretation of the site and the region in which it is situated, more synthetic work directed at specific archaeological problems, and a closer integration of osteological data with other sources of evidence, would all serve the west midlands region well. It is, of course, an issue as to where such assemblages might be identified. The inclusion of such requirements within the brief for a study of a rural settlement, evoking comparisons with the approach taken at Wharram Percy, clearly has much to recommend it. However, it has also been pointed out that Coventry has a concentration of medieval chapel sites with attached graveyards, having no post-medieval successors, which potentially also makes the city a valuable research tool in this regard.

### 6.4.3. Material culture

Traditionally, material culture is at the heart of the study of archaeology, and while archaeology has broadened its brief, this remains the case. Artefactual studies remain a defining aspect of the discipline. While the medieval period benefits, like others, from initiatives such as the Portable Antiquities Scheme, the west midlands region has not seen much work in recent years on the study of medieval artefacts other than ceramics.

Material culture in the region is represented primarily by two sets of material, although the distinction is an artificial one. There is that material already held in museum collections and other archives, and then the material produced by ongoing excavation work or other discoveries. In the case of the first category of material, apart from the occasional opening of a new gallery or exhibition, as in Shrewsbury and Birmingham, medieval artefacts have not attracted any sustained study or review. Since much of the material in collections was accessioned many years ago, and has been supplemented by more recent excavated material, much of it in storage and as yet insufficiently studied, the time is ripe to address it. A coherent review of the collections needs to be undertaken on a regional basis, and there would seem to be merit in encouraging their publication as a regional assemblage, rather than institution by institution. This effectively builds on work previously commissioned by the West Midlands Area Museums Service (now, Museums and Libraries Association), and on studies conducted by the West Midlands Archaeological Collections Research Unit. The volumes recently published by the Museum of London dealing with medieval finds from excavations in London (eg Clark 1995) offers inspiration, although online publication offers opportunity for regular updating. However it is approached, accessible works of synthesis and comparative studies are urgently required.

In the case of material produced in current or recent excavations, the situation is inevitably variable and if an evaluation does not lead to a larger-scale excavation, there is unlikely to be further analysis of finds. Major excavations like those at Burton Dassett and Deansway have added to the material available, but such excavations are relatively few in number and interventions which are developer-led, while they have the potential to add to the record, in reality rarely add much of note beyond ceramic material. The chance finds of metal detectorists and fieldwalkers are of no less importance here.

In reality, the prospect of adding significantly to the region's material culture assemblage is only likely to be forthcoming in the wake of major excavation projects. Even so, it must be remembered that many sites are relatively disappointing in the material that they produce, and their 'productivity' in this regard can be affected by many different factors, related to type and function of site, conditions for survival, and excavation strategies.

In the case of the west midlands region, there is no aspect of the medieval material culture where more is not needed. The existing artefacts are in need of more detailed study, not only by typology, but also through an examination of the materials and methods of manufacture. Most recent additions have derived from urban contexts, so there is a particular need for artefacts from rural sites, and also from high status sites, such as castles and manorial complexes. The prospect of significant artefactual discoveries on church sites will always be relatively low, although such sites can present other perspectives on material culture, through church furnishings and decoration. For example, many churches preserve wall painting schemes, as at Claverley (Shropshire), while excavations, as at Coventry Priory, can add further significant examples, here in the form of the Chapter House Apocalypse Panels (Rylatt and Mason 2003, 83-9; Fig. 6.6). The region can also boast a significant corpus of sculptural decoration, including the celebrated Romanesque Herefordshire School of Sculpture, a regional school that has attracted much attention (eg Hunt and Stokes 1997; Thurlby 1999; Hunt 2004). The study of such material within the context of the society that produced and used it is an ongoing objective.

## 6.5. Making a living

### 6.5.1. The agricultural resource

With the possible exception of field patterns, the agricultural economy has often been overlooked by archaeologists in the west midlands, this area being left primarily to documentary research. To some degree, this is inevitable, given the nature of the evidence, and the absence of a large-scale, settlement-focused project, within which such themes might be pursued.

**Fig 6.6** Coventry Priory Chapter House, Apocalypse painting (copyright Coventry Museum)

However, the agricultural economy was the core activity of the vast majority of the population and deserves close attention. Work is ongoing around the region recording the 'physical infrastructure' of the rural economy, such as agricultural buildings and farmsteads (eg Hodder 2004, 101) and the fields that surrounded them. The recording of these field patterns, and of ridge and furrow, is an essential activity of landscape surveys, and can reveal distinctive local profiles. For example, at Walker's Heath in Birmingham, ridge and furrow has been found to post-date 13th- and 14th-century features in the field (Hodder 2004, 125). Archaeobotanists and archaeozoologists have not been lax in their study of the agricultural economy and integral issues such as diet, drawing on sites such as Burton Dassett and Boteler's Castle, but there is an urgent need for their researches to be brought together in a work of synthesis. The generally poor survival of bone in the region has handicapped studies of livestock, although some important assemblages have been studied, as at Dudley Castle (Thomas 2002). However, there is clearly a need for large assemblages of animal bone that might facilitate studies of local population types, of pathology, and possible indicators of animal husbandry methods.

There are clearly some important gaps in our knowledge of the agricultural economy. Developer-associated work will continue to reveal isolated examples of hearths associated with domestic industrial activity, but we currently lack an archaeological perspective on the intensity, organisation and development of such activities within a rural settlement.

More specifically, mill sites, so common in the documentary record, are essentially unknown in the archaeological record of the region. This reflects the need for broadly based fieldwork across the region, attempting to translate mill locations into sites that might be suitable for excavation. While opportunities might arise in urban areas, as was recently the case for the water mill in Stafford (Hislop et al 2006), and at Edgbaston mill, Birmingham (Hodder 2004, 150; first mentioned in the 13th century), they are less likely to occur in the countryside as a result of development work.

Within this broader issue of medieval mills, there is a more specific need to address the topic of fulling mills. Wool production, especially in the west and south of the region, together with the cloth industry, was of great importance in the medieval economy. However, at what point does this become archaeologically accessible? The fulling mill, so frequently mentioned in estate surveys and the extents associated with inquisitions post mortem, is a likely point. They are widely instanced across the region, and demonstrate that wool was being processed into textiles locally. In Coventry for instance, the predominant trade was in dyed blue woollen cloth, woven in Coventry, which was at its zenith in the 14th century (Soden 2005). The presence of good waterlogged deposits here is perhaps promising for an approach based on the recovery of biological remains. Fulling mills, and more widely, archaeological perspectives on wool and cloth production, are themes not well researched archaeologically, either regionally or nationally. A necessary first step must be to ensure that HERs are confident in the data that they hold on the distribution of such sites within their area as indicated in the documentary record.

### 6.5.2. Industry in town and country

The industrial profile of the region in the medieval period was varied and, being rich in the necessary raw materials, it was very likely more important within the local economy than has sometimes been allowed. Regionally, it ranges from highly specialised activities, as at Droitwich, to the more general industrial activity located in urban and rural contexts. Nevertheless, it is widely acknowledged that our knowledge of medieval industry in the west midlands region is wholly inadequate, and that in order to take this agenda forward, there is an urgent need for works of synthesis bringing together both documentary and archaeological approaches.

While industrial activity was a feature of both towns and the countryside, it is the former that is better represented archaeologically, provided primarily through the excavation of the backyard areas of tenements, and particularly where the industries concerned required structures set into the ground. Unlike other aspects of urban archaeology, it is the excavation of backyards rather than frontages that has more to reveal on industrial activities. Among the examples of industrial activity thus demonstrated, it is possible to cite tanning at Warwick, Birmingham, Hereford and perhaps Lichfield (Hurst 2003; Tavener in prep; cf Nichol and Ratkái 2004); the distinctive evidence of bell founding and other copper alloy casting has been found at Worcester and Ludlow (Carver 1980; Hurst 2003; Dalwood and Edwards 2004), and metal working has been widely demonstrated, as at Birmingham and Dudley (Hurst 2003; Hodder 2004, 93-4). Also in Worcester, two tile kilns in the suburbs, in Silver Street and in the Tything, produced both roof tiles and floor tiles (Brown 1991; Miller et al 2004), while other identified activities have included flax retting in Leominster, possible dyeing in Hereford, and pottery manufacture in Warwick and Birmingham (Hurst 2003; Hodder 2004, 94-5). Despite the presumed ubiquity of this latter industry, the region actually has very few identified, and even fewer excavated, kiln sites. The salt industry in Droitwich has also attracted particular attention in recent years, excavations revealing much about the structures and equipment associated with production, including the site of the main brine well at Upwich (Hurst 1997).

Industrial activity in the countryside is much more elusive. The pottery industry illustrates the difficulties. Even where petrological analysis has provided indicators of production areas, locating these more precisely on the ground can be difficult, even when dealing with major potters' sites. Such was the case with the potters operating in Hanley (Worcestershire), producing Malvernian wares over some 400 years. Fieldwork enabled Hurst (1990; 1994) to locate a pottery kiln of 15th- to 16th-century date, but their medieval antecedents remain problematic. The division between agriculture and industry was not a sharp one in the medieval period, with most crafts located at scattered sites, most probably in or near woodland settings. It may be that the medieval Hanley potters can be characterised as small-scale rural potters over a large area working in a common tradition, but there remains scope to debate the extent to which major industries, like the Malvernian, can be described in any sense as secondary or seasonal activities. Production was considerable, but its organisation remains largely unknown.

There were many other industries operating within rural contexts about which we know as little, or even less. Given the size and importance of the building industry in medieval

Fig 6.7 Wolseley glassworks on Cannock Chase under excavation in 1992 (copyright John Hunt)

England, those industries that supplied it must have been large. Notwithstanding the evidence for tile production in urban centres like Worcester, brick and roof tile industries were perhaps mainly rural, but there is little archaeological evidence of it to hand. A tile kiln has recently been found close to the city of Worcester, and floor tile kilns are known from Malvern Priory and St Mary's church, Droitwich. Stone quarries were also integral to the needs of the building industry, but with the exception of Shropshire, where quarries have been identified, very little is known.

Mineral extraction, by its nature, was also to be found within the countryside and was widely practised across the region, and the iron industry was another notable regional activity, particularly in south-east Herefordshire, north Staffordshire and the Dudley area. Apart from metal working hearths in towns, most of the evidence tends to be documentary in nature, although Staffordshire can illustrate some recent archaeological contributions that complement the documentary record. Excavation and survey work at Oldfurnace Cottage and Eastwall Farm in Oakamoor have demonstrated medieval bloomery sites in the Churnet valley (Harding 2004), while similar fieldwork has revealed the activities of medieval glass-makers on Cannock Chase and in Bagot's Park at Abbots Bromley (Welch 1997; Linford 2001; Fig. 6.7). In Warwickshire, medieval smithies have been excavated at Burton Dassett and at Cawston (Palmer 2003).

The archaeological process has inevitably meant that ceramics is the most intensively studied of all the industries active in the region but, as has been noted above, there remain some significant issues to address. As might be expected, there are a number of assemblages still awaiting publication, among which is material from Worcester, Stafford and Coventry. However, this backlog in publication compounds the issue of gaps in our knowledge, dealing as we are with a region of disparate ceramic traditions, and a region in which there are relatively few good stratigraphic sequences. Indeed, some of the divisions, such as that which separates Warwickshire from Worcestershire and Herefordshire, may be traced back into the Roman period and do not seem to arise from economic factors alone. These diverse ceramic traditions are reflected by the number of type series in the west midlands, access to which could be greatly eased if they were published on the internet.

It would be opportune to re-examine what we already have, to reassess the products of kiln sites, review site archives, and study the distribution of wares, particularly with a view to 'commodity-trade' based pottery distribution patterns. More use might also be made of site specific distribution plots of vessel forms, a technique that is potentially informative on spatial relationships on a site. The socio-economic dimension is a particularly important one to explore in more sophisticated ways, not only from the point of view of how pottery production worked as an industry, but also for other aspects that it might inform upon. This might encompass such as the study of hinterlands, or manorial economies and seigneurial links through travelling households. Does the frequency of Coventry type wares and Nuneaton wares at Brackley (Northants) reflect links arising from the wool trade, and of what nature? (Ratkái 2003)

There is clearly much ground to cover on the archaeology of medieval industry, with questions to address at all levels. There is a general lack of identified industrial sites, particularly in the countryside, and all aspects of production, distribution and consumption require study. The wider context of industrial activity, including its setting within the landscape and impact on its hinterland, on which environmental evidence can inform, needs to be addressed; the interrelationship between different industries certainly needs to be more forcefully explored. At the most basic, it is a matter of the relationship between the extraction and use of raw materials. There are also issues such as identifying the point at which industrial activity transcends localised need, and the question of transition between the medieval and post-medieval periods. What were the factors that 'drove' production? There is clearly no shortage of questions to address, but the evidence base from which to do so is relatively limited. Furthermore, our information on medieval industries is often derived from consumer sites, but the distinction between production and consumer sites is an important one, and the latter category presents only a partial picture of medieval industry. Clearly, we need to maximise what the 'consumed' products can tell us about production.

What key steps might be advocated?

- Undertake a multidisciplinary overview and synthesis of what is currently known.

- There is considerable merit in undertaking some key case studies, particularly in places such as the Ironbridge Gorge or the Black Country, where the precursors to post-medieval activity might be explored.

- Programmes of proactive fieldwork are needed particularly with regard to rural industry, including work along waterways to seek out possible mill sites.

- The organisation of industry within its wider setting is another key target, taking account of landscape contexts, communication networks, areas of economic connectivity, and the socio-economic perspectives of medieval industry.

- As in most other categories, the opportunity to study any waterlogged deposits is of the utmost importance.

### 6.5.3. Organisation, marketing and communications

The organisation of medieval industry, including the factors that drive production, the acquisition of raw materials and the distribution of products, has not received a great deal of archaeological attention. This is not surprising, as these have seemingly been difficult themes to address archaeologically, the lead being taken by those working with documentary sources. However, there are aspects that have potential, particularly for multidisciplinary approaches.

A fundamental element, central to patterns of acquisition, production and consumption, is the communications network. Thus, in the case of Birmingham, it has been suggested that coal, and lime for tanning, came from the Black Country in the 13th century, and subsequent products were marketed within the region. Here, at the very least, a network into the Black Country must have been central to Birmingham's developing economic vitality.

Reconstruction of communications networks – involving roads and tracks, waterways, and the vessels that plied them – is a major task, and a challenging one. Work to date is patchy. The most consistent contributions have been made from the study of early medieval charters (eg Hooke 1990), with which the region is relatively well provided, identifying routeways that in many cases likely continued in use throughout the medieval period, although this has not generally been specifically demonstrated. The work of geographers like Hindle has pointed to patterns of routes, but is generally not sufficiently detailed to inform on this theme. There have also been more localised studies, such as the routeways mapped in association with reporting on excavations at Stafford Castle (Darlington 2001, 6, 19-20, 91) but, in this case, the network traced is not sufficiently extensive to assist. What is required is a reconstruction of communication networks within the context of hinterlands.

This will inevitably take some time to achieve. However, something of the skeletal framework can be addressed at county and regional level relatively quickly, most obviously by the mapping of medieval bridges, fording places and ports, representing as they do key parts of the communications infrastructure. In Warwickshire, for instance, a preliminary survey has been made of the 40 bridges recorded as existing before 1550 (Palmer 2003). Such studies need to be amplified by embracing other crossing points, and by establishing a chronology for the development and expansion of the network.

Another aspect in need of study is the infrastructure of distribution supported by the communications network. In particular, it is important to look at seasonal and non-seasonal activities, and at rural markets and fairs. The likely sites of the latter are being discovered, particularly with the aid of metal detector finds of coins in fields adjacent to villages. It must be a regional priority to identify possible market and fair sites, and remain aware that developer-led interventions have the potential to reveal such sites.

## 6.6. Honors and manors

### 6.6.1. Castles

The agenda for castle studies has developed considerably in recent years and the west midlands region can illustrate both why that agenda has moved on, and offer the potential for more diverse and sophisticated studies which will benefit not only the region but also enhance our understanding of castles nationally. As elsewhere, although the castles of the west midlands have attracted interest since antiquarian times, there remains much work to do. Some parts of the region have attracted more attention than others, and there are relatively few sites that have attracted the levels of intensive study enjoyed at such as Kenilworth and Hen Domen. The situation is further complicated by the fact that some key sites which have been the subject of excavations, with the potential to address the problem of poor stratigraphy associated with many of the published sites, still await full publication. Sites in this category include Dudley, Wigmore and Castle Bromwich. The publication of this excavation backlog is urgently needed.

An audit of recent work in the region is relatively patchy. There has been survey and recording work at Warwick, and some excavation at Kenilworth and Beaudesert (Warwickshire). In Herefordshire, in addition to the study of Wigmore, there have been detailed surveys of Longtown and Richard's Castle, and Weobley Castle has been the subject of a multidisciplinary project exploring the relationship between the castle and its attendant borough (Nash and Children 2003). However, in Worcestershire there has been very little work, the only modern excavations being small-scale evaluations on

**Fig 6.8** Chartley Castle, Staffordshire (copyright John Hunt)

demolished sites at Evesham and Worcester, although there has been some documentary work elsewhere (eg, Toomey 2001; Field 1996).

By contrast, Staffordshire has fared reasonably well. Historians working in the 1960s and 70s established a working gazetteer of castle sites within the county as a preliminary towards more detailed studies (eg Cantor 1966; Palliser 1972), but may have missed some sites that were not obviously documented. For example, survey in advance of the Audley to Alrewas gas pipeline has identified a possible motte not previously recorded (Network Archaeology 1997). There have been excavations of varying levels of scale on castle sites at Tamworth, Dudley, Stafford, Tutbury, Alton, Newcastle, and Eccleshall, while at Chartley there has been a survey of the fabric and earthworks (Fig. 6.8). This apparently enviable record (subject to final publications in some cases), which certainly includes some important excavations informing on individual sites, none the less conveys no great sense of major contributions to the wider debates on the place of castles in their broader socio-political, economic and landscape contexts.

In many respects, some of the most stimulating and innovative of recent work has taken place in Shropshire and the March, particularly in relationship to designed landscapes, already familiar at sites like Kenilworth and Bodiam. The most spectacular of the Shropshire examples is the FitzAlan castle at Clun. Aerial photographs have shown the presence of a reflecting lake and pleasance (water garden) below the great lodgings block of *c* 1300, with an adjacent 'little park' (Stamper 1996, plate 6). Clun is not alone. At Whittington, some earthworks relate to the documented garden, all within a controlled, watery, mere-like setting (Brown 2003). Stafford Castle too has two areas more controversially interpreted as garden earthworks, the western gardens intended to be viewed from the keep of 1348. Unlike the Shropshire examples, these are not watery settings (Darlington 2001, 99), but a watery setting has recently been suggested by work in 2003 by Warwickshire Museum on the north side of the great hall at Caludon Castle, Coventry (I Soden, pers comm).

Such work reflects a more sophisticated appreciation now being brought to castle sites and points to the potential that a systematic survey of other castle sites might have for the revelation of more designed landscapes. In Shropshire for example, at Wattlesborough, a tower house of late 13th-/early 14th-century date sits on a great ditched platform, perhaps the moat that was noted in 1379. These earthworks were bulldozed some years ago, but the tower house may have shared this platform of 40 sq m with a garden, orchards and ornamental features. A site that is particularly deserving of further survey work is Stokesay Castle, purchased in 1281 by Lawrence of Ludlow. The fenestration and position of the hall proclaims it as a building 'with a view', looking out across the surrounding countryside. To the west of the castle there is a sheet of water, and to the south a complex arrangement of ponds and water channels. These elements are suggestive of a sophisticated building within, and enhanced by, a watery designed setting.

There is no part of the west midlands region that does not stand to benefit from more work on castle sites, including fairly fundamental work such as mapping, density and distribution on a local and a regional basis, alongside determining the extent of individual sites within their landscapes.

Furthermore, castle studies are a particularly strong contender for multidisciplinary approaches, even though this is a position that might be reasonably argued for medieval archaeology as a whole. Revisionism and increasingly sophisticated perceptions of castles in medieval society has been a trend as evident in the work of historians as it has been in that of archaeologists, while the landscape, broadly defined, offers one context that might readily bring these disciplines together. The work that has been done in Shropshire on designed landscapes needs to be extended not only within that county, but also across the region as a whole. Apart from establishing that this is a norm, there is also a need to determine the various forms that it might take, the social range of the sites with which they are associated, and the chronological framework within which they appear. Are they features of castles from the earliest times, or do they appear over time? At what point, and to what extent, do they appear on sites of 'lower' social standing, and may they be associated with the development of 'gentry culture'? These are key questions to address. Similarly, with regard to symbolic or status arrangements in the landscape, the means by which castle sites were approached is in need of closer attention, and the vistas with which they were associated, as part of a fuller appreciation of how they were to be perceived within the landscape.

The castles of the region also need to be studied within their wider contexts, those of the manor and of the honor. This provides the opportunity to examine castles within constructs and infrastructures that were meaningful to contemporaries, and facilitates our understanding of castles within socio-economic and socio-political landscapes and frameworks. This approach also enables consideration of any 'hierarchy' that might occur, ranging across those sites which served as a 'caput', to sub-honorial centres, and others that might come about for entirely different reasons, such as Symons Castle (Powys). Some preliminary work on this has taken place (eg Hunt 1997), but there is considerable scope to undertake much more, with many sites around the region that recommend themselves. While excavation should form a part of this work, it is clear that such ambitions will only be realised with the deployment of the fullest range of survey and interpretative techniques that are available. Projects currently taking shape in Staffordshire and Herefordshire have the potential to make a contribution to this agenda.

Finally, despite the proximity of the celebrated excavations at Hen Domen (Montgomeryshire) (Barker and Higham 1982; Higham and Barker 2000), the examination of a relatively modest earthwork site, such as the Warwickshire motte and bailey at Seckington, would be highly beneficial on several counts. All the points made above are relevant here. However, in addition, such research would enhance our opportunity to look at the hierarchy of sites, to examine the chronology and development of earthwork castle sites, and address the relative 'imbalance' within the region that has seen most work conducted on relatively large, stone-built castle sites.

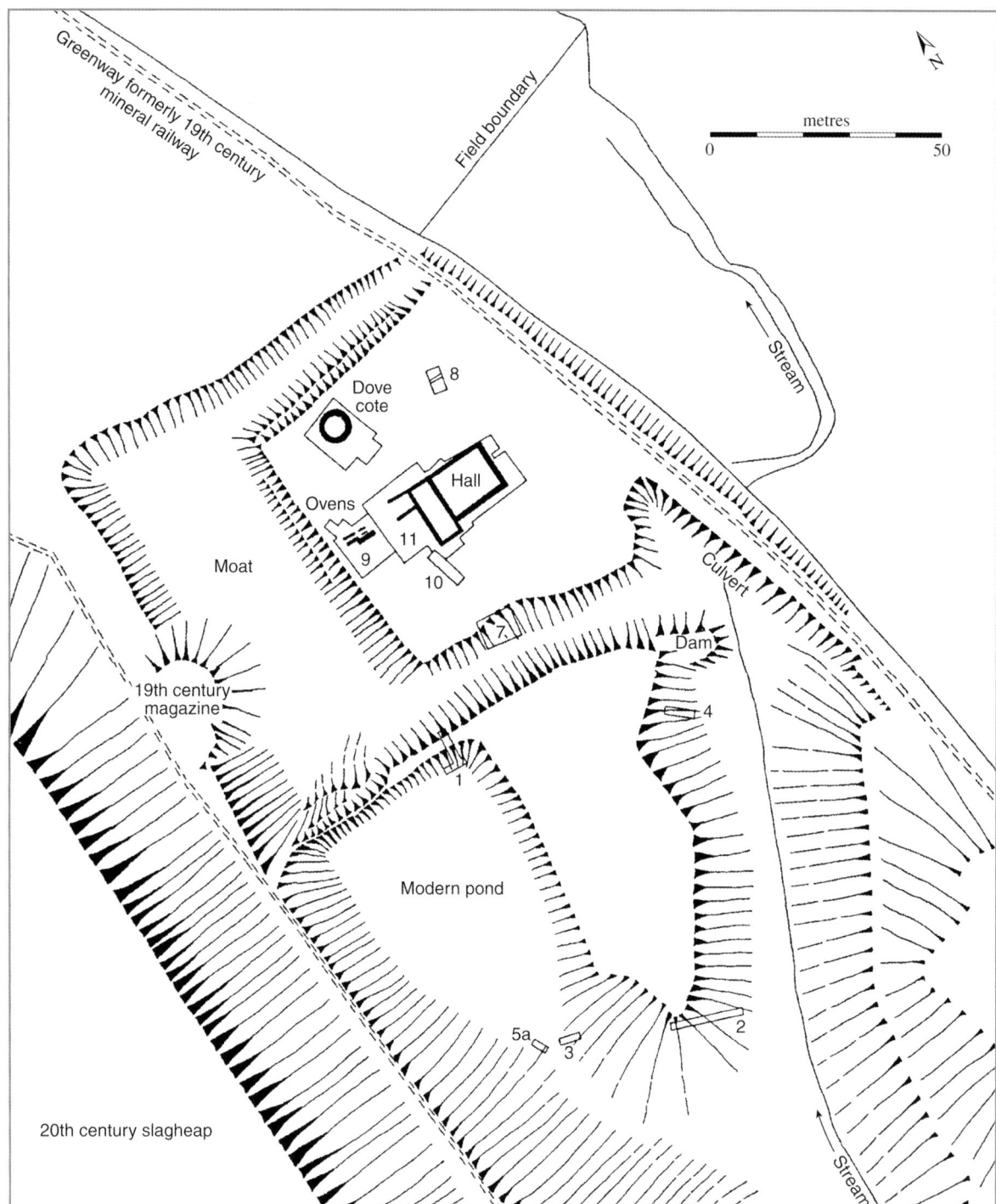

**Fig 6.9** Lawn Farm moated site (copyright Noel Boothroyd)

## 6.6.2. Moated sites and manorial complexes

Moated sites are widely regarded as one of the classic field monuments of the medieval period and are characteristic of much of the west midlands region, being particularly associated with woodland landscapes. Although moated sites have attracted the attention of historians, geographers and archaeologists, and are often perceived as having been intensively researched, the impression is to some extent a misguided one, with considerable variations in our knowledge across the region. The distribution of such sites across the region is generally well known, stimulated by the scheduling process that took place in the 1990s, although many were scheduled well before this. However, fundamental though such mapping is, it is generally the case that this dot on the map is the full extent of our knowledge of the site. Thus, the excavator on one recent project, at Lawn Farm near Stoke-on-Trent in Staffordshire, found it difficult to find sites with sufficient levels of information to enable comparative studies (N Boothroyd, pers comm; Fig. 6.9).

Several sites have been surveyed, but rather fewer excavated. When moated sites have been the subject of closer study, this has generally concentrated on the platform or the moat in the form of a survey and perhaps an excavation. Thus at Burton's Farm, Kingshurst (Warwickshire), recent excavations stripped the entire platform, revealing a possible medieval stone building, but a paucity of finds (Palmer 2003). At Old Hall Street in Wolverhampton, recent excavation in advance of redevelopment actually had little option other than to examine the moat of the former 16th-century manor house. Relatively few attempts have been made within the region to set a moated site within its wider landscape context, although one recent exception is the work that was undertaken at Lawn Farm (Klemperer and Parkes 2000; Boothroyd 2002).

As these examples reflect, the most recent activity has taken place in Warwickshire and Staffordshire. In Warwickshire there have been more recent excavations at Old Knowle Hall, and small-scale work at Coughton Court, Baddesley Clinton, Lower Woodcote (Leek Wootton) and Chilvers Coton Manor, together with research projects at Hurley Hall and Old Berry Hall. These are all sites located within the Arden region, the woodland nature of which may be associated with the greater density of such sites. However, they are also to be found in the Feldon, at sites such as Wormleighton, although the only recent Feldon excavation has been limited work at Cawston, and work at Hunningham which remains unpublished. In Staffordshire, apart from the excavations at Lawn Farm, the most recent work was that on Drayton Bassett in the 1980s, an important and impressive site that remains unpublished. The importance of this site is given further weight by the fact that its origins may well go back to the early post-Conquest period (Hunt and Hodder 1992). This has a bearing on the problem of the chronology of moated sites. As has been pointed out before, the study of moated sites is disadvantaged by the lack of secure dating, the chronological frameworks that are frequently offered being characterised by a misplaced sense of confidence (Hunt 1997, 98).

These recent projects join an older corpus of work within the region which includes excavated sites such as Eyeswell Manor, Sinai Park, and Shareshill, all in Staffordshire; West Bromwich and Walsall in the Black Country (medieval Staffordshire); Durrance Moat at Upton Warren (Worcestershire); Birmingham Moat, Hawkesley Farm and Kent's Moat (Birmingham), Gannow Green (Worcestershire), Weoley Castle (medieval Worcestershire, now Birmingham) and Sydenhams Moat near Solihull. Inevitably this older generation of work, as well as some of the more recent work, does not engage with more current research issues.

Despite the spate of activity in the 1990s that led to the recording and scheduling of moated sites, an activity that was, of course, facilitated by the high visibility of most sites in the field, there was rarely any incentive or opportunity to look beyond the scheduled area. In short, these sites were being divorced from the wider context in which they operated. Furthermore, the relative ease with which moated sites might be recognised also led to a tendency to overlook cognate but non-moated sites. Moated and non-moated sites are simply sub-groups of what might be described as manorial complexes, leaving aside for the moment the issue of non-seigneurial homestead moats. The moated site is often only distinctive because it has a moat. While the moat is clearly a feature of note, the purpose of which has been much debated (this writer would place the greatest emphasis upon the status connotations of a moated enclosure), its presence has tended to detract from a wider and more important observation. Namely, that we are dealing with manorial complexes of varying sizes and sophistication. Some sense of this aspect of moated sites may be gained from the work undertaken on sites outside the west midlands region, such as that at Chalgrove in Oxfordshire. Manorial complexes represent a neglected theme in the medieval archaeology of the west midlands region, and should become more of a focus in our research efforts. Integral to such studies should be the proper contextualisation of associated features, such as fishponds, which can sometimes be prone to examination as isolated field monuments.

Therefore, there is a need to look at moated sites within wider frameworks than has customarily been the case, engaging with wider landscapes and the tenurial patterns within them. This is, effectively, developing further those studies that have already examined such sites within the context of assarting and landscape colonisation, and addressing matters such as the impact of subinfeudation and estate division, manorial re-organisation and manorial economies and the socio-economic context in which these estates operated.

While these observations represent the main thrust of where future work is needed, there also remain some fundamental and long-standing issues to address. There are some areas where work on moated sites is needed to address previous 'neglect', such as Worcestershire, Shropshire and the Feldon of Warwickshire. There is also the problem of 'identity'. It is well known that moated sites might arise in various contexts. Some are seigneurial, whereas others are 'homestead' sites. There are also hunting lodges and monastic granges represented within this class of field monument. The ability to distinguish between them is as important as it ever was, and is still as unlikely. The paucity of finds on many sites leaves one sceptical as to how helpful excavation might be, and the documentary record varies in its usefulness. However, a clearer understanding of the context in which these often anonymous sites occur may offer indicators.

Despite their apparent ubiquity, moated sites still have much to reveal. In terms of the PPG16 process, close attention to the 'hinterlands' of such sites is called for, as it is essential not to view these as single, isolated features within the medieval landscape. This is as true for non-seigneurial sites as it is for seigneurial sites. However, there is one further point of concern. The visibility of these sites in the present landscape generally arises from the survival of all or part of the moat. There were also many instances throughout the region of non-moated manorial complexes, which are often not so readily recognised. Excavations at sites such as the celebrated preceptory at South Witham (Lincolnshire) (Mayes 2002), or the survey of the earthworks of the north manor house at Wharram Percy (Yorkshire) (eg Beresford and Hurst 1990, 23; Rahtz and Watts 2004, 3-6), demonstrate the potential of such complexes. These need to be identified as a matter of urgency so that they may be incorporated into the same academic and planning policy frameworks that are developed to address the issues presented by moated sites.

## 6.7. The Church

### 6.7.1. The monastic church in town and country

The study of monastic sites has a pedigree reaching back into the work of antiquarians, but much of the work that has been done has tended to be very site specific, that is, work tightly focused on the church and cloister. While such studies are still prevalent, work in the region has clearly recognised the need to examine monastic sites within the context of their wider setting and landscapes. The 'flagship' project is undoubtedly the long-running study of Bordesley Abbey (Worcestershire). In addition to an examination of the church itself, there has been an investigation of the impact that this Cistercian house had upon its landscape in the Arrow valley, and an important excavation of a metal-working site, which has contributed to an appreciation of the Abbey within its hinterland and economic environment (Astill 1993).

More modest projects have included studies of Dieulacres and Hulton Abbeys (Cistercian) and Sandwell Priory (Benedictine) in Staffordshire, the latter comprising extensive excavations of the church and claustral buildings, set within a study of the surrounding landscape (Hodder 1991). More recently, some significant survey work has been undertaken by English Heritage in Shropshire. At Haughmond Abbey (Augustinian) this has greatly illuminated our understanding of the layout of the site (Pearson 2003; Fig. 6.10). Earthworks within the scheduled area have been demonstrated to be part of a more extensive complex, which has led to the identification of the monastic precinct boundary confining these earthworks. This work has not only demonstrated the need to revise the scheduled area, but also takes us closer to appreciating the 'mentalité' of the site. What was the vision of the founders? What were the zones that made up the site, their interconnections with the wider landscape of fields, woods, roads and the like, and

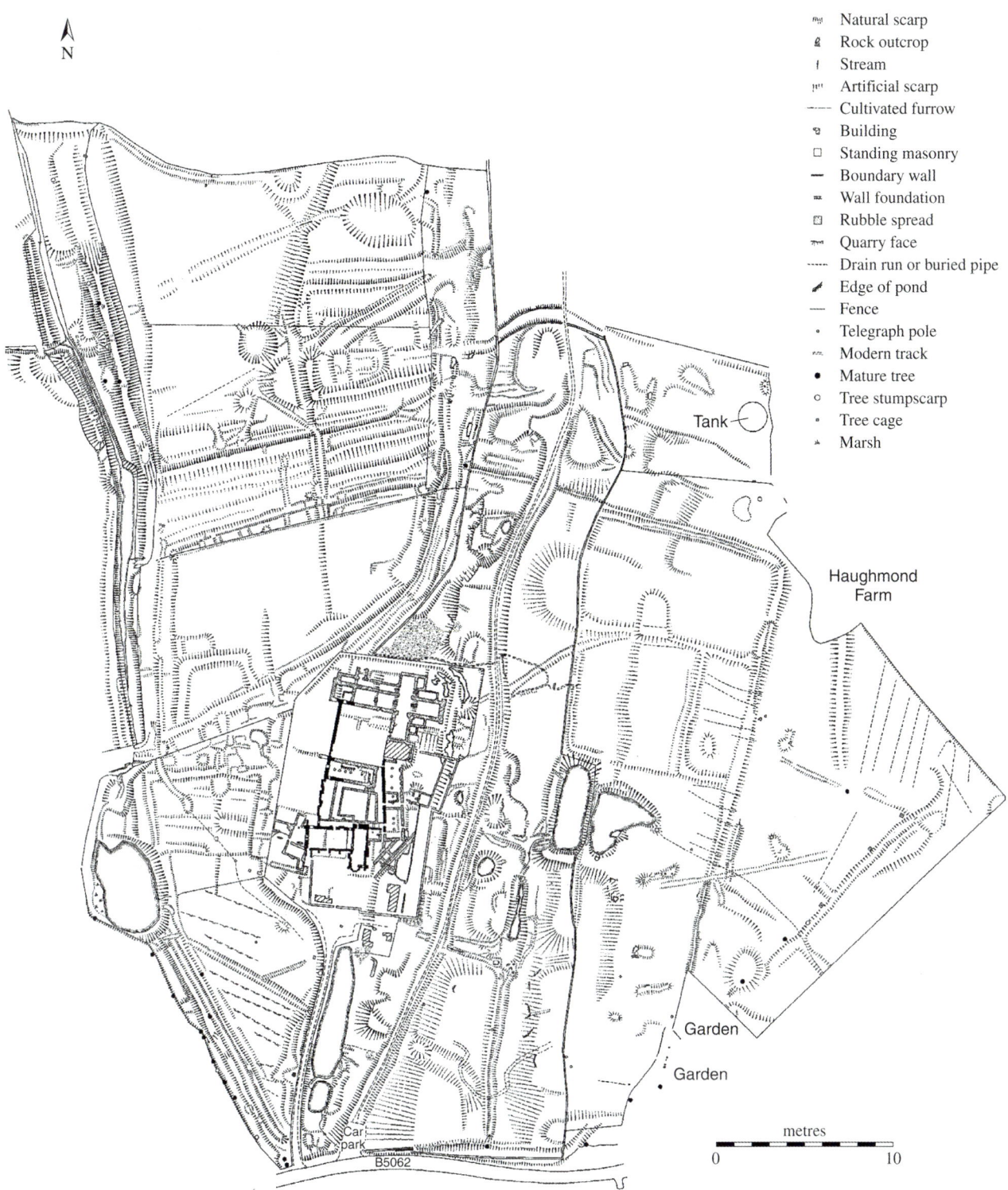

Natural scarp
Rock outcrop
Stream
Artificial scarp
Cultivated furrow
Building
Standing masonry
Boundary wall
Wall foundation
Rubble spread
Quarry face
Drain run or buried pipe
Edge of pond
Fence
Telegraph pole
Modern track
Mature tree
Tree stumpscarp
Tree cage
Marsh

**Fig 6.10** Haughmond Abbey, Shropshire; plan of earthworks survey (copyright English Heritage)

the importance of features such as springs in determining the layout of a site? A similar survey has been undertaken at Buildwas Abbey (Savignac, then Cistercian) which revealed monastic remains, post-medieval water meadows and a Second World War searchlight complex. A study of the natural setting has led to the suggestion that the monastery was deliberately sited as close as possible to the edge of the floodplain of the Severn, perhaps representing a 'special' zone of cultural or religious significance (Brown 2002).

These surveys in Shropshire have also served to illustrate a point that is generally true of monastic archaeology across the west midlands region. In certain key respects, our knowledge of monastic sites, even of major ones, remains poor. Sites like Buildwas and Haughmond are well known, but only recently have these surveys demonstrated how poorly they were actually understood. The same point may be made of most sites across the region, even more so in areas like Herefordshire, where monastic archaeology is not a current research activity. There is uncertainty regarding monastic boundaries, the location of farm courts and outer courts, of industrial areas, and of water and drainage systems. Nor has there been much targeted work on granges and monastic farms. These are very basic questions in need of urgent attention, one approach to which must be more survey work of this kind.

In Warwickshire, the most significant recent work has taken place on the Cistercian abbeys of Stoneleigh and Combe, although monastic sites are still relatively poorly researched within the county. Earlier work included excavations of varying scale at Kenilworth Priory (Augustinian), the nunnery at Polesworth (Benedictine) and at Nuneaton Priory (Benedictine) (Andrews et al 1981). There has been survey work at the Augustinian priories of Studley and Maxstoke, and at Alcester Abbey (Benedictine) (Palmer 2003). However, although the unpublished earlier work on Warwick Priory (Augustinian) is now being re-examined, it is the case that there is a particular lack of significant work on urban monasteries.

This lacuna is partially addressed through work that has taken place in Coventry. This has included excavations at the Carthusian priory (Soden 1995), the Carmelite Friary and, most recently, the Cathedral and Priory of St Mary, Coventry (Rylatt and Mason 2003), and can be set alongside key urban projects such as the excavations of Shrewsbury Abbey (Baker 2002).

In Staffordshire, although there has been some work touching on the Franciscan friary in Lichfield (eg Welch 1991; Stone 1999), urban sites are also generally poorly understood. The most significant recent project has been the work at Hulton Abbey focused on the church and chapter house, an important aspect of which has included the excavation of some eighty graves (Klemperer and Boothroyd 2004). More limited survey work has been undertaken at Croxden Abbey (Cistercian) and St Thomas' Priory (Augustinian), together with some work on Burton Abbey, and an architectural and sculptural study of Tutbury Priory (Alexander and King 1999).

Perhaps surprisingly, given the generally high profile of monastic sites in the region's landscape, there is a large research agenda still to be met. This has arisen partly as the nature of our questions change, and as recent survey work has underscored the extent to which our understanding of monastic sites is 'falling short'. Our knowledge of small rural monastic houses, and of urban monastic sites, notwithstanding the excavation of friary sites such as Ludlow, Bridgnorth and Coventry, is generally poor, while there is an acute lack of knowledge of sites associated with the military orders. Of particular importance has been the survey work in Shropshire that has challenged our perceptions of monastic sites and highlighted the importance of spatial relationships in their layouts. The implications of these results must now be fully integrated into our research agendas. This sits alongside the longer established recognition of a need to investigate monastic sites within the context of their estate infrastructures, economic regimes and wider landscapes. There is a need to know much more about the interaction between monastic houses and their hinterlands, rural and urban.

Thus, two broad and consistent points emerge from this review, both of which reflect the partial nature of the work undertaken to date.

First, many would advocate the value of a large-scale excavation of a monastic site as a regional project, to establish a kind of type-site against which the more piecemeal information obtained via the development control process might be assessed. While such a project clearly has immense potential, it is not unproblematic. The likelihood of such an excavation seems remote, and currently can only be regarded as an aspiration. However, given the range of questions and contexts that need to be addressed, one single project seems unlikely to be sufficient.

Second, as has been discussed above, it is necessary to approach the study of monastic sites from a much wider perspective than that of church and cloister. It is necessary to move through a spectrum of understanding individual buildings within the context of the core site itself, the dynamic of spatial relationships, and the wider landscape setting in its various manifestations – tenurial, economic, environmental and so on. An important preliminary in this context is to ensure that all grange sites have, at the very least, been located, mapped and recorded.

While a large-scale regional project may well prove elusive, there is clearly potential to undertake key case studies that develop our capacity to understand and appreciate the range of monastic sites within the region. Haughmond and Buildwas to some extent point the way. While this requires the opportunity to obtain good field evidence, it would also be beneficial to examine, where possible, sites which also have a good documentary record, particularly cartularies, estate surveys and account books. Within these studies, the other questions may also be addressed, such as the relation of churches to earlier sites, the development of the early church, and the role of monastic sites in the development of towns. Development-led work clearly has only limited capacity to deliver on this complex raft of research questions, particularly in the absence of a reliable 'model' or 'baseline' for contextualisation.

### 6.7.2. The secular church in town and country

Although there are similarities at some points, the secular church presents a rather different set of issues from the monastic church, particularly because of close associations with settlement history. As in other areas, work to date has had a tendency to overlook wider contexts and focus instead on what is visible in the standing structure.

**Fig 6.11** Clifton Campville church, Staffordshire (copyright John Hunt)

There is widespread recognition that our current approaches to the archaeology of church sites, led primarily by the small-scale interventions of contract archaeologists, often in graveyards, is largely uninformative. However, there are occasional exceptions. At Dodderhill (Worcestershire), it has been possible to identify a research question that small-scale trench excavations might address, namely, the presence or absence of an earlier minster, suggested by the discovery of earlier foundations on a different alignment to that of the medieval church.

The level of work on parish churches is relatively low key, related at least in part to the restrictions imposed upon archaeological investigations on such sites. This tends to arise in the wake of small developments, such as drainage work, new toilets, small extensions and the like. Churches in use fall outside the normal planning controls, the management of church archaeology being conducted through the Faculty process, and tensions can occur from the contrast between the church as a historic monument, and as a working community building. We are often seemingly better informed, through fabric surveys, on churches above ground, but this is illusory, as standing fabric reflects only one aspect of church development.

In Warwickshire, early foundations have been seen at Merevale and Temple Balsall, and there have been several seasons of work recording the fabric of the north porticus at Wootton Wawen. Evidence for the development of the church has also been forthcoming from Chadshunt (Palmer 2003). However, other west midland counties are less well informed. Shropshire is particularly poorly addressed in this respect, and one wonders if hints of a Romano-British church, and a residual British church into the mid Saxon period, as claimed in Herefordshire, might not also be sought here as suggested by excavations at Much Wenlock priory in the 1980s (Woods 1987). In Worcestershire and Staffordshire there are good levels of information on the locations of churches, a reasonable documentary base, and a number of fabric and architectural studies (eg Clifton Campville, Staffordshire, Fig. 6.11), but, with the exception of Dodderhill, little archaeological investigation beyond that associated with development control.

A still more crucial gap in the archaeological record relates to the urban parish church; work in towns has tended to focus on the greater churches. There have been very few informative excavations or surveys. In Shrewsbury none of the four former minster churches have been investigated since the 19th century, while in Worcester only one of the ten parish churches has attracted any attention. In Stafford, there has been nothing of significance since the work on St Bertelins in the 1960s. In contrast to the situation in the east and south of England, archaeology currently has little to offer on the fabric, use, development or origins of the urban parish church in the region.

Therefore, the research agenda to be addressed is substantial and fundamental in its nature. The problem is that development-led work seems unlikely in most instances to address the principal questions, certainly on a regional basis, and therefore only a carefully designed research programme seems likely to take us forward.

The origins of the parish church remain a key priority, in which this region needs to be tested against the models developed in others. Where and when did they arise, and in what context? Are we dealing primarily with seigneurial foundations between the 10th and 12th centuries? What relationship do church sites have to earlier ritual sites or central places? In reality, the means of addressing such questions, and key related issues such as the phases in church development, can only be met through excavation.

At the same time, it is essential to avoid seeing the parish church in isolation. It sat at the heart of the medieval community, and was in many respects a manifestation of the parish community, and an integral part of the settlement within which it was situated. Approaches to the research of the secular church must recognise and accommodate this fundamental perspective.

How, then, might these research needs be progressed?

- There is a need to establish a consistent baseline survey and archaeological characterisation for each church. Part of the 'Statement of Significance', this should include a summary of the research aims for each individual church. In order to achieve this, it is likely that it will be necessary to address outstanding issues on the data currently held, or awaited, in HERs. Only once this process has been tackled will the numerous contractor briefs and subsequent small-scale interventions have any real chance of being meaningful. Furthermore, this is work that needs to be interdisciplinary in nature.

- There must be a strong recommendation for the establishment of a regional research project, the fundamental objective of which is the excavation of a suitable parish church that might provide a type-site to test models from elsewhere, and against which more piecemeal information might be assessed. This is, in essence, recognising a need in the west midlands for a project similar to Wharram Percy in Yorkshire, where a church might be fully examined within the context of the community and settlement that it served. Sites of redundant churches, like that of Pendock in Worcestershire, seem potentially highly appropriate to this kind of project.

- For all of the work that has been done, there remains value in fabric surveys that are undertaken to a common standard and format. These have the potential to inform on regional and sub-regional patterns of patronage and building, and again to illustrate how churches related to their communities in various ways, reflecting, for example, patterns of prosperity and decline. Patterns of regional styles and workshops in church decoration will also be properly assimilated into the HER through this process. In surveys of this kind, the value of antiquarian writings, informing particularly on church furnishings and glass, should not be overlooked. The recording of churchyard monuments should also form a part of this process.

While these points outline the main thrust of what needs to be done, it is also necessary to maintain a wider perspective still – to be aware of the possibilities of 'lost' churches, and to look also for opportunities to study the burials and focal points of other faiths, particularly synagogues.

## 6.8. Research priorities and approaches

In many respects, the medieval period is a part of our past that feels among the most familiar to us. Considerable progress has been made in our understanding of medieval life and society, but archaeologically there remain some outstanding issues and developing focal points. Research issues have been identified for each of the themes discussed in the body of the text. Therefore, in conclusion, it is not the intention to reiterate these, but rather to highlight the key broad-based trends that emerge. In many respects, they are unsurprising, and may be summarised as follows.

- In many of the areas discussed, it is recognised that there is an urgent need to clear backlogs in publication, and to undertake works of synthesis to consolidate data and establish clear baselines. Given that archaeology will continue to be dominated by development-based investigations, such works of synthesis and comparison will provide essential tools for the interpretation of sites. This is a tool that once established will require periodic updating.

- It is essential to overcome tendencies to see themes in isolation; they all interlock. Approaches that facilitate such aspirations must include more multidisciplinary working, particularly between historians and archaeologists and across all disciplinary specialisms. Similarly, in the majority of the themes discussed, the value of whole, landscape-based, approaches is recognised. There has been a number of landscape studies around the region, essentially exploring change in the landscape over time (eg Hodder 1991-2), or mapping elements that make up particular blocks of landscape – fields, woodland, parks, settlement, and the like. These approaches should be further developed as the mechanism best suited to examining many of the themes discussed. Consideration should also be given to how the historic landscape characterisation process might be applied to support these objectives.

- While landscape-focused approaches are strongly recommended, it is clear that there are some questions and issues that can only be satisfactorily approached through excavation and related studies. Work undertaken in the train of PPG16 is not sufficient to address this although, given its prominence, it is important to maximise the returns through this process. However, there are very strong grounds for identifying regional research projects, including large-scale excavations, as a means of moving the research agenda forwards, and providing a framework for the better understanding of the results produced through development-led interventions. This will also help to determine if the results from PPG16 trial trenching warrant extension to more substantial investigations. Similarly, it is vital that the contributions of artefactual specialists are fully recognised and integrated into this research process, given their potential to inform on a wide range of themes and issues.

Identifying the most appropriate organisational practice for delivering on these key points lies beyond the scope of this review. However, it seems clear that redefined and enhanced Historic Environment Records departments offer a particularly apposite locus and means to drive and inform the Research Agenda, and to disseminate the results.

## Bibliography

Alexander, J S, and King, J F, 1999   The Architecture and Romanesque Sculpture of Tutbury Priory, in *Staffordshire Histories. Essays in Honour of Michael Greenslade. Collections for a History of Staffordshire*, 4th Series 19 (eds P Morgan and A D M Phillips), Stafford and Keele, 13-46

Andrews, D, Cook, A, Quant, V, Thorn, J C, and Veasey, E A, 1981   The archaeology and topography of Nuneaton Priory, *Trans Birmingham Warwickshire Archaeol Soc* 91

Astill, G G, 1993   *A Medieval Industrial Complex and its Landscape: The Metalworking Watermills and Workshops of Bordesley Abbey*, CBA Res Rep 92

Atkin, M, 1993   Ecclesiastical Archaeology in the West Midlands, *West Midlands Regional Research Framework* (Seminar 5)

Baker, N (ed), 2002   *Shrewsbury Abbey: Studies in the Archaeology and History of an Urban Abbey*, Shropshire Archaeological and Historical Society, Monograph Ser 2

Baker, N, 2003   *The Archaeology of the Larger Medieval Towns, West Midlands Regional Research Framework* (Seminar 5)

Barker, P, and Higham, R, 1982   *Hen Domen Montgomery. A Timber Castle on the English-Welsh Border,* Volume 1, Exeter

Bartley, D D, and Morgan, A V, 1990   The palynological record of the King's Pool, Stafford, England. *New Phytology* 116, 177-194

Bayley, J (ed), 1998   *Science in Archaeology. An agenda for the future*, London

Beresford, G, 1975   *The Medieval Clay Land Village: Excavations at Goltho and Barton Blount*, Society for Medieval Archaeology Monograph 6

Beresford, M, and Hurst, J, 1990   *Wharram Percy. Deserted Medieval Village*, London

Booth, F, 1998   *A Study of Human Skeletons from Greyfriars Cemetery, Stafford*, Unpub thesis, York University

Boothroyd, N, 2002   *Archaeological Excavation at Lawn Farm Moated Site. Interim Report on 2002 Season*, Potteries Museum Field Archaeology Unit, Report 117

Brown, D L, 1991   *Salvage recording at St Oswald's Almshouses, Worcester*, County Archaeological Service, Hereford and Worcester County Council, Report 83

Brown, G, 2002   *Earthworks at Buildwas Abbey, Shropshire*, English Heritage Archaeological Investigation Report Series AI/9/2002

Brown, P, 2003   *Whittington Castle Guidebook*

Bryant, V, 2003   Medieval Worcestershire: priorities and potential. *West Midlands Regional Research Framework* (Seminar 5)

Buteux, S, 2003   *Beneath the Bull Ring*, Warwickshire

Cantor, L M, 1966   The Medieval Castles of Staffordshire, *North Staffordshire J Field Stud* 6, 38-46

Carver, M (ed), 1980   Medieval Worcester. An Archaeological Framework, *Trans Worcestershire Archaeol Soc,* 3rd series 7

Carver, M, 1981   *Underneath Stafford Town. Archaeology in Stafford*, Birmingham University Field Archaeology Unit

Clark, J (ed), 1995   *Medieval Finds from Excavations in London: 5. The Medieval Horse and its Equipment c1150-c1450*, London

Dalwood, H, 2000   The archaeology of small towns in Worcestershire, *Trans Worcestershire Archaeol Soc*, 3rd series 17, 215-221

Cuttler, R, Hunt, J and Rátkai, S, 2009 Saxon Burh and Royal Castle: Re-thinking Early Urban Space in Stafford. *Trans Staffordhire Archaeol Hist Soc* XLIII, 39-85

Dalwood, H, 2003   Small Places with Large Consequences - the Archaeology of Small Towns in the west midlands. *West Midlands Regional Research Framework* (Seminar 5)

Dalwood, H, and Edwards, R, 2004   *Excavations at Deansway, Worcester, 1988-89: Romano-British small town to late medieval city*, CBA Res Rep 139

Darlington, J (ed), 1997   *An Archaeological Desk Based Assessment of Land off Tipping Street, Stafford*, Stafford Borough Council, Unpub Archaeology Section Report 11

Darlington, J (ed), 2001   *Stafford Castle. Survey, Excavation and Research 1978-1998. Volume 1 - The Surveys*, Stafford

Dodd, L J, Garner, D J, Robinson, D J, Ayres, K, Carruthers, W J, and Ambers, J, 2004   *Construction of a new Wine Bar at 25-27 Gaolgate Street, Stafford, Staffordshire. A Programme of Archaeological Investigations*, Earthworks Archaeological Services, Project E286. Unpub report

Dyer, C, 1986   English peasant buildings in the later middle ages (1200-1500), *Medieval Archaeology* XXX, 18-45

Dyer, C, 1990   Dispersed Settlements in Medieval England. A case study of Pendock, Worcestershire, *Medieval Archaeology* XXXIV, 97-121

Dyer, C, 1991   *Hanbury: Settlement and Society in a Woodland Landscape*, Leicester

Dyer, C, 1996   Rural settlements in medieval Warwickshire, *Trans Birmingham Warwickshire Archaeol Soc* 100, 117-132

Dyer, C, 2000   *Bromsgrove: A small town in Worcestershire in the Middle Ages.* Worcestershire Historical Society Occasional Publications 9

Dyer, C, 2001   Review of Roberts and Wrathmell, An Atlas of Rural Settlement in England, *Landscape History* 23, 117-118

Dyer, C, Jones, R, and Page, M, 2002   The Whittlewood Project, *Medieval Settlement Research Group, Annual Report* 17

Esling, J, Howard, R E, and Litton, C D, 1989   Recent tree-ring dating results in the West Midlands, *West Midlands Archaeol* 32, 22-9

Field, R K, 1965   Worcestershire Peasant Buildings, Household Goods and Farming Equipment in the Later Middle Ages, *Medieval Archaeology* IX, 105-145

Field, R K, 1996   The Beauchamp Earls of Warwick and the Castle at Elmley, *Trans Worcestershire Archaeol Soc*, 3rd series 15, 135-146

George, M, 1997   *The Deserted Village of Chartley (with reference to related earthworks)*, Unpub MA thesis, Univ of Keele

Harding, P, 2004   *Oldfurnace Cottage and Eastwall Farm Oakamoor, Staffordshire. Archaeological Evaluation and an Assessment of the Results*, Wessex Archaeology

Higham, R, and Barker, P, 2000  *Hen Domen Montgomery. A timber castle on the English-Welsh border. A Final Report*, Exeter

Hilton, R H, and Rahtz, P A, 1966  Upton, Gloucestershire, 1959-1964, *Trans Bristol Glouc Archaeol Soc*

Hilton, R H, 1983  *A Medieval Society. The West Midlands at the End of the Thirteenth Century*, Cambridge

Hislop, M, 1985-6  Reeve End Cottage, Yoxall: A Medieval Aisled Timber-Framed House, *Trans South Staffordshire Archaeol Hist Soc* XXVII, 48-52

Hislop, M, Ramsey, E, and Watts, M 2006  Stafford Mill: An Archaeological Excavation 2003, *Trans Staffordshire Archaeol Hist Soc* XLI

Hodder, M, 1991  Excavations at Sandwell Priory and Hall 1982-1988, *Trans South Staffordshire Archaeol Hist Soc* XXXI

Hodder, M, 1991-2  The Development of the North Warwickshire Landscape: settlement and landuse in the parishes of Wishaw and Middleton, *Trans Birmingham Warwickshire Archaeol Soc* 97, 41-56

Hodder, M, 2004  *Birmingham. The Hidden History*, Stroud

Hooke, D, 1990  *Worcestershire Anglo-Saxon Charter-Bounds. Studies in Anglo-Saxon History II*, Woodbridge

Hoverd, T, 2003  Medieval Herefordshire, *West Midlands Regional Research Framework* (Seminar 5)

Hunt, J, and Hodder, M, 1992  An early manorial enclosure at Curdworth, Warwickshire, and its affinities, *Warwickshire History* 8, 162-74

Hunt, J, 1997  *Lordship and the Landscape. A documentary and archaeological study of the Honor of Dudley c.1066-1322*, BAR British Series 264, Oxford

Hunt, J, and Stokes, M A, 1997  Sculpture and Patronage in a Shropshire Manor: A Group of Twelfth Century Sculptures from Alveley, *Journal of the British Archaeological Association* CL, 27-47

Hunt, J, and Klemperer, W, 2003  The Archaeology of Medieval Staffordshire: An Overview, *West Midlands Regional Research Framework* (Seminar 5)

Hunt, J, 2003  Whose handmaiden? Historical and archaeological approaches to the Middle Ages, *West Midlands Regional Research Framework* (Seminar 5)

Hunt, J, 2004  Sculpture, Dates and Patrons: Dating the Herefordshire School of Sculpture, *Antiquaries Journal* 84

Hunt, J, 2007  *Newcastle-under-Lyme. Historic Character Assessment Report January 2007. Staffordshire Extensive Urban Survey*, Unpub Report for Staffordshire County Council

Hurst, J D, 1990  Documentary evidence for medieval potters in Worcestershire, *Transactions of the Worcestershire Archaeological Society 3rd series* 12, 247-50

Hurst, J D, 1994  A medieval ceramic production site and other medieval sites in the parish of Hanley Castle; results of fieldwork in 1987-1992, *Trans Worcestershire Archaeol Soc,* 3rd series 14, 115-28

Hurst, J D, 1997  *A multi-period salt production site at Droitwich: excavations at Upwich 1983-84*, CBA Res Rep 107

Hurst, J D, 2003  Medieval Industry in the West Midlands, *West Midlands Regional Research Framework* (Seminar 5)

Hurst, J G, Andrews, D D, and Milne, G (eds), 1979   *Wharram. A Study of Settlement on the Yorkshire Wolds, I, Domestic Settlements, I: Areas 10 and 6*, Society of Medieval Archaeology Monograph Series 8

Johnson, M, 2002   *Behind the Castle Gate. From Medieval to Renaissance*, London

Jones, C, Eyre-Morgan, G, Palmer, S, and Palmer, N, 1997   Excavations in the Outer Enclosure of Boteler's Castle, Oversley, Alcester, 1992-93, *Trans Birmingham Warwickshire Archaeol Soc* 101, 1-98

Jones, R, and Page, M, 2003a   Medieval Settlements and Landscapes in the Whittlewood Area: Interim Report 2003-4, *Medieval Settlement Research Group, Annual Report* 18, 37-45

Jones, R, and Page, M, 2003b   Characterising Rural Settlement and Landscape: Whittlewood Forest in the Middle Ages, *Medieval Archaeology* XLVII, 53-83

Klemperer, W, and Parkes, A, 2000   *Berryhill Fields. History and Archaeology*, Stoke on Trent

Klemperer, W, and Boothroyd, N, 2004   *Excavations at Hulton Abbey, Staffordshire 1987-1994*, Society for Medieval Archaeology Monograph 21

Linford, P, 2001   *Bagot's Park, Abbots Bromley, Staffordshire. Archaeomagnetic Dating Report*, London

Mayes, P, 2002   *Excavations at a Templar Preceptory. South Witham, Lincolnshire 1965-67*, Society for Medieval Archaeology Monograph 19

Mays, S, 1998   The archaeological study of medieval English human populations, AD 1066-1540, in *Science in Archaeology. An agenda for the future* (ed J Bayley), London, 195-210

Meeson, R, 2001   Archaeological Evidence and Analysis. A Case Study from Staffordshire, *Vernacular Architecture* 32, 1-15

Meeson, R, 2003   *Hill Farm, Wychnor. An archaeological Assessment*, Unpub Report 03/24

Mercer, E, 2003   *English Architecture to 1900: The Shropshire Experience*, Logaston

Miller, D, Griffin, L, and Pearson, E, 2004   *Programme of archaeological work at 9-10 the Tything, Worcester*, Worcestershire Historic Environment and Archaeology Service Report 1150

Morgan, P, and Phillips, A D M (eds), 1999   *Staffordshire Histories. Essays in Honour of Michael Greenslade. Collections for a History of Staffordshire Fourth Series* 19, Stafford and Keele

Murphy, P, 2001a   *Review of Wood and Macroscopic Wood Charcoal from Archaeological Sites in the West and East Midlands Regions and the East of England*, Report 23/2001, London

Murphy, P, 2001b   *Review of Molluscs and Other Non-Insect Invertebrates from Archaeological Sites in the West and East Midlands, and the East of England*, Report 68/2001, London

Nash, G, and Children, G (eds), 2003   *An Anatomy of a Castle: The Weobley Castle Project*, Logaston

Network Archaeology 1997   *Audley to Alrewas Gas Pipeline. Archaeological Desk-Based Assessment*, Unpub Report 107

Nichol, K, and Ratkái, S, 2004   Excavations on the north Side of Sandford Street, Lichfield, Staffordshire, *Trans Staffordshire Archaeol Hist Soc* XL, 58-121

Palliser, D M, 1972  Staffordshire Castles: A Provisional List, *Staffordshire Archaeology* 1, 5-8

Palmer, N 2003  Warwickshire (and Solihull) – the Medieval Period, *West Midlands Regional Research Framework* (Seminar 5)

Palmer, N and Dyer, C, 1988  An Inscribed Stone from Burton Dassett, Warwickshire, *Medieval Archaeology* XXXII, 216-19

Pearson, E, and Grieg, J, Jordan, D, 1999  *Environmental Remains from a Watching Brief at Lammascote Road, Stafford,* Worcestershire Archaeological Service, Project 1668, Unpub Report 767

Pearson, T, 2003  *Haughmond Abbey, Shropshire,* English Heritage Archaeological Investigation Report Series AI/10/2003

Perring, D, 2002  *Town and country in England: frameworks for archaeological research,* CBA Res Rep 134

Rahtz, P A, and Watts, L, 2004  *The North Manor Area and North-West Enclosure. Wharram IX,* York

Ratkái, S, 2003  That Earthern Lot: Ceramics in the West Midlands, *West Midlands Regional Research Framework* (Seminar 5)

Razi, Z, 1980  *Life, Marriage and Death in a Medieval Parish. Economy, Society and Demography in Halesowen 1270-1400,* Cambridge

Roberts, B K, 1965  Moated Sites in Midland England, *Trans Birmingham Warwickshire Archaeol Soc* LXXX

Roberts, B K, 1968  A Study of Medieval Colonisation in the Forest of Arden, *Warwickshire Agricultural History Review* 16(2)

Roberts, B K, and Wrathmell, S, 2000  *An Atlas of Rural Settlement in England,* London

Roberts, B K, and Wrathmell, S, 2002  *Region and Place. A study of English rural settlement,* London

Robinson, M, 2003  *English Heritage Reviews of Environmental Archaeology: Midlands Region Insects,* Report 9/2003, London

Rylatt, M, and Mason, P, 2003  *The Archaeology of the Medieval Cathedral and priory of St Mary, Coventry,* Coventry

Shaw, M, 2003  Priorities for the Archaeology of the Black Country and Birmingham in the Medieval Period, *West Midlands Regional Research Framework* (Seminar 5)

Soden, I, 1990  *Excavations on the town wall, Friars Road, Coventry,* Coventry Museums Archive Report

Soden, I, 1995  *Excavations at St Anne's Charterhouse, Coventry, 1968-87,* Coventry Museums Monograph 4, Coventry

Soden, I, 2003  Coventry's Archaeology: Summary of the Medieval Resource. *West Midlands Regional Research Framework* (Seminar 5)

Soden, I, 2005  *Coventry: The Hidden History,* Stroud

Stamper, P, 1996  *Historic Parks and Gardens of Shropshire,* Shropshire

Stamper, P, 2003  Medieval Shropshire: Research Priorities, *West Midlands Regional Research Framework* (Seminar 5)

Stone, R, and Appleton-Fox, N, 1996  *A View from Hereford's Past. A report on the archaeological excavation of Hereford Cathedral Close in 1993,* Logaston

Stone, R, 1999  *1 Bird Street, Lichfield, Staffordshire. Report on a watching brief,* Unpub report, Marches Archaeology Series 103

Tavener, N, in prep  An excavation and watching brief on land to the rear of 15 Sandford Street, Lichfield, Staffordshire

Thomas, R, 2002  *Animals, economy and status: the integration of historical and archaeological evidence in the study of a medieval castle,* Unpub PhD thesis, Univ of Birmingham

Thorpe, H, 1965  The Lord and the Landscape, Illustrated Through the Changing Fortunes of a Warwickshire Parish, Wormleighton, *Trans Birmingham Warwickshire Archaeol Soc* 80

Thurlby, M, 1999  *The Herefordshire School of Romanesque Sculpture,* Logaston

Toomey, J P (ed), 2001  *Records of Hanley Castle, Worcestershire, c 1147-1547,* Worcestershire Historical Society New Series 18

Welch, C M, 1991  *The Franciscan Friary, Lichfield. A Reassessment,* Unpub report, Staffordshire County Council

Welch, C M, 1997  Glass-making in Wolesley, Staffordshire, *Post-Medieval Archaeology* 31, 1-60

Williamson, T, 2003  *Shaping Medieval Landscapes. Settlement, Society, Environment,* Macclesfield

Woods, H, 1987  Excavations at Wenlock Priory, 1981-6, *Journal of the British Archaeological Association* CXL

Wright, S M, 1982  Much Park Street, Coventry: the development of a medieval street. Excavations 1970-74, *Trans Birmingham Warwickshire Archaeol Soc* 92, 1-132

# 7. 'The archaeology of everything' – grappling with post-medieval, industrial and contemporary archaeology

Paul Belford

paul.belford@nexus-heritage.com

## 7.1. Introduction

It is a cold frosty morning in February in the closing years of the reign of Queen Elizabeth. Four well-wrapped figures are working hard at the frozen ground, digging trenches through the clay. Elsewhere others are creating roads and earthworks. The land they are all working on has recently been acquired by an entrepreneurial developer keen to profit from the rapidly shifting shapes of an emerging new world. This is a world characterised by investment in overseas enterprise, ongoing international conflict over religion and resources, and the ever-present tension between core and periphery in European society. Such matters may seem far from the blistered hands and frozen feet of the workers hacking at the clay. But only one of them is local. The others have arrived seeking better prospects or fleeing from religious persecution elsewhere. And they are helping to build a new centre for a rapidly developing technology that will be crucial in the development of a new England and a new world.

The place is Wednesbury, in the heart of the west midlands. The date could be 1597 or 2007. In the 16th century a water-powered forge was built here; it was first mentioned in the documentary record in 1597 as the result of a legal dispute. The forge was built by a man whose father obtained land during the dissolution of the monasteries. The dissolution saw the greatest ever transfer of property in English history, and set changes in motion which eventually led to the industrial revolution and the development of a consumer society. The first English colony in Virginia had been established a decade earlier; ten years later the settlement at Jamestown would begin the process of invasion, clearance and 'civilisation' which would lead to the creation of modern America. During the 17th and 18th centuries our forge at Wednesbury made guns and other weapons; during the 18th and 19th centuries it also made tools for cutting and digging – axes, scythes, hoes and spades. The new empire was built and defended with goods from Wednesbury Forge. In the 19th century the owner built a church, a sports club and housing for his workers; he also connected his expanding factory to the new railway network. Wooden water wheels were replaced by steam engines and high-speed turbines.

Despite these investments the world moved on. A Great War cut down a generation in the fields of Flanders. Recession. Fascism. Another war to end all wars. Gradually the apron strings of Empire were severed. The forge was bought by a major national manufacturer. Within a generation this company had been taken over by an international conglomerate and the spectre of rationalisation loomed. Cheaper products could be made in Eastern Europe, India and China. Twentieth-century consumers – like their forebears in the 16th century – discriminated mainly on price rather than quality. The site was acquired for redevelopment and, finally, after more than 400 years, the forge closed down. A new industrial estate will be created, the sort of place where computer software will be developed and service industry workers will be trained; there will

**Fig 7.1** Blistered hands and frozen feet. Excavations in advance of development at Wednesbury Forge (Sandwell) in 2007. The two site assistants are clearing out the silted-up brick-built 17th-century watercourse which was constructed directly over its 16th-century timber-framed predecessor, evident in the background. It went out of use in the 19th century; finds included an 18th-century Irish penny defaced with Nationalist graffiti, a 17th-century pewter spoon and a 16th-century brass thimble (copyright Paul Belford)

also be a new hotel and playing fields for the local school. So here we are on our frosty morning in February. A gang of Romanians are stripping the site of anything burnable – shelves, patterns, drawings of tools, records of production – and piling it high on the funeral pyre of English industry. A small team of archaeologists work in the shadow of the encroaching development, carefully extracting the story of the forge from the clay subsoil into which its first timbers were laid (Fig 7.1).

This paper is an inevitably personal view of the archaeology of the last few hundred years. Between the 16th and 21st centuries the world has changed radically, despite the outward similarities in the two scenes at Wednesbury. It has also produced a lot of 'stuff'. This 'stuff' consists of both the material culture (artefacts, buildings, documents and so-on) with which archaeologists are so familiar, and also a non-material culture – a much more evanescent but essential component of everyday life incorporating sounds, smells, emotions and ideas. No historical or archaeological period has as much resonance in our lives today. Moreover, the overwhelming extent of the evidence makes a conventional audit and analysis of the resource impossible to achieve even with a generous word allowance from the editors. Consequently, unlike the other chapters in this volume there is no 'resource assessment' *per se*. Instead, this chapter provides an overview of the historical and theoretical development of the discipline itself, an analysis of some of the themes that have emerged from archaeological study hitherto, and discussion of how we might deal in practical terms with this superabundance of 'stuff'.

## 7.2. Framing the past in the future

The title of this chapter comes from a discussion between David Barker and myself in 2004. We had co-organised the period seminars in Coalbrookdale and Stoke-on-Trent, and had been discussing ways in which we could present the archaeology of the region's period in a coherent 'framework'. We were returning by train from an event in Nottingham organised by the Association for Industrial Archaeology in an attempt to develop a national framework of their own. We were critiquing the event, and also attempting to define what was significant and interesting about the archaeology of the last 500 years for our own region. Before the train had reached Derby (where engineering work forced us to decant to separate buses) the interconnectedness of so many themes had forced the conclusion – in David's words – that we were talking about 'the archaeology of everything'. Attempting to order 'everything' into a neat list of archaeological priorities is akin to herding cats or Border Terriers.

### 7.2.1. What are we talking about?

The original brief for the framework seminars was to look at two periods. These were 'Post-medieval', covering the period from *c* 1500 to *c* 1750; and 'Industrial' which took the period *c* 1750 to *c* 1900. This was felt to be an artificial and somewhat old-fashioned subdivision of a single period which in fact contained considerable continuity. The conventional starting point is essentially the dissolution, although this episode was an English material reflection of wider European reformation which had been in progress for more than a hundred years. There was also concern about the cut-off date of *c* 1900, which seemed to imply that archaeology had nothing to contribute to our understanding of the post-Victorian period. Yet archaeological analysis of the region's 20th-century industries began a generation ago with the late Michael Stratton's work on car factories and electricity and this has been followed by extensive work on subjects as wide-ranging as the Defence of Britain during the Second World War and the archaeology of 1960s tenement houses (Collins and Stratton 1993; Stratton 1994; Stratton and Trinder 2000; Denison 2002; Belford and Ross 2004). In the last five years there has been the exciting development and maturation of the discipline of 'contemporary archaeology', and a growing acceptance of the value of the archaeology of the very recent past (Buchli and Lucas 2001; Bradley et al 2004; Lamb 2004). The study of 'contemporary archaeology' in the UK context has become a significant interface between the disciplines of archaeology, ethnography, anthropology and sociology. Therefore for this volume the three periods have been brought together and the period consequently covers, give or take a generation here or there, the five centuries before today.

**Fig 7.2** Excavations during restoration of Jackfield Tile Museum (Shropshire) in 2005. An encaustic tile works was built in 1873 on the site of a 17th-century 'mughouse' in an area with a long tradition of ceramic production. This updraught kiln was built in the early 19th century in the last phase of pottery manufacture, where 17th-century-style 'Staffordshire' slipwares were still being made. Technologically similar to contemporary kilns in Stoke-on-Trent, it was converted to a downdraught kiln in the 1870s to fire tiles. The workers on this site were also consumers of Jackfield ware, as finds in the area have revealed (copyright Paul Belford)

The debate about what we actually call the period and/or its constituent parts is still ongoing. The terms 'post-medieval', 'industrial' and 'contemporary' are all used in the title of this paper, and all have different meanings to different archaeologists. This is partly a result of the origins of the different elements of the discipline which the terms represent. There is arguably a dichotomy between the middle-class, humanities-based origins of 'post-medieval archaeology' and the working-class, science- and engineering-based approaches of 'industrial archaeology'. This has sometimes polarised the discipline and diverted energies away from cooperation in understanding the archaeology itself (Cranstone 2004). Many see value in the term 'post-medieval', but choose to ignore (or subvert) the expression by the founders of the Society for Post-Medieval Archaeology that the period ends at 'the onset of industrialisation' (Anon 1967, 2). Indeed the Society itself has recently produced volumes entitled *The Archaeology of Industrialization* and *Cities in the World 1500-2000*, which explicitly accept a broader timespan for the 'post-medieval' period (Barker and Cranstone 2004; Green and Leech 2006). Defining a period by what it is not (post-medieval – not medieval, but what?) does raise issues for some. However, it is wrong to suggest, as Susie West did in 1999, that post-medieval archaeology is the last refuge of 'traditionalist archaeology', operating as an empirical data-gathering exercise without theoretical rigour (West 1999, 6-7).

Outlining the scope of 'industrial archaeology' is also fraught with difficulty, and meetings of the Association for Industrial Archaeology have grappled with this subject. Certainly the subject has moved a long way from the days when one of its founding fathers,

Kenneth Hudson, could state that 'the very point of Industrial Archaeology…[is]…to provide facts about the history of industry and technology' (1967, 9). Instead, its most innovative practitioners prefer to explore 'social transformations…power relations, new systems of control and the creation of a work ethic' (Gould 1999, 153). Marilyn Palmer has written of the 'long pre-history of industrialisation' which preceded the industrial revolution, and has acknowledged that industrialisation was 'one of the key developments in the post-medieval British economy and society' (2004, 1). So 'industrial archaeology' is today generally acknowledged as a subset of 'post-medieval archaeology', but with a specific focus on the issues surrounding the process of industrialisation (Palmer and Neaverson 1998; Fig 7.2). Like post-medieval archaeology, it has in the past been an easy target for those who accuse it of having 'neglected almost all theory' and focused on steam engines and mills (Grant 1987, 118). This situation has certainly changed in recent years, with theoretically informed studies being produced by industrial archaeologists such as James Symonds (2002) and Michael Nevell. The publication of papers from the 2004 conference referred to above has been a helpful step forward in articulating some of the issues concerned (Gwyn and Palmer 2005).

These home–grown approaches to the study of the recent past are part of a much wider global study of 'historical archaeology' (Andren 1998; Hall and Silliman 2006). Outside Europe there is less of a problem in identifying a starting point, for the term 'historical archaeology' is usually synonymous with the period following European contact. In North America the discipline was quick to advance beyond empirical approaches and developed a comprehensive armoury of theoretical weapons. Some colleagues have looked rather enviously across the Atlantic and bemoaned the academic marginalisation of the discipline here; however, their attempts to apply American approaches to UK situations have not always been wholly successful. Others have noted the shortcomings for British archaeology in some of the key tenets of traditional American historical archaeology, witness the widespread backlash in the 1990s against James Deetz's influential 'Georgian Order' theory (Deetz 1977; Hall 1992; Courtney 1996). It has recently been said that American practitioners 'often do not know much about historical archaeology outside of north America' (although there are many notable exceptions), and for some the use of the term 'historical archaeology' in a UK context has been regarded as a form of US cultural imperialism (Hall and Silliman 2006, 6; Mark Horton, pers comm). There is clearly a need to continue developing our own set of models and theories, yet it is evident that in studying a period which created the modern globalised society, we can only do justice to the study of our own region with reference to the wider world and to its understanding of the same period and the events and processes within it.

### 7.2.2. Constructing an archaeological framework

The seemingly semantic debate over what the period is called is critical, since it is at the heart of our identity within the broader church of archaeological enquiry. David Cranstone has tentatively suggested a name for our subject might be the 'archaeology of the later second millennium' (Cranstone 2004). The arbitrariness of starting in the year 1500 is attractive, as is the all-encompassing nature of the phrase which advocates doing away with studies of industry, consumption and landscape (and all the rest) as separate sub-disciplines. The unwieldiness of the phrase is the main disadvantage, together with its implicit Euro-centricity. Agreement amongst colleagues specialising in the period is not readily forthcoming, and I have my own personal unease about the use of the terms 'industrial archaeology' (for the implied narrowness of the field) and 'historical archaeology' (for its inappropriateness as a period descriptor in a European context, when much medieval, Roman and even Iron Age archaeology also uses contemporaneous written sources). Consequently, in the rest of this chapter, the term 'post-medieval' will be used to describe the period from *c* 1500 to the present day.

It is clear that there are a number of issues around the construction of an archaeological research framework. One of the reasons for developing the framework in the first place has been to try and come to terms with the vast quantity of data emerging from PPG16-led archaeology. However, there is still a tendency amongst some archaeologists to dismiss the 'overburden' of later deposits in the quest for the remains of earlier periods (Lawrence 2006, 308). Malcolm Atkin has suggested that some colleagues are under the 'impression that post-medieval archaeology is less important than earlier periods' (Atkin 2003, 1). This situation is more acute for the post-medieval period than for prehistoric or Roman periods, although the urban archaeology of the medieval period has also suffered (Hunt, this volume). Part of the problem is a failure of communication between the three branches of the archaeological profession – academics, contractors and curators. Richard Bradley's recent survey of prehistoric archaeology has shown that archaeological contractors are actually very much in the vanguard of research, particularly when they have developed a localised or subject-specialised interest (Bradley 2006). This is very true for the post-medieval period, as we shall see later. Another issue is the question of geographical cohesion, as John Hunt has already mentioned in his chapter on the medieval period. The west midlands region, as defined by this volume, has never been a coherent cultural entity. It also excludes the vital communication nodes of Gloucester and the Mersey Basin, through which most of the industrial output of the conurbations, the Severn hinterland and north Staffordshire (coal, iron, steel, pottery, porcelain, textiles and so-on) was directed.

Colleagues constructing frameworks for the post-medieval period elsewhere in the country have had mixed approaches. Yorkshire stands at one extreme, where little space in the published volume was devoted to the last 500 years, notwithstanding the significance in that time frame of (for example) the port of Hull, Sheffield's steel and cutlery trades, and the West Riding textile industries. At the other end of the scale the contributors to the north-west framework used the opportunity to promote Manchester as the 'epicentre' of industrialisation (McNeil and Newman 2006a and b). In the north-east, north-west and south-west, large amounts have been written under the heading 'Resource Assessment', with the implication that fieldwork has already identified the full nature, extent and character of the resource. Only in the north-east has the archaeology of the 20th century been given equal consideration to that of other periods (Petts and Gerrard 2006). The approach of the London research framework is more refreshing in this regard –four out of the total of 120 pages comprises the resource assessment (Museum of London 2002). Like Simon Esmonde Cleary (this volume), I would argue that the creation of a traditional resource assessment would simply echo the 'history of the development of the specialisms' within the discipline of archaeology and do little to develop a framework for future understanding. In terms of the pace and extent of social, cultural and technological change, the last 500 years are probably equivalent to dealing with the Neolithic, Bronze Age, Iron Age and Roman periods in one synthetic whole.

## 7.3. Variations on a theme of transition

Transition pervades the entire period. Sometimes this was a gradual transition, such as the gently rolling snowball of industrialisation. At other times transition occurred sharply, even violently, through processes of reformation and revolution. The archaeology of this period deals with transition at every level, from the dissolution of the monasteries to the closure of Longbridge. In many places and situations there are several overlapping transitions going on at the same time. All of these different layers of change impacted upon people in different ways, and will have different manifestations in the archaeological record. They will also resonate most powerfully with present–day consumers of archaeology – ourselves, our clients and our public – who ultimately this is all for and for whom we need to start telling stories.

### 7.3.1. Some broad issues

It has been successfully argued that the archaeology of this period is to an extent the 'archaeology of capitalism' (Leone 1995; Johnson 1996; Leone and Potter 1998). Matthew Johnson employed a broad definition of the term, which included notions such as the increasing privatisation of social space, as well as conventional material activities such as trade and the consumption of artefacts. Post-medieval archaeology has traditionally been very good at identifying where and how goods were produced and consumed, and in more recent years has begun to use artefacts to tell more complex stories about the people who used them. We have been less successful in trying to understand some of the more subtle and shifting nuances of meaning that have been created in our sites, buildings and landscapes by the ever-developing processes of capitalism. Johnson and others have used the term 'commodification', by which the notion of capitalism 'embraces other concepts such as privacy, individualism and sentiment' (Johnson 1996, 87-90; Tarlow 1999, 265). The development of capitalism was already underway when the dissolution of the monasteries created new patterns of asset ownership from the 16th century. This in turn provoked widespread and ongoing adjustment of social structures and power relations. Everything in the new post-medieval age had its social, cultural and economic price and the continual (re)negotiation of value is one of the key drivers of the development of the modern world.

One of the most obvious manifestations of capitalism was the process of industrialisation, which occurred very early in our region. Mining, pottery manufacture, iron- and glass-making had been steadily colonising the wastes, those helpful interstices between civilised and ordered towns and fields, since the 13th century. As the grip of traditional asset-holders (monasteries and aristocrats) began to slacken, capitalist entrepreneurs seized more opportunities to make money by making things. In 15th-century Rugeley, Ralph Wolseley put money into industrial plant for brewing and dyeing; by the mid 16th century the enterprising Robert Brooke had begun substantial capital investment to create Coalbrookdale's industrial landscape (Welch 2001; Belford and Ross in prep). From this followed the massive industrial expansion of the 17th and 18th centuries, characterised by increasing mechanisation and mass production. The creation of these sorts of capital-intensive production infrastructures required the construction of new physical landscapes and mental adjustment to new (and continually adjusting) power relations between men, women and children. Enclosure of all sorts of spaces was a particularly post-medieval phenomenon and formed part of this process of commodification and alienation (Johnson 2007). As well as the phenomenon of agricultural enclosure, there was also re-colonisation of 'marginal' land, improvement of meadow systems and increasingly sophisticated woodland management (Welch 2000; Stamper 2003; Gledhill 2004). Landscapes of industrial production and transportation created new types of buildings and structures, and new hierarchies of relations between them. In urban spaces the same processes were evident, from the increasing partition and subdivision of existing townscapes to the regularised expansion of suburbs from the 17th century onwards.

Closely linked with the development of industrialised capitalism was the creation of a consumer society; money was made by mass-producing objects for sale – from iron bars to chocolate bars. Increasing consumption of 'stuff' can be seen as a marker of modernity and individuality (Johnson 1996). However, consumption studies have traditionally had art-historical origins rather than archaeological ones and have therefore tended to focus on groups and individuals from well-documented sections of society (Courtney 1996; Johnson 2007). The archaeology of consumption can be studied at all levels – from the appropriation of medieval landscape features by wealthy landowners, to the use of pub tokens by urban workers. Perhaps one of the greatest strengths of post-medieval archaeology is its ability to look at sections of society traditionally marginalised by (the absence of) documentary records. Archaeology in the west midlands has the potential to challenge, for example, the traditional perception of urban (or London or European) core and rural (or provincial or colonial) periphery. Consumption of food, for example, was not undertaken in a cultural vacuum, but was informed by prevailing social conditions and resulted in the acquisition, modification and use of an array of metal, glass and ceramic artefacts. In spite of mass production, many of these items were imbued with particular personal and social meanings, as studies on both sides of the Atlantic have shown (Yentsch 1991; Pennell 1999). It is important not to separate production and consumption – the workers in the ironworks or pottery kilns were also consumers, and stories about identity and social networks can be teased out of both manufacturing and domestic sites. Changes in the consumption of space are also significant, not only 'private' domestic space but also 'public' spaces such as streets, railway carriages, art galleries and brothels.

The increasing *crescendo* of consumerism was assisted by the development of trade, transport and communication links. Improved navigability of rivers and the development of canal, railway and road networks resulted from the need to move raw materials and finished goods around (Quartermaine et al 2003; Trinder 2005). Improved communication also increased the consumption of ideas – ideas about God, governance and the way the world was (and could be) put together. Not only was a new world being manufactured at home, but the New World abroad was being 'discovered', mapped and colonised. The colonial experience for existing and new inhabitants of these places – from 17th-century Ireland to 20th-century Australia – has been extensively studied from a variety of viewpoints and in all of these places we find the consumer products of the industrial capitalism of the west midlands (Egan and Michael 1999; Barker 2003; Given 2004; Horning 2006). However, the means by which many of these goods appeared at home and abroad – the role of Birmingham munitions in the slave trade, for example, or the role of slaves in the tobacco trade which sustained the clay pipe makers – have often been overlooked (Higgins 1999; Hicks 2003; Johnson 2006). Furthermore the existence of the New World had impacts on European and English society, both in terms of ideas (the rise of European nation-states can be seen as a response to the 'other' represented by colonial experience, for example) and material remains. Hence the lavish houses built on the proceeds of slavery, and also the sometimes fiercely resisted processes of enclosure and improvement (itself a form of colonialism). There is tremendous scope to examine patterns of migration and notions of identity and ethnicity through material culture. Such studies will not simply illuminate the processes of globalisation in the past but may also provide assistance as we struggle with some of its effects in the present.

This rather superficial analysis suggests that the *leitmotif* of transition can be broken down into four broad and over-arching thematic groups which are characteristic of the development of human society in the west midlands over the last 500 years. These are:

- Capitalism (including the commodification of social and personal space).

- Industrialisation (and its associated cultural and social changes).

- Consumption (of place, meaning, identity and self, as well as artefacts).

- Globalisation (including all of the above, colonialism and communication).

Of course it will always be difficult to directly relate these groups to the daily experience of confronting a 'mid-grey-brown silty clay' deposit, extracting its fragments of pot, tile and slag, and trying to understand its stratigraphic relationship with neighbouring layers of grey-brown mud. (Although of course archaeologists themselves are physically enacting all of these themes, with developer-funding, machine-assisted trial trenching, tea-drinking, bacon butties from the local greasy spoon and cheap Chinese-made waterproofs). Very rarely will a single artefact or feature speak so eloquently and directly of capitalism, industry and global consumption as the ones illustrated here, although some of these topics should be emerging at the level of an individual site or assemblage (Fig 7.3 and 7.4).

### 7.3.2. Interconnecting themes

Present within all of these four main thematic groups is a number of subjects which will more readily manifest themselves in the archaeological record, or at least in our interpretation of it. These are very much interconnecting and overlapping; thus an archaeology of conflict may also be present in a gender-based archaeology of the home; or it might equally be evident in an investigation of scientific developments in the workplace. These themes include (but are by no means restricted to) the following areas, which have been arranged in alphabetical order.

### Conflict

The subject of battlefield archaeology has matured significantly in recent years, with practitioners such as John Carman moving the subject away from its close association with military history and placing it within a broader archaeological discourse. By emphasising the significance of place (rather than the event), Carman and others have sought to make a 'distinctive archaeological contribution to...debates about...war itself' (Carman and Carman 2001, 280). However, the area of conflict archaeology in the post-medieval period is potentially much wider. It should encompass the changing functional and symbolic roles of the medieval castle, the creation of new types of fortification to meet the changing nature of gunfire, the development of arms and munitions and the social and industrial ramifications, 19th- and 20th-century developments and the archaeology of the Cold War (Johnson 2002; Saunders 2002; Brown et al 2006). It should also concern itself with non-military forms of conflict. Thus we should be exploring the way in which industrial space was constructed, archaeologies of civil unrest at times of economic hardship, political agitation, trade unionism, overt and covert forms of industrial resistance (from the Levellers to Red Robbo), suffragettes and civil rights, peace demonstrators, anti-road protestors and the Countryside Alliance (Ludlow Collective 2001; Schofield et al 2002).

**Fig 7.3** 'Jacare – Fabricada Na Inglaterra'. A mid 20th-century enamel sign found during clearance of standing buildings at Wednesbury Forge. Part-finished examples of the product depicted were found during excavation, and the dies for their forging recorded during demolition of the factory. An eloquent testimony to the widespread influence of English manufactured goods around the world (copyright Paul Belford)

### Death and disease

The archaeology of death is certainly a well-established field in prehistoric, Roman and medieval archaeology, and is also developing into a serious part of post-medieval archaeology. Several large assemblages of post-medieval human skeletal remains have been examined, and probably the most significant regionally is the work done by Birmingham Archaeology at the Bullring site (Brickley et al 2006). Such analysis is not only important for understanding populations in the broad sense, but is also able to determine pathologies of disease, injury and disability during life. For the 19th century there is considerable potential to look at individual biographies and see how the stresses of work and life impacted on people's bodies. There is also the archaeology of commemoration, understanding the social role played by acts of burial and remembrance. Detailed analysis of gravestones and coffin furniture, for example, has proved particularly fruitful in elucidating social attitudes amongst the living (Mytum 2002 and 2006). Analysis of the interplay between identity and ethnicity within and between groups is also possible; Quakers, Methodists, Jews and Muslims all have different practices of burial and commemoration that are manifest in the archaeological record.

### Home

There was a transformation in domestic life during this period; the main trends in the use of space evincing increasing density, privatisation of space and regularisation of form. The creation, use and modification of the built environment is the result of prevailing cultural modes and it has been clearly shown that an archaeological study of housing can provide a 'route into the mentality of people who lived in the past' (Leech 2006, 302). The evolution of housing forms does show considerable localised variation and retention of vernacular elements continued well into the 19th century. Studies elsewhere have shown that an investigation of this process can illuminate the extent to which this was the conscious (re)creation of identities (Leech 1981; Leech 1996; Guillery and Herman

**Fig 7.4** 'Neverbend in Bermuda'. This shovel was made at Wednesbury Forge in the late 1980s and sold to the Bermuda National Trust. It has been used on a variety of archaeological excavations and conservation projects, and is depicted here resting from duties excavating a test-pit which discovered slave quarters on a plantation dating to c 1700 (copyright Emma Dwyer)

1999; Burton and Guillery 2006; Figs 7.5 and 7.6). Infilling of existing urban spaces and expansion to create new suburbs, as well as the creation of specifically industrial forms of housing, all redefined the notion of home. Company housing schemes often had an explicit agenda of control and domination, although this was frequently subverted; the same may be true of later local authority schemes. It is certainly possible to investigate the changing dynamics of households (and within them gender, class and other forms of personal and group identity) through exploring the ways in which interior space and material culture were given meaning, as projects elsewhere have shown (Shackel 1996; Beaudry and Mrozowski 2001; Praetzellis and Praetzellis 2004). Research excavations in the region, for example at Coalbrookdale and Stoke-on-Trent, have shown how assemblages of domestic material culture demonstrate the continuity of regional networks, links and identities well into the 20th century (Belford and Ross 2004; Barker 2003). Further work of this nature needs to be made a more frequent part of developer-funded projects.

### Identity

This is a substantial topic, bound up with intangible notions of ideas and ideology. At an individual level it is possible to reconstruct notions of personal identity by developing, for example, an archaeology of gender. Gender study in archaeology is now beginning to mature away from an overtly feminist agenda which sought to explore heterosexual male/female tensions, to a more sophisticated and nuanced approach which also examines homosexual, transgendered and transsexual identities (Spector 1993; Casella 2000; Schofield and Anderton 2000; Voss 2006). There is also scope to develop archaeologies of masculinity, childhood and old age. A number of studies concerning ideas of class or group identity have been extremely influential. Work on the industrial complex of Boott Mills, for example, has demonstrated that a working–class identity was developed through differential use of clay pipes, costume jewellery and alcohol; and that this behaviour was identifiable in the archaeological record (Beaudry and Mrozowski 2001). In Shropshire, excavation of a 1930s Tartan linoleum floor covering in workers' housing prompted questions about identity – did it form a conscious manifestation of Scottish cultural heritage, or was it simply the cheapest offcut available at the time? (Belford and Ross in prep). At the other end of the social scale, it has been shown that post-medieval rebuilding of castles and monastic sites represented appropriation of a medieval past to give substance to modern identities. This has been demonstrated by Pete Brown's ongoing investigations at Whittington Castle (Shropshire); and also by recent work at Chesterton (Warwickshire) which suggests the deliberate creation of a house and landscape setting to make a complex ideological statement during the turbulent mid 17th century (Brown et al 2006; Paul Everson, pers comm; Bowden 2003). Widening further still we can look at cultural identities shaped by religion, belief, membership and geography. There is almost certainly a 'border identity' along the Welsh Marches, for example, which provokes consideration of 'English' and 'Welsh' identities; the region has a contribution to make to the archaeology of Britishness and its components. There is also the legendary dichotomy between Birmingham and the Black Country, as well as numerous other local rivalries. How old these identities are, and how they rank in significance to different people at different times, are some of the questions post-medieval archaeology can begin to answer.

**Fig 7.5** Home and identity? Madeley Court, Shropshire. Originally the grange of Much Wenlock Priory, this house was acquired by the Brooke family at the dissolution, who adapted it into a substantial Elizabethan mansion using wealth from their industrial activities at Coalbrookdale. The retention of substantial parts of the medieval house was probably a deliberate attempt to legitimise the new ownership and control through heritage (copyright Paul Belford)

### Labour

The archaeological recording of industrial production sites has been ongoing for the last fifty years. However, it is only in the last decade that we have moved beyond the recording of process to the beginnings of an understanding of the social 'world of the workshop' (Belford 2006). Intentions behind the design of workspaces were often to divide, subjugate and observe the workforce to ensure that their time spent at work was time spent working. The use of courtyards as defensible and controllable spaces was widespread in many industries (Belford 2004b). However, workers were able to overcome these intentions, and detailed archaeological investigation of place and material culture – notably in the new world – has been able to illuminate these processes of resistance and subversion (Shackel 1996; Beaudry and Mrozowski 2001; Fig 7.7). It is important to remember that factories were not the only workplaces. In the west midlands, where industrialisation happened at such an early stage, the scale of operations was often smaller and less proscriptive than it was in the Manchester mills and Sheffield steelworks. The quasi-independent social worlds of the chain- and nail-making industries of Worcestershire and the Black Country were typical. The role and social position of itinerant labourers, such as 16th-century potters, 18th- and 19th-century navvies (or 21st-century archaeologists and Romanian demolition workers for that matter) is also worthy of further investigation.

### Leisure

The development of an industrialised society brought about clear demarcation between 'work' and 'other' time, and a formalisation of leisure pursuits (Fig 7.7). At least, such is the conventional historical wisdom, although it is evident that using time at work for leisure

**Fig 7.6** Less than 1km from Madeley Court is Station Road. This road was part of the original medieval town plan, leading off the lower High Street towards the Church and open fields. The building in the foreground was originally a farm and forge, but was rebuilt as the 'Railway Inn' in the 1850s when the new station was built opposite. Beyond is a pair of 17th–century cottages, refronted in two phases during the 19th–century to reflect changing aspirations and identities of their occupants (copyright Paul Belford)

activities has a long and noteworthy tradition – from sly games of cribbage on the workshop bench to surfing the net in the manager's office. Outside the workplace, the archaeology of sex is a particularly interesting theme, bound up with notions of sexuality, gender and identity explored above. The recovery of a 17th-century condom from excavations at Dudley Castle, for example, is a rare example of the survival of material culture directly associated with sex as leisure; other items such as sex toys and masturbation aids have been found in prehistoric contexts and are known from documentary sources, but remain hitherto unidentified in the region's post-medieval material culture (Gaimster et al 1996; Taylor 1996). Archaeological investigation of the full range of more formalised leisure pursuits is becoming more widely accepted, and the study of football grounds, theatres, cinemas and pubs is now developing a substantial literature (Smith 2001; Richardson 2005; Wood 2005). Contemporary archaeology has much to contribute to the study of leisure, as Julian Lamb has shown in his analysis of Mell Square shopping centre in Solihull, which sought to examine 'the mesh of differing and shifting understandings, meanings and significances' experienced by present-day users of the site (Lamb 2004, 135). The use of 'industrial' transport networks to access leisure – such as journeys to the seaside by road and railway – and the concomitant development of servicing facilities en route, from coaching inns to Little Chefs, is also worth investigation.

### Scientific enquiry

The evolution of modern capitalist, industrialised consumer society was bound up with the post-reformation Enlightenment and the development of humanist ideals leading to the emergence of scientific techniques, methods and ideas. One of the great stimuli to

**Fig 7.7** Towards an archaeology of industrialisation. Work at Tean Hall Mills, Staffordshire during 2005-6 was undertaken on many levels. Starting with the recording of two successive phases of power transmission in the main mill building, the project went on to develop a comprehensive understanding of the phasing of the buildings on site – from the conversion of a 17th-century timber-framed house into a weaving shop in the late 1700s, through the creation of a purpose-built 'fireproof' building in the 1820s, to the construction of new weaving sheds in the 1950s. Analysis of graffitti, posters and other 'subversive' traces left by the workers also enabled reconstruction of the social world of the (predominantly female) workplace (copyright Paul Belford)

these developments was the exploration and description of the new world during the 16th, 17th and 18th centuries; encounters at the fringe of knowledge which profoundly affected English society (Sloan 2007). Encounters with temporal as well as spatial fringes were also increasingly common and the emergence of archaeology itself was a key development – the pioneering work of Leland, Camden, Aubrey, Stukeley and others ultimately led to the formation of the Society of Antiquaries in 1707 and the development of the modern profession; a pattern mirrored in other disciplines. Existing systems of measuring the world began to be standardised and improved, and new methods developed – thus Gunter's 22-yard long surveying chain was in widespread use by the mid 1600s and, for example, affected the allocation and sizes of enclosed plots of land. In our region the importance of the Lunar Society, whose members included key figures of 18th-century rationalism such as Matthew Boulton, Erasmus Darwin, Joseph Priestley, James Watt and Josiah Wedgwood, cannot be underestimated (Uglow 2002). Archaeological work can reveal, for example, the progress of the installation of gas lighting following William Murdoch's developments at Soho; the emergence of new medical and post-mortem practises through analysis of human remains; or the role of the region's instrument makers in the beginnings of scientific industrialism.

## 7.4. Post-medieval archaeology in practice

The themes outlined above provide a possible framework for exploring the archaeology of the post-medieval period in our region. It is now worth addressing some of the

**Fig 7.8** The context of archaeological research. The often restricted and difficult conditions under which most developer-funded archaeology is undertaken sometimes precludes wider landscape investigation or detailed comparison with analogous sites. However, the results are often well worth the extra effort, which should be encouraged at curatorial level (copyright Paul Belford)

key issues which we face in trying to implement such a study. In terms of fieldwork we should be moving beyond the stage where post-medieval remains are dealt with superficially in order to arrive at earlier features underlying them. Some colleagues persist in seeing archaeology as the 'handmaiden of history' (Andren 1998, 106). Thus Malcolm Atkin suggests that the role of post-medieval archaeology is still perceived as being 'largely confined to *illustrating* an already well-dated historical framework' (his emphasis), and John Hemingway argues the need for historical evidence to be 'proved archaeologically' (Atkin 2003, 1; Hemingway 2003, 4). Certainly the temptation is there, in this extraordinarily well-documented period, to confine ourselves to confirming the sequence of building construction here or to filling the gap in production records there. However, this is like picking at the side salad of the wondrously rich feast that post-medieval archaeology has to offer. Rather, we should be seeking to develop a uniquely archaeological viewpoint for the human story of the last 500 years. Instead of answering questions thrown to us like scraps from the table by historians, geographers, sociologists, ethnographers, architects, conservationists and others, we should be stamping our muddy boots on the tablecloth and hurling great slabs of meat towards our colleagues in sister disciplines. More importantly we should also be serving up tasty morsels for non-professionals and non-archaeologists.

### 7.4.1. Sites in context

The work by Birmingham Archaeology on the cemetery at St Martin's in the Bullring, or more recent work by Ironbridge Archaeology on the multi-period forge site at Wednesbury, shows that large-scale developer-funded archaeological projects can embrace post-medieval archaeology – even to the extent, in the latter case, of recording

21st-century material culture (Brickley et al 2006; Belford and Mitchell in prep). These projects worked well because of close collaboration between archaeological curators and contractors, and because of the support of the developers themselves. It has been possible to place them in the context of the development of the urban landscape through time (Belford 2004a). However, in the world of developer-funded archaeology it is sometimes difficult to think of a site in its full landscape context, let alone any other form of context such as an historical, social or cultural one (Fig 7.8). Arguably the development of syntheses is the work of curatorial archaeologists, but in most cases they are overworked simply dealing with the daily demands of development control. Where local and national curators are able to facilitate inter-contractor cooperation the results can be very useful – as in the case of recent near simultaneous excavations by Ironbridge Archaeology and Birmingham Archaeology on two physically separate 17th-century pottery production sites in Wednesbury; or in tying together the results of temporally separate interventions on the same site in Edgbaston by the same two organisations (Sandwell Metropolitan Borough Council and Birmingham City Council respectively).

The dearth of local specialist knowledge has been noted by David Barker in relation to the Staffordshire pottery industries (Barker 2003) and this is a much more widespread problem which sees many of us duplicating the work of colleagues as a result of ignorance of previous research. Essentially this is a call for common courtesy – if a unit is undertaking work in an area traditionally the 'patch' of another, they can certainly make contact and ask for advice; equally the unit being asked can supply useful information

**Fig 7.9** Standing buildings are a key part of the post-medieval historic environment. Best practice should encourage the study of buildings in their historical, archaeological and landscape settings – as well as within the tradition of architectural history. Convergence in heritage protection will be increasing in the future, and dialogue between archaeologists, conservation officers and planning professionals will need to be at the core of delivering proper understanding and management of the historic environment (copyright Sophie Watson)

without compromising commercial confidentiality. The 'Frameworks' collaboration between Oxford Archaeology and the Wessex Trust is an interesting example of this kind of development, as is the Channel Tunnel Rail Link project involving five separate contractors (David Jennings, pers comm; Frank Meddens, pers comm). Experience of these and other projects suggests, however, that very clearly defined methodologies and managerial structures need to be in place (and firmly understood by all parties) before work begins. On a wider scale, we need to be looking far afield for comparative examples. As noted above, the west midlands region is an entirely artificial modern construct. For example, fieldwork on an early 19th-century domestic site in Oswestry is as likely to have parallels with similar work in Powys and Cheshire as it is with a project looking at a site of the same period in Stratford-on-Avon. Notwithstanding the importance of locale, it is equally the case that the sites in Oswestry and Stratford will certainly have similarities with domestic sites in Virginia and New South Wales.

### 7.4.2. Not all archaeology is below ground

It is unfortunate that archaeology is often regarded as the study of artefacts and features dug out of the ground rather than as a methodology for investigation of past societies. In the post-medieval period particularly, we rely on a wide range of resources that are not buried. These include documents, memories, landscapes and buildings. Documents have a dual role as artefacts; they were of course created for a specific purpose in the past and therefore provide as much information about the people who produced them and the circumstances in which they were produced as they do about the subject they are purportedly about. Moreover they were usually part of an expression of established power and authority, which our archaeologically derived narratives should attempt to counterbalance. The role of oral history is also particularly interesting for archaeologies of the very recent past. Work by Ironbridge Archaeology during the excavation of tenement houses demolished in the 1960s, for example, found the anecdotes of former residents extremely helpful in understanding the function and meaning of the place for its 20th-century inhabitants (Belford 2003). Elsewhere oral history has proved more problematic, particularly when tempered with robust west midlands humour, with people born in the 1950s seeming to remember buildings that were demolished in the mid 19th century (Dwyer and Mitchell 2006). Nevertheless, talking to people about the past (and their perceptions of it) is an important part of the study of post-medieval archaeology.

The archaeology of buildings is a well-established component of the discipline (English Heritage 2006a; Fig 7.9). Recent work has revealed a great deal about prevailing attitudes to mind, body and society in a variety of circumstances, ranging from analyses of 19th-century workhouses, jewellery factories and textile mills, through to investigation of Soviet communal housing (Lucas 1999; Buchli 1999; Cattell et al 2002; Watson 2006). Archaeologists dealing with buildings are developing increasingly sophisticated analyses of the way space was defined, used and developed over time – in terms of industrial buildings for example there has been considerable movement away from purely functional understandings to a more complex realisation of social and cultural use of space. Much of this can be built into building recording specifications as part of PPG15 or PPG16, as Gould (1999) has pointed out. However, problems have arisen when 'buildings' and 'archaeology' are considered as separate and unrelated entities. Yet it is clearly nonsense to try and understand the standing remains of post-medieval housing without excavating the rubbish dumped in its back yard or to attempt an exploration of the archaeology of a lead-smelting site without recording the extant standing remains of the former smelt mill at the centre of it.

### 7.4.3. Not all archaeology is done in the field

The role of archaeological science is key to developing our understanding of the post-medieval period. However, the discipline of post-medieval archaeology has such firm roots in the arts and humanities that it has at times been slow to grasp the opportunities offered by science-based archaeology (Astill 1998). Partly this is the result of the overwhelming scale of the evidence; the extent of process residues left by 19th-century ironworking, for example, makes a conventional 50% sample impossible to remove from site. There is also a persistent feeling that the period is so well documented that such analyses are unnecessary or redundant (English Heritage 2006b). However, many processes are not at all well documented, whether through inadequate record keeping or a desire for secrecy, particularly at the early stages of their evolution. In the ferrous industries for example, very little is known about the adoption of coke for refining wrought iron in the 18th century. Cort's puddling process emerged fully fledged and well documented in the 1780s, but the metallurgical details of experimentation prior to this are not clear (King 2003). Equally, where processes were well documented (particularly in the 20th century) then archaeology can be helpful as a 'control' for other periods. The role of archaeometallurgy and the scientific analysis of glass and ceramics is particularly important for understanding the development of industrial processes during this period (English Heritage 2001; English Heritage 2006b).

Studies of industrial development are also enhanced by the work of environmental archaeology (Mighall and Chambers 1993; Murphy and Wiltshire 2003). Quite localised studies have the potential to determine, for example, the effects of industrial pollution on specific ecosystems or changes in woodland management as a result of a switch from coppice-wood to mineral fuel. On a wider scale there is potential to look at longer-term impacts of industrialisation, as studies in Worcestershire and Shropshire have shown (Pittam 2003; Pittam et al 2006; Belford and Ross in prep). This has a particular resonance today with the rapid onslaught of global warming. Coming to terms with the contribution of formerly industrialised societies (such as ours) to this situation may help in dealing with the future impact of the now rapidly-industrialising economies such as China

**Fig 7.10** Public archaeology programmes, such as the one seen here being run at the Ironbridge Gorge Museum, are just one of the many ways in which archaeologists are engaging with the public. Post-medieval archaeology has a unique potential to be accessible to people from all walks of life, in a way in which the remains of more distant periods are not (copyright Simon Roper)

and India. Pollen, seed and faunal analysis can of course assist in our understanding of food, diet, agriculture and landscape during the post-medieval period just as much as for earlier periods (Pearson 2003). Environmental sampling should ideally become a routine part of work on post-medieval sites, even where the work is relatively small-scale – for, as Liz Pearson has pointed out, 'some of the best environmental evidence has been recovered from the smallest of watching briefs' within the region (Pearson 2003, 6). Dendrochronology, archaeomagnetic and thermoluminesence dating methods are also applicable. Finally, it is worth mentioning the potential for osteoarchaeology. The importance of human skeletal assemblages has been noted above; however, analysis of animal bone from urban sites can reveal a great deal of information about processes such as tanning, and secondary industries like handle- and button-making.

### 7.4.4. Not all archaeology is done by archaeologists

The role of amateurs is arguably more important in post-medieval archaeology than elsewhere. This is partly due to the historical development of the specialism outside mainstream academic archaeology. There is an extremely long amateur 'pre-history' to post-medieval studies, and the 19th-century volumes of local antiquarian groups are often full of fascinating studies of folklore, buildings, landscapes, documents and ways of life that are very definitely part of the study of modern post-medieval archaeology. The tradition of local history and local 'industrial archaeology' as essentially amateur pursuits continues today – many present–day stalwarts of such groups would recognise the sentiments expressed by the author of an early textbook on industrial archaeology, who 'became an industrial archaeologist in his spare time because of his love for windmills and watermills' (Major 1975, 9). A number of investigators in this field still are non-professionals – whose dogged determination to extract definitive detail far exceeds the time and energy of professionals – and their contribution should be valued. Knowledgeable expertise often appears in surprising contexts. Re-enactment groups, for example (one of which includes a county archaeologist from our own region) are often extremely well informed about particular fields of interest, be it traditional long-bows, musket balls, clay pipes, slipware or buttons, which can be very helpful. Encouraging members of the public to assist with excavation and post-excavation processes can be difficult, but is worthwhile.

### 7.4.5. Very little archaeology is done for archaeologists

Finally, it is worth remembering, in the self-referential world of archaeology, that very few people actually read archaeological site reports. Indeed I often comment to my staff (in my more sadistic moments) when editing their site reports – the grey literature which satisfies the client's planning conditions and ends up in the 'public domain' of the relevant HER – that only three people will ever read the results of their intensive labours: themselves, myself and the curatorial archaeologist. There is no published data on exactly how many people visit their local HER and access the grey literature. However, as Richard Bradley has suggested, it seems likely that very few people from outside the profession and the network of local history groups actually get through the door (Bradley 2006). In practice many of our developer clients have been extremely interested in our findings and we have discovered (perhaps surprisingly) that the more recent the archaeology, the more interesting it is to the non-archaeologist. On several public open days on a variety of sites, people have consistently been drawn to recognisable artefacts from their own lifetimes – particularly the period from c 1930- c 1960, and to clearly identifiable objects like stoneware jars and bottles (Fig 7.10). Enthusiasm for archaeology is high amongst all sectors of the population and post-medieval archaeology has potential to really engage people. We know, for instance, that the hilltop settlement of medieval Wednesbury was probably on an earlier hill fort. Yet this abstract knowledge of a vanished Iron Age landscape (however romantic and evocative it may be) appears to have little resonance for the modern citizens of the place. Instead our open day at Wednesbury Forge showed that the locals had real appetite for understanding their fathers', grandfathers' and great-grandfathers' workplace, the role Wednesbury had in building the modern world and the reasons why the (18th-century) watercourses, the (19th-century) streets and the

(20th-century) houses were the way they were. We ignore this audience at our peril. We must publish more synthetic and accessible accounts of our work, and we must not be afraid to ask developers to pay for them.

## 7.5. Conclusion

At the beginning I remarked that this was an entirely personal view of the research potential of post-medieval archaeology. No doubt many colleagues would have produced a very different paper. An attempt at a global synthesis of the archaeology of the last 500 years was made by Anders Andren almost a decade ago with only partial success; like most of us he found himself struggling in what Martin Hall and Stephen Silliman have more recently described as 'a field of enquiry that is resistant to classification' (Andren 1998; Hall and Silliman 2006, 7). This paper has attempted to look at the period for a much smaller geographical area than the whole world; nevertheless the abundance of material remains from the last 500 years has proved to be overwhelming. However, the conscientious creation of a comprehensive catalogue of the 'resource' would not only be extremely boring to read but would do little for the development of a research agenda (it would also not fail to exclude someone's particular pet topic). Hence the extraction of a few key themes, for which the potential for development will largely depend on the specific circumstances of an individual project. Priorities to pursue for the archaeology of the west midlands include:

- **Capitalism**. Studies should try and explore the way in which the social changes wrought by the adoption of capitalism manifest themselves in the archaeological record: the processes of enclosure and improvement, the commodification and privatisation of space and the development of new identities as evinced through landscape, buildings and material culture. This theme would also include study of the development of 'quasi-urban' landscapes in places like the Black Country, north Worcestershire, east Shropshire and north Staffordshire. Careful investigation of the changing role of medieval centres such as Hereford, Coventry and Lichfield should move beyond simply noting 'decline' and look at (for example) aspects of identity and migration.

- **Industrialisation**. For industrial process sites, greater emphasis should be placed on exploring the earlier and smaller-scale industries for which traces above ground or in the documentary record are relatively slight. Building recording should be allied with below–ground investigations. Below–ground investigations must include provision for appropriate specialist scientific analysis. As much effort needs to go into understanding the social world of the workplace as its physical and technological aspects; themes such as gender- and class-identity can be fruitfully explored, as well as dialogues of 'domination and resistance'. Understanding the interactions between different sites (and along linear systems) within the landscape – both rural and urban – is critical.

- **Consumption**. The rise of consumerism is one of the defining characteristics of the age. The richness of the material culture, and the opportunity to combine with documentary sources, means that archaeology has the potential to revolutionise our understanding of the development of the consumer society. Complex patterns of trade, exchange, identity and communication should all be evident in the archaeology of the post-medieval period. Consumption studies should not, of course, be restricted to 'things'; rather we should be looking at the consumption of landscapes (for example through the development of tourism), the consumption of spectacle (an archaeology of sport and leisure) and the consumption of ideas (evident in practises of burial and commemoration, for example).

**229**

- **Globalisation**. The rise of the 'new world' may seem an odd topic to study from within the only English region without a coastline. However, the role of our region in the development of the new world was critical, as has been the impact of that world on our own. Useful topics to consider include the role of the region's industries in the development and continuation of the slave trade, the role played by scientific and industrial development in exploration and colonial exploitation, patterns of trade and migration and the impact of the 'other' on our own society – a theme with particularly direct resonance for the archaeology of the later 20th century.

It is worth pointing out that the actual implementation of archaeological research is to a large extent determined by the day-to-day decisions made at project officer or project manager level within commercial archaeological organisations. However, with clear vision and understanding, and the support of a well-written and comprehensive curatorial brief, then a hugely exciting archaeology of the last 500 years can begin to emerge from the west midlands. This period of transition is still ongoing; the west midlands was and is a key contributor to the development of modern society, and the evidence is there in the people, documents, buildings and below-ground remains. The global impact of our region is attested through the presence of 'our' material culture on historical sites around the world; we are still coming to terms with the impact of the rest of the world on ourselves and archaeology has an important part to play in that process as well. Hopefully the 'archaeology of everything' can be a positive force for changing our future, as well as enabling us to understand how we got here in the first place. Even on a cold frosty morning in February.

## Acknowledgments

This paper would not have been possible without the support and assistance of two people: Roger White (University of Birmingham) who provided much-needed guidance and advice; and Kate Page-Smith (English Heritage) who provided equally much-needed love and support. The original seminars at Coalbrookdale and Stoke-on-Trent in 2003 were co-organised with David Barker – speakers were: Malcolm Atkin, Andy Boucher, Mark Bowden, James Dinn, John Hemingway, Mike Hodder, Jeremy Milln, Jonathan Parkhouse, Liz Pearson, Rebecca Roseff, Ian Soden, Paul Stamper, Barrie Trinder and Chris Welch, to whom many thanks for their contributions. The final version has incorporated comments made on draft versions by David Cranstone, Ian George, Keith Hinton, William Mitchell, Simon Roper, Anna Wallis and Sophie Watson. I am also grateful to Kenneth Aitchison (Institute of Field Archaeologists), Justine Bayley (English Heritage), Mary Beaudry (University of Boston), Geoff Egan (Museum of London), Paul Everson (English Heritage), David Gaimster (Society of Antiquaries), David Jennings (Oxford Archaeology), Mark Horton (University of Bristol), Frank Meddens (Pre-Construct Archaeology), Kirsty Nichol (Birmingham Archaeology), Stephanie Ratkai and John Schofield (English Heritage) amongst many others, for providing helpful information along the way. Sarah Watt, Ian George and John Hunter have been unstinting in their support during the lengthy pause before the paper's eventual gestation. The style, errors and omissions in this chapter are entirely my own, and comment and criticism is very welcome; please direct it to me archaeology@ironbridge.org.

## Dedication

This paper is dedicated to the memory of my grandmother Dorothy Smith (1917-2006). Her ability to laugh, sing, and consume vast quantities of tea all over the world should be an inspiration to us all.

## Bibliography

Andren, A, 1998  *Between Artifacts and Texts: Historical Archaeology in Global Perspective* (trans A, Crozier), New York

Anon, 1967  Editorial, *Post-Medieval Archaeology* 1, 1-2

Astill, G, 1998  Medieval and later: composing an agenda, in *Science in Archaeology: an agenda for the future* (ed J Bayley), London, 169-178

Atkin, M, 2003  Archaeology in Worcestershire 1500-1750, *West Midlands Regional Research Framework* (Seminar 6)

Barker, D, 2003  Ceramic Industries, *West Midlands Regional Research Framework* (Seminar 6)

Barker, D, and Cranstone, D (eds), 2004  *The Archaeology of Industrialization*, Society for Post-Medieval Archaeology Monograph 2, Leeds

Bayley, J (ed) 1998  *Science in Archaeology: an agenda for the future*, London

Beaudry, M C, and Mrozowski, S A, 2001  Cultural Space and Worker Identity in the Company City: Nineteenth-Century Lowell, Massachusetts, in *The Archaeology of Urban Landscapes: Explorations in Slumland* (eds A Mayne and T Murray), Cambridge, 118-131

Belford, P, 2003  Forging Ahead in Coalbrookdale: Historical Archaeology at the Upper Forge, *Industrial Archaeology Review* 25, 59-63

Belford, P, 2004a  Urban Industrial Landscapes: Problems of Perception and Protection, in *The Archaeology of Industrialization* (eds D Barker and D Cranstone), Society for Post-Medieval Archaeology Monograph 2, Leeds, 165-180

Belford, P, 2004b  Monasteries of Manufacture: Questioning the origins of English industrial architecture, *Industrial Archaeology Review* 26, 45-62

Belford, P, 2006  The World of the Workshop: Archaeologies of Urban Industrialisation, in *Cities in the World 1500-2000* (eds A Green and R Leech), Society for Post-Medieval Archaeology Monograph 3, 133-150

Belford, P, and Ross, R A, 2004  Industry and domesticity: exploring historical archaeology in the Ironbridge Gorge, *Post-Medieval Archaeology* 38, 215-225

Belford, P, and Ross, R A, in prep  *Upper Forge, Coalbrookdale*, Ironbridge Archaeology Monograph 3

Belford, P, and Mitchell, W, in prep  *Wednesbury Forge, Wednesbury*, Ironbridge Archaeology Monograph 2

Bowden, M, 2003  Earthworks, *West Midlands Regional Research Framework* (Seminar 6)

Bradley, A, Buchli, V, Fairclough, G, Hicks, D, Miller, J, and Schofield, J, 2004  *Change and Creation: historic landscape character 1950-2000*, London

Bradley, R, 2006  Bridging the Two Cultures – Commercial Archaeology and the Study of Prehistoric Britain, *Antiq J* 86, 1-13

Brennand, M (ed), 2006  The Archaeology of North West England. An *Archaeological Research Framework for North West England: Volume 1, Resource Assessment*, CBA North West, ALGAO and English Heritage

Brickley, M, Buteux, S, Adams, J, and Cherrington, R, 2006  *St. Martin's Uncovered: Investigations in the churchyard of St. Martin's-in-the-Bullring, Birmingham, 2001*, Oxford

Brown, P, King, P, and Remfry, P, 2006  Whittington Castle. The Marcher Fortress of the FitzWarin Family, *Trans Shropshire Archaeol Hist Soc* 79, 106-127

Buchli, V, 1999  *An Archaeology of Socialism*, New York

Buchli, V, and Lucas, G (eds), 2001  *Archaeologies of the Contemporary Past*, London

Burton, N, and Guillery, P, 2006  *Behind the Façade: London House Plans, 1660-1840*, Reading

Carman, J, and Carman, P, 2001  Beyond military archaeology: battlefields as a cultural resource, in Freeman, P W M, and Pollard, A (eds), *Fields of Conflict: Progress and Prospect in Battlefield Archaeology*, British Archaeological Reports International Series 958, 275-281

Casella, E C, 2000  Doing Trade: A Sexual Economy of Nineteenth-Century Australian Female Convict Prisons, *World Archaeol* 32, 209-221

Cattell, J, Ely, S, and Jones, B, 2002  *The Birmingham Jewellery Quarter: an Architectural Survey of the Manufactories*, Swindon

Collins, P, and Stratton, M, 1993  *British Car Factories from 1896: A Complete Historical, Geographical, Architectural and Technological Survey*, Godmanstone

Courtney, P, 1996  In small things forgotten: the Georgian world view, material culture and the consumer revolution, *Rural History* 7, 87-95

Cranstone, D, 2004  The Archaeology of Industrialization – New Directions, in *The Archaeology of Industrialization* (eds D Barker and D Cranstone), Society for Post-Medieval Archaeology Monograph 2, Leeds, 313-320

Deetz, J, 1977  *In Small Things Forgotten: The Archaeology of Early American Life*, Garden City, New York

Denison, S, 2002  Fortress Britain, *British Archaeology* 65

Dwyer, E, and Mitchell, W, 2006  Forging Past? Archaeology and Memory at Wednesbury, West Midlands, paper presented at the *Contemporary and Historical Archaeology in Theory* conference, Bristol, 11th November 2006

Egan, G. and R.L. Michael (eds) 1999  *Old and New Worlds*, Society for Post-Medieval Archaeology and the Society for Historical Archaeology, Oxford: Oxbow Books

English Heritage 2001  *Archaeometallurgy*, London

English Heritage 2006a  *Understanding Historic Buildings: A guide to good recording practice*, Swindon

English Heritage 2006b  *Science for Historic Industries: Guidelines for the investigation of 17th- to 19th-century industries*, Swindon

Gaimster, D, Boland, P, Linnane, S, and Cartwright, C, 1996  The archaeology of private life: the Dudley Castle condoms, *Post-Medieval Archaeology* 30, 129-142

Given, M, 2004  *The Archaeology of the Colonized*, London

Gledhill, T, 2004  Woodland, industry and common rights – a conflict of interest, in *The Archaeology of Industrialisation* (eds D Barker and D Cranstone), Society for Post-Medieval Archaeology Monograph 2, 89-93

Gould, S, 1999  Planning, Development and Social Archaeology, in Tarlow, S, and West, S (eds), *The Familiar Past*, London, 140-154

Grant, E G, 1987  Industry, landscape and location, in *Landscape and Culture* (ed J M, Wagstaff), Oxford, 96-117

Green, A, and Leech, R (eds), 2006  *Cities in the World 1500-2000*, Society for Post-Medieval Archaeology Monograph 3, Leeds

Guillery, P, and Herman, B, 1999   Deptford Houses: 1600 to 1800, *Vernacular Architecture* 30, 58-84

Gwyn, D, and Palmer, M (eds), 2005   *Understanding the Workplace: A Research Framework for Industrial Archaeology in Britain*, Industrial Archaeology Review 27

Hall, M, 1992   Small things and the mobile: conflictual fusion of power, fear and desire, in *The Art and Mystery of Historical Archaeology: Essays in Honor of James Deetz* (eds A Yentsch and M Beaudry), Boca Raton, 373-399

Hall, M, and Silliman, S W, 2006   *Historical Archaeology*, Oxford

Hemingway, J, 2003   West Midlands Industry 1485-1750, *West Midlands Regional Research Framework* (Seminar 6)

Hicks, D, 2003   Archaeology unfolding: diversity and the loss of isolation, *Oxford Journal of Archaeology* 22, 315-329

Higgins, D A, 1999   Little Tubes of Mighty Power: A Review of British Clay Tobacco Pipe Studies, in *Old and New Worlds*, SPMA / SHA (eds G Egan and R L Michael), Oxford, 310-321

Hodder, M A, 2003   The archaeology of the early post-medieval period 1550-1750 in Birmingham and its surroundings, *West Midlands Regional Research Framework* (Seminar 6)

Horning, A, 2006   English Towns on the Periphery: 17th-Century Development in Ulster and the Chesapeake, in *Cities in the World 1500-2000* (eds A Green and R Leech), Society for Post-Medieval Archaeology Monograph 3, 61-82

Hudson, K, 1967   *Handbook for Industrial Archaeologists*, London

Johnson, M H, 1996   *An Archaeology of Capitalism*, Oxford

Johnson, M H, 2002   *Behind the Castle Gate: From Medieval to Renaissance*, London

Johnson, M H, 2006   The Tide Reversed: Prospects and Potentials for a Postcolonial Archaeology of Europe, in *Historical Archaeology* (eds M Hall and S Silliman), Oxford: Blackwell, 313-332

Johnson, M H, 2007   *Ideas of Landscape*, Oxford

King, P W, 2003   *The Iron Trade in England and Wales 1500-1815: the charcoal iron industry and its transition to coke*, Unpub PhD thesis, Univ of Wolverhampton

Lamb, J, 2004   The Contemporary Archaeology of Mell Square: Developing an Interpretive Theoretical Framework and Research Strategy for the 'Preservation by Record' of a 1960s Shopping Precinct in the West Midlands, *Industrial Archaeology Review* 26, 129-140

Lawrence, S, 2006   Overburden – the importance of the archaeology of the modern period in Britain, in *Cities in the World 1500-2000* (eds A Green and R Leech), Society for Post-Medieval Archaeology Monograph 3, 307-319

Leech, R H, 1981   *Early Industrial Housing: The Trinity Area of Frome*, Royal Commission on Historical Monuments England, Supplementary Series 3, London

Leech, R H, 1996   The Prospect from Rugman's Row: The Row House in late 16th and Early 17th Century London, *Archaeol J* 153, 201-242

Leech, R H, 2006   Portsmouth – a window on the world?, in Green A, and Leech, R (eds), *Cities in the World 1500-2000*, Society for Post-Medieval Archaeology Monograph 3, 299-306

Leone, M, 1995   A historical archaeology of capitalism, *American Anthropologist*, 97, 251-268

Leone, M, and Potter, P B (eds), 1998   *An Historical Archaeology of Capitalism*, New York

Lucas, G, 1999   The archaeology of the workhouse: the changing uses of the workhouse buildings at St Mary's, Southampton, in *The Familiar Past* (eds S Tarlow and S West), London, 125-139

Ludlow Collective 2001   Archaeology of the Colorado Coal Field War 1913-1914, in *Archaeologies of the Contemporary Past* (eds V Buchli and G Lucas), London, 94-107

Major, J K, 1975 *Fieldwork in Industrial Archaeology*, London

Mayne, A, and Murray, T (eds), 2001   *The Archaeology of Urban Landscapes: Explorations in Slumland*, Cambridge

McNeil, R, and Newman, R (eds), 2006a   The Post-Medieval Period Resource Assessment, in *The Archaeology of North West England. An Archaeological Research Framework for North West England: Volume 1, Resource Assessment* (ed M Brennand), 145-164

McNeil, R, and Newman, R (eds), 2006b   Industrial and Modern Period Resource Assessment, in *The Archaeology of North West England. An Archaeological Research Framework for North West England: Volume 1, Resource Assessment* (ed M Brennand), 165-194

Mighall, T M, and Chambers, F M, 1993   Early mining and metalworking: its impact on the environment, *Historical Metallurgy* 27, 71-83

Murphy, P, and Wiltshire, P E J (eds), 2003   *The Environmental Archaeology of Industry*, Symposia of the Association for Environmental Archaeology 20, Oxford

Museum of London 2002   *A Research Framework for London archaeology 2002*, London

Mytum, H, 2002   A Comparison of Nineteenth and Twentieth century Anglican and Nonconformist Memorials in North Pembrokeshire, *Archaeol J* 159, 194-241

Mytum, H, 2006   Popular attitudes to memory, the body, and social identity: the rise of external commemoration in Britain, Ireland and New England, *Post-Medieval Archaeology* 40, 96-110.

Nevell, M (ed), 2003   *From Farmer to Factory Owner: Models, Methodology and Industrialisation*, Archaeology North West 6, CBA, University of Manchester Archaeological Unit and Chester Archaeology, US

Palmer, M, 2004   The Archaeology of Industrialization: Introduction, in *The Archaeology of Industrialisation* (eds D Barker and D Cranstone), Society for Post-Medieval Archaeology Monograph 2, 1-4

Palmer, M, and Neaverson, P 1998   *Industrial Archaeology: Principles and Practice*, London

Pearson, L, 2003   Environmental archaeology in the west midlands in the post-medieval period. Do we really need environmental archaeology?, *West Midlands Regional Research Framework* (Seminar 6)

Pennell, S, 1999   The Material Culture of Food in Early Modern England *c* 1650-1750, in *The Familiar Past* (eds S Tarlow and S West), London, 35-50

Petts, D, and Gerrard, C (eds), 2006   *Shared Visions: The North East Regional Research Framework for the Historic Environment*, Durham

Pittam, N J, 2003   Reconstructing the Midlands Landscape during Medieval and Historical Times: A Case Study from Kyre Pool, Worcestershire, *West Midlands Regional Research Framework* (Seminar 6)

Pittam, N J, Mighall, T M, and Foster, I D L, 2006   The Effect of Sediment Source Changes on Pollen Records in Lake Sediments, *Water, Air, & Soil Pollution: Focus*, 6, 677-683

Praetzellis, M, and Praetzellis, A (eds), 2004   Putting the 'There' There: Historical Archaeologies of West Oakland, 1-880 Cypress Freeway Replacement Project, http://www.sonoma.edu/asc/cypress/finalreport/index.htm

Quartermaine, J, Trinder, B, and Turner, R, 2003   *Thomas Telford's Holyhead Road: The A5 in North Wales*, CBA Res Rep 135

Richardson, S, 2005   Welcome to the Cheap Seats: Cinemas, Sex and Landscape, in *Understanding the Workplace: A Research Framework for Industrial Archaeology in Britain* (eds D Gwyn and M Palmer), Industrial Archaeology Review 27, 145-152

Saunders, N J, 2002   Excavating memories: archaeology and the Great War, 1914-2001, *Antiquity* 76, 101-108

Schofield, J, and Anderton, M, 2000   The Queer Archaeology of Green Gate: Interpreting contested space at Greenham Common Airbase, *World Archaeol* 32, 236-251

Schofield, J, Johnson, W, and Beck, C M (eds), 2002   *Materiel Culture: The Archaeology of Twentieth Century Conflict*, London

Shackel, P A, 1996   *Culture Change and the New Technology: An Archaeology of the Early American Industrial Era*, New York

Sloan, K, 2007   *A New World: England's First View of America*, London

Smith, J, 2001   An introduction to the archaeology and conservation of football stadia, *Industrial Archaeology Review* 23(1)

Soden, I, 2003a   Early Post-Medieval Coventry: Resource Assessment *c* 1539-*c* 1750, *West Midlands Regional Research Framework* (Seminar 6)

Soden, I, 2003b   Late Post-Medieval Coventry: Resource Assessment *c* 1750-1940, *West Midlands Regional Research Framework* (Seminar 7)

Spector, J D, 1993   *What This Awl Means: Feminist Archaeology at Wahpeton Dakota Village*, St. Paul

Stamper, P, 2003   The Post-Medieval Countryside, *West Midlands Regional Research Framework* (Seminar 6)

Stratton, M, 1994   *Ironbridge and the Electric Revolution*, London

Stratton, M, and Trinder, B, 2000   *Twentieth Century Industrial Archaeology*, London

Symonds, J (ed), 2002   *The Historical Archaeology of the Sheffield Cutlery and Tableware Industry 1750-1900*, British Archaeological Reports 341

Tarlow, S, 1999   Strangely familiar, in *The Familiar Past* (eds S Tarlow and S West), London, 263-272

Tarlow, S, and West, S (eds) 1999   *The Familiar Past: archaeologies of later historical Britain*, London

Taylor, T, 1996   *The Prehistory of Sex: Four Million Years of Human Sexual Culture*, New York

Trinder, B, 2003   Issues Relating to Transport, *West Midlands Regional Research Framework* (Seminar 7)

Trinder, B, 2005   *Barges and Bargemen: a social history of the upper Severn navigation 1660-1900*, Chichester

Uglow, J, 2002  *The Lunar Men: The Friends who made the Future*, London

Voss, B, 2006  Engendered Archaeology: Men, Women, and Others, in *Historical Archaeology* (eds M Hall and S W Silliman), Oxford, 107-127

Wagstaff, J M (ed), 1987  *Landscape and Culture: Geographical and Archaeological Perspectives*, Oxford

Watson, S, 2006  *Archaeological Survey and Recording at Tean Hall Mills, Tean, Staffordshire*, Unpub report, Ironbridge Archaeology (IAS 191)

Welch, C M, 2000  Elizabethan Ironmaking and the Woodlands of the Churnet Valley, Staffordshire, *Staffordshire Studies*, 17-73

Welch, C M, 2001  Ralph Wolseley, A Fifteenth Century Capitalist, *Trans Staffordshire Archaeol Hist Soc* 39, 22-27

Welch, C M, 2003  Early Post-medieval Staffordshire, *West Midlands Regional Research Framework* (Seminar 6)

West, S, 1999  Introduction, in *The Familiar Past* (eds S Tarlow and S West), London, 1-15

White, R, 2003  The Archaeology of Shropshire in the 19th and 20th centuries: an industrial backwater?, *West Midlands Regional Research Framework* (Seminar 7)

Wood, J, 2005  Talking Sport or Talking Balls? Realising the Value of the Sports Heritage, in *Understanding the Workplace: A Research Framework for Industrial Archaeology in Britain* (eds D Gwyn and M Palmer), Industrial Archaeology Review 27, 137-144

Yentsch, A E, 1991  Chespeake artefacts and their cultural context: pottery and the food domain, *Post-Medieval Archaeology* 25, 25-72

Yentsch, A E, and Beaudry, M C (eds), 1992  *The Art and Mystery of Historical Archaeology: Essays in Honor of James Deetz*, Boca Raton

# 8. West Midlands Regional Research Framework priorities: Historic Landscape Characterisation (HLC)

## Michael Shaw

Mike.Shaw@wolverhampton.gov.uk

One of the problems of archaeological research in the 20th century was a tendency to concentrate on individual sites or groups of sites rather than the wider landscape. Increasingly towards the end of the century the need to look at the landscape of an area as a whole was recognised but tended to lead to a concentration on those landscapes regarded as particularly 'special'.

The principles of Historic Landscape Characterisation (HLC) have been adopted to overcome both of these biases and have, since the mid 1990s, become increasingly accepted as a model for the analysis, management, protection and enhancement of the historic environment. Starting with Cornwall, English Heritage has encouraged the undertaking of, and largely financed, a series of HLC projects with the intention that there should eventually be national coverage. Initially there was a concentration on rural county areas but more recently similar studies have commenced in urban metropolitan areas, and areas with particular development pressure such as for new housing.

Within the west midlands, HLC has been undertaken or is underway in Herefordshire, Shropshire (Fig 8.1), Staffordshire, Warwickshire and Worcestershire. Additionally, a detailed Urban Historic Landscape Characterisation is underway for the Black Country.

HLC aims to look at the entire landscape, dividing it up into basic character types such as 'woodland' or 'industrial', etc. These are subdivided into narrower types such as 'orchard' or 'metal works'. Time depth is added by describing previous landscape type as shown on historic mapping or by professional judgement, for example 'quarry', 'former open field', etc. (Fig 8.2) Computerised mapping (Geographic Information Systems – GIS) and a database is used, enabling the data to be analysed and presented in a wide variety of ways. Importantly no judgement is made at the initial stage about the value of one piece of land over another but, once the basic work is completed, areas with similar character types can be combined to form historic landscape areas or zones with policies defined to protect and enhance their local character and identity.

Properly applied HLC has a number of advantages over more traditional studies. In particular it ensures that the landscape of entire areas is studied to the same depth rather than particular areas being picked out and given priority. It has been all too easy in the past for the same special areas to be defined and given badges of honour and for adjacent areas to be ignored. In addition HLC by its very nature, and by its use of GIS, fits well with Central Government requirements for Regional Spatial Strategies and is already endorsed as a technique for planning in European, National and Regional legislation.

What does this mean for the west midlands archaeological community? No one is pretending that the technique itself is particularly revolutionary. Historical geographers

N

**Fig 8.1** Historic Landscape Characterisation (HLC) map of Shropshire showing Current HLC Types (copyright Shropshire County Council)

Shropshire
County Council

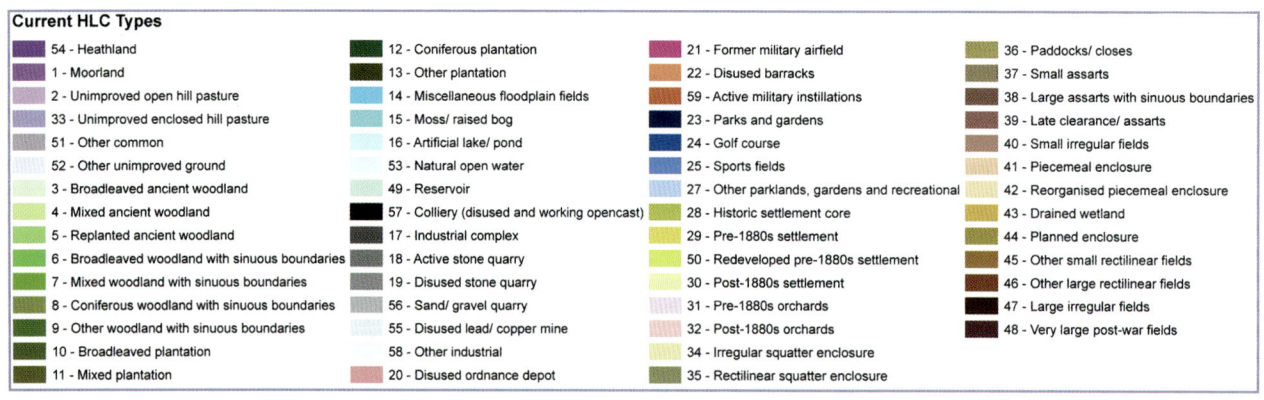

**Current HLC Types**

| | |
|---|---|
| 54 - Heathland | |
| 1 - Moorland | |
| 2 - Unimproved open hill pasture | |
| 33 - Unimproved enclosed hill pasture | |
| 51 - Other common | |
| 52 - Other unimproved ground | |
| 3 - Broadleaved ancient woodland | |
| 4 - Mixed ancient woodland | |
| 5 - Replanted ancient woodland | |
| 6 - Broadleaved woodland with sinuous boundaries | |
| 7 - Mixed woodland with sinuous boundaries | |
| 8 - Coniferous woodland with sinuous boundaries | |
| 9 - Other woodland with sinuous boundaries | |
| 10 - Broadleaved plantation | |
| 11 - Mixed plantation | |

| | |
|---|---|
| 12 - Coniferous plantation | |
| 13 - Other plantation | |
| 14 - Miscellaneous floodplain fields | |
| 15 - Moss/ raised bog | |
| 16 - Artificial lake/ pond | |
| 53 - Natural open water | |
| 49 - Reservoir | |
| 57 - Colliery (disused and working opencast) | |
| 17 - Industrial complex | |
| 19 - Disused stone quarry | |
| 56 - Sand/ gravel quarry | |
| 55 - Disused lead/ copper mine | |
| 58 - Other industrial | |
| 20 - Disused ordnance depot | |

| | |
|---|---|
| 21 - Former military airfield | |
| 22 - Disused barracks | |
| 59 - Active military instillations | |
| 23 - Parks and gardens | |
| 24 - Golf course | |
| 25 - Sports fields | |
| 27 - Other parklands, gardens and recreational | |
| 28 - Historic settlement core | |
| 29 - Pre-1880s settlement | |
| 50 - Redeveloped pre-1880s settlement | |
| 30 - Post-1880s settlement | |
| 31 - Pre-1880s orchards | |
| 32 - Post-1880s orchards | |
| 34 - Irregular squatter enclosure | |
| 35 - Rectilinear squatter enclosure | |

| | |
|---|---|
| 36 - Paddocks/ closes | |
| 37 - Small assarts | |
| 38 - Large assarts with sinuous boundaries | |
| 39 - Late clearance/ assarts | |
| 40 - Small irregular fields | |
| 41 - Piecemeal enclosure | |
| 42 - Reorganised piecemeal enclosure | |
| 43 - Drained wetland | |
| 44 - Planned enclosure | |
| 45 - Other small rectilinear fields | |
| 46 - Other large rectilinear fields | |
| 47 - Large irregular fields | |
| 48 - Very large post-war fields | |

18 - Active stone quarry

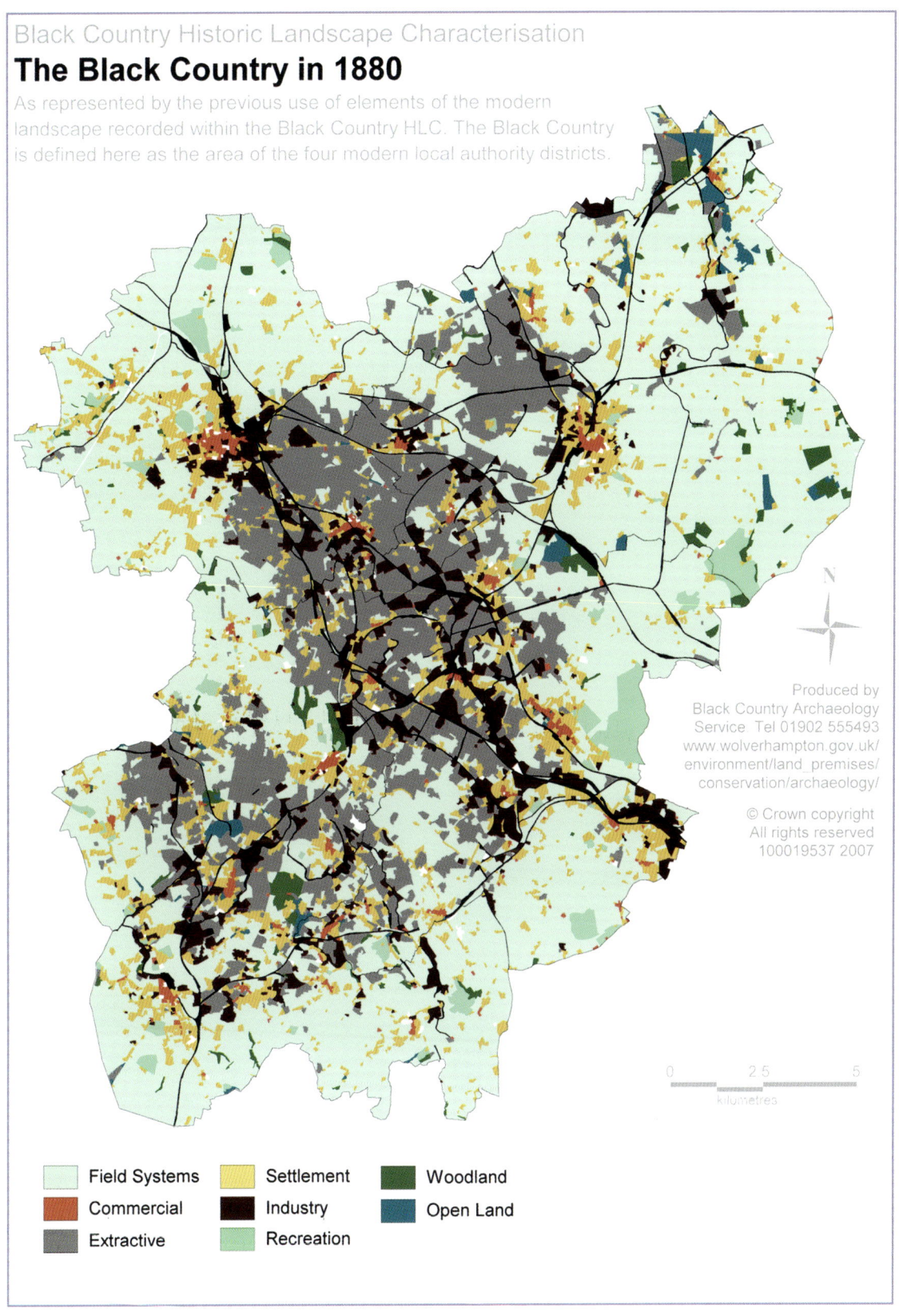

Black Country Historic Landscape Characterisation

## The Black Country in 1880

As represented by the previous use of elements of the modern landscape recorded within the Black Country HLC. The Black Country is defined here as the area of the four modern local authority districts.

Produced by
Black Country Archaeology
Service Tel 01902 555493
www.wolverhampton.gov.uk/
environment/land_premises/
conservation/archaeology/

0        2.5        5
kilometres

**Legend:**
- Field Systems
- Commercial
- Extractive
- Settlement
- Industry
- Recreation
- Woodland
- Open Land

in particular have been dividing areas up into character zones for many years. However, its widespread use will make it easy to compare and contrast historic settlement areas throughout the region, and its widespread endorsement will make it easier to protect and enhance the local character and identity of our region. Archaeological and historical research which can be tied in to characterisation should find it easier to attract funding.

**Fig 8.2** The Black Country in 1880

What can we do?

- Support the undertaking of HLC for the whole of the west midlands area at a broad level.

- Press for detailed HLC to be undertaken in areas with particular development pressures in order to ensure that development respects, protects and enhances local character and identity.

- Seek to work with other related specialists such as conservation officers, planning officers and urban designers to ensure that the results of detailed HLC are used to inform and influence development frameworks.

- Seek to tie archaeological and historical research into characterisation and study of the development of the landscape of the region.

- Seek to engage local communities with their surroundings using the visual results of HLC as a catalyst.

# 9. A common vision: priorities for Historic Environment Records (HERs) within the west midlands region

## Victoria Bryant and Michael Shaw

Vbryant@worcestershire.gov.uk and Mike.Shaw@wolverhampton.gov.uk

### 9.1. Introduction

One concern has been foremost during the extensive programme of seminars and discussion groups generated by the need to produce research frameworks for the west midlands. How do we maintain the momentum and create a research cycle where management and fieldwork priorities are informed by, and in turn inform, a research agenda?

The general consensus seems to be that the region's Historic Environment Records (HERs), imperfect though they are, are the only tool we have which could realistically achieve this, but that they are incapable of performing this function in their present form. HERs have developed out of Sites and Monuments Records (SMRs). The name change is in recognition of the wider role which these records need to achieve to meet future requirements and aspirations. In particular it has become clear that without the development of HERs the information generated by fieldwork, prompted and informed by the developing research agendas, will be largely inaccessible and the impetus will be lost. HERs **can** be the catalyst to making a research agenda an essential and dynamic part of the process of data collection and synthesis.

We are all aware of the very real problems, not least lack of finances, which hinder or prevent development of SMRs/HERs. Because of this, it was felt important to agree a common vision and define a set of priorities which could be used to argue the case for moving forward. This document is an attempt to outline such a vision and priorities.

### 9.2. National background

For the purposes of this document a SMR is considered to be a record containing a closely defined range of archaeological and heritage data whose collection policy is largely driven by its role within the planning process. For example data on buildings is often patchy and undefined. An HER is a record containing a wide range of archaeological, historical, heritage and non-heritage data and synthesis whose collection policy is driven by its role as provider of data useful to a wider range of users. Data on buildings is comprehensive and not limited to listed and locally listed examples.

SMRs have developed over the last 30 to 40 years, latterly primarily for development control purposes, ie to identify areas of archaeological interest in order that they can be considered during the planning control process. This focus, along with the limitations of the available technologies, has had a profound effect on the way information has been ordered within the various systems and on staffing and other resources.

The result has been records which provide basic descriptive and locational information but are often inconsistent within themselves and can vary considerably between local authorities.

The process of collecting region-wide data for the research framework seminars has highlighted the problems with the type of data held and the accuracy and ease with which one or more SMRs can be searched.

It is clear that old-style SMRs, with their emphasis on single buried archaeological sites, are too narrow in their remit. It is now recognised that such records should have a wider role as an academic and educational resource and for public enjoyment of, and involvement in, the historic landscape. They should become HERs.

The need to make this change has been recognised nationally (English Heritage 2000; English Heritage/ALGAO 2002). The Department of Culture Media and Sport (DCMS) undertook a consultation on the future of HERs. The results of the consultation were included in the *Review of Heritage Protection: The Way Forward* (DCMS 2004). In March 2007 the *Heritage Protection White Paper* was published (DCMS 2007). This proposed, amongst other things, enhancing local historic environment services by introducing a statutory requirement for local authorities to have access to Historic Environment Records. In response to the white paper The Archaeology Forum[1] has identified the need for clear government guidance on the functions of a local authority historic environment service and a programme of training and capacity building to be in place in advance of the proposed legislation.

## 9.3. A vision for HERs in the west midlands

Assuming the draft Heritage Protection Bill becomes law, local authorities will have a statutory duty to maintain and enhance an HER for their area. This provides an unparalleled opportunity for HERs to become the central point for the storage, retrieval, dissemination and encouragement of research upon the historic environment as a whole. In order to do so, however, HERs need to develop the mechanisms to encourage and facilitate synthesis of data. This will greatly increase their power as a development control tool as well as enabling them to act as the focal point for research and education. Issues of operational systems need to be addressed but complex HERs cannot run themselves and more staff with the appropriate range of skills will be needed to deliver such a dynamic service. In the west midlands region we aim to:

- Create HERs which contain consistent and comprehensive datasets which can be searched to provide high quality data for a wide range of users, including local authority Conservation Officers (Fig 9.1).

- Create HERs where a wide range of heritage and non-heritage datasets and expert knowledge are used to develop and map models of past landscapes.

- Use these models and associated research questions to provide an academic context for all fieldwork and research within the west midlands and use the results of fieldwork and research to modify the models.

- Improve access to all users and create HERs which are used extensively in education and outreach and play a key role in social, economic and environmental development.

## 9.4. Priorities for HERs in the west midlands

In order to achieve these aims we need to set a number of priorities for development. These break down into two groups; the first group are those that will allow all west midlands HERS to meet the first and second stage HER performance measures (English Heritage and ALGAO 2002). Of particular importance in this region are:

**Fig 9.1**  3D reconstruction of landuse at Elmley Castle, Worcestershire in 1843. View created using data derived from the original tithe maps and apportionment books and held within the Worcestershire HER

- A dedicated HER officer for all authorities.

- Developed GIS systems for the fully integrated management of spatial and map-based data linked to databases and text-based information. Cleaning and enhancement of the records will be needed to make full and effective use of GIS.

- Provision of dedicated, supervised work areas for researchers, appropriately equipped and with facilities for copying, etc.

- Developed provision for remote access to the HERs through the internet.

- Developed programmes of outreach activities to create new audiences and promote wider use of resources. Many of these will be in partnership with other individuals and organisations.

- Updating of records to modern standards (English Heritage 2007). For example, best practice is to separate events from sites/monuments. All HERs should do this with any newly entered records but most have large amounts of earlier material which needs to be altered to conform to modern standards.

- The elimination of backlogs – many SMRs have a backlog of material for entry onto their databases.

- Ensuring that studies of the historic environment in the area are undertaken in such a way that the results of these studies are easily integrated into the HER rather than becoming yet another backlog for entry. In particular the data from such studies should be stored on a computerised database linked to a GIS system.

Such work will create very much improved HERs but will not of itself help to create an information cycle which will push forward research in the west midlands. For this to succeed a second group of priorities needs to be defined. These might be seen as a regional response to Benchmark 2.2b (English Heritage and ALGAO 2002, 6) which advocates 'enhanced coverage...additional datasets... networked arrangements for shared access to distributed systems...collaborative projects creating multidisciplinary information resources with libraries, museums and record offices.' These priorities are

- To develop models of the landscape over time which include research questions framed for that period or type of landscape. These are subjective point-of-time interpretations that, at least in their early stages, will be very crude. They should be clearly differentiated from more objective HER data such as activities, buildings, SAMs, etc. Such models would require a multidisciplinary approach.

- To be proactive in the development of enhancement programmes led by HERs and driven by local research agendas.

- To continue to undertake enhancement projects such as Historic Landscape Characterisation, Extensive Urban Surveys and Urban Archaeological Databases and to ensure they are fully integrated with the HERs.

- To create comprehensive and consistent records of finds and environmental data linked to museum collections.

- To work towards interoperability of records between HERs. Ultimately it might be beneficial to have a single entry portal for all HERs within the region. Rather than attempting to create a separate Regional HER, the best and most cost effective way of achieving this would be to ensure that the records of the various HERs work together.

All these priorities have staffing and financial implications which must be addressed by the local authorities but these mirror national aspirations and in some cases there are identified sources of funding available, for example, Heritage Lottery Funding and the Aggregates Levy.

## 9.5. Conclusion

We believe that the provision of high quality HER information for the entire region should be one of the major priorities of the west midlands archaeological community. HERs should become pivotal in the creation of a research cycle within the west midlands. Such a research cycle would mean that curatorial decisions are informed by a high level understanding of the resource and its potential; fieldwork and post-excavation is informed by an understanding of the context of any discoveries; and researchers at all levels can gain easy access to high quality data and synthesis.

## Notes

### The Archaeology Forum

The Archaeology Forum is a grouping of the key, non-governmental organisations concerned with archaeology in the UK. Its members include the Association of Local Government Archaeological Officers UK, The Council for British Archaeology, the Institute of Conservation, The Institute for Archaeologists, the Institute of Historic Building Conservation, The National Trust, the National Trust for Scotland, Rescue, the Society of Antiquaries of London, the Society of Antiquaries of Scotland, the Standing Conference of Archaeological Unit Managers and the Society of Museum Archaeologists.

## Bibliography

ALGAO 1999   *Local Records – National Resource: an ALGAO strategy for Sites and Monuments Records*, London

ALGAO 2001   *Strategy 2001-2006*, London

Baker, D, and Baker, E, 1999   *An Assessment of English Sites and Monuments Records for the Association of Local Government Archaeological Officers*, Chelmsford

DCMS Architecture and Historic Environment Division 2004   *Review of Heritage protection: the way forward*, London

DCMS 2007   *Heritage protection for the 21st century*, London

English Heritage 2000   *Power of Place: the future of the historic environment*, London

English Heritage 2007   *MIDAS Heritage – a data standard for the historic enviroment,* available online at http://www.english-heritage.org.uk/server/show/nav.18041/

English Heritage and ALGAO 2002   *Historic Environment Records: Benchmarks for Good Practice*, London

# 10. Curatorial practice

## Mike Hodder

Mike.Hodder@birmingham.gov.uk

## 10.1. Introduction

This paper has been produced in the context of the Research Framework and Agenda, in recognition that implementation of much of the Agenda will be dependent on curators (ie those responsible for advising on the management of the archaeological resource, principally but not exclusively through the planning process). It is not a general statement on curatorial practice in the region, nor can it address specialist aspects in detail.

The purpose of this paper is to identify issues relating to curatorial practice that arise from the seminars, circulated papers, web-published papers and agenda discussions, and subsequent comments stimulated by these. These points need to be addressed by curators when giving advice at a strategic and policy level, in site-specific advice and in the preparation of site-specific briefs, and in monitoring fieldwork and post-excavation work. Such advice is given in the context of a wide range of processes which affect the historic environment, including large-scale urban regeneration, infrastructure schemes (communications and services), extensive aggregate extraction and a massive change to rural landscapes as agriculture is transformed, as well as the cumulative attrition of historic environment assets by smaller-scale development.

It is taken for granted that all archaeological work in the region is required to comply with the Code of Conduct and appropriate Standards and Guidance of the Institute for Archaeologists, and is required to be in accordance with guidelines produced by English Heritage and specialist groups.

## 10.2. General

It is essential that briefs prepared by curators address the particular regional issues identified in the Research Framework and Agenda. The fitness for purpose of specifications, project designs, project proposals, written schemes of investigation and post-excavation assessments produced by consultants and contractors must likewise be assessed against these criteria.

Details for each period are contained in the summaries, but a few key points arising from the Framework process merit reiteration here:

- The number of prehistoric, especially earlier prehistoric, and Roman sites and landscapes in the region is much greater than had previously been assumed.

- The proven or likely occurrence of earlier settlement on sites mainly occupied at a later date, and vice versa, such as Iron Age or post-Roman on mainly Roman sites, and Roman or early medieval on later medieval sites.

- Evaluation, excavation and post-excavation strategies must take into account the fact that artefactual assemblages from prehistoric and early medieval settlements and even Roman rural settlements may be sparse and difficult to date.

- Some soil types in the region make it difficult to detect or examine sites by aerial photography or geophysics.

- Different elements of extensive sites need to be addressed, for example the suburbs as well as the cores of Roman, early medieval, medieval and post-medieval towns.

- A broader approach needs to be taken for a fuller understanding of sites of all periods. This demands more on- and off-site palaeoenvironmental work, greater involvement of geoarchaeologists to understand site formation processes and more multidisciplinary contact, such as documentary historians, historical geographers and historic building specialists for the medieval and post-medieval periods.

- Curators need to work closely with other related professionals such as conservation officers, urban designers, landscape architects, and ecologists.

- A Regional Standards Document should be considered.

- The Research Framework and Agenda need to be formally adopted by local authorities and other organisations who are advised by curators.

## 10.3. Dating

The occurrence of few or poorly dated finds on sites of all prehistoric periods and of early medieval date emphasises the importance of scientific dating. Therefore, a requirement for a sampling strategy for scientific dating needs to be included in briefs for work that is likely to encounter deposits of these dates. The use of radiocarbon dating with appropriate statistical analysis should be routine, even on sites where artefacts are relatively abundant, using AMS where required, and accompanied by other dating methods such as TL and OSL. Consequently, attention needs to be paid to the sampling and recovery of dateable material during the excavation process, not afterwards. Undated human burials, which could be any date from early prehistoric onwards, should be routinely radiocarbon dated and the radiocarbon dating of burials otherwise dated by artefacts would strengthen regional chronologies. Samples should be taken from existing buildings or excavated timbers for dendrochronology wherever possible and appropriate. Opportunities for dating production sites (eg archaeomagnetic dating of kilns) should not be missed.

## 10.4. The palaeoenvironment

More environmental data is required in the region for all periods: it will be a long time before the law of diminishing returns applies to palaeoenvironmental or geoarchaeological work anywhere in the region. Therefore, environmental work should be more prominent in briefs, requiring a sampling rationale and methodology, and adequate time and funding for appropriate processing of environmental samples. With pressures for contractors to keep staff costs low, it is important that curators are informed about the qualifications of specialist staff.

Reservoirs of palaeoenvironmental data, such as former stream channels at burnt mounds, should be identified and sampled on site. Off-site 'natural deposits' which can provide environmental data, such as alluvial sequences, palaeochannels, and peat deposits, should be sampled by appropriate specialists, including geoarchaeologists, and radiocarbon dated. Such sampling should be identified as a core evaluation activity. These deposits, which also survive in urban locations, are not solely relevant for earlier periods: even in the medieval and post-medieval periods, on-site and off-site deposits can provide information on the impact of industry and on agricultural improvements, including introduction of exotic plants and animals.

Charred plant remains are relatively sparse in the west midlands. Negative evidence is therefore even more important, ie samples must be sufficiently large to demonstrate that absences of charred plant material are genuine, rather than the consequence of inadequate sampling. Larger samples are also sometimes needed to obtain larger assemblages of material that can be better interpreted. Unusual and early plant taxa need to be AMS dated as often as possible to make sure that early introductions are accurately identified and that intrusive material can be recognised and excluded.

Industrial residues should be analysed, including metallurgical investigation. The possibility of such residues being found, and a statement of the action to be taken if they are, should be routinely built into briefs. More guidance is needed about the range of analyses available and when it would be appropriate to apply them, for instance in trying to see the effects of industry upon the countryside, where industrial pollutants might occur in environmental deposits. Equally, we need to know where such analysis would not be worthwhile. We may in the first instance need to look for circumstances where we can test new methodologies. For example, would it be possible to identify different coal types? Industrial pollutants might also be detectable in the human skeleton. Very few substantial groups of human remains have been studied from the west midlands from any period that could provide information on demography, disease and diet.

## 10.5. Artefact Analysis

A requirement for an appropriate level of artefact analysis should be written into briefs. Appropriate specialists should be involved from an early stage in the evaluation and excavation processes. If they are not involved until well into the post-excavation phase it may by then be too late to get answers to the questions that need asking. Allowance should be made for investigative conservation of artefacts because of its potential to provide information on the technology of artefact manufacture and the effects of the burial environment after deposition.

There should be a full quantitative study of ceramic assemblages, together with petrological analysis, residue analysis and other analyses where appropriate. Established fabric and form series, where available, should be used as an integral part of the identification and analysis of the ceramics. Where local ceramic fabric series exist briefs should require that they are used by all pottery specialists working in that area. If a pottery specialist creates a fabric series for an area they should be required to deposit a copy of it at a local museum or appropriate institution so that it can be used by future researchers.

More artefact research is generally needed for all periods, with more well-stratified medieval and post-medieval finds assemblages being especially required from dateable contexts. For example, in the post-medieval period a key area may be the sources of ceramics supplying newly emerging towns. Also in the post-medieval period, squatter camps ought to provide closely dated assemblages.

## 10.6. Prospection strategies

More emphasis needs to be placed on non-invasive mapping strategies: fieldwalking, microrelief, aerial photographs, geophysics and geochemical survey. Geochemistry in particular is underused as a mapping technique.

Because of the low quantities of objects, fieldwalking is not a suitable method for locating prehistoric settlements, nor is it reliable for the location of Roman rural settlements in some parts of the region. However, heat-shattered stones may be an important site indicator. It is unclear what some surface scatters represent and to what extent chance finds, ie objects found other than in deliberate search, especially Roman coins and material recorded in the Portable Antiquities Scheme, should be used in site prediction. There needs to be proper geospatial analysis of the distribution of individual findspots.

In general, the use of aerial photography needs to be encouraged. At present there is little indication that full use is being made of the available resource at either the evaluation or excavation stages. It is essential that all potential sources are examined as a matter of course, not just those closest to hand or those taken just for archaeological purposes.

Although the region contains extremely variable near-surface geology, specialists consider that most geophysical techniques will produce useful results, with appropriately skilled operators. Given the difficulties with geophysics on many west midlands soils, there is a need for better integration of geophysical and geoarchaeological results to better inform future use of geophysical techniques. Curators may need to look at requiring a wider range of prospection and survey techniques.

## 10.7. Evaluation strategies

The conventional trenching method and conventional percentage evaluation are not adequate for several periods and areas. A higher evaluation percentage is needed for dispersed and ephemeral prehistoric remains, consisting of a regular array of wide excavation trenches and gridded trial pits, or even the excavation of large areas from the outset, rather than trenching. For sites represented by flint scatters, the ploughsoil needs to be evaluated as well as the subsoil. This principle should also apply to other site types that can also be severely affected by later agricultural attrition, such as rural medieval settlements.

Where colluvium or alluvium covers or contains the archaeological remains, evaluation trenches should be wide, in order to see sufficiently large areas under it. Trenching should be preceded and accompanied by borehole data, test pits and augering, and geoarchaeologists should be involved. Similarly, in densely built-up urban areas where archaeological deposits frequently survive as 'islands' at some depth, large-scale evaluation is required, consisting of trenches dug to a sufficient width to reach the undisturbed natural. When open spaces within present day urban areas are affected by development, whether or not they are within historic town cores, evaluation should usually be required, even if no specific sites have previously been recorded.

Small towns, whether they are still small or were so in the past (such as medieval Birmingham), often have a very different deposit history to that of larger towns, consisting of shallower and more disturbed deposits. They therefore require larger evaluation trenches or area stripping from the outset. Their deposits are often more like those of rural settlements and may therefore require similar extensive investigation to fully realise their potential. Medieval and early post-medieval suburbs in the larger towns and cities seem to share many characteristics with the small towns.

## 10.8. Excavation strategies

The excavation strategy for sites of all periods needs to include an appropriate sampling strategy for all features and deposits encountered. Percentages of excavation of particular features always need to be justified for each site, in relation to the site type, its location and its geology. Various percentages of excavation of different types of features for sites of different periods were suggested during the Research Framework process. To maximise information and artefact recovery, prehistoric, early medieval and even some Roman sites require large-scale excavation and the excavation of a greater proportion of individual features than is often the case. On colluvial or alluvial sites, overburden stripping requires an approach which provides alternating long sections and areas in plan, in order to record the alluvial or colluvial sequence as well as the archaeological features and deposits.

The likely use of clay and cob walling and free-standing timber-framed buildings constructed on areas of hard standing should also be considered for sites of Roman and other periods. Therefore, sites which have no obvious structural remains but which produce large assemblages of domestic debris (for instance from enclosure ditches) should be considered as potentially representing settlement sites and sample levels should be adjusted accordingly.

For sites of all periods, to reduce nil results from watching briefs, full excavation of sample areas may be more appropriate than a watching brief of the entire site. It is likely that many deposits are lost without record because they cannot be seen in section in foundation and service trenches, but would be visible in plan.

Where briefs are drawn up for very large projects it would generally be sensible for these to have a staged approach and, on linear projects in particular, negative results should not be accepted as necessarily conclusive without the conducting of a watching brief during groundworks at the outset of construction.

## 10.9. Above-ground archaeology

Above- and below-ground archaeology must be integrated. More building studies are required, including dating by dendrochronology where possible. The apparently poor survival of medieval and post-medieval deposits in some towns, particularly small towns, emphasises the importance of recovering information from surviving buildings.

Much of the post-1840 built environment is poorly served by designation. Study of industrial buildings, not just the exceptional but also the typical, would be useful. This demands close working with building conservation officers to ensure that the appropriate requirements are imposed when demolition or alteration is proposed, although this may be difficult where such buildings are not listed or locally listed or within conservation areas.

In the same way as we need to look at complete landscapes rather than individual monuments, we need also to assess the complete building stock of areas rather than just picking out individual buildings. Such studies are often associated with detailed historic landscape characterisation of urban areas and can help in the definition and retention of local character and distinctiveness. Archaeologists need to work in collaboration with conservation officers and others such as urban designers in these studies but may have the most appropriate skills within an authority to specify the way that such work is undertaken.

The value of garden archaeology has been demonstrated. In rural landscapes, the importance of features such as landmarks, trees, water features and paths must be recognised. Here collaboration is required with ecologists, landscape architects and landscape historians.

## 10.10. Public information and engagement

We need to encourage the provision of public information and other forms of engagement as an integral part of projects wherever appropriate and feasible, since the entire process is predicated upon a concept that archaeological endeavour is of public benefit. Such provision may also be of benefit to the developers who have been required to undertake the archaeological work. Although physical access may sometimes be restricted or precluded by health and safety considerations, visual access is often possible and can be supplemented by other activities and intellectual access can be provided through a variety of media.

## 10.11. A Regional Standards document

A Regional Standards document for the west midlands, like that for East Anglia, would refer to the Regional Research Framework and Agenda. It could include many of the issues in this document and expand on subjects such as excavation percentages. The Regional Standards document would need to be formally adopted by the local authorities and other organisations who are advised by curators.

### 10.12. Formal adoption of the Regional Research Framework and Agenda as policy

To carry weight in a local government context, the Regional Research Framework and Agenda need to be formally adopted as policy. This could be achieved by their inclusion in Supplementary Planning Documents for Archaeology or the Historic Environment at an individual local authority level and beyond this as part of the Regional Spatial Strategy.

### Acknowledgements

I am extremely grateful to all those curators, contractors and specialists who commented on earlier drafts of this paper.